THE PRIEST AND THE GREAT KING

BIBLICAL AND JUDAIC STUDIES FROM THE UNIVERSITY OF CALIFORNIA, SAN DIEGO

Volume 10

edited by William H. C. Propp

Previously published in the series:

1. *The Hebrew Bible and Its Interpreters*, edited by William Henry Propp, Baruch Halpern, and David Noel Freedman (1990).
2. *Studies in Hebrew and Aramaic Orthography*, by David Noel Freedman, A. Dean Forbes, and Francis I. Andersen (1992).
3. *Isaiah 46, 47, and 48: A New Literary-Critical Reading*, by Chris Franke (1994).
4. *The Book around Immanuel: Style and Structure in Isaiah 2–12*, by Andrew H. Bartelt (1996).
5. *The Structure of Psalms 93–100*, by David M. Howard Jr. (1997).
6. *Psalm 119: The Exaltation of Torah*, by David Noel Freedman (1999).
7. *Between Heaven and Earth: Divine Presence and Absence in the Book of Ezekiel*, by John F. Kutsko (2000).
8. *The Storm-God in the Ancient Near East*, by Alberto R. W. Green (2003).
9. *Le-David Maskil: A Birthday Tribute to David Noel Freedman*, edited by Richard Elliott Friedman and William H. C. Propp (2004).

THE PRIEST AND THE GREAT KING
Temple-Palace Relations in the Persian Empire

Lisbeth S. Fried

EISENBRAUNS
Winona Lake, Indiana
2004

Published for Biblical and Judaic Studies
The University of California, San Diego
by
Eisenbrauns
Winona Lake, Indiana

Cataloging in Publication Data

Fried, Lisbeth S.
The priest and the great king : temple-palace relations in the Persian Empire / Lisbeth S. Fried
p. cm. — (Biblical and Judaic studies from the University of California, San Diego ; v. 10)
Revision of the author's thesis (doctoral)—New York University
Includes bibliographical references and indexes.
ISBN 1-57506-090-6 (cloth : alk. paper)
1. Iran—Politics and government. 2. Iran—History—To 640. 3. Temples—Middle East—History—To 1500. 4. Religion and politics—Middle East—History—To 1500. I. Title. II. Biblical and Judaic studies ; v. 10.
DS275.F67 2004
322'.1'0935—dc22

2004009806

The paper used in this publication meets the minimum requirements of the American National Standard for Information Sciences—Permanence of Paper for Printed Library Materials, ANSI Z39.48-1984.⊗™

Dedicated to

GERDA SELIGSON (ז"ל)
(1909–2002)

Valē

Contents

Preface

When I began graduate school in 1989, the Persian period, unlike others, was the Dark Age of Jewish history. The years between the temple's destruction and the rise of Alexander were a blank that the books of Ezra and Nehemiah could not fill. Noticeably missing was a description of the change in Judah from monarchy to theocracy. At the time of the First Temple's destruction, a Davidic king ruled Judah. Under Alexander and the Ptolemies, the high priest reportedly led the Jewish nation. The book Ezra–Nehemiah could not get us from here to there, from monarchy to theocracy.

More than by the theocracy's unknown origin, I was haunted by the conflicting views toward it. In Josephus, Philo, and Ben Sira, the high priest was God's emissary on earth. According to biblical scholars, however, the Mosaic theocracy was rigid, legalistic, a "dead work," "estranged from the heart," a source of opprobrium.[1]

I want to know if the Jewish priesthood did accrue secular power, and if so, how it exercised this power in relation to the imperial forces that surrounded it. I write in an unabashed attempt to defend it. I do so by setting it in its ancient Near Eastern context. Rather than focusing on the Judean priesthood, I try to understand the role of any priest in the ancient world. I want to know if theocracies arose in other parts of the Persian Empire, and if so, how, and if not, why not. I believe that the Jews and the Jewish priesthood were not unique and that whatever was true of other temples and other temple cities in the face of imperial domination and control would also be true of the Temple of YHWH and of Jerusalem.

Acknowledgments

This book is a complete revision of my Ph.D. dissertation. Neither the dissertation nor this book could have been written without help and wise instruction. The dissertation was conceived in the classrooms of Peter Machinist and Haim Tadmor at the University of Michigan but was brought to the birthstool at New York University's Department of Hebrew and Judaic Studies. At the risk of belaboring the metaphor, I would add that its midwives were my adviser, Baruch A. Levine, and my committee: Daniel Fleming, Gernot Windfuhr, William Arnal, S. David Sperling, and Lawrence

1. E.g., Wellhausen, *Prolegomena*, 425. Please note that in this book source references are abbreviated in the footnotes. The full citations are found in the bibliography.

Schiffman. I add Bezalel Porten who, although not on the committee, read every word of the dissertation and made critical suggestions at every point. Although he may not agree with its conclusions, this book bears the stamp of his imprint. Gary Beckman, Lester Cole, Eugene Cruz-Uribe, Victor Horowitz, Yonatan Nadelman, Carolyn Thorpe, and Norman Yoffee were there when I needed them for suggestions, counsel, and advice. Thank you.

I want to express a special note of gratitude to David Noel Freedman for his interest and concern, and for mentoring me all through my graduate career and beyond. It is greatly appreciated; I hope I continue to merit it. I thank William Propp and his committee for accepting this book into their series, and for their critical suggestions.

The dissertation and now the book could not have been written without the University of Michigan's Department of Near Eastern Studies. Their willingness to provide me a home, library, e-mail, and access to their outstanding faculty is gratefully appreciated. It would not have become a book, however, without the efforts of Beverly McCoy and Jim Eisenbraun and all of the folks at Eisenbrauns; their efforts are greatly appreciated.

I want to thank my husband, Michael, who suffered through four years without a wife while I commuted to New York every week. He has supported me unflinchingly and without complaints in all my endeavors. He has been the wind beneath my wings. Finally, I dedicate this book in love to the memory of my teacher and friend Gerda Seligson, ז״ל, of the University of Michigan's Classics department. She patiently taught me Greek, Latin, and so much more. *Valē.*

Abbreviations

General

AO	Antiquités orientales: Tablets in the collections of the Musée du Louvre
BIN	Babylonian Inscriptions in the Collection of James B. Nies
BM	Tablets in the Collections of the British Museum
BRM	Babylonian Records in the Library of J. Pierpont Morgan
CBS	Tablets in the Collections of the University Museum of the University of Pennsylvania, Philadelphia
DB	Bihistun (Bisitun) Inscription of Darius
DNa	Inscription A of Darius at Naqš-I-Rustam
DNb	Inscription B of Darius at Naqš-I-Rustam
DSe	Inscription E of Darius at Susa
DSf	Inscription F of Darius I at Susa
ET	English translation
FdX	Fouilles de Xanthos
LXX	Septuagint (Greek translation of the Hebrew Bible)
MT	Masoretic (Hebrew) Text
NRSV	New Revised Standard Version of the English Bible
P.	Papyrus
PBS	Publications of the Babylonian Section, University Museum, University of Pennsylvania
PN	Personal name
PTS	Cuneiform Tablets in the Princeton Theological Seminary
RhM	Rheinisches Museum
VAT	Tablets in the Collections of the Staatliche Museen, Berlin
XPh	Inscription H of Xerxes at Persepolis
Y	Yasna
YBC	Tablets in the Babylonian Collection, Yale University Library

Reference Works

AASOR	Annual of the American Schools of Oriental Research
AB	Anchor Bible Commentary Series
ABC	*Assyrian and Babylonian Chronicles.* A. K. Grayson. Texts from Cuneiform Sources 5. Locust Valley, N.Y., 1975. Reprinted: Winona Lake, Ind., 2000

ABD	*Anchor Bible Dictionary.* Edited by D. N. Freedman. 6 vols. New York, 1992
ABRL	Anchor Bible Reference Library
ABL	*Assyrian and Babylonian Letters.* Edited by R. F. Harper. 14 vols. Chicago, 1892–1914
AfO	*Archiv für Orientforschung*
AHw	*Akkadisches Handwörterbuch.* W. von Soden. 3 vols. Wiesbaden, 1959–81
AMI	*Archäologische Mitteilungen aus Iran*
ANET	*Ancient Near Eastern Texts Relating to the Old Testament.* Edited by J. B. Pritchard. 3rd edition. Princeton, 1969
AnOr	Analecta Orientalia
AOAT	Alter Orient und Altes Testament
AoF	*Altorientalische Forschungen*
AOS	American Oriental Series
ArOr	*Archiv Orientální*
ARAB	*Ancient Records of Assyria and Babylonia.* Edited by D. D. Luckenbill. 2 vols. Chicago, 1926–27
ASOR	American Schools of Oriental Research
AUWE	*Ausgrabungen in Uruk-Warka: Endberichte*
AW	*Ancient World*
BA	*Biblical Archaeologist*
BaMi	*Baghdader Mitteilungen*
BAR	*Biblical Archaeology Review*
BASOR	*Bulletin of the American Society of Oriental Researches*
BDB	*A Hebrew and English Lexicon of the Old Testament.* By F. Brown, S. R. Driver, and C. A. Briggs. Oxford, 1907
BEFAR	Bibliothèque des École françaises d'Athenes et Rome
BHT	*Babylonian Historical Texts Relating to the Capture and Downfall of Babylon.* Translated by S. Smith. London, 1924
BIDR	*Bolletino dell'Istituto di dritto romano*
BIFAO	*Bulletin de l'Institut français d'Archéologie orientale*
BZAW	Beihefte zur Zeitschrift für die alttestamentliche Wissenschaft
CAD	*The Assyrian Dictionary of the Oriental Institute of the University of Chicago.* Chicago, 1956–
CANE	*Civilizations of the Ancient Near East.* Edited by J. Sasson. 4 vols. New York, 1995
CBQ	*Catholic Biblical Quarterly*
CdE	*Chronique d'Égypte*
CHI	*Cambridge History of Iran.* 7 vols. Cambridge, 1968–91
CRAIBL	*Comptes rendus de l'Académie des Inscriptions et Belles-Lettres*
CT	Cuneiform Texts from Babylonian Tablets in the British Museum
Cyr.	*Inschriften von Cyrus.* J. N. Strassmaier. Leipzig: Pfeiffer, 1890

DAE	*Documents araméens d'Égypt.* Edited by P. Grelot. Paris, 1972
Dar	*Inschriften von Darius, König von Babylon.* J. N. Strassmaier. Leipzig: Pfeiffer, 1893–97
DHA	*Dialogues d'Histoire Ancienne*
DPB	*Demotische Papyri aus den Staatlichen Museen zu Berlin, I and III, Papyri von der Insel Elephantine.* Edited by K.-Th. Zauzich. Berlin: Akademie, 1978–93
EDB	*Eerdmans Dictionary of the Bible.* Edited by D. N. Freedman. Grand Rapids, Mich., 1992
EPE	*Elephantine Papyri in English: Three Millennia of Cross-Cultural Continuity and Change.* Edited by B. Porten. Leiden, 1996
ErIsr	*Eretz-Israel*
EVO	*Egitto e Vicino Oriente*
FAT	Forschungen zum Alten Testament
GCCI	*Goucher College Cuneiform Inscriptions.* Edited by R. P. Dougherty. 2 vols. New Haven, Conn., 1923–33
GRBS	*Greek, Roman, and Byzantine Studies*
HALOT	*Hebrew and Aramaic Lexicon of the Old Testament.* Edited by L. Koehler, W. Baumgartner, and J. J. Stamm. Translated and edited under M. E. J. Richardson. 4 vols. Leiden, 1994–99
HEP	*L'histoire de l'empire perse: De Cyrus à Alexandre.* P. Briant. Paris, 1996
HSM	Harvard Semitic Museum Publications
HSS	Harvard Semitic Series
HTR	*Harvard Theological Review*
IEJ	*Israel Exploration Journal*
INJ	*Israel Numismatic Journal*
ISMEO	Istituto per il Medio e Estreme Oriente
JAOS	*Journal of the American Oriental Society*
JARCE	*Journal of the American Research Center in Egypt*
JASR	*Journal of Achaemenid Studies and Researches*
JBL	*Journal of Biblical Literature*
JCS	*Journal of Cuneiform Studies*
JE	*Journal d'Entrées.* Egyptian Museum, Cairo
JEA	*Journal of Egyptian Archaeology*
JESHO	*Journal of the Economic and Social History of the Orient*
JHS	*Journal of Hellenic Studies*
JNES	*Journal of Near Eastern Studies*
JSOT	*Journal for the Study of the Old Testament*
JSOTSup	Journal for the Study of the Old Testament, Supplement
JTS	*Journal of Theological Studies*
KAJ	*Keilschrifttexte aus Assur juristischen Inhalts.* Edited by E. Ebling. Osnabruck: Zeller, 1968

LS	*A Greek-English Lexicon.* Edited by H. G. Liddell, R. Scott, and H. S. Jones. 9th edition. Oxford: Clarendon, 1996
MDAIK	*Mitteilungen des Deutschen Archäologischen Instituts, Kairo*
Mnem.	*Mnémosyme*
MOS	Midden Oosten Studies
NABU	*Nouvelles Assyriologiques Brèves et Utilitaires*
Nbn.	*Inschriften von Nabonidus, König von Babylon.* J. N. Strassmaier. Leipzig, 1889
NICOT	New International Commentary on the Old Testament
OBO	Orbis Biblicus et Orientalis
OEANE	*The Oxford Encyclopedia of Archaeology in the Near East.* Edited by E. Meyers. 4 vols. New York, 1997
OIP	Oriental Institute Publications
OrAnt	*Oriens Antiquus*
OTL	Old Testament Library
PEQ	*Palestine Exploration Quarterly*
PFT	*Persepolis Fortification Tablets.* Edited by R. T. Hallock. Chicago, 1969
PIHANS	Publications de l'Institut historique: Archéologique néerlandais de Stanboul
Pohl	*Neubabylonische rechtsurkunden aus den Berliner Staatlichen museen.* Edited by A. Pohl. Rome: Pontifical Biblical Institute, 1933–34
PSBA	*Proceedings of the Society of Biblical Archaeology*
RA	*Revue archéologique*
RB	*Revue Biblique*
RdE	*Revue d'égyptologie*
REA	*Revue des études anciennes*
RLA	*Reallexikon der Assyriologie*
RT	Recueils de travaux relatif à la philologie et à l'archéologie égyptiennes et assyriennes
SBAW	Sitzungsberichte der bayerischen Akademie der Wissenschaften
SPAW	Sitzungsberichte der preussischen Akademie der Wissenschaften
SSEA	Society for the Study of Egyptian Antiquities
TAD	*Textbook of Aramaic Documents from Ancient Egypt.* Edited by B. Porten. Jerusalem, 1986–99
TBER	Textes babyloniens d'époque récente
TEBR	*Textes économiques de la Babylonie récente.* F. Joannès. Paris, 1982
TCL	Texts cunéiformes du Louvre
VT	*Vetus Testamentum*
VTSup	Supplements to Vetus Testamentum
WBC	Word Biblical Commentary
WHJP	*World History of the Jewish People*
WO	*Die Welt des Orients*

YBT	Yale Oriental Series, Babylonian Texts
YNER	Yale Near Eastern Researches
YOS	Yale Oriental Series
ZA	*Zeitschrift für Assyriologie*
ZABR	*Zeitschrift für altorientalische und biblische Rechtsgeschichte*
ZAS	*Zeitschrift für ägyptische Sprache und Altertumskunde*
ZAW	*Zeitschrift für die alttestamentliche Wissenschaft*
ZPE	*Zeitschrift für Papyrologie und Epigraphik*

Chapter 1
Introduction

Persian domination in Judah (539–333 B.C.E.) apparently created a sea-change in Judah's form of government. In two centuries it seems to have gone from a monarchy to a theocracy. In 520, Zerubbabel, great-grandson of Jehoiachin and heir to the Davidic throne, governed Judah as *peḥâ*, פחה (1 Chr 3:18; Hag 1:1). In 445, the non-royal Nehemiah was פחה (Neh 5:14), and his primary interlocutor and antagonist in Judah was Eliašib, the high priest. What happened to the Davidic heir? According to Josephus (*Ant.* 11.317), by the time Alexander invaded Judah in 332, Yaddua, the high priest, was in charge. He controlled auxiliary troops, military equipment, and provisions, with the power to open the gates of the city to Alexander or to resist him (*Ant.* 11.326–27). Had Judea become a theocracy?

Ancient writers characterize the Judean state as being controlled by the high priest. Indeed, Josephus coined the term *theocracy* in an effort to describe the Jewish form of government (*Ag. Ap.* 2.164):

> There is endless variety in the details of the customs and laws which prevail in the world at large. To give but a summary enumeration: some peoples have entrusted the supreme political power to monarchies, others to oligarchies, yet others to the masses. Our lawgiver, however, was attracted by none of these forms of polity, but gave to his constitution (πολίτευμα) the form of what—if a forced expression be permitted—may be termed a "theocracy" (θεοκρατίαν), placing all sovereignty and authority in the hands of God. (*Ag. Ap.* 2.165)

Hecataeus of Abdera, writing during the time of Alexander the Great and Ptolemy I, describes the Jews as follows:

> [Moses] picked out the men of most refinement and with the greatest ability to head the entire nation, and appointed them priests; and he ordained that they should occupy themselves with the temple and the honors and sacrifices offered to their God. These same men he appointed to be judges in all major disputes, and entrusted to them the guardianship of the laws and customs. For this reason the Jews never have a king, and authority over the people is regularly vested in whichever priest is regarded as superior to his colleagues in wisdom and virtue. They call this man the high priest, and believe that he acts

as a messenger to them of God's commandments. (Quoted in Diodorus Siculus 40.3:5)

The Problem

These two citations suggest that the Jewish government was viewed as strange, a thing to be explained, not the usual practice. This study investigates the apparent transition from Davidic heir to high priest. Did Judean priests obtain secular power during the Persian period, and if so, did the empire foster or impede the priesthood's authority? Current scholarship holds that, as long as Jerusalem sent funds to Susa, the Persian administration was lax and nondirective, permitting the Jews to develop their own form of government according to their own traditions. In this vein, Frei and Koch propose a theory of Persian imperial authorization. They argue that royal representatives in the provinces authorized local norms and customs, transforming them into locally applied imperial laws.[1] The local priesthood's rise to power was due to a local mandate, imperially legitimated. In contrast, Eisenstadt proposes a theory of bureaucratic empires in which Persia would have opposed any local accrual of power.[2] In this view, if the high priest amassed secular authority, it would have been in spite of, not because of, the Persian ruler.

The Theory of Self-Governance

Recently articulated by M. Dandamayev, the theory of self-governance holds that the Persians interfered as little as possible in the traditional political and social structures of the provinces.[3] The Achaemenids realized that if they were to rule nations that had thousands of years of cultural traditions behind them, they had to demonstrate a high degree of respect for these traditions. Cyrus and Cambyses retained with practically no alterations the local administrative, economic, and legal institutions in Media, Babylonia, and other countries they conquered. Although Darius organized the empire into 20 administrative units and created its bureaucracy, it was marked more by variety and diversity than uniformity. As long as the districts sent funds to Susa, they were able to develop autonomously.[4] Each province remained an

1. Frei and Koch (eds.), *Reichsidee und Reichsorganisation im Perserreich*; Frei, "Zentralgewalt und Lokalautonomie im achämenidischen Kleinasien"; idem, "Persian Imperial Authorization." For a critique of the theory, see the essays in Watts, *Persia and Torah,* especially the essay by Ska, "'Persian Imperial Authorization': Some Question Marks."

2. Eisenstadt, *The Political Systems of Empires.*

3. Dandamayev, "Achaemenid Imperial Policies and Provincial Governments"; see also idem, "Achaemenid Mesopotamia," 129.

4. Dandamayev and Lukonin, *Culture and Social Institutions of Ancient Iran,* 97.

independent socioeconomic unit with its own social institutions, internal structure, local laws, customs, traditions, systems of weights and measures, and monetary units. According to one form of this theory, the Persians not only allowed but commanded their subjects to develop their own life within the limits dictated by the necessities of imperial politics.[5] The Achaemenids were benign and did not interfere in local social and economic structures or existing traditions, since "such a control would have contradicted traditional social institutions and popular psychology."[6] Subjects were therefore free to develop their own intellectual and religious life. Because the Persian government was tolerant and supportive of local governance, and because the satrap did not interfere in the internal affairs of the communities in his district, the priesthood's rise to secular authority was driven by pressures within Judah itself.[7] A more sophisticated form of this view stresses that Persian rulers used local elites and their familiarity with local conditions and customs to create acceptance of their power. Local traditions and systems were maintained but exploited by the king for his own purposes.[8] Knoppers argues that

> it is true that in a few instances the Persian authorities supported local sanctuaries with gifts and endowments. But there is no clear documentation to suggest that such efforts led to any larger attempt to micromanage the daily operations of local communities within the great range of societies found within the enormous Achaemenid empire. Rather, the Persian kings seem to have given local appointees significant leeway to govern their communities in accordance with larger strategic priorities.[9]

The Theory of Persian Imperial Authorization

Frei and Koch ask to what degree local communities within an empire had the authority to regulate their own interests. They conclude that since "[imperial] ruling classes were not in a position to build quickly a complex and efficient administration that could be managed by its own members, . . . it was imperative to concede administrative responsibilities to the conquered."[10] The Achaemenid Empire created a process by which, "not only were the

5. Noth, *The History of Israel*, 302–3. "The Great King, as far as possible, allowed the peoples to preserve their traditional customs and institutions" (Widengren, "The Persian Period," 519). See also, Meyers and Meyers, *Haggai, Zechariah 1–8*, xxxii.

6. Dandamayev, "Achaemenid Imperial Policies," 280.

7. Ibid.; Hanson, *Dawn of Apocalyptic.*

8. Kuhrt, *The Ancient Near East c. 3000–330* B.C., 656–64; Knoppers, "An Achaemenid Imperial Authorization of Torah in Yehud?" 130–34.

9. Ibid., 131. By local appointees, Knoppers means locally appointed leaders. I assume that by "larger strategic priorities," he means priorities established by the Persians. Knoppers admits that the highest echelon of political authority was held by Persians.

10. Frei, "Persian Imperial Authorization," 6.

norms established by a local authority approved and accepted by the central authority, but adopted as its own."[11] Laws proposed by subordinates were legitimated and issued in writing by the central government. Imperial authorization was not essential or obligatory but was desired by the communities, since through it "the legal norms of a local body with subordinate status were elevated to the status of imperial legislation."[12] The most that the central authority would do would be to order local communities to codify their laws and norms and so publicize their use for authorization and enforcement. In this way, locally determined laws and customs became imperialized.

Thus, according to the theory of self-governance, as long as tribute was sent to Persia, cities and provinces were self-directing. Judah's choice of government resulted from internal pressures and desires within the Jewish community itself. Persian demands and goals did not influence it. I label this view *Hypothesis 1: The Hypothesis of Self-Governance.* In one version of self-governance, local laws and traditions were authorized, legitimated, and imperialized by the empire. This is *Hypothesis 2: The Hypothesis of Imperial Authorization.*

The Model of Bureaucratic Empires

Both of these theories of self-governance conflict with Shmuel N. Eisenstadt's model of bureaucratic empires.[13] Eisenstadt bases his model on an in-depth study of five such empires: (1) Sassanid Persia, (2) the Byzantine Empire, (3) T'ang China, (4) the Spanish-American Empire, and (5) the Hapsburg Empire and other European countries in the Age of Absolutism. The Achaemenid Empire was not a direct object of study. A brief outline of his model follows:

The ruler. Rulers of all bureaucratic empires needed to control the economic, military, and human resources in their empires for immediate deployment anywhere. These resources could not be tied to or dependent upon any power other than the ruler himself. This need was paramount and governed all the ruler's actions.[14] It meant he strove to "disembed" power from the strata of society that ordinarily controlled the resources and allocate it to himself. In Judah, these strata included the Davidic descendant, the priesthood, the landed aristocracy and nobles—the very men who would have wielded power according to the theory of self-governance.

The traditional ruling elites. The traditional ruling classes did not passively adjust themselves to the wishes of the ruler. Most groups had their own

11. Ibid., 7.
12. Ibid., 38.
13. Eisenstadt, *The Political Systems of Empires.* See also Yoffee, "Orienting Collapse."
14. Eisenstadt, *The Political Systems of Empires,* 117.

basic interests and objectives; and political conflict resulted from the struggle between the policies of the rulers and those of other major social strata.[15] According to Eisenstadt, when a society had been newly conquered, "[local] aristocratic groups, patrician, or some more traditional urban groups, and traditional cultural elites . . . felt menaced by the new objectives and activities of the ruler. . . . [T]hey considered the ruler as a renegade, upstart, or barbarian. . . . [T]hey felt that their positions were threatened by the trend to political centralization; and they were not willing to help to implement this trend. Therefore, they frequently attempted to deny the rulers resources and support, and plotted and worked against them either in open political warfare or by sleight of hand, infiltration, and intrigues."[16] If traditional ruling classes of Judah—priests, nobles, or elders—controlled resources in Persian period Judah, then it would have been *in spite of* the wishes of the Persian rulers. It would not have been because the Persians encouraged local control.

The bureaucracy. Separate from the traditional elites was the bureaucracy. This was composed of men appointed by the ruler, who exercised power in his name. Like traditional elites, the bureaucracy strove to obtain political autonomy for itself and to limit the control of the ruler.[17] Its members typically identified with the aristocracy: they desired to equal its wealth and status and to be recognized as part of it. According to Eisenstadt, bureaucrats "strove to acquire aristocratic or semi-aristocratic symbols of status and to establish their hereditary transmission. . . . [T]he bureaucracy often strove to make [their] titles more or less hereditary, and to develop a strong cohesion as a status group."[18] Officials that were originally appointed to positions of power and prestige by the ruler sought autonomy. They attempted to limit the control of the ruler; to put wealth and power under their own control; and to make their office—and the status, the wealth, and the power that went with it—hereditary. They strove to join the landed aristocracy.

According to Eisenstadt's model, rulers of bureaucratic empires did not permit traditional local elites to maintain power or to control resources. If local priesthoods gained control of resources, it would have been in opposition to the forces of the Persian Empire. I label this view *Hypothesis 3: The Hypothesis of Foreign or Central Control.*

The purpose of my study is to determine the extent to which the Judean priesthood attained secular authority during Achaemenid occupation and to test the three hypotheses as explanations of the Persian Empire's role in their rise to power.

15. Ibid., 156.
16. Ibid., 14.
17. Ibid., 162.
18. Ibid., 163.

Methodology

In the following pages, I examine the three hypotheses against archival and inscriptional data from the temples of the western satrapies of Babylon, Egypt, and Asia Minor with a view toward establishing the relationship between the Achaemenid ruler and the temples. I assume that if the relationship uncovered between the Great King and local priesthoods is constant across the western satrapies, then it will also describe Judah. In his seminal report on *Achaemenid Imperial Administration in Syria–Palestine* during the period of Ezra and Nehemiah, Hoglund laments that documentation of the imperial system of the Neo-Babylonian Empire (both before and after the Achaemenid takeover) is scarce.[19] Moreover, few texts pertain directly to the administration of imperial territories in the west. He regrets that "the economic tablets that might provide a reflection on the interaction with outlying territories number in the thousands, making a synthetic analysis still unattainable."[20] Hoglund's response has been to focus on the writings of the Greek historians and on the archaeology of the Levant.

Being concerned with the growth of local priesthoods, I examine the subset of these "thousands" of texts that pertains to the power and economic resources of temples. I identify temple elites in power before the Achaemenid conquest and chronicle their history under Achaemenid rule. I investigate their role in land rents, sales, and taxation to understand who controlled temple land and resources. The goal is to determine whether local temple elites lost, maintained, or accrued power during Persian hegemony. Did new, nontraditional temple elites appear who owed their authority solely to the Persian conquerors, or did the central government maintain the power and status of indigenous temple families? Was the Persian role supportive or hostile, or did the Achaemenid ruler play no role at all relative to local priesthoods' accrual of power?

Data from the three western satrapies under investigation (Babylon, Egypt, and Asia Minor) are compared with textual, archaeological, and numismatic data from Judah. To anticipate my conclusions: Eisenstadt's model of bureaucratic empires provides a better descriptor of temple-palace relations in the Achaemenid Empire than does the model of self-governance. Power is the ability to control resources, both human and material. Under the Achaemenids, all power was in the hands of the king and his representatives. Local priesthoods had no control over the land or the manpower in

19. Hoglund, *Achaemenid Imperial Administration*, 5.

20. Ibid. I note a similar unfortunate neglect of administrative and economic tablets in Vanderhooft's *Neo-Babylonian Empire and Babylon in the Latter Prophets.* He bases his discussion of Babylonian administration policy on inscriptional data and the biblical text.

their domains. If the high priest Yaddua was able to surrender the Jewish province to Alexander, it was only because the Persians had abandoned the city in the face of Darius's retreat.

Chapter 2

Temple-Palace Relations in Babylonia

Temple and palace were two of the three great institutions around which social life in Mesopotamia flourished.[1] In this chapter I discuss these two institutions, the relations between them, and the changes that occurred, if any, as a result of the Achaemenid conquest. I test the three hypotheses outlined in the introduction: the theory of self-governance, the theory of imperial authorization, and the theory of central control. Did local priests manage the temple without central interference? Were temple norms authorized by the king? Or did local priests bow to the monarch's will? Who controlled the economic and human resources of the temples? Was it the local indigenous temple hierarchy or the Persian ruler? Were temple resources under the control of the priesthood, or did the king appropriate them for his use anywhere in the realm?

Sources and Methodological Limitations

Two temples (Eanna at Uruk and Ebabbar at Sippar) in Mesopotamia left extensive archives from the Neo-Babylonian and Persian periods. These archives consist primarily of receipts of goods and rents, of orders for goods, and of contracts. Left with little else, scholars have directed their attention to the list of parties to the receipts and witnesses of the contracts that provide personal names, patronymics, often family names, and the titles of the individuals who played a significant role in the life of the temple. The titles of the signatories appear in fixed order, yielding the official hierarchy of the priesthood. Receipts and contracts are dated, enabling scholars to detect when changes in personnel or in the titles of temple offices occurred and whether they correlate with changes in the monarchy.

In addition to the restricted nature of the archive, a second frustration is the lack of data from the Eanna Temple after Darius I's second year in office (520) and from the Ebabbar Temple after Xerxes (486–465). It is not clear

1. Oppenheim, *Ancient Mesopotamia,* 95. The third was the city. Economically speaking, however, there may have only been the two; see the essays in Bongenaar, *Interdependency of Institutions and Private Entrepreneurs.*

why these temple archives stopped. A switch to papyrus is possible, but cuneiform temple archives exist from Babylon in the Seleucid period. Whatever the reason, the archives of the Eanna and Ebabbar temples are limited to the Neo-Babylonian period and to the early years of Achaemenid rule. In spite of these restrictions, the archives may be used to determine if Nabonidus's system of governing continued under the Achaemenids and if Achaemenid rule led to an increase or a decrease in local control.

Temple Personnel

The appointment of personnel to traditional positions of power reveals the political struggle in bureaucratic empires. According to Eisenstadt's model, the ruler seeks to control the flow of resources (monetary and human) and to direct them to himself. The officials at the head of the temples control temple resources, so the ruler must control these officials. The final section of this chapter charts the flow of resources controlled by the great temples of Babylon in the late Babylonian and early Achaemenid periods. The present section asks who the elite temple officials were, how they were selected, and to whom they were responsible.[2]

The Eanna Temple at Uruk

The ranking of administrative positions at the Eanna at Uruk can be reconstructed from the witness lists as follows:

zazakku
šākin ṭēmi Uruk
ša rēši šarri bēl piqitti Eanna
qīpu ša Eanna
šatammu Eanna

The Zazakku

The *zazakku* (ideogram DUB.SAR.ZAG.GA) appears for the first time during the reign of Nabonidus. It was once thought that he replaced the *mākisu*-scribe (ZAG.HA) mentioned in texts from the Old and Middle Babylonian periods as well as in the Middle and Neo-Assyrian periods. In these early texts, the word *mākisu* indicated a high-ranking official in charge of the national tax system who calculated the share of the yield of a field that was owed to the palace (PBS 7 89:36; TCL 1 152:4).

2. Except where noted, this section is based on San Nicolò, *Beiträge zu einer Prosopographie*; Kümmel, *Familie*; Ebeling, "Beamter"; and Sack, *Cuneiform Documents*; as well as the *CAD* and von Soden's *AHw.*

The *mākisu* is not attested in the Neo-Babylonian period when the *zazakku* (DUB.SAR.ZAG.GA) starts to appear. In the witness lists of two texts from the temple at Uruk (YOS 6 238:17 and AnOr 8 25:1) the *zazakku*, Bēl-uballiṭ, is listed first, followed by several other high officials. In a third text (YOS 6 198:10), the *zazakku* official (again Bēl-uballiṭ) accepts delivery of 500 kur of barley from two high officials at the king's quay. In addition to Uruk, Bēl-uballiṭ is also active in Sippar, Nippur, and Babylon. Most suggestive is a letter from the crown prince, Belshazzar: "I am sending you herewith the *zazakku*-official Bēl-uballiṭ. Give him all the gold he asks for so that he can accomplish the work in Ekur (the temple of Enlil in Nippur)" (TCL 9 136:7). In the 17th year of Nabonidus (his last), the *zazakku*-official, Rīmût, is recorded as receiving the *malītu*-dues of the Temple of Adad (Nbn. 1055:9, 11) and is described standing at the side of King Nabonidus in the Nabonidus Verse Account (*BHT* pl. 9, 5:24). The letter from Belshazzar and the presence of Rīmût next to Nabonidus in the Verse Account indicate he was an extremely highly placed royal official. When present at a temple, he is listed first on witness lists. He was not attached to any one place but was an official of the empire.

Because it was once thought that the *zazakku* filled the role of the *mākisu*-scribe, he was identified in the literature as "the official in charge of tax collection, directly under the *bēl pīḫāti*, the provincial governor."[3] He was called the *Katasterdirektor*[4] and "the one in charge of the land registry on which the entire system of *imittu* was based."[5] This has been disputed recently.[6] References to *zazakku* in Neo-Babylonian documents show no evidence that this official was involved in estimating yields of fields or gardens, in compiling cadastral documents, or even that he was a tax collector. He was simply the chief officer of the king who transmitted the king's orders and intervened in temple and civil affairs serious enough to warrant the king's attention.

The Babylonian version of the Behistun inscription also mentions a *zazakku*. Line 31 reads, "Nidintu-Bēl, the son of Kinzer, who is called *zazakku*" (if the restoration is correct).[7] Although it is not clear whether Nidintu-Bēl or his father is the *zazakku*, the title seems to have been in use up to the beginning of the reign of Darius. Since no other Achaemenid text refers to this

3. Ebeling, "Beamter," 453–54.

4. *AHw*, 1517, with references.

5. Joannès, *TEBR*, 224 (the *CAD* defines *imittu* as rent for lands, fixed in advance, on the basis of the projected harvest).

6. Dandamayev, "The Neo-Babylonian *Zazakku*," 39; Joannès, "À propos du *Zazakku*"; MacGinnis, "A Further Note on the *Zazakku*."

7. Dandamayev, "The Neo-Babylonian *Zazakku*." Cf. von Voigtlander, *Bisitun*, 19–20.

title, Darius must have abolished the office.[8] If either Nidintu-Bēl or his father was the *zazakku* under Cyrus or Cambyses, then his office may have put him in a position to rebel against the king. Taking the name of Nebuchadnezzar III, Nidintu-Bēl rebelled and brought a large army to the Tigris to fight against Darius. Suffering defeat there, Nidintu-Bēl fled to Babylon but met Darius again with a second large army on the Euphrates (DB I 80–81, 83–96). Nidintu-Bēl's role as *zazakku* may have provided him with power and money sufficient to furnish both soldiers and equipment, which he turned to his own use. If so, the power and resources that Nidintu-Bēl was able to command would have been reason enough for Darius to abolish the *zazakku* office.

The šākin ṭēmi Uruk

The *šākin ṭēmi* appears in texts from the Eanna most often as *šākin ṭēmi* (*ša*) *Uruk*^{ki}. The *šākin ṭēmi* (ideogram LÚ.GAR.KU or LÚ.ŠA.KU) denotes the *Beschließender* or decision-maker, the one who lays down the edicts. The title is derived from the expression *ṭēma šakānu,* which means variously: 'to make a decision', 'to utter a decree', 'to put a case before someone', 'to inform someone of something', or 'to give orders, instructions'. It is used most often with kings and royalty. For example, ^{lú}*darišu šarru ṭēmu iltakan umma* 'King Darius has made a decision, as follows . . .' (*Dar.* 451). Another example reads: *ina libbīkunu mannu ki šarrumma ṭēma išakk*[*anu*] 'who among you gives orders as king' (*AfO* 10 2:6). In a third example: "they will undergo the river ordeal," [*ša*] *ikkallu šarru ṭēma išakkan* 'the king will pronounce judgment on the one who refuses' (HSS 9 7:26). Except for what can be gleaned from a study of temple or private archives, little of the *šākin ṭēmi*'s duties can be known.

Prior to 850, the office appears in Babylon at the bottom of witness lists, suggesting a minor administrative official. In texts dated after 850, the title appears at the top and denotes the governor of a province or mayor of a large city and its associated villages. It is usually identified with the civil bureaucracies of large urban centers such as Uruk, Babylon, and Borsippa. Even though the *šākin ṭēmi* belonged to the city bureaucracy, he had a strong influence over the temple, often heading its administrative hierarchy. He had priority over temple officials and sat at the head of the temple's court of justice (YOS 7 7:6 [538/537]; YOS 7 198:1 [528/527]; ArOr 4 [1932], 343). For example, a text dated to the time of Cambyses reads: 'PN$_1$, the mayor of Uruk (*šākin ṭēmi Uruk*^{ki}), PN$_2$, the temple administrator of Eanna, and the assembly of Babylonians and Urukians gave a verdict concerning them' PN,

8. Dandamayev, "The Neo-Babylonian *Zazakku.*"

^{lú}*šākin ṭēmi Uruk* . . . PN_2 *šatam Eanna puḫur Bābili u Urukayya elišunu iprusû* (TCL 13 147:9). The text belongs to the temple archives, yet the *šākin ṭēmi* is the first official listed, above the temple administrator. In a more telling case (BIN 2 134) dated to Cyrus's fourth year, the *šākin ṭēmi* of Uruk settled a dispute between the temple administration and three cousins, private individuals who had inherited a house from their grandfather; the house was mortgaged to the temple. The relevant section reads as follows:

> Nabû-aḫḫē-bulliṭ, the provincial governor (*šākin māti*), sent PN^1, PN^2 and PN^3 [the three cousins] along with Nidintum-Bēl, the director of the temple (*šatammu Eanna*), . . . [and] Nabû-aḫḫē-iddin, the royal commissioner of the temple (*ša rēši šarri bēl piqitti Eanna*), . . . and temple scribes (*ṭupšarru*^{meš}) to stand before Imbiya, the mayor of Uruk (*šākin ṭēmi Uruk*), . . . and the judges (*dayyānu*^{meš}) of Nabû-aḫḫē-bulliṭ, the governor, so they may make a decision regarding them.

The *šākin ṭēmi Uruk* thus stood above and outside the temple administration and had the judicial authority (delegated by the *šākin māti*) to decide between it and external parties.

The *šākin ṭēmi*s of Uruk had family affiliations that are only partly known. A few belong to well-known scribal families of the temple: Gimil-Nanā, Ḫunzû, and Kidin-Marduk. One text (YOS 16 8:7), for example, reveals the patronymic (Nabû-balaṭsu-iqbi) and family name (Gimil-Nanā) of Marduk-šuma-iddina, the *šākin ṭēmi* of Uruk during the first years of Nabonidus (555–553).[9] A recently published tablet (YBC 4038) dated to the first year of Amēl-Marduk (561–560) shows this same man working with the administrator (*qīpu*) of Eanna. At that time he supervised receipts of commodities from other temples by the temple at Uruk. Thus, he was part of the temple hierarchy prior to becoming *šākin ṭēmi* of the city. Sack suspects that many of the great scribal families (Egibi, Ekur-zākir, Baʾiru, and Gimil-Nanā) not only provided scribes to the temple but also *šākin ṭēmis* to the city.[10] Beyond the case of a few men, and a father-son pair of *šākin ṭēmis* from the Ḫunzu family, this was not a general practice, however. Except for these, there are no linkages to the great scribal families or any indications of previous temple activity for other *šākin ṭēmi*s of Uruk.[11]

If they did not arise from within the temple hierarchy, who appointed the *šākin ṭēmis*, and to whom were they accountable? A theory of self-governance, of noninterference, predicts that the local population selected its own leaders. A theory of central control predicts that the ruler (whether monarch or emperor) appointed the mayors of these towns. Several texts from the reign of

9. Sack, *Cuneiform Documents,* 17.

10. Ibid.

11. Kümmel, *Familie,* 109.

Šamaš-šum-ukīn (667–648) make it clear that these officials were appointed by the king as early as the 7th century. One document reads, 'PN[1], the brother of PN[2], to whom Šamaš-šum-ukīn had entrusted the office of mayor of Uruk' (*lúšākin-ṭēmūtu ša Uruk [irḫ] uṣušu*; CT 54 496:4). Another reads, "The king wrote to PN: Do not worry, the mayorship of Uruk is yours (*lúšākin-ṭēmūtu ša Uruk attūka*), I will not give it to anyone else" (ABL 965:7). In a third document we read, "PN, whom the king, my lord, sent to [take over] the mayorship (*šākin-ṭēmūtu*) of Marad, is now in Nippur with me" (ABL 238:9). These texts from the Neo-Babylonian period indicate that the *šākin ṭēmi* was appointed by the king and answerable to him. Texts cited above, dating to the time of Cyrus and Cambyses, show that in the Achaemenid period the *šākin ṭēmi* ranked above the temple and had the power to adjudicate between it and external parties. Whether he was also appointed by the Persian ruler in the Achaemenid period will be discussed below.

The ša rēši šarri bēl piqitti Eanna

The title *ša rēši šarri bēl piqitti Eanna* (LÚ.SAG LUGAL LÚ.EN *piqitti ša Eanna*) appears in the archives of Eanna for the first time early in the reign of Nabonidus and continues for the duration of the archive. Although it occurs as a single unit only in the reign of Nabonidus, the separate elements, *ša rēši šarri* and *bēl piqitti*, appear earlier.[12] In the Neo-Babylonian period, the title *ša rēši šarri* indicated an officer of the king, an inspector or comptroller, assigned by the king to either province or temple. Bongenaar translates the phrase *ša rēši šarri* as 'courtier' to stress that he was "chosen from the king's inner circle of confidants" and from outside the temple hierarchy.[13] The title *bēl piqitti* was the general term for an 'administrative official'. The combined title *ša rēši šarri bēl piqitti Eanna* indicates a royal commissioner and administrative official associated with the Eanna Temple.

It was once thought that the position of *ša rēši šarri bēl piqitti Eanna* appeared only from the third year of Nabonidus on. That Nabû-šarra-uṣur held this office on the second day of the third month of Nabonidus's first regnal year, May 31, 555, is now certain (PTS 2097).[14] Only a little more than a month before, on the 28th of Nisannu (April 27), he appeared at Eanna simply as *ša rēši šarri* (YOS 6 10).[15] The complete title must have been created in the interval between these dates.

12. Saggs, "Two Administrative Officials," 29; Sack, *Cuneiform Documents*, 20. Tadmor ("Was the Biblical *Sārîs* a Eunuch?") demonstrates that the title *ša rēši* should be translated 'eunuch'.

13. Bongenaar, *Neo-Babylonian Ebabbar*, 100.

14. Frame, "Nabonidus," 38.

15. Ibid., 55–56.

From the very beginning of his appointment, Nabû-šarra-uṣur received his orders from the king himself (PTS 2097) and from a high royal official, the keeper of the seals (YOS 6 10). He relayed them to other temple officials and to the mayor of Uruk. Acting on orders from the king, Nabû-šarra-uṣur distributed food allotments in Eanna, saw to the repair of the temple, allocated temple land, and appointed and dismissed temple personnel. Through his *ša rēši šarri bēl piqitti Eanna,* Nabonidus controlled the minutiae of temple life at Eanna from the very first days of his reign.

The *ša rēši šarri bēl piqitti Eanna* appeared most often with the *qīpu* and *šatammu.* From the time of Nabonidus on, these three officials formed the highest administrative body of the temple. This was not always the case. Prior to this king, the *qīpu, šatammu,* and the *ṭupšar bīti ša Eanna* (the official secretary of Eanna) formed the temple's highest administrative body. For these periods, *tupšar Eanna* should be translated 'temple secretary' or 'temple accountant' rather than 'scribe', since the holder of this office is never listed as the person responsible for composing a tablet. Upon his appointment, however, Nabû-šarra-uṣur as *ša rēši šarri bēl piqitti* arrogated the prerogatives of the *ṭupšar Eanna,* whose prestige was thereby greatly reduced. The title disappears from the records then; when it reappears in Nabonidus's 12th year, it had changed drastically. No longer a position of status and prestige, it was now held jointly by several officials.

Before Nabonidus, the occupation of scribe was the starting point for many high positions in the economic and administrative spheres at Eanna. The names of scribal families of Uruk, for example, Gimil-Nanā, Ḫunzû, and Kidin-Marduk, were well known from the 7th and 6th centuries down to Seleucid times. Before Nabonidus, every scribe and hence every official belonged to one of these great scribal families, and the possibility of promotion from simple scribe to 'Scribe of Eanna' *ṭupšar Eanna* was well attested. From the time of Nabonidus, however, and throughout the Achaemenid period, there is no clear linkage to these scribal families for any holder of the key positions of Eanna. The top positions were royal appointees and came from outside Uruk. We never know their family names and only very occasionally their fathers'.

Even though Nabû-šarra-uṣur was appointed by Nabonidus from outside the temple scribal families, as *ša rēši šarri bēl piqitti Eanna* he had priority within the three-member board that supervised temple affairs. When the three officials are mentioned, he is first. The role and status of the three officials can be seen from YOS 6 232 (year 12 of Nabonidus).[16] Nabû-šarra-uṣur is listed first in his role as *ša rēši šarri bēl piqitti Eanna,* followed by the *qīpu,* and then the *šatammu.* A *ṭupšar Eanna* is not listed. These three are then fol-

16. Ibid., 70.

lowed by two ordinary scribes (lú*ṭupšarrī*) of Eanna. According to this text, these officials order a number of tax assessors (lú*ēmidē*) to swear to determine correctly the rent due to Eanna on some fields. As royal representative at Eanna, Nabû-šarra-uṣur was in close communication with the crown prince, Belshazzar, during the absence of the king (YOS 6 71, 150; TCL 9 132, 136, 137), the only temple official for whom this was true.[17]

Nabû-šarra-uṣur was actively involved in almost every sphere of the administration of the Eanna.[18] As *ša rēši šarri bēl piqitti Eanna* he leased out temple land; assigned rights and obligations in connection with canals; supervised the assessment, collection, transportation, use, and distribution of the products of the land and canals (including cattle and fish); and kept the accounts associated with these activities. He also played a major role in judicial matters. Under Nabonidus, he became the highest authority within the temple complex. In one case (YOS 6 137), two persons caught with stolen property were brought to him for questioning.[19] On another occasion (YOS 6 144), a guard caught a man who had stolen cattle belonging to the temple, and handed him over to Nabû-šarra-uṣur, the *qīpu*, and other officials of Eanna for interrogation.[20]

A contract provides insight into the nature of the *ša rēši šarri bēl piqitti*.[21] This contract specifies that a person known as the 'man-over-the-tax-on-dates' (*ša muḫḫi sūti*) was to deliver dates to the 'government house' (*ekalli ša šarri*) that is *ina muḫḫi Eanna* 'over Eanna'. This last phrase is ambiguous. It could in theory be taken in a topological sense to denote a hill overlooking the temple, or it could be taken in an administrative sense, 'in charge of Eanna'.[22] The presence of an *ekalli ša šarri* at Eanna suggests a palace established on the command of the king. This passage therefore must mean 'over' in the sense of 'controlling affairs at' Eanna. The presence of the *ša rēši šarri bēl piqitti* in a royal government house over Eanna suggests the real role of the *ša rēši šarri bēl piqitti*: to manage the temple as an economic unit on behalf of the king. The introduction of this office at Eanna under Nabonidus reveals unmistakably that the king had usurped the autonomy of the temple.[23] By this single appointment, the Eanna Temple became the personal fiefdom of the king.

17. Ibid., 71–72; Beaulieu, *Reign of Nabonidus*, 126.
18. Frame, "Nabonidus," 79.
19. Ibid., 73–74.
20. For other examples, see ibid., 75 nn. 91–95.
21. Saggs, "Two Administrative Officials," 32; Pinches, "Two Late Tablets."
22. Saggs, "Two Administrative Officials," 30.
23. San Nicolò, *Beiträge zu einer Prosopographie*, n. 72.

The qīpu ša Eanna

The word *qīpu*, written [lú]*qi-i-pi* or [lú]TIL(.LA).GÍD.DA, from *qâpu* 'entrust', is 'the person authorized, entrusted'. Together with the *šatammu* and the *ṭupšarru bīti*, or later (from the time of Nabonidus) with the appointed royal commissioner (*ša rēši šarri bēl piqitti Eanna*), the *qīpu* constituted Eanna's highest administrative body. As with the *ša rēši šarri bēl piqitti Eanna*, we never know their family names and only occasionally their fathers'. Their origin and appointment were from outside Uruk.

The Šatammu Eanna

The *šatammu* (LÚ ŠÀ.TAM) was the *Verwaltungsdirektor* or the 'chief temple administrator' of Eanna. He sat on the three-member board of the temple's highest administrative body. The elevated status of his position is shown in the fact that in 559–558 the *šatammu* of Ezida married a daughter of the reigning king, Nergal-šarru-uṣur.

As a member of the temple administration, the *šatammu* managed temple estates, temple personnel, and the cult.[24] He was the only one on the board with cultic responsibilities and so the only one to be appointed from among the temple families of Uruk. Together with the other two members, he hired and leased temple land; assigned rights and obligations toward associated canals; supervised the assessment, collection, transportation, use and distribution of the products of temple land and canals; and kept the accounts associated with these activities.

The *šatammu* exercised his responsibilities from his office within the temple. The *ša rēši šarri bēl piqitti* supervised activities directly at the estate or canal and sent reports back to the *šatammu*. For example, in two separate cases (YBT 3 17 and 19) the *ša rēši šarri bēl piqitti* supervised a large work of canal excavation and sent letters back to the *šatammu* at the temple.[25] The bearers of the letters were local tenant farmers who worked on the excavation; the letters were orders to the *šatammu* to pay the bearers. The *šatammu* controlled the records and the accounts at the temple. He also controlled a special fund for temple expenses. At Eanna, in the year 588–587, a certain Innina-zēru-ušabši was named *ša muḫḫi quppi ša šatammu* ('the one in charge of the fund [literally, cashbox] of the *šatammu*').

Was the *šatammu* a royal appointee, or was he selected by temple personnel? A theory of self-governance predicts that temple personnel would choose their own *šatammu*. A theory of central control predicts that the king (whether monarch or emperor) would appoint him. In Neo-Babylonian times, he was appointed by the king. One text reads, "Now I will assume [the position of] *šatammu*, no one may appoint a[nother] *šatammu* to serve along-

24. Saggs, "Two Administrative Officials," 29.

25. Ibid., 31.

side you, since my lord the king gave the *šatammu*-ship (*šatammūtu*) to me" (ABL 1016 rev. 6ff. + CT 54 470). Another text from the Neo-Babylonian period reads: "it is the king who confers the office of *šatammūtu* and of governor" (Landsberger, Brief no. 116; Dietrich, WO 4 70). A new monarch resulted in a new *šatammu*. Because of his cultic responsibilities, he was necessarily selected from among the temple families; yet he was selected by the king and owed his allegiance only to him.

The Ebabbar Temple at Sippar

During the Persian period, the chief administrative personnel of the Ebabbar[26] at Sippar were the *šangû* and the *qīpu*.[27]

The šangû ša Ebabbar

The *šangû* is attested at the Ebabbar from the reign of Nabopolassar on (625–605).[28] According to the witness lists, the *qīpu* ranked above the *šangû* from the reign of Nabopolassar to the end of the reign of Cyrus (529), but from the beginning of the reign of Cambyses on, the *šangû* ranked above the *qīpu*. The duties of the *šangû* included the receipt, issuance, and administration of barley, emmer, flour, bread, dates, sesame, pastry, mustard, sheep, cattle, birds, beer, wine, salt, wool, clothing, silver, gold, iron, bronze, reeds, wood, boats, tools, plows, baked brick, and bitumen. He drew up and checked accounts, carried out inspections of temple stores, supervised receipts of the temple's various revenues, and dealt with problems arising on the rented estates owned by the temple. He oversaw shepherds and shearing, provided seed for land worked by temple laborers, and maintained the canal system.[29] In the company of the *qīpu*, he leased out temple lands, houses, and water rights.[30] He was the head of the huge conglomerate that was the temple.

The *šangû* typically came from well-known families in Sippar. Many of these families are attested as *ērib bīti*s or 'temple enterers' of *Šamaš*. The role of *ērib bīti* included cultic functions with prebendary privileges.[31] In the Chaldaean period, during the reigns of Nabopolassar, Nebuchadnezzar, and Neriglissar, a single family, appropriately called the *Šangû-Sippar* family, provided the *šangû*s of Sippar. A change occurred with Nabonidus. A new family, Šangû-Ištar-Bābili, supplied the *šangû*s from the second year of Nabonidus's reign on. This family continued in office under Cyrus and

26. The following discussion is based on Bongenaar, *Neo-Babylonian Ebabbar*, unless otherwise noted.

27. MacGinnis, *Letter Orders*, 114.

28. San Nicolò, *Beiträge zu einer Prosopographie*, 34ff.

29. MacGinnis, *Letter Orders*, 114–15, with references there.

30. Ibid., 115.

31. The prebend system is discussed below.

Cambyses.[32] Darius's reign brought in a new dynastic family of *šangû*s, and another new family was installed during the accession year of Xerxes. Thus, a new monarch inaugurated a new *šangû* family. The Šangû-Ištar-Bābili family, which provided the *šangû*s under Nabonidus and the early Achaemenid rulers, did not totally lose their grip over Ebabbar when Darius came to power, however. This family provided nearly all the college scribes from the reign of Nabonidus until the archive ended in the second year of Xerxes. These 'scribes of Ebabbar' (lúUMBISAG.MEŠ (*ša*) É.BABBAR.RA = *tupšar Ebabbar*) ranked immediately behind the *šangû* and the *qīpu* in the hierarchy at Ebabbar. They served as direct assistants to the *šangû* and the *qīpu* and owned prebends in the temple. Two of the *šangû*s appointed by Darius moved into the position of *šākin ṭēmi* of Babylon later in Darius's reign.

The qīpu ša Ebabbar

The rank of the *qīpu* at Ebabbar also changed over time. According to the witness lists, during the reign of Kandalanu (647–627) the *qīpu* was the second ranking official after the *šatammu*. At the beginning of Nabopolassar's reign (625–605), he became the highest official and the *šangû* became second; the office of *šatammu* then disappears from our sources. At the beginning of Cambyses' reign (529–522), the *qīpu* became second in rank again, and the *šangû* first.

The family affiliation of those holding the title *qīpu* at Sippar, like those holding this title at Uruk, is not stated in the texts, indicating that they were appointed from outside. Since many *qīpu* at Sippar had a personal name made from the component *šarru* 'king', Bongenaar offers the intriguing suggestion that these were "nobodies" from outside the temple community who proved loyal to the king and received new names with their commission.[33] The *qīpu* shared equally with the *šangû* in the management of the temple. Yet clear differences between them resulted from the fact that the *qīpu* was appointed from outside, while the *šangû* was appointed from within the temple community. Unlike the *šangû*, the *qīpu* did not have private business at Ebabbar, nor did he own prebends in the temple. Unlike the *šangû*, he had no part in the temple's cultic aspects. That the *qīpu* was supported by the state, not the temple, is corroborated by a text from Sippar, now in the British Museum (BM 68777).[34] It is badly damaged, but it contains a list of bundles of something, possibly reeds or arrows, allocated to the *qīpu*s of the major temples of Babylonia (Ezida, Eanki, Esagila, Emeslam, Eankikugga, and so on) from one central source. It is likely that the source was the state,

32. Why Cyrus and Cambyses retained this family is discussed below.
33. Bongenaar, *Neo-Babylonian Ebabbar*, 34.
34. MacGinnis, "Qīpu's Receive."

and if so, it appears that these temples and their *qīpu*s were centrally organized and centrally controlled.

The *qīpu* appears in many types of texts, often in the company of the *šangû*. One of the most characteristic texts at Ebabbar is the letter order, in which two senders order a recipient to pay out commodities to a third party.[35] The senders are either the *šangû* or the *qīpu* plus one or more of the official college scribes. The addressee, either the one in charge of the rents (*ša muḫḫi sūti / rab sûti*) or the one in charge of the tithes (*ša muḫḫi ešrî*), is ordered to pay commodities to temple personnel such as bakers, brewers, or craftsmen.[36] A second type of text is the judicial document. These texts are depositions that begin "PN says to the *šangû* (or to the *qīpu*) as follows"; or "PN swore in the presence of the *šangû* (or in the presence of the *qīpu*) that. . . ." In most of these documents, no settlement is indicated; but in those in which it is indicated, the outcome is decided administratively. Suits involving nontemple personnel are referred to a court of justice in Babylon. Promissory notes as well as contracts for various work assignments and so on were written in the presence of the *šangû* or *qīpu*.

The *qīpu* was involved in the administration of the temple as an economic institution. He issued and received commodities, supervised temple personnel, and managed the estate belonging to the god Šamaš. In this regard, he rented out houses and agricultural land, one of the temple's largest sources of income. Both the *šangû* and the *qīpu* figure in these texts. The *šangû* and the *qīpu* were also involved in contracts regulating the fishing rights of Ebabbar. Together these two officials allocated work assignments of temple personnel, regulated apprenticeship contracts, and supervised the hiring out of oblates.

One of the *qīpu*'s primary responsibilities was the organization and supervision of crews of laborers working outside of Sippar. From the food ration texts, it appears that more than 60 people worked for him. According to one text, the *qīpu* received provisions for 50 workmen (*ṣābū ēpeš dulli ša qīpi*), plus 10 guards, 2 carpenters, a blacksmith, and a chief of oblates (*rab širkī*; CT 56 633). From the beginning of the reign of Darius, texts indicate that crews of workmen directed by the *qīpu* were loaned from Ebabbar to Elam for construction projects. These work crews included men in charge of sheep, cows, and birds, men in charge of feeding these animals to the workers, as well as boatmen, and a man over the "cash-box." These workmen become associated with the *qīpu* only during the reign of Nabonidus. From the beginning of Nabonidus's reign (Nbn. 1), they were called 'workmen working for the *qīpu*' (*ṣābū ēpeš dulli ša qīpi*). Before this, they were simply

35. This letter form was studied extensively by MacGinnis, *Letter Orders*.

36. More on the tithe below.

"oblates working out of town," supervised by the chief of the oblates.[37] Thus, under Nabonidus, workmen were taken from under the aegis of the *rab širkī* of the temple and placed under the *qīpu*, under the control of a royal appointee. Nabonidus thus took direct control over the system of compulsory service that the temple rendered to the state.

Temple-Palace Relations under Nabonidus and Cyrus

Nabonidus and the Marduk Priesthood

According to two Akkadian literary texts, the Cyrus Cylinder and the Nabonidus Verse Account, Nabonidus was despised by the Marduk priesthood, which welcomed Cyrus with open arms. The Verse Account states that Nabonidus had committed every possible sacrilege: he abolished the Akītu festival, he built an abomination and installed it in a temple, he mixed up the rites, confused the oracles, uttered blasphemies, and threatened to turn over the Esagil of Marduk to the god Sîn![38] Oppenheim concludes that "the king appeared to many of his contemporaries as a mad dreamer and reformer, dangerous to the stability of the country, and unfit to be ruler of Babylonia."[39] Dandamayev agrees that Nabonidus was planning to change the Babylonian Temple of Marduk, the supreme god of the land, into a temple of Sîn, causing the Marduk priesthood to side with the Persians.[40] He also argues that the conflict between Nabonidus and the populations of the old sacred cities of Babylon, Borsippa, Nippur, Larsa, Uruk, and Ur reflects the traditional struggle between these cities' popular assemblies and the kings who strove to abolish their privileges.[41] Smith argues that Persian propagandists had persuaded the Marduk priesthood to side with Cyrus.[42] These priests then influenced city leaders to open the gates of Babylon to the foreign conqueror. Vanderhooft recently argues that Nabonidus's attempt to ex-

37. MacGinnis, "Royal Establishment," 205.

38. Translations of the Nabonidus Verse Account and the Cyrus Cylinder may be found in *ANET,* 312–16 with references. For the Cyrus Cylinder, see also Walker, "A Recently Identified Fragment of the Cyrus Cylinder"; Berger, "Der Kyros-Zylinder mit dem Zusatzfragment BIN II Nr. 32 und die akkadischen Personennamen im Danielbuch"; and recently Schaudig, *Die Inschriften Nabonids von Babylon und Kyros' des Großen,* 550–62. For the Verse Account, see pp. 563–78. See also Machinist and Tadmor, "Heavenly Wisdom."

39. Oppenheim, "The Babylonian Evidence of Achaemenid Rule in Mesopotamia," 540–41.

40. Dandamayev (*A Political History of the Achaemenid Empire,* 40) later warns against becoming a victim of Cyrus's propaganda ourselves; ibid., 53.

41. Dandamayev (ibid., 41 n. 1) attributes the idea to V. A. Jakobson, but gives no reference.

42. M. Smith, "II Isaiah and the Persians," 416.

alt Sîn above the other gods resulted in a diminution of the role of Babylon and hastened the collapse of the state.[43]

Smith's view that Cyrus sent advance men to secure good relations with influential local priesthoods is also put forward by Harmatta, who suggests that Cyrus had "good relations" with the Marduk priesthood even before his rebellion against the Medes.[44] Harmatta bases his argument on lines 11–13 of the Cylinder:

> [Marduk] scanned and looked (through) all the countries, searching for a righteous ruler willing to lead him [i.e., Marduk] (in the annual procession). (Then) he pronounced the name of Cyrus (*Ku-ra-aš*), king of Anshan, and declared him [lit., pronounced (his) name] to be(come) the ruler of all the world.

Harmatta proposes that, before his rebellion against the Medes, Cyrus had planned to conquer Babylon and sought to guarantee in advance the good will of the Marduk clergy.[45] In turn, the priests of Marduk received restoration of their rights and royal support for the cult.[46] To Harmatta, this view is substantiated by the Cyrus Cylinder:

> As to the inhabitants of Babylon . . . [I abolished] the corvée. . . . I brought relief to their dilapidated housing. . . . I established for (the gods) permanent sanctuaries.

Since Cyrus agreed to end corvée labor for the citizens of Babylon, to rebuild their houses, and rebuild the sanctuaries of the gods, Harmatta infers that a positive relationship, a quid pro quo, existed even before Cyrus's conquest of Media.

The difficulties with this view have been pointed out by Kuhrt.[47] To begin with, as Harmatta already suspected, the Cyrus Cylinder was based on Babylonian building inscriptions, especially those of Ashurbanipal.[48] Harmatta's hypothesis was confirmed by a fragment that fits the broken end of the cylinder and supplies portions of lines 36–45.[49] These last lines refer to Cyrus's additional offerings to the Temple of Marduk and to his restoration of the city's fortifications. They conclude by stating: "In it (the gateway of the city?) I saw inscribed the name of my predecessor, King Ashurbanipal." Laato

43. Vanderhooft, *The Neo-Babylonian Empire*, 55–57.

44. Harmatta, "Modéles littéraires," 38–39.

45. Ibid., 40.

46. Ibid., 43.

47. Kuhrt, "Nabonidus and the Babylonian Priesthood," 143–44; so also Stolper, *Entrepreneurs and Empire*, 2.

48. Harmatta, "Modéles littéraires," 31–38.

49. Berger, "Der Kyros-Zylinder mit dem Zusatzfragment"; Walker, "A Recently Identified Fragment of the Cyrus Cylinder."

has shown many strong similarities between the Cyrus Cylinder and previous royal inscriptions, the most salient being the titulary.[50] Cyrus's flamboyant titulary in the cylinder is that of the Assyrian kings who ruled Babylon, Ashurbanipal in particular. Akkadian royal inscriptions provided a close model for the authors of the Cyrus Cylinder, suggesting that it was not a spontaneous outburst of affection for the new monarch.

Nevertheless, Beaulieu argues that the Marduk priesthood represented a fifth column in Babylon under Nabonidus. The authors of the Verse Account were "enraged," because "Nabonidus' science and knowledge were alien to Babylonian culture."[51] Beaulieu suggests that the Verse Account reflects Nabonidus's actual attempt to turn the Esagil over to Sîn. His evidence is a dedicatory inscription of the ziggurat of Sîn at Ur.[52] It speaks of the Esagil, the Ezida, and the Egišnugal (all Babylonian temples) as Sîn's dwelling places and begs Sîn to speak favorable words for "the temples of your great godhead."

Beaulieu dates the inscription to 540–539, Nabonidus's 16th year, when Cyrus controlled all of Asia Minor, Urartu, and Elam. The Nabonidus Chronicle records that the gods moved to Babylon in Nabonidus's 17th year as Cyrus approached (III 9–11).[53] It is highly likely that statues of Sîn moved to Babylon from Ḫarran, Ur, and other outlying areas much earlier, in the 16th year, when Cyrus was threatening these areas. If so, the Esagil, the Ezida (the cella of Nâbu in the Esagil[54]), and the Egišnugal (also a Temple of Sîn in Babylon[55]) would have housed Sîn's statues during Cyrus's advance. In fact, the text (Schaudig 150 2:8–12) indicates that the god was not present in the ziggurat at Ur:

> *ana bīti šuāti ḫādiš ina erēbika damqat Esagil Ezida Egišnugal bītat ilûtika rabīti liššakin šaptukka*
>
> When you enter this temple joyfully, may good things for Esagil, Ezida, [and] Egišnugal, temples of your great godhead, be placed on your lips.

Rather than being a usurpation of Marduk's and Nabû's Temples and an exaltation of the god Sîn, this prayer in the inscription for Sîn's ziggurat at Ur may simply have been an acknowledgment of the fact of Sîn's temporary shelter in Babylon at this frightful time.[56]

50. Laato, *The Servant of YHWH and Cyrus,* 47–68; Harmatta, "Modéles littéraires," 35.

51. Beaulieu, *The Reign of Nabonidus King of Babylon (556–539 B.C.),* 217–18.

52. Ibid., Beaulieu's Number 17. The inscription is presented with transliteration and translation in Schaudig, *Die Inschriften Nabonids,* 350–53.

53. Grayson, *Assyrian and Babylonian Chronicles,* 109.

54. George, *House Most High,* 160, #1237.

55. Ibid., 114, #654.

56. It is also possible that Sîn was at his temple in Babylon while the temple in Ur was being repaired; see Hurowitz, "Temporary Temples."

Other than this inscription cited by Beaulieu, no evidence but the Cyrus Cylinder and the Verse Account has been brought forth to express the putative conflict between Nabonidus and the Marduk priesthood. This is because data contemporaneous with Nabonidus's reign do not indicate antagonisms either between him and local priesthoods or between him and city assemblies.[57] Indeed, such data could not exist, for the priest who voiced dislike of the reigning king would, at the very least, have been relieved of his duties. References to Cyrus in the Verse Account and in the Cyrus Cylinder confirm that the negative statements toward Nabonidus were written after the latter's defeat. They could have been written shortly after the conquest or several years later. Kuhrt argues that the Marduk priesthood supported Nabonidus to the end but, after his defeat, switched its allegiance and wrote paeans to Cyrus. She suggests that "the fact of [Nabonidus's] defeat indicated the Babylonian gods supported Cyrus and condemned Nabonidus."[58] Marduk rejected Nabonidus, so the Marduk priesthood rejected him as well. Rather than reflecting their attitudes prior to the conquest, these texts represent the priests' necessary about-face after Cyrus's victory.

Machinist and Tadmor disagree and suggest that the subtle play of literary references in the Verse Account on phrases from Nabonidus's own inscriptions reveals a conflict between Nabonidus and the author of the Verse Account, which characterizes the entire history of Nabonidus's reign.[59] According to Machinist and Tadmor,

> [Kuhrt's] thesis is that the Verse Account does not reflect any real opposition to Nabonidus during his reign that would have come from priestly supporters of Marduk; it was rather a text composed after Nabonidus' defeat by Cyrus, and its condemnation of Nabonidus' actions as king is its own doing, simply a logical consequence of its aim to legitimize his defeat, following a well-established theological and literary pattern. One may agree with Kuhrt about the post-defeat date of the Verse Account, and agree as well that it is part of a long tradition of apologies for changes of rulership. But to go on from there to describe the condemnation in the text as a mechanical reflex of what all apologies do and thus to dismiss it as a witness to pre-defeat tensions in Babylon simply ignores the specificity and sharpness of the kind of argument in the text that we have been examining.[60]

Yet no matter how specific and sharp the condemnation of Nabonidus in the Verse Account is, these post-Cyrus documents cannot testify to a predefeat conflict between Nabonidus and the Marduk priesthood. It is evident that

57. This is also argued by Kuhrt, "Nabonidus and the Babylonian Priesthood"; and Weisberg, "Polytheism and Politics: Some Comments on Nabonidus' Foreign Policy."

58. Kuhrt, "Nabonidus and the Babylonian Priesthood," 143.

59. Machinist and Tadmor, "Heavenly Wisdom."

60. Ibid., 150 n. 34.

the priests who wrote the Cyrus Cylinder and the Verse Account believed that Marduk had rejected Nabonidus and had installed Cyrus, as Kuhrt surmises. In this way they reflect the psychology of the collaborator.[61] But were these really the priests who managed the temple under Nabonidus? I suspect that they were not, that those priests remained loyal to Nabonidus to the end. I suggest it was other priests, newly installed by Cyrus, who wrote the Cyrus Cylinder and the Nabonidus Verse Account.

Cyrus and the Priests of Uruk, Sippar, and Babylon

Whether or not Nabonidus was despised by the Marduk priesthood, texts contemporary with his reign will not reveal it.[62] The strong control he held over the temple and city hierarchy would have prevented such revelations. The data surveyed above indicate that throughout the Neo-Babylonian period the king appointed the mayors (*šākin ṭēmi*s) of the large urban metropolises, as well as the governing boards of the temples within them. The *ša rēši šarri bēl piqitti* of Eanna, the *qīpu*s of Eanna and of Ebabbar, the *šatammu* of Eanna, and the *šangû* of Ebabbar were all appointed by the king. Except for the *šangû* and the *šatammu*, who alone had cultic responsibilities, they were appointed from outside the temple community. Yet, whether they were selected from within or from without the great temple families, they were appointed by the king and owed their allegiance only to him.

Data show that Cyrus exercised the same prerogatives of kingship as did every Babylonian king: he replaced top temple and city officials with his own appointees when he conquered an area.[63] The top officials at Uruk and Eanna were replaced immediately after Cyrus's conquest of Babylon: A new *šākin ṭēmi* of Uruk (TCL 13 124:12) and a new *qīpu* of Eanna (GCCI 2 102:11) were appointed during Cyrus's first regnal year.[64] A new *šatammu* of Eanna and a new *ša rēš šarri bēl piqitti Eanna* (PTS 2301) were appointed even earlier, during the first four months of Cyrus's accession year.[65] Ilī-rēmanni,

61. Lloyd, "The Inscription of Udjaḥorresnet." The psychology of the collaborator will be discussed below in the section on Udjaḥorresnet in the chapter on Egypt.

62. This section has benefited from the comments of John MacGinnis and F. Joannès on an earlier draft.

63. Pace Dandamayev (*A Political History*, 55), who states that "the majority of the officials (possibly all of them) maintained their position in the state administration. . . . These people included judges, governors, etc." Pace also Kuhrt (*The Ancient Near East*, 660) and Stolper (*Entrepreneurs and Empire*, 2), who argue that "when Cyrus took Babylonia he tampered little with it. Radical change was neither desirable nor . . . practical." Stolper cites as evidence the Cyrus Cylinder.

64. Kümmel, *Familie*, 140–41. San Nicolò, *Prosopographie*, did not know that Sula, son of Tabija, was appointed in Cyrus's 1st year.

65. Ibid.

the previous *ša rēš šarri bēl piqitti Eanna,* and Kurbanni-Marduk, the previous *šatammu,* are last attested in the 12th month of Nabonidus's 16th year. Nabû-aḫa-iddin, the new *ša rēš šarri bēl piqitti Eanna,* and Nabû-mukīn-zēri, the new *šatammu,* are attested in the archive four months later, in Cyrus's accession year.[66] Admittedly, this is the 17th year of Nabonidus. Yet, the fact that Nabû-aḫa-iddin continued in office throughout the reign of Cyrus and into the 4th year of Cambyses suggests that he was a Cyrus appointee.[67] Nabû-mukīn-zēri is attested only until the 1st year of Cyrus; but one of his sons became *šatammu* after him, continuing until Cyrus's 5th year (AnOr 8 37; AnOr 8 50). His brother followed after that as *šatammu* and continued through Cambyses' 6th year (AnOr 8 51; YOS 7 198). This suggests that this family, the Dabibi family, one not previously cited among the *šatammu* families at Eanna, had been installed by Cyrus.

Yet, if the new *ša rēš šarri bēl piqitti Eanna* and the new *šatammu Eanna* are attested in the beginning of Nabonidus's 17th year, prior to the conquest of Babylon, could they not have been appointed by Nabonidus himself in the last months of his reign and simply retained by Cyrus and Cambyses? The beginning of the broken third column of the Nabonidus Chronicle implies that Persian armies were operating in the south in the winter of 540–539. The Nabonidus Chronicle (III 1, 2) states:

> . . . *killed/defeated/massacred* (GAZ). The river . . . Ishtar Uruk . . . [arm]ies of Per[sia] . . . [The *seventeenth* year

This reading of the text, supported by Beaulieu,[68] may refer to a Persian defeat of a Babylonian army near the Eanna Temple of Ishtar/Inanna and the city of Uruk. If so, the new *ša rēš šarri bēl piqitti Eanna* and the new *šatammu* may have been installed by Cyrus, not Nabonidus. These men were Babylonian, but the length of their tenure into the reigns of Cyrus and Cambyses indicates that they had collaborated with the Persians. Lloyd discusses the reasons for priestly collaboration with the conquerors.[69] Beyond personal aggrandizement, the primary motivation was their desire to obey the wishes of their god.

Several events are recorded for the last months of Nabonidus's reign. The Nabonidus Chronicle notes that the Akītu festival took place as normally,

66. Beaulieu, "An Episode in the Fall of Babylon to the Persians"; Frame, "Some Neo-Babylonian and Persian Documents Involving Boats."

67. The same may be true of Širikti-Ninurta, the *šakin ṭemi* at Nippur from the 17th year of Nabonidus to the 7th year of Cambyses (Joannès, *TEBR,* 3); he is actually called the *šandabakku* at Nippur, but the functions were the same.

68. Grayson, *ABC,* 282; Beaulieu, *The Reign of Nabonidus,* 220 and n. 52.

69. Lloyd, "The Inscription of Udjaḥorresnet." This notion of priestly collaboration is presented more fully below in the section on Udjaḥorresnet (pp. 63ff.).

but that until the 6th month (Ulul) of Nabonidus's 17th year the gods of Marad, Zababa, Kish, and Hursagkalamma[70] entered Babylon (III 9–11). The gods were brought to Babylon to prevent their being destroyed or captured by the approaching Persian armies.[71] Beaulieu suggests an additional reason: Nabonidus ensured the loyalty of the Babylonian cities by keeping their gods in Babylon.[72] A city's loyalty to Nabonidus was guaranteed as long as its gods were held hostage to him in the capital. Put another way: if a god showed support for Nabonidus by fleeing to Babylon, his priests (no matter who appointed them) could not be true to the god and at the same time support Cyrus. A city could not switch outward allegiance from Nabonidus to Cyrus as long as Nabonidus held its gods in his power.

The goddess Inanna/Ishtar of Eanna had fled Uruk after the defeat of the Babylonian army there and had entered Babylon early in Nabonidus's 17th year. A text (YOS 19 94) dated to the 5th month (Abu), day 5, of the 17th year of Nabonidus records a deposition before the assembly of the *mār banî* of Uruk:

> (These are) the *mār banî* in whose presence Zēriya, son of Ardiya, has thus spoken: Bazuzu, son of Ibni-Ištar, descendant of Gimil-Nanaya, has brought a boat from Babylon to lease it fo[r the sum of xxx], and he said thus: "I will take the barley for the regular offerings of the Lady-of-Uruk to Babylon."[73]

The goddess Inanna/Ishtar was in Babylon by the end of the 4th month. Indeed, six times between the last days of Duzu (the 4th month) and the 6th day of Ulul (the 6th month) the Eanna Temple rented boats.[74] In agreement with Beaulieu, I would suggest that this high number of boat rentals in a little over one month plus the fact that they were witnessed by the (new) *šatammu* and *bēl piqitti* indicate that the rentals were to supply the regular offerings of the goddess at Babylon, and that she had entered Babylon by the end of the 4th month.[75] She would not have left her city if there was no danger from the Persian armies, and she would necessarily have left Uruk before the Persian capture of the city, or she could not have left at all. The new (Persian-

70. This area is also at Kish and contains the Temple of Ištar; George, *House Most High*, 101.

71. They were not brought to Babylon to increase the cities' dependence on the capital, pace Weinfeld, "Cult Centralization in Israel in the Light of a Neo-Babylonian Analogy." For a discussion of this practice, see Meissner, *Babylonien und Assyrien*, 126–28; Cogan, *Imperialism and Religion: Assyria, Judah and Israel in the Eighth and Seventh Centuries, B.C.*, 30–34; Beaulieu, "An Episode in the Fall of Babylon to the Persians," 241–43; and my "Land Lay Desolate."

72. Beaulieu, "Episode in the Fall of Babylon," 223.

73. Ibid., 245.

74. Frame, "Documents Involving Boats"; Beaulieu, "Episode in the Fall of Babylon."

75. Ibid.

appointed?) officials ensured the continued support of the cult of Inanna even while she was at the temple in Babylon. Their first duty would have been to the god, wherever she was.

One more text (YOS 3 145) must be considered, an undated letter.

> Letter of Rī[mūt] to Nabû-[mukīn-zēri], *šatammu* of the E[anna], and Nabû-aḫa-id[din], *bēl piqitti* [of the Eanna], my brothers. May Nabû and Marduk bless my brothers! Send me one leather mat and five (inflated) goatskins for the boat concerning the La[dy] of the Eanna via the soldiers who will bring the boat parts to me, (so that) the Lady of the Eanna may go to Babylon on the Euphrates.[76]

The addressees are Eanna's newly appointed *šatammu* and *bēl piqitti.* The letter must have been written early in Nabonidus's 17th year. Although Rīmūt is a common name, the sender may have been the *zazakku* official who served at the end of Nabonidus's reign.[77] Beaulieu interprets the text as a demand from Rīmūt to the officials at Eanna to send the goddess to Babylon from her temple in Uruk. Yet, nowhere does the text state that the goddess herself be sent, only a boat and boat parts. Beaulieu suggests further that Rīmūt must be in Babylon, since that is the location of the two gods Nabû and Marduk, from whom he requests a blessing. However, Rīmūt wants the boat and boat parts sent to *him,* so that the goddess may travel to Babylon on the Euphrates. This suggests that the goddess is with Rīmūt, not in her temple, and that Rīmūt needs the boats to bring her up to Babylon. Rīmūt is not in Babylon; rather, he and the goddess must be somewhere in the south, on the Euphrates between Uruk and Babylon, and they lack the necessary equipment to continue their journey. Rīmūt had very likely gone to Uruk to snatch Inanna in advance of a possible Persian conquest of the city. They had started out for Babylon, but got into trouble, lost their boats, and needed replacements. Rīmūt's demand for boats and boat parts included a reference to Babylonian soldiers, suggesting that there were hostile armies in the area.

Contrary to the situation in Uruk, the officials of the Ebabbar Temple at Sippar were not replaced by Cyrus. The Šangû-Ištar-Bābili family, appointed in Nabonidus's 2nd year, continued in office under Cyrus and Cambyses. The *qīpu,* Bêl-aḫḫê-iqîša, appointed in Nabonidus's 9th year, continued into Cyrus's 4th. Also contrary to the situation at Uruk, Sippar surrendered without a battle (Nabonidus Chronicle III:14), and the gods of Sippar did not attempt to enter Babylon (III:11). They sided with Cyrus. Cyrus seems to have replaced officials of temple cities that resisted his armies and whose gods had fled (e.g., Uruk), but did not replace officials of temple cities that did not

76. Idem, *The Reign of Nabonidus,* 221.
77. Idem, "Episode in the Fall of Babylon."

resist him and whose gods stayed in place (e.g., Sippar). If this is accurate, one may ask whether Babylon resisted the Persian attack and whether Cyrus replaced the top officials of Babylon and of the Esagil when he entered that city.

The Nabonidus Chronicle suggests that the priests of the Esagil in Babylon resisted the Persian onslaught. I cite column III:

> . . . *killed/defeated.* The river . . .[78] . . . Ishtar Uruk . . . [arm]ies of Per[sia][79] [The *seventeenth* year: N]abû [came] from Borsippa for the procession of [Bēl. Bēl came out]. [In the month] Tebet the king entered Éturkalamma. In the *temple* [. . .] . . . He made a libation of wine. . . . [. . . . B]el came out. . . . They performed the Akītu festival *as in normal times.* In the month [. . .] [the gods] of Marad, Zababa and the gods of Kish, Ninlil [and the gods of] Hursagkalamma entered Babylon. Until the end of the month Ulūlu the gods of Akkad [. . .] which are above and below [the wall?] were entering Babylon. The gods of Borsippa, Kutha, and Sippar did not enter (Babylon). . . . the river [Tigris]. In the month Tashritu when Cyrus (II) did battle at Opis on the [*bank of*] the Tigris against the army of Akkad, the people of Akkad retreated. He (Cyrus) carried off the plunder (and) slaughtered the people. On the fourteenth day, Sippar was captured without a battle. Nabonidus fled. On the sixteenth day Ugbaru, governor of the Guti, and the army of Cyrus entered Babylon without a battle. Afterwards, after Nabonidus retreated, he was captured in Babylon. Until the end of the month the shield-(bearing troops) of the Guti surrounded the gates of the Esagil. (But) there was no interruption (of rites) in Esagil or the (other) temples and no date (for a performance) was missed. On the third day of the month Marcheshvan Cyrus entered Babylon.[80]

The events of Nabonidus's last year can be reconstructed as follows: the Persians defeated a Babylonian army near Uruk at the end of Nabonidus's 16th year, in Adar (March) at the latest (III:1, 2). In consequence, Inanna fled Uruk, arriving in Babylon by the end of the 4th month of Nabonidus's 17th year. Persia's southern offensive would have been the second prong of a pincer attack, for Herodotus (1.190) places Cyrus's armies at the headwaters of the

78. Pace Dandamayev (*Political History,* 44), who follows Cameron ("Cyrus the 'Father,'" 46) and S. Smith (*Babylonian and Historical Texts*) in restoring "Tigris" as the name of the river, but the name is not in the text. The river is probably the Euphrates. Uruk was well watered and situated on a network of tributaries from the Euphrates River (Boehmer, "Uruk-Warka").

79. This reconstruction was suggested by von Voigtlander (*A Survey of Neo-Babylonian History*) and accepted by Cameron ("Cyrus the 'Father'"); by Grayson (*ABC,* 282), who agrees that ^{kur}*Pa*[*r-su*(?) . . .] at the end of III:3 is preferable to ^{kur}*ta*[*m.*(*tim?*). . . .]; and by Beaulieu (*Reign of Nabonidus,* 219–20; idem, "Episode in the Fall of Babylon," 260 n. 50).

80. Grayson, *ABC,* 108–10.

Diyala River, above Opis, in the spring of that same year.[81] Cyrus must have met stiff resistance there, for the Chronicle reports that the gods were safely entering Babylon until the end of Ulul (September 26). By the 1st of Tashritu (September 27), after many months of fighting, Cyrus had made his way downriver to Opis. The Babylonian army (the people and army of Akkad), which had been defending the city, fled. Cyrus destroyed the city, took the plunder, and slaughtered the remaining inhabitants.[82] He then moved on to Sippar, on the Euphrates, across from Opis. This city surrendered on the 14th of Tashritu without a battle. Nabonidus escaped to Babylon. By then almost his entire kingdom had been taken, north and south (above and below the wall?—III:11), and only the city of Babylon remained.[83]

On the 16th of Tashritu (October 12), Ugbaru and his army attacked Babylon and entered it. The center of the Neo-Babylonian city of Babylon was the temple precinct of the Esagil, devoted primarily to Marduk. After his losses at Opis and Sippar, Nabonidus fled to Babylon and then to the Esagil. The army of Ugbaru entered Babylon without a battle and laid siege to the temple precinct. *Until the end of the month the shield-(bearing troops) of the Guti surrounded the gates of the Esagil.* This siege lasted 14 days. During this period, the rites of the Esagil continued. At the end of the 14-day siege, the Esagil and Nabonidus surrendered, and the city was conquered.

The Marduk priesthood did not throw open the gates to Cyrus. The temple precinct of the Esagil resisted the Persian attack. This suggests that as he did at Opis, Cyrus slaughtered the defenders of the Esagil, replacing the temple priesthood and Babylon's top officers with men of his own choosing. This is indicated at the end of the third tablet of the Nabonidus Chronicle. After the conquest of Babylon, and after Cyrus's triumphal entrance into the city, the Nabonidus Chronicle reports that Cyrus's governor, Gubarvaya, appointed new officials for Babylon (III:20):

> *Gubaru pāḫatišu pāḫatūti ina Bābili ipteqid.*
>
> Gubaru, his governor, appointed officials in Babylon.

The officials whom Gubarvaya appointed in Babylon would have included the leadership of the Esagil, the Temple of Marduk, the *šākin ṭēmi*, and the officials of the city. The temple and city officials whom he appointed

81. If Cyrus engaged in irrigation efforts on the Diyala, according to Herodotus (1.189) it was during the previous summer, the summer of 540, not the summer in which he attacked Babylon. Further, it would have been in the part of the Diyala that was in Media.

82. The plunder would have included the city's gods. See Younger, *Ancient Conquest Accounts.*

83. The biblical book of Kings records that Sennacherib took all of the fortified cities of Judah before he attacked Jerusalem (2 Kgs 18:13).

would owe their allegiance only to him. Like every Babylonian king, Cyrus sought to commandeer the temple's huge wealth for himself. It would have been these priests, newly installed, who wrote the Cyrus Cylinder and the Nabonidus Verse Account.

Priestly Collaborators

Who were the new priests installed in the Esagil by Cyrus and Gubarvaya? They were not Iranians. Dandamayev finds little evidence of Iranians in high-ranking temple positions anywhere in Babylonia under the Achaemenids.[84] They were Babylonians, and they were collaborators.[85] They enabled Cambyses to take the hand of Marduk and be legitimated as king of Babylon in the Akītu festival that spring, as is suggested by the Nabonidus Chronicle.[86]

> On the night of the eleventh of the month Marcheshvan, Ugbaru died. In the month [. . .] the king's wife died. From the twenty-seventh of the month Adar to the third of the month Nisan [there was] (an official) mourning period in Akkad. All of the people bared their heads. On the fourth day when Cambyses (II), son of C[yrus (II)], went to Egidrikalammasummu the . . .-official of Nabû who . . . [. . .] When he came, because of the Elamite . . . (dress) . . . the hand of Nabû [. . .] . . . [. . .] [sp]ears and quivers from [. . .] . . . crown prince to the [. . .] Nabû to Esagil . . . before Bēl and the son of B[ēl . . .].[87]

The date is the 4th of Nisannu, the precise date during the Akītu festival for the king to travel to Borsippa to retrieve the god Nabû and escort him back to his father, Bēl, at the Esagila.[88] Instead of going to Borsippa as was usual, Cambyses went to the Temple of Nabû of the *ḫaru* in east Babylon.[89] Unfortunately, the text breaks off here; there is no information about subsequent days. However, there is no indication that Cambyses did not complete the ceremony appropriately, especially since it is clear he immediately became king of Babylon and shared a co-regency with Cyrus. Several texts are dated to the 'first year of Cyrus, king of lands, and Cambyses, king of Babylon' ^{m}*Ku-ra-aš* LUGAL KUR.KUR ^{m}*Ka-am-bu-zi-ja* LUGAL TIN.TIR^{KI}.[90] It

84. Dandamayev, *Iranians in Achaemenid Babylonia.*

85. The issue of priestly collaborators and their motivation will be discussed in the section on Udjaḥorresnet in the chapter on Egypt.

86. Pace Kuhrt and Sherwin-White, who argue that there is no evidence that any Persian king ever participated in the Akitu festival (Kuhrt and Sherwin-White, "Xerxes' Destruction of Babylonian Temples," 79–80).

87. Grayson, *Assyrian and Babylonian Chronicles,* Chronicle 7, iii 22–28, pp. 110–11.

88. Black, "The New Year Ceremonies in Ancient Babylon."

89. George, *House Most High,* 132 n. 878.

90. BM 55089 [82-5-22, 1421], BM 67848 [82-9-18, 7846], BM 61307 [82-9-18, 1282], Zawadzki, "Cyrus-Cambyses Coregency."

would have been in exchange for these new priests' collaboration with the conqueror that Cyrus abolished the city's obligation for corvée labor (the yoke):

> As to the inhabitants of Babylon, whom he (Nabonidus) against the wil[l of the gods] the yoke, which for them was not appropriate, made them pull. For their exhaustion I provided rest, I removed the yoke. (lines 25–26, Cyrus Cylinder)[91]

Cyrus's Mode of Administration

By participating in the Akītu festival, Cambyses had himself legitimated by the traditional modes of Babylonian kingship. In so doing he arrogated to himself the theology of the local king. Cyrus used the existing administrative system to legitimate himself, but he installed his own men in the positions of power. Nabonidus had created the position of *ša rēši šarri bēl piqitti* to enhance his control over the temple and its assets, a practice the Achaemenids continued. Except for officials directly responsible for the cult—necessarily members of local priestly families—the Achaemenids, like the Neo-Babylonian dynasty before them, brought in men from outside who owed their allegiance only to themselves.

Although the administrative system continued nominally much as before, crucial differences resulted from the conversion of a free and independent state to a satrapy within the Persian Empire. Primary among these was the installation of the Persian Gubarvaya as satrap over Babylon and Beyond the River (*pāḫat Babili u Ebir-nāri*) at the moment of conquest.[92] He is recorded in this role again in Cyrus's 4th year (Pohl I 43:16, 18) and regularly thereafter until August 525.[93] The lack of texts with Gubarvaya's name or title from Cyrus's 2nd and 3rd years and the presence of two documents from this period with Nabu-aḫḫê-bulliṭ named as *šākin māti Babili*[ki], holding similar functions, have suggested to some that the two men worked alternately, not simultaneously.[94] However, a difference between two texts and no texts is not significant when compared with the thousands of texts that exist from this period. It is more likely that both held office during these years, that

91. Schaudig, *Die Inschriften*, 553, 556.

92. Nabonidus Chronicle III:20. Petit, *Satrapes et satrapies*, 49–59. The administration of the region thus did not remain as it was before, pace Joannès, "Pouvoirs locaux," and Briant, *HEP*, 82–83, 919. Briant claims that the evidence used by Petit is "incomplete."

93. San Nicolò, *Beiträge zu einer Prosopographie*, 56 n. 1; Stolper, "The Governor of Babylon and Across the River," 289–90.

94. San Nicolò, *Beiträge zu einer Prosopographie*, 61–64; Briant, *HEP*; Joannès, "Pouvoirs locaux"; Tuplin, "Achaemenid Administration," 114.

the *šākin māti* served under Gubarvaya, the satrap, and that sometime after the 4th year the position of *šākin māti* was eliminated. If this is so, then the power, status, and prestige of the *šākin māti* would have been drastically reduced at the moment of the Persian conquest.

Under the reigns of Cyrus and Cambyses, the Persian satrap Gubarvaya (^{lú}*pāḫat Babili*^{ki} *ù* ^{kur}*Ebir-nāri*) appointed judges and high civil and temple officials.[95] He supervised judicial decision-making, the excavation and cleansing of canals, and the repair of official buildings and temples; and he regulated commercial activities in the interest of the state. His commands were enforced by troops recruited from within the satrapy, most likely through the *bīt ritti*, to be discussed below.

Like his predecessors, Cyrus legislated through his own royal edicts and through the edicts of the officials he appointed. There were no legislative assemblies. A search among the Neo-Babylonian and Persian period instances of the word *puḫru* ('assembly') and *paḫāru* ('to assemble') reveals the nature of this institution. A *puḫru* was called for judicial decisions, such as when a sheep was stolen or land needed to be reassigned. No legislative sessions are recorded.[96] The parties to the transaction spoke before judges, who gave their opinion, and a scribe drew up the case. The witnesses listed agreed that the matter occurred and that the decision was rendered as described. The people who were called to testify during the proceedings were not the same ones who are listed as the witnesses to the proceedings, although the same term is used (*mukinnu*). The 20 or 30 men listed as witnesses to the trial and to the ultimate decision formed the *puḫru*.[97] These members (*mār banī*) of the assembly (*puḫru*) did not speak. The provincial governor, mayor, judges, or temple leaders announced the verdict. Although the decisions were rendered in the name of the assembly, rather than in the names of the specific judges, the assembled *mār banī* simply witnessed the decisions. They did not

95. Petit, *Satrapes et satrapies*, 55–56 and nn. 183–88, based on more than twenty texts.

96. Van de Mieroop (*The Ancient Mesopotamian City*, 120) argues that this is an accident of scribal practices. Mesopotamian records are primarily concerned with the transfer of property, and no exchanges took place between government and citizenry. However, this cannot be the whole story. Ultimate powers of legislation belonged to the king. Whether or not citizens advised, the responsibility was the king's or the king's surrogates. If citizens advised, this advice would not be given publicly in assembly but in private audience, and not recorded. (I am indebted to Martha Roth, Tim Collins, and Linda McLarnan of the Chicago Oriental Institute for their help in searching their database.)

97. The only exceptions to this come from literary texts (ibid., 118–41, with bibliography; idem, "The Government of an Ancient Mesopotamian City"; Bloom, *Ancient Near Eastern Temple Assemblies*).

contribute to the decision-making process.[98] The purpose of trials before an assembly of respected citizens was so that trials would be open and decisions rendered in full view of the public. Dandamayev points to the literary composition "Advice to a Prince," in which it is stated that, if a citizen is unjustly convicted, "Shamash will establish foreign rule in his country."[99] The public nature of trials and dispositions ensure justice. Yet, as Dandamayev also makes clear, the centuries-old rivalry between the royal court and the popular assembly of the temple communities had already ended under the Chaldaean kings with the defeat of the [legislative] assembly.[100] There was no vehicle for local control of either the city or the temple under Nabonidus and none under the Achaemenids.

Like previous kings, Cyrus governed through the judges that he appointed. After the Achaemenid occupation of Babylon, local judges were replaced by Persians.[101] The "judge of the canal of Sîn" was the Persian Ishtabuzanu; later his son, Humardātu, took over the post. A document on the receipt of a loan of 45 *mina* of silver by Marduk-naṣir-apli of the house of Egibi was registered in the presence of the Iranian judge Ammadātu.

The judges appointed by Cyrus and his officials were the vehicle through which royal edicts were enforced. The ubiquitous Mesopotamian law codes did not restrict these decisions. Law collections, inscribed on steles set up in temples or in the market place, or buried as foundation deposits in temple walls, were intended to demonstrate the ruler's concern to establish truth and justice, not to serve as a system of law. The term *law code* is a misnomer. The goal of modern law codes is to provide a complete and comprehensive list of the laws and prescriptions that govern a legal jurisdiction. To this end, they are continually revised and updated. In this sense, the ancient law collections

98. Pace Dandamayev, "The Neo-Babylonian Elders"; idem, "Babylonian Popular Assemblies"; idem, "State and Temple in Babylonia"; idem, "Social Stratification in Babylonia"; and Dandamayev and Lukonin, *The Culture and Social Institutions of Ancient Iran,* 361. In all of these, Dandamayev argues that the most important questions (of temple administration) were resolved by an assembly of the citizens of the temple district in question. He should say "before" an assembly. . . . The evidence adduced only indicates that the *mār banî* served as witnesses to the decision which was made by the judges or ranking officials. There is no indication that they spoke, voted, or gave assent. Athenian trials cannot be used as a model of Mesopotamian ones. In Athens, where a trial could be before hundreds of citizens, there were no judges, few witnesses, and the verdict was rendered according to the majority vote of the assembled. This was not the case in Mesopotamia under the Persians.

99. Dandamayev, "Babylonian Popular Assemblies."

100. Idem, "State and Temple in Babylonia," 591.

101. Dandamayev and Lukonin, *The Culture and Social Institutions of Ancient Iran,* 122–23.

are not codes. They are notoriously incomplete.[102] Whole areas of law are missing; yet, they were never revised to add these missing sections.[103] Hammurabi's Code, for example, does not deal with cases of arson, treason, theft of livestock, surety, barter, murder, manumission, or sale.[104] These omissions are even more surprising when placed against the hundreds of court cases extant.[105] Problems and conflicts arise that are never mentioned in the codes, yet they are not emended to account for them. Moreover, among the dozens of court cases extant, none refers to any article from these law codes, even when the case deals with a subject that the codes cover.[106] Indeed, many cases are resolved differently from the procedure suggested by the codes, as if the codes did not exist.[107] The notion of written law as binding on judges is a modern concept. It was not part of the understanding of the ancient Near East. As is often pointed out, there is no Akkadian word for "law," and such expressions as "to observe the law," "the validity of the law," or even "convicted according to law #x" never appear.[108]

Hammurabi's Code, for example, contains more than 280 separate articles, each structured in the form of a conditional proposition. They begin with a protasis, introduced by the conjunction *šumma* 'if', and end with an apodosis, describing a concrete situation. This casuistic formula has caused scholars to label these articles as case law and to conclude that they record actual verdicts.[109] However, normal judicial decisions were not phrased as conditional sentences.[110] The purpose of Hammurabi's stele was not to proclaim law; rather, it was to demonstrate that the king had established justice in the land. To set up a physical stele was to set up abstract justice. Hammurabi states:

102. Westbrook, "Biblical and Cuneiform Law Codes"; Bottéro, "The 'Code' of Ḫammurabi," 161.

103. Hittite laws may be an exception. See Westbrook, "What Is the Covenant Code?"

104. E.g., Bottéro, "The 'Code' of Ḫammurabi"; Westbrook, "What Is the Covenant Code?" Greengus, "Some Issues Relating to the Comparability of Laws and the Coherence of the Legal Tradition."

105. Bottéro, "The 'Code' of Ḫammurabi," 161.

106. As Westbrook points out, cancellation of debts, reorganization of the royal administration, and the fixing of prices and wages fall into the arena of royal edicts. These form an exception to the rule (Westbrook, "What Is the Covenant Code?" 24–25).

107. Bottéro, "The 'Code' of Ḫammurabi"; see my discussion in "You Shall Appoint Judges."

108. Landsberger, "Die babylonischen Termini für Gesetz und Recht."

109. E.g., Greengus, "Legal and Social Institutions of Ancient Mesopotamia," 472.

110. Rather than being law, these codes are in fact a treatise on justice. See my "You Shall Appoint Judges," for a discussion.

> In order that the mighty not wrong the weak, to provide just ways for the waif and the widow, I have inscribed my precious pronouncements upon my stele and set it up before the statue of me, the king of justice, in the city of Babylon, the city which the gods Anu and Enlil have elevated, within the Esagil, the temple whose foundations are fixed as are heaven and earth, in order to render the judgments of the land, to give the verdicts of the land, and to provide just ways for the wronged.
>
> Let any wronged man who has a lawsuit come before me, the king of justice, and let him have my inscribed stele read aloud to him, thus may he hear my precious pronouncements and let my stele reveal the lawsuit for him; may he examine his case, may he calm his troubled heart, and may he praise me.[111]

The implication is not that a wronged man may see his case inscribed on the stele and feel relieved about its outcome. The odds are not good that his particular case will be included. Rather, what he will see on the stele are instances of *justice itself.* He sees these and is reassured.

Because these lists did not function as law codes, judges based their decisions on their own socially constructed values of right and wrong. Royal judges, appointed by the king, were often Iranian. The men who decided cases for the temple community comprised the temple's governing board and, though Babylonian, were selected by the king. Cases involving both the temple and external parties were decided by the *šākin ṭēmi,* also appointed by the king. There were no professionally trained judges, and there was no independent judiciary.

Eisenstadt's model of central control predicts that the Achaemenid rulers put their own men on governing boards of temples and cities in order to funnel temple resources to themselves. Frei's theory of Imperial Authorization predicts that these royal appointees used their positions to authorize indigenous temple norms. The theory of noninterference predicts that the royal appointees stayed out of local affairs as long as tribute continued to be funneled to the king. The following section investigates these three hypotheses.

The Resources of the Temple and Their Allocation

Eisenstadt's model defines the political struggle between ruler and local elites as a competition for control of resources: agricultural, monetary, and human. Under the Achaemenids all of these fell under the direct control of the king, and resources followed a one-way path from temple to palace. I discuss this allocation through: (1) land and its usufruct, (2) the prebendary system, and (3) the slave and corvée labor.

111. Quoted in Roth, *Law Collections,* 133–34.

Temple Land and Its Usufruct

Temple Land

The land around the city of Uruk was owned either by the king, by private individuals, or by the Eanna Temple.[112] Lands acquired by the king or his governors by encroachment on land previously owned by others was called *gizzātu*. Royal lands were exploited directly by the king or distributed as fiefs to those meriting his favor. Royal lands were often let out to temples or temple personnel as *bīt ritti* 'hand estates'.[113] Some land was owned by private individuals, and often the owner did not live in Uruk. But the primary owner of the surrounding lands was the Eanna, and this land was immense. The temple alone occupied an area of 300 × 200 m; the sanctuary itself measured 90 × 90 m, with 150 service and warehouse facilities adjoining it.[114] The temple also possessed lands at Marad, on the seacoast, and at Sippar. Similarly, other temples (for example, Ebabbar at Sippar) owned land in areas around Uruk.

Prior to Nabonidus, small farmers—*errēšu* and *ikkaru*—worked the land for the profit of the temple. For their labor, these tenant farmers, or sharecroppers, received a portion of the crop. The *ikkaru* received a fixed amount as rations; the *errēšu* received a percentage share of the produce. [115] In many cases, oxen and manual labor (slaves or hired workers) were furnished by the temple to these lessee farmers. Besides the leased lands, the temple also ceded certain areas as prebends (*isqu*) to people associated with the temple. The date palm groves of Ḫallat had this status. They were assigned as prebendary property to master workers (^{lú}GAL.DÙ^{meš} = *rab bāni*). The owners of the prebends as well as the lessees paid rent to the temple. In addition, all the land around Uruk was subject to a tithe.

Who allocated the leases? Who distributed the prebends? Who controlled the usufruct? On the 8th day of the 1st month of his 1st regnal year, Nabonidus issued the so-called "Charte du 28 Nisan" when Šum-ukīn and Kalbaia asked him to give them annually 6,000 kur (almost 80 square km) of arable land belonging to Eanna, plus date groves, 400 workers (*ikkaru*), 400 oxen, and 100 cows.[116] For the first year, they requested an additional 3,000 kur of seed barley (ca. 540,000 liters) and 10 talents of iron with which to forge farm implements. In return for all this, they agreed to give 25,000 kur of bar-

112. This section is based primarily on Cocquerillat, *Palmeraies.*

113. Joannès, "Pouvoirs locaux." Beginning with the period of Darius I, they appear to have had a military function. This is discussed more fully below (pp. 42ff.).

114. Dandamayev and Lukonin, *The Culture and Social Institutions of Ancient Iran,* 360.

115. Kümmel, *Familie,* 97–98.

116. Joannès, *TEBR,* 126; Beaulieu, *The Reign of Nabonidus,* 117. Three copies of the text are extant (YOS 6 11, VAT 8418, and AO 19924).

ley (4.5 million liters) and 10,000 kur of dates (1.8 million liters) to Eanna each year.[117] Nabonidus agreed to the request; the contract was concluded.

The witnesses to the contract included: the governor (*šākin māti*); the chief slaughterer (*rab ṭābiḫī*); the governor of Bit Ada (*bēl pīḫāti bīt Ada*); the chief of the [royal] seals (*rab unqāti*); the chief of the army (*rab kiṣri*); the chief of troops (*rab ṣābī*); the mayor of Uruk (*šākin ṭēmi Uruk*); Nabû-šarra-uṣur, at that time still only entitled *ša rēši šarri*; and a scribe, Aplaia, son of Bēl-Iddin, of the family Egibi.[118] All were royal appointees, answerable only to the king. Noticeably absent were the *šatammu*, the *qīpu*, and the *ṭupšar Eanna*, who constituted the temple's governing board at the time. That the witness list included the army chief (*rab kiṣri*) and the chief of troops (*rab ṣābû*) suggests compulsion. The absence of local high temple personnel hints that the temple did not comply willingly.

Two years later, a second contract of this type was concluded. According to this contract (YBT 6 41), Nergal-nāṣir requested temple land, not from the king, but from Nabû-šarru-uṣur, now titled *ša rēši šarri bēl piqitti Eanna*. He stood *in loco regis*, leasing temple land as the king did before him. Several temple officials (*bēl piqitti Eanna*) witnessed the contract, including the chief of the brewers.[119] The *qīpu*, the *šatammu*, and the *ṭupšar bīti* again were absent. A third contract (YBT 6 40), dated to the 3rd year of Nabonidus, is similar to the previous one.[120] Nabû-šarra-uṣur, in his role as representative of the king, leased out temple land to a private individual. Witnesses to this contract included the chief of the flocks (*rab būli*) and the chief of the archers of the royal herds (*ša muḫḫi* ^{lú}*qašti ša* ^{lú}*re'û ša šarri*).[121] Again, the *šatammu*, the *qīpu*, and the *ṭupšar bīti* were absent. A fourth contract (TCL 12 90), identical to these two, is dated to the 8th year of Nabonidus, while the king was at Taima.

These contracts created a system of agricultural administration called *ferme générale*.[122] A private individual or group, known as the *fermier général* (*ša muḫḫi sūti*; lit., 'the man over the rents'), was allocated land belonging to the temple for the cultivation of barley and dates. The temple assigned the *fermier général* a certain number of workers and cattle annually, as well as iron for building and repairing equipment. In the first year of the contract, the temple provided barley seed. In return, the *fermier général* agreed to pay

117. Joannès, *TEBR*, 137–38. A kur is a measure of volume. It is also used to describe area. It is the area of land that a kur of seed will sow.

118. Ibid., 138–39.

119. Cocquerillat, *Palmeraies*, 39–40, 108–9; Joannès, *TEBR*, 140.

120. Cocquerillat, *Palmeraies*, 40, 109.

121. Joannès, *TEBR*, 140.

122. Cocquerillat, *Palmeraies*, 37ff. See also, Joannès, "Relations entre intérêts privés et biens des sanctuaries à l'époque néo-babylonienne"; and Kessler, *Uruk*.

a rent in barley and dates (the *sūti*) fixed in advance. By agreeing to a fixed sum, the *fermier général* assumed all the risk. The system begun in the 1st year of Nabonidus continued at Eanna for the duration of the archive.

The so-called Edict of Belshazzar (YBT 6 103) later formalized the system. Promulgated in the 7th year of Nabonidus by Belshazzar, the crown prince, on the order of his father, the king, the edict set forth the terms under which land belonging to the Esagil in Babylon could be leased.[123] Although the document directly concerned only the estates of the Esagil, it was found among the archives of Eanna in Uruk. The system established at the Esagil governed land-lease for all the temples in the king's realm.

The first line of the Edict reads: "[Regarding the] Land of Bēl which in Nisan of year 7 of Nabonidus, king of Babylon, Belshazzar, the crown prince, assigned to the *fermiers généraux* (LÚ.GAL.MEŠ GIŠ.BÁN.MEŠ = *ša muḫḫi sûti*)."[124] Belshazzar, and not a member of the Esagil, assigned temple lands to individual rent-farmers. That this Edict was everywhere in force is shown in a contract (YBT 6 150) from the Eanna, dated to the 11th year of Nabonidus, in which the request to rent temple farmland is made not to Nabû-šarra-uṣur, the *ša rēši šarri bēl piqitti Eanna*, but to Belshazzar himself.[125] The document begins as follows: "Ibni-Ištar, son of Balaṭu, oblate (*širku*) of the Lady of Uruk, requests of Bēl-šar-uṣur, the son of the king, his lord, in these terms: May the son of the king, my lord, give me 625 *kur* of arable land from a cultivated area among the grain producing lands of the Lady of Uruk." The terms of the contract follow those set forth in the Edict. The Edict formalized a system of central control over the diverse estates of all the temples of the realm. Local temple governing boards had no part in the system. One document from the time of Darius (BRM 1 101) states that Uštanu, the satrap of Babylon and Beyond the River, ordered the *šangu* of Sippar to report to him concerning the stipulations required to lease temple land.[126] By the last half of the 5th century, most of the real properties witnessed in the Murašû archive were completely under the administrative control of the Persian satrapal office in Babylon.[127] The Murašû texts witness to the large landed estates around Nippur owned by members of the royal family, courtiers, and officials of the Persian crown.[128] Temple control of the

123. The 7th year of Nabonidus was the first year the king was away in Teima, and the first year in which Belshazzar served as regent.

124. Van Driel, "Edict of Belshazzar," 63.

125. Cocquerillat, *Palmeraies,* 42, 109–10.

126. Dandamayev, "Achaemenid Mesopotamia," 229.

127. Stolper, *Entrepreneurs and Empire,* 36, 41–45.

128. Ibid., 26. These included a queen during the time of Artaxerxes I; Queen Parysatis, wife and half-sister of Darius II; Arsames, prince of the royal household, and satrap of Egypt; and eleven other men entitled "prince."

land had disappeared.[129] In 5th-century Nippur, the disposal of temple lands was administered by an independent firm of general contractors hired by agents of the king—the house of Murašû. The Sîn Canal watered property on "land of (the god) Bēl," for example, yet in the 5th century, rents on it were collected by the Murašû firm and leased out by it. There was no visible involvement of the temple's administrative board.[130] The canal was the temple's in name only. By the middle of the 5th century, the power of the temple as an economic institution had been completely eroded. It was replaced by that of the monarchy and its attendant bureaucracy, composed of the friends and family of the king.

Canals and Water Rights

The limiting factor on Babylonian agriculture was water, and during the Neo-Babylonian and Achaemenid periods, irrigation systems were expanded by the state and enhanced with a series of interlocking grids. Parallel main canals were crossed by a series of secondary channels that greatly increased the area of irrigated land and improved drainage. This increased the output, but the canals and the water also became objects of sale and lease. The canals and the water rights were conferred by agents of the crown; these rights could be leased but could not be alienated from the state.

Use of a canal obligated the individual to its repair and upkeep. One text from Uruk dated to the 2nd year of Cambyses (TCL 13 150) required a certain canal manager named Aqrija to muster ten men from among his farmers (^{lú}ENGAR^{meš}) for work on the canal or suffer the sanction of the satrap (*ḫiṭu ša* ^{m}*Gūbāri šadādu*). The canal managers were subject to another official called the *mašennu*. These were usually members of the royal household, as was the satrap himself.[131]

The Usufruct

The Achaemenids took over the system established by Nabonidus. The Achaemenid king not only leased temple land and water rights to whomever he wished, he controlled the usufruct.[132] On the 28th of Tashritu, in the 2nd year of Cambyses (528–527), the king ordered the Eanna to bring 100 ewes and 100 nanny-goats from Eanna to the temporary palace of the king in Abanu (Pohl 1.67). They were to be slaughtered there for the king's meal (*ana naptani ša šarri*). Failure to bring the animals to Abanu by the 28th of Araḫsamnu (Marḫeshvan), the following month, would result in punishment by

129. Ibid.
130. Ibid., 42–44.
131. Ibid., 45–47.
132. This section is based primarily on San Nicolò, "Verproviantierung."

the king (*hīṭu ša šarri išaddadū*). The punishment would be directed against Zēriya, son of Nanā-ēreš, and Arad-Bēl, son of Šarru-ukīn, the men in charge of small animals at Eanna (*rabi būli*).

Two weeks later, on the 12th of Araḫsamnu, Nabû-aḫu-iddin, then *ša rēši šarri bēl piqitti Eanna*, received a request from Gubarvaya (satrap of Babylon and Beyond the River) for an additional 80 sheep to be delivered to Abanu (GCCI 2 120). He and Nabû-mukīn-apli, the *šatammu Eanna*, then ordered Zēriya, son of Nanā-ēreš (one of the *rab būli* mentioned in the previous document), to take 80 additional full-grown sheep to the king's temporary palace at Abanu for the provisioning of the king (*šuṣbūtu ša šarri*). They were to be brought there by the 17th. If Zēriya did not keep this deadline, he would suffer punishment from Gubarvaya.

Two weeks later still, on the 25th of Araḫsamnu, Arad-Bēl, son of Šarru-ukīn, one of the two animal-keepers of Eanna, swore before Nabû-aḫu-iddin, the *ša rēši šarri bēl piqitti Eanna*:

> Truly, on the 30 of Araḫsamnu, I will take, lead, and hand over in Abanu to Nabû-mukīn-apli, the *šatammu* of Eanna, the son of Nādinu, the descendant of Dābibi, and to Nabû-aḫu-iddin, *ša rēši šarri bēl piqitti Eanna*, the full-grown billy-goats and the male kids of the small animals belonging to Ishtar of Uruk. . . . I will also pay for and maintain the sheep and male lambs for the regular sacrifice of the Lady of Uruk and all the gods of Eanna, up to the end of the month of Kislev. If [I do] not provide the male sheep and lambs for the regular sacrifice of the Lady of Uruk for the entire month of Kislev, or if [I do] not deliver the fully-grown billy-goats and the male kids to Abanu by the 30th of Araḫsamnu, [I] will suffer the punishment of the king (*ḫīṭu ša šarri*). (YBT 7 123)

Thus, on three occasions in a single month, in the late fall of 528, Cambyses' 2nd year, the Eanna Temple had to deliver sheep and goats to the palace in Abanu. This was by order of the king or of Gubarvaya, the satrap. The amounts were enormous: 200 sheep and goats, followed shortly thereafter by 80 more sheep, and a few days later by an additional number of goats. Only a few months earlier, the temple had to turn over to the palace at Abanu 200 kegs of beer made from the date groves there (YBT 7 129). This was also for the "provisioning" of the king's table (*ana šuṣbutum ša šarri*).[133] Three years earlier (531–530), when the king was also at Abanu, Eanna had to deliver spices for the "provisioning of the king" and had to purchase them for the not small amount of $1\frac{1}{2}$ minas of silver (YBT 7 86).[134] These deliveries were *ana naptani* or *ana bīt šuṣbutti ša šarri*—that is, for the "meals" or "provisioning" of the king's table and not part of the regular fixed tax. It was an obligation

133. Ibid., 324; *CAD* Š/3 377.

134. San Nicolò, "Verproviantierung"; *CAD* Š/3 377.

imposed on the temple simply by the temporary residence of the court in nearby Abanu. The king had jurisdiction over the temple and everything in it.

This explains why Nabonidus and his son were involved in the day-to-day management of the temples and the leasing of temple lands. It explains why they created the system of *ferme générale*: an increase in temple income was an increase in deliveries to the palace.[135] By usurping the power to control the allocation of temple land and the usufruct, the king severely reduced the autonomy of the officials of Eanna.[136]

The Prebendary System

Temple personnel were remunerated for their services to the god with plots of land and distributions of temple offerings, the god's "leftovers."[137] The services range from baking bread and cakes or delivering fish for the divine banquet to cultic duties to the mundane tasks of guarding, carrying, and measuring. Members were assigned plots of land plus a share of the food and drink offerings, according to status. The offices and their perquisites were called prebends (GIŠ.ŠUB.BA = *isqu* 'share, income, right'), and they could be inherited, sold, or leased.[138] Originally they may have been passed down only to the oldest son, but they were eventually subdivided among all of them, so that by Neo-Babylonian and Achaemenid times individuals might hold an office for only an hour a year. Nonprebendary professions (mostly craftsmen) appear in food ration (*kurummātu*) distribution lists, whereas prebendary professions appear in texts that record the issue of commodities for the offerings. Those who manufactured, washed, and mended the garments of the gods, for example, were prebendaries, as opposed to those who manufactured and cared for human clothing.

The king also held a prebend in the temples. The *ša rēši šarri ša muḫḫi quppi ša šarri ša* (*ina*) *Eanna* was the 'royal commissioner in charge of the cash-box (*quppu*) of the king at Eanna'.[139] The full title first appeared in Nabonidus's reign, but it was often reduced to its second component, *ša muḫḫi quppi*, literally, 'the one over the box'. He was the chief administrative official in charge of the king's income from the temple receipts of Eanna and from his prebendary share of the sacrifice.[140] In the first year of Nabonidus, Nabû-

135. Frame, "Nabonidus," 61.

136. Ibid.

137. An excellent discussion of the prebendary system is in Bongenaar, *Neo-Babylonian Ebabbar*, 140–295; Jursa (*Das Archiv des Bēl rēmanni*) has now published the archive of one prebendary family of Ebabbar.

138. Postgate, *Early Mesopotamia*, 125; Bongenaar, *Neo-Babylonian Ebabbar*, 140.

139. San Nicolò, *Beiträge zu einer Prosopographie*, n. 91.

140. Ibid.

dīni-epuš, the keeper of the royal seals (*rab unqāti*), reminded Nabû-šarru-uṣur, the new *ša rēši šarri bēl piqitti Eanna*, to "put the breast of the large sheep from the morning [meal of the god] into the king's box (*ša quppi ša šarri*)" (PTS 2097).[141] The full title *ša rēši šarri ša muḫḫi quppi ša šarri* does not appear in our texts until the 3rd year of Nabonidus. Yet, the existence of the cash box in his 1st month and the installation of the *ša rēši šarri bēl piqitti* suggest this position too was created in the beginning weeks of Nabonidus's reign.[142]

The abbreviated title *ša muḫḫi quppi* is attested at the Ebabbar at Sippar from the 6th year of Nabonidus; but the additional designation *ša šarri* does not appear until the 4th year of Cyrus.[143] Even without the additional clarification, it is likely that the cashbox of the king is meant.[144] A hint of this is found in the mention of one Nadin, who "accompanies the *quppu* to Babylon," the site of the king's palace (Nbn. 1058).[145] In addition to the god's leftovers from the sacrifices, silver jewelry and vessels were also placed in these boxes. The silver was then melted down and made into ingots for the king's treasury.[146] Texts also mention people in charge of the 'rations of the king' (*ša muḫḫi kurummāti ša šarri*).[147] These men brought rations to the king from the temple. One text records them bringing "choice offerings" to the king; another records them bringing him silver; another records them bringing rations to the crown prince.[148]

The Tithe and the bīt ritti

Temple land was not unencumbered. Anyone who obtained an income from the temple, whether through leased temple land or prebend, was obligated to pay a tithe on it, the *eśrû*.[149] This included royal land leased to the temple and then subleased.[150] The term (and the tithe itself) goes back to Sumerian times and was paid in gold, silver, or in kind, usually barley and dates. Those who leased land from more than one temple owed the tithe to

141. Regarding the king's share of the morning and evening meals, see MacGinnis, "A Royal Share in the Meals of Šamaš."

142. So also Beaulieu, *Reign of Nabonidus*, 126.

143. Bongenaar, *Neo-Babylonian Ebabbar*, 100.

144. *CAD* Q 308.

145. MacGinnis, "Royal Establishment," 206.

146. Oppenheim, "A Fiscal Practice."

147. MacGinnis, "Royal Establishment," 203.

148. Ibid., 204.

149. Dandamayev, "Der Tempelzehnte"; Salonen, *Über den Zehnten im alten Mesopotamien*; Giovinazzo, "The Tithe *eśrû* in Neo-Babylonian and Achaemenid Period."

150. Royal land leased out by the temple was not always obligated by a strict tithe; "Zehnt ist nicht gleich Zehnt" (Jursa, *Der Tempelzehnt*, 11).

each, as well as the rent. This could amount to 55% of the yield.[151] The priests, the temple and city officials, even the king, were obligated. For example, the crown prince, Belshazzar, paid one mina of silver to the Eanna in the year 551 (GCCI 1 322), and in the year 549 he paid to the Ebabbar a fattened ox and five sheep (Nbn. 272).[152] There were some exceptions. Those who worked the land for rations, that is, for a fixed salary from the temple, were not obligated by the tithe, and the requirement of the tithe could be expressly excluded from the agreement of the *fermier général* (TCL 12 73).[153] After the conquest of Babylon, however, there is no record, among the many thousands of documents extant, of a tithe being paid to the temples by any Persian king.[154] In this way, the Achaemenids enhanced their receipts from the temples' wealth.

Some of the temple land referred to in the archives of Ebabbar and Eanna had evidently been ceded to the temple by the king as fiefs. In addition to the rent and the tithe, holders of these lands, called either *bīt ritti* ('hand land') or *bīt qašti* ('bow land'), were obligated to supply and equip either a manual laborer or an archer for the army.[155] This practice of using fiefs to raise and equip soldiers and archers, while well known from the time of Nabonidus, has recently been observed to have existed in Babylon from the 35th year of Nebuchadnezzar on.[156] Although the system was utilized by the Achaemenids at least from the time of Darius I to raise and equip an army, it is difficult to interpret the *bīt ritti* in this framework. Joannès suggests instead that the temple's *bīt ritti* was used to support labor that the temple owed the king.[157]

151. If the rent amounts to 50%, the tithe is 5% of the yield—10% of the 50% remaining to the renter.

152. Dandamayev, "Der Tempelzehnte."

153. Jursa, *Der Tempelzehnt*, 5.

154. Ibid., 89.

155. Cardascia, "Le fief dans la Babylonie achéménide"; idem, "Armée et fiscalité dans la Babylonie achéménide"; Dandamayev and Lukonin, *The Culture and Social Institutions of Ancient Iran*, 232–33. In some cases the tithe was not demanded; Jursa, "Exkurs: *bît ritti* und das neubabylonische Militärwesen," in idem, *Der Tempelzehnt*, 13–18. The term *bît ritti* appears in the Murašu documents, but no service or fiscal encumbrances are associated with the references there (Stolper, *Entrepreneurs and Empire*, 25 n. 97). I suspect that the holders of these fiefs were obligated to do manual labor, but it may not have required mention in the texts.

156. Jursa, "Bogenland schon under Nebukadnezar II"; however, Postgate (*Taxation and Conscription*, 223) notes a single Assyrian reference to a "bow field," ABL 201:6. There appears little difference between the *ilku* service used by the Assyrian kings to obtain men and supplies for the army and the system used by the Persian kings described here.

157. Joannès, *TEBR*, 11.

Corvée Labor and the Slave

In addition to the land and the enormous herds of sheep and goats, the temple owned slaves.[158] The primary source of such slaves was prisoners of war, whom both Nebuchadnezzar and Nabonidus presented to the temples as gifts. Under the Achaemenids, the practice stopped; prisoners of war remained slaves of the state. A second source was private individuals. The devout dedicated their slaves to the temples, often in their wills. The temple also received slaves in payment of debts. The children of slaves were slaves, as were the offspring of marriages between slaves and nonslaves.

The term for temple slave is *širku*, from the verb *šarāku* 'to dedicate, bestow'.[159] This is customarily translated 'oblate'. The 'oblate' *širku* was socially, judicially, and economically bound to the temple but was not involved in the performance of the cult.[160] Collectively, temple slaves were called *ṣābu* 'workers' of the temple. The work they performed was *ēpeš dulli* 'corvée labor'.

Like the temple's land and usufrucht, the oblates were controlled by the king, and the satrap was kept regularly informed about dead or runaway slaves.[161] A primary task of the *qīpu* at Ebabbar was to supervise the temple's work force. This group consisted of about 50 male slaves (*širkû*) divided into crews of some 10 to 13 workers, each headed by a *rab ešerti* (literally, 'chief of ten').[162] These were most often employed outside the city of Sippar. Under Nabonidus, they were called 'workmen assigned to the *qīpu*' (*ṣābu ēpeš dulli ša qīpi*). Before Nabonidus, they were referred to as 'oblates outside the town' (*širkû ša ṣēri*) or 'workers outside the town' (*ṣābû ša ṣēri*). Under Nabonidus, they were reassigned from a temple official to the *qīpu*, an appointee of the king.

An important use of temple slaves was to provide corvée labor for the fabulous gardens, the *pardēsū*, of the Achaemenid kings.[163] A letter (CT 22 198) from a certain Rīmūṭ to the *šangû* of the Ebabbar at Sippar requests the *šangû* to send at least 15 workmen from the temple to prepare a *pardēsu*, or royal garden, and to plant grapevines there. The letter is dated to the end of the reign of Nabonidus. A second text (Cyr. 212) also involves a *pardēsu* and the Ebabbar. According to this text, dated to the 5th year of Cyrus, Šāpik-zēri of Ebabbar received one shekel of silver from Marduk-rīmanni for the shift

158. This section relies on Dandamayev's discussion on temple slavery in his book *Slavery in Babylonia.*

159. Ibid., 469; *CAD* Š/3 106ff.

160. *CAD* Š/3 110.

161. Dandamayev, "Achaemenid Mesopotamia," 229; Scheil, "Gobryas de la Cyropedie"; and Clay, "Gobryas."

162. Bongenaar, *Neo-Babylonian Ebabbar*, 40–45.

163. Dandamayev, "Royal *Paradeisoi*."

workers of the *pardēsu*. A royal *pardēsu* evidently existed near the Ebabbar, and the temple was charged with the work.

A third text (YOS 3 133) is a letter from the archive of Eanna at Uruk.[164] In this letter, a certain Innin-ālik-pāni informs the *qīpu* of the temple (no name is given) and Nabû-aḫa-iddina, the *ša rēši šarri bēl piqitti Eanna*, that he is in charge of some work for the palace, *dullu ša ekalli*. According to the letter, Innin-ālik-pāni was commanded to plant date palms and make bricks, as well as to till the *pardēsu* (*dullu ša pardēsu*). He complains to the leaders of Ebabbar that the work is too hard, the men are escaping. Of 50 workmen, 20 have already escaped. He also requests money to buy bread and water for the workmen. Thus, the Eanna had also been ordered to furnish labor for the royal, non-temple *pardēsu* near it. Indeed, *pardēsus* may have been placed near temples specifically to take advantage of the labor available there.

Another task of the workforce of Ebabbar was brickmaking.[165] On one occasion 2,000 bricks were brought by Šamaš-mukīn-apli, chief of the oblates, to where Mušēb-Marduk, the *šangû* of Ebabbar, supervised a construction site (*Nbn.* 643). The bricks were manufactured at the site, since clay, the main building material, was readily available. Brickmaking involved four activities: (1) digging out the clay and putting it in molds to dry, (2) firing or baking the sun-dried bricks in a kiln, (3) piling up the bricks, and, if necessary, (4) transporting the bricks to the construction site. If not made on site, bricks had to be transported by donkey or by boat, often long distances. Projects outside of Sippar often entailed enormous transportation costs.

Archival texts show that the workforce of the *qīpu* of Ebabbar participated in numerous brick-laying projects in Susa, the capital of the empire.[166] Projects at Susa were initiated at the instigation of the king, of course, not the temple. The temple workforce was simply another temple commodity available to him. This is readily seen in the inscription of Darius I at Susa (DSf) (the italicized sections refer to the role of Babylon).

> *Lines 22–27.* This palace which I built at Susa, from afar its ornamentation was brought. Downward the earth was dug, until I reached rock in the earth. When the excavations had been made, then rubble was packed down, some 40 cubits in depth, another [part] 20 cubits in depth. On that rubble the palace was constructed.
>
> *Lines 28–30. And that the earth was dug downward, and that the rubble was packed down, and that the sun-dried brick was molded, the Babylonian people, they did it [these tasks].*

164. Ibid.
165. Bongenaar, *Neo-Babylonian Ebabbar*, 43–44.
166. Ibid., 37–38, plus references there.

Lines 30–35. The cedar timber, this—a mountain by name Lebanon—from there was brought. The Assyrian people, they brought it to Babylon; from Babylon the Carians and the Ionians brought it to Susa. The *yaka* timber was brought from Candara and from Carmania.

Lines 35–40. The gold was brought from Sardis and from Bactria, which was worked here. The precious stone lapis-lazuli and carnelian which was worked here, this was brought from Sogdiana. The precious stone turquoise, this was brought from Chorasmia, which was worked here.

Lines 40–45. The silver and the ebony were brought from Egypt. The ornamentation with which the wall was adorned, that was brought from Ionia. The ivory which was worked here, was brought from Ethiopia and from Sind and from Arachosia.

Lines 45–49. The stone columns which were worked here, a village by name Abiradu, in Elam, from there were brought. The stone-cutters who worked the stone, these were Ionians and Sardians.

Lines 49–55. The goldsmiths who worked the gold, those were Medes and Egyptians. The men who worked the wood, those were Sardians and Egyptians. *The men who worked the baked brick, those were Babylonians.* The men who adorned the wall, those were Medes and Egyptians.

Line 55. Says Darius the King: At Susa a very excellent [work] was ordered, a very excellent [work] was [brought to completion].[167]

This inscription provides royal confirmation of the archival texts from Sippar. The foundations of Darius's palace at Susa in Elam were laid by Babylonians (lines 28–30). Babylonians made the bricks (lines 49–55). Archives from Sippar list food rations for temple slaves doing corvée labor in Elam in the first years of Darius I, evidently to make the bricks for Darius's palace in Susa. The Old Persian version of the inscription refers to Babylonians; the Babylonian version refers to "men of Akkad,"[168] "Akkad" in this period being a term for all Babylonia.[169]

In her investigation of king and kingship in Achaemenid art, Margaret Cool Root observes that the art and the texts on it strive to present the king as he wanted to see himself.[170] According to this inscription from Susa, Darius saw himself as the recipient of all the world's resources. He names the peoples from all over the empire who came to build the palace. He lists the materials involved in its construction and stresses their rarity and the great distances they traveled. Darius did not intend to provide a record of palace-building but to show the vastness of his empire and the immense resources that lay at his command.[171] The inscription expresses his view not only of

167. Kent, *Old Persian*, 142–44.
168. Lecoq, *Les inscriptions de la perse achéménide*, 235.
169. Foster, "Akkadians."
170. Root, *King and Kingship*, 17–23.
171. Roaf, *Cultural Atlas*, 212.

himself but of his role in the empire. This self-image, preserved in three languages, serves as propaganda and as warning: the purpose of the empire is to provide for the king.

Conclusion

The Persians ruled by arrogating to their own ends the mechanisms of control put in place by Nabonidus: they appointed judges, mayors, and governors—and these were Iranian. They appointed the temples' governing boards. The tithe and the donations of slaves and booty of war that the Babylonian kings paid to the temples stopped under the Achaemenids. Funds and resources traveled a one-way street from temple to palace.

Admittedly, the Persians utilized local forms of governance and adopted local modes of kingship. However, now the locus of control was Susa, not Babylon, and the decision-maker a Persian, not a Babylonian. Prior to Nabonidus, the temple hierarchy was appointed from among the great temple families, but from the time of Nabonidus on they were appointed from outside.[172] This could not have pleased temple elites. That Belshazzar required the chief of the army and the chief of troops to be present when he instituted the system of *ferme générale* may suggest force. Even so, there never was a revolt against Nabonidus such as there was against Darius in 522 and Xerxes in 482. Nabonidus's rule was accepted in a way that Persian rule was not.

According to Eisenstadt's model of bureaucratic empires, rulers strove to limit the power and influence of the indigenous strata of society that had traditionally controlled resources. According to the models of self-governance and imperial authorization, local institutions were free from outside influence, except for taxes due the king, and may even have had their local norms and customs authorized by the king's appointees. This chapter examined these alternative models against archival data from the great temple institutions of Uruk and Sippar in Babylonia. The data are consistent with the hypothesis of central control proposed by Eisenstadt and are not consistent with the hypotheses of self-governance or imperial authorization. Persian rulers (and Nabonidus) strove to limit the power of indigenous elites. Central authorities did not allow self-government by local institutions. Nabonidus and the Achaemenid rulers who followed him actively sought to control the governing boards of local temples. They appointed the upper echelon of temple officials from outside the temple community, men who would be loyal only to themselves. They also appointed judges, city mayors, and provincial governors from outside the locale that they were to govern, and often

172. Except the personnel who oversaw the cult.

appointed Iranians. Temple elites from local scribal families lost control and prestige as a result of the Persian conquest. Temples lost control of the economic and human resources held in their name. The king diverted temple resources for his own use anywhere in his realm anytime he wished. Babylonian temples had become the private fiefdoms of the kings.

These conclusions refer to Babylonia, near the center of the Persian Empire. Can they be generalized to its periphery? Perhaps temples at the periphery were left alone; perhaps those temples were truly autonomous. To test this possibility, I investigate archival data from the temples of Khnum and Yhw at Elephantine in chap. 3. In chap. 4 I examine inscriptions from the Greek cities of Asia Minor. In these chapters I question whether the Achaemenid rulers controlled the temples of the far-flung western satrapies as tightly as they did those of Babylon. In the final chapter I ask if the answer from Babylon, Egypt and Asia Minor can be applied to Judah.

Chapter 3

Temple-Palace Relations in Egypt

Historians of Persian-period Egypt are blessed with several archives in Aramaic, Greek, and Demotic, even including a collection of letters from Arsames, Egypt's satrap in the last quarter of the 5th century. The largest archive is from the island of Elephantine, an island in the upper Nile, opposite Aswan (ancient Syene). The Aramaic material has been conveniently collected, photographed, copied, edited, and translated by B. Porten and A. Yardeni in a four-volume set: *Textbook of Aramaic Documents from Ancient Egypt.* Demotic texts from Elephantine (many dating to the Persian occupation) have been newly edited by C. Martin in *The Elephantine Papyri in English* (B. Porten, editor) and by K.-T. Zauzich, *Demotische Papyri aus den Staatlichen Museen zu Berlin, III: Papyri von der Insel Elephantine.* Many inscriptions in hieroglyphs also provide evidence about Persian administration in Egypt.

The great wealth of material permits a test of the two major hypotheses whose comparison underlies this study: the hypothesis of self-governance and the hypothesis of foreign control. According to the theory of self-governance, as long as tribute was sent to Susa, the Persians did not intervene in local affairs and customs; they encouraged peoples to cultivate their own national traditions. According to this view, the Persian governor would have had little role in the internal affairs of the province, either legislative or judicial; internal affairs would have been managed by indigenous elites. This view has been reiterated recently:

> The higher classes of Egyptian society accepted Persian rule as the Persians maintained a policy of only moderate interference in day to day activities, leaving upper class Egyptians in power situations within the conquered Egyptian society.[1]

In one version of this model, the theory of imperial authorization, Persian authorities would be actively involved but only to support and authorize

---

Author's note: This chapter has benefited from the comments of E. Cruz-Uribe on an earlier draft. Remaining errors are my own.

1. Cruz-Uribe, "The Invasion of Egypt by Cambyses." See also Johnson, "The Persians and the Continuity of Egyptian Culture."

local norms. According to Eisenstadt's model of bureaucratic empires, however, the Persian king would have attempted to dominate the economic, military, and human resources of the provinces in his realm. He would have tried to usurp control over legislative, cultic, and judicial arenas of society and to manage each satrapy as his own private fiefdom.

In this chapter I survey the nature of temple-state relations prior to the Achaemenid conquest and then examine the effect of Persian domination.

The Pharaoh

Pharaoh was the state; Egypt cannot be understood without understanding his role.[2] He was, primarily, the god Horus, the all-powerful owner of the soil and its resources, responsible for the overflow of the Nile, the rising of the sun, and the birth of living beings and plants.[3] He was also the physical son of the sun-god, Re, the state god of Egypt. Local gods, in order to enhance their prestige, were assimilated to Re. Pharaoh became their son too, and the natural mediator between mankind and the gods. As the physical son of the gods, he had to care for his fathers; he thus became every god's high priest. Not only was he their high priest, but according to Egyptian understanding he was the *only* priest. Temple reliefs show no other priest but him. He alone built the temples; he alone worshiped the gods and brought the offerings.[4] He also inherited from his father: the king owned the property of every temple and was lord of all its personnel.[5] Egyptian temples were the "repositories for the revenues from the empire."[6] The temples paid no taxes to the state, because the state was the pharaoh, and the temples were his.

As the son of every god, he received from his fathers complete power over the earth to maintain the divine order. By his edicts, he administered the country; managed the economy, labor pool, and taxes; and guaranteed individual rights. Royal commands affected nominations, promotions, dismissals, and payments—his every statement had the force of law.[7] Besides all this, he maintained and led the army.[8] According to ideology, he was the army. In the reliefs, he alone destroys the enemy, who falls dead at his feet.[9]

2. Except where otherwise noted, the following discussion is based on Blackman, "Priest, Priesthood (Egyptian)."

3. Sauneron, *Les prêtres de l'ancienne Égypte*, 29.

4. Blackman, "Priest, Priesthood (Egyptian), 117–18; Sauneron, *Les prêtres de l'ancienne Égypte*, 31.

5. Janssen, "The Role of the Temple," 509.

6. Ibid., quoting Redford, *The Akhenaten Temple Project*, 1.123.

7. Valbelle, "L'Égypte pharaonique," 31–33.

8. Sauneron, *Les prêtres de l'ancienne Égypte*, 31.

9. Frankfort, *Kingship and the Gods*, 3–12, figs. 1–16.

This principle remained constant as an ideal throughout much of Egypt's long history.[10] The reality varied. During the Old Kingdom, Pharaoh was god incarnate. During the Intermediate periods, the image of the perfect god decreased; various nomarchs vied for supremacy, and his privileges were shared with princes and high functionaries.[11] His portraits began to describe his weaknesses.[12] Yet throughout, he remained between god and man, champion of Maʾat, justice and order, who vanquished the forces of darkness, who ensured the well-being of Egypt agriculturally by maintaining the irrigation system, and militarily, by defending it against external enemies. This is illustrated by the Nitiqret Adoption Stele in which Psammetichus (Psamtek) I (664–610) commemorated the installation of his daughter as the powerful "god's wife" in the Temple of Amun at Thebes. Psammatichus, previously installed by the Assyrians as a viceroy in the nome of Sais, was gradually able to expand his influence throughout the Delta and to shake off the Assyrians. By installing his daughter as one of the highest officials in Upper Egypt, Psammatichus cemented his conquest of the south and the reunification of the Two Lands. In the stele, he is shown taking on the traditional role of Pharaoh:

> I [Psamtek] have acted for him [Amun] as should be done for my father. I am his first-born son, one made prosperous by the father of the gods, one who carries out the rituals of the gods: he begat [me] for himself so as to satisfy his heart. To be 'god's wife' I have given him my daughter, and I have endowed her more generously than those who were before her. Surely he will be satisfied with her adoration and protect the land of him who gave her to him. . . . I will not do that very thing which ought not to be done and drive out an heir from his seat inasmuch as I am a king who loves truth—my special abomination is lying—the son and protector of his father, taking the inheritance of Geb, and uniting the two portions while still a youth.[13]

Again, in Pharaonic Egypt, Pharaoh was the state. He was the entire source of positive law, the only legislator.[14] In actuality, this was a fiction. The king delegated his functions to specialists: generals, judges, and clergy.

10. Valbelle, "L'Égypte pharaonique," 15.

11. Taylor, *Oxford History of Ancient Egypt*, 330–68; Kitchen, *The Third Intermediate Period in Egypt (1100–650)*; O'Connor, "New Kingdom and Third Intermediate Period, 1552–664 BC"; Valbelle, "L'Égypte pharaonique," 17; Myśliwiec, *The Twilight of Ancient Egypt: First Millennium B.C.E.*

12. Spalinger, "The Concept of the Monarchy during the Saite Epoch."

13. Lloyd, *Herodotus Book II: Commentary 2.16–17*, quoted in Lloyd, "The Late Period," 376; see also Myśliwiec, *The Twilight of Ancient Egypt*, 112–17.

14. Positive law refers to legislated or decreed law. It is opposed to natural law, or custom. This blanket statement about the pharaoh should be modified depending on the degree of centralization in Egypt. See, for example, Théodorides, "La 'Coutume' et la 'Loi' dans l'Égypte Pharaonique," 39–47.

Yet, ideologically speaking, these people served only as representatives of the king, carrying out their tasks in his place. As H. Frankfort has succinctly said, "the whole apparatus of government was but an implement for the execution of the royal command."[15] The structure of government was delegated personal power.[16] Pharaonic law, or the *hp* of the pharaoh, refers to the pronouncements of the king or his governors or his appointed judges. These were all called the *hpw* of the pharaoh. There were no law codes, no references to written legislation, only pharaonic decrees.[17] A comprehensive study of judicial cases dating from the Old to the New Kingdom shows that a reference to a specific ruling (*hp*) was a reference to a royal edict.[18] Lorton cites three examples from texts from Deir el-Medina:

> Now, "give the goods to the burier," so says it, namely the law (*hp*) of Pharaoh. (P. Cairo 58092 recto 10–11)
>
> Now, Pharaoh (Life! Prosperity! Health!), has said, "Let each man do his desire with his goods." (P. Turin 2021 recto 2, 11)
>
> Now, Pharaoh (l.p.h.) says, "Give the *sfr* to each woman for her (own use)." (P. Turin 2021 recto 3, 4–5)[19]

15. Frankfort, *Ancient Egyptian Religion*, 32.

16. Ibid., 33.

17. Pace Lorton, "The Treatment of Criminals in Ancient Egypt through the New Kingdom." Blenkinsopp makes this point in "Was the Pentateuch the Constitution of the Jewish Ethnos?"

18. Lorton, "The Treatment of Criminals in Ancient Egypt through the New Kingdom"; idem, "Legal and Social Institutions of Pharaonic Egypt," esp. p. 356.

19. Lorton, "The Treatment of Criminals," 63. Lorton suggests that Egypt had written law codes, but they simply haven't been discovered yet. According to Lorton: "Since these citations occur in statements to the court, it seems doubtful that they are verbatim quotations, but rather that they are references to the substance of the *hpw* in question. The fact that such references are made, however, greatly confirms the impression that all areas of law were treated by detailed written statutes of royal origin in ancient Egypt, and that the courts did not operate with a 'traditional,' unwritten law." In my opinion, these three examples (the only ones he brings) cannot show either that laws were written or that these royal pronouncements covered every aspect of law. Lorton also cites Diodorus (1.75) as evidence, but Diodorus wrote during the time of Julius Caesar. The only law code in Egypt I know stems from Ptolemaic times (cf. Allam, "Réflexions sur le 'code legal' d'Hermopolis dans l'Égypt ancienne"; Pestman, "L'origine et l'extension d'un manuel de droit égyptien"; Zauzich, "Weitere Fragmente eines juristischen Handbuches in demotischer Schrift"). See Redford ("The So-Called 'Codification' of Egyptian Law," 158–59), who argues based on the content and style of the Hermopolis law codes that they do not go back to the time of Darius, nor should they even be considered a law code. He suggests that they form a manual for writing up summonses and leases and form part of the instructional literature for the incoming Ptolemaic regime. See also Shupak, "A New Source for the Study of the Judiciary and Law of Ancient Egypt: 'The Tale of the Eloquent Peasant.'"

These statements refer to royal decrees (*wd-nsw*). Such references were not the norm. The case of Peteesi is typical. It deals with events from the reigns of Psammetichus I through Cambyses but could describe any period.[20] Peteesi was a priest at the Temple of Amun at Teuzoi (El-Hîbeh) under Darius I. According to Peteesi's petition, every wrong done his family over the generations necessitated a trip downriver to plead the case to the district governor. The governor heard both sides and rendered his decision. He cited no law, he referred to no royal pronouncement; as stand-in for Pharaoh, he was the law. The literary "Tale of the Eloquent Peasant" also illustrates the judicial system.[21] A peasant, wronged, took his case to the district head who personally adjudicated it. No law is cited.

A variety of officials, judges, and district heads composed edicts in the name of the king. Pharaoh through his agents bore the responsibility for every aspect of government. This included "the direction of the economy, the administration of justice, the maintenance of civil order, the defense of the realm, and the organization of the divine cult."[22] As is discussed below, this was true in the Persian period as well.[23] In pharaonic times, the vizier headed the official hierarchy; in Persian times, the satrap played the role of vizier, while the Great King in Susa played Pharaoh. The hierarchical aspect of Egyptian law did not change with the advent of the Persians; Persian officials simply took it over.

Under the pharaohs, there was no professional judiciary. Pharaoh or his agents judged or appointed others to do so on an ad hoc basis; litigants argued their own cases. From the time of the emergence of the state, the authorities in a district (both religious and civil) met to decide cases.[24] In a few cases a single judge would decide. As there were no professional judges, there was no professional school. District officials judged according to previous legal decisions in their district, custom, and their own ideas of fairness and right (*Maʾat*). They also attended to the occasional edict from the king if applicable. This is explicit in a text dated to the 3rd year of Neb-kheperu-Re Antef, founder of the 17th Dynasty. An official at the Temple of Min at Koptos had committed a crime. The text of this royal decree was found inscribed on the temple door. It reads as follows:

20. Griffith, "The Petition of Peteesi." The following remarks are true whether or not the petition is fictitious. See Vittmann, "Eine mißlungene Dokumentenfalschung: Die 'Stelen' des Peteese I (P. Ryl. 9, XXI–XXIII); idem, "Der demotische Papyrus Rylands 9, Teil I und II."

21. Shupak, "The Tale of the Eloquent Peasant."

22. Lorton, "Legal and Social Institutions of Pharaonic Egypt," 354.

23. This aspect of Egyptian law under native and Persian pharaohs is discussed in Menu, "Les juges égyptiens sous les dernières dynasties indigènes," 237.

24. Allam, "Richter."

> The king [Pharaoh Antef] commands the royal seal-bearer and first of the registry of Koptos Min-em-hat [the chief civil authority at Koptos], the king's son and commandant of Koptos Qi-nen [the chief military authority at Koptos], the royal seal-bearer, stolist of Min and scribe of the temple Nerfer-hotep, the entire army of Koptos, and the lay priesthood of the temple in its entirety:
>
> Behold, this command is brought to you to inform you with regard to (the fact) that my majesty, life!, prosperity!, health!, has sent the scribe and god's seal-bearer of Amun si-Amun, and the elder of the portal Amun-user, to perform an audit in the temple of Min with regard to (the fact) that the lay priesthood of the temple of my father Min approached my majesty, l., p., h., saying, "An evil matter has reached the point of happening in this temple. An enemy has been taken (in) by . . . Teti son of Min-hotep."
>
> Let him be expelled from the temple of my father Min, etc. . . .[25]

The king commanded royal officials to hear the case. These were not professional judges but highly placed individuals in the king's court. The king dictated the punishment. This illustrates normal practice under the pharaohs. The district head (or his surrogate) conducted the investigations (here termed an "audit"). The district head (or his surrogate) would judge the case, determine the facts of the matter, and mete out the punishment. He based his decisions on his own understanding of what was appropriate in the matter before him. Laws were not cited.

The Temple

The Temple's Economic Role

The economic structure of Ancient Egypt was a combination of two spheres.[26] At the base was a local subsistence economy: peasants and artisans produced what they needed and acquired by exchange what they could not make for themselves. Tomb paintings portray barter between peasants and artisans at the riverside. On top of this base was the state sphere, the sphere of redistribution. The state collected surplus produce and manufactured goods, then redistributed these to its employees. These were numerous: high officials, soldiers, necropolis workmen, police, and the priesthood. The primary institutions for redistribution were the royal granary, the royal treasury,

25. Lorton, "The Treatment of Criminals," 19–20. Numerous onerous punishments are ordered by the king, but I do not detail them here.

26. The following discussion is based on Janssen, "The Role of the Temple in the Egyptian Economy during the New Kingdom." He describes the New Kingdom (1550–1080), but his conclusions hold for later periods as well. For a more comprehensive overview, see Shaw, *The Oxford History of Ancient Egypt.*

and the temples. The granary collected grain as taxes and distributed it as rations to state workers. Necropolis workmen, for example, earned monthly $5\frac{1}{2}$ sacks of grain (wheat), 4 sacks of emmer for bread, and $1\frac{1}{2}$ sacks of barley for beer. These were sufficient for a family of 6–8 adults. The treasury collected metal, cattle, and flax as taxes and distributed these on special occasions, such as holidays and festivals.

The temples were also a major organ of taxation and redistribution. Like the great Mesopotamian temples, Egyptian temples were the estates, the residences, of the gods. Like every other estate in antiquity, they aspired to self-sufficiency.[27] Temple estates included houses and gardens for staff, plus storehouses, workshops, and slaughter yards.[28] The permanent staff of the temple at Medinet Habu was estimated at 150 men and their families. These included high-ranking ritualists and administrators, as well as peasants and artisans. All of these lived within the temple confines. In the time of Ramses III (1198–1166), when the god Amun was in favor, his temple at Thebes recorded 81,322 people in his service.[29] These included priests, peasants who worked the land, hunters, boatmen, administrators, craftsmen, builders, scribes, police, chief of the scribes, chief of police, herdsmen, chief of herdsmen, director of the fields, chief of the granary, treasurer, chief of the treasurers, "chief of all that is placed under the seal of Amun"—and their families. A papyrus lists 125 separate occupations.[30] The temple owned at that time 433 gardens, 2,393 km^2 in fields, 83 boats, and 46 workshops. It received the taxes from 65 neighboring villages in gold, silver, and copper, cloth, grain, animals, and birds; numerous scribes were needed to keep accounts. This was exceptional. Other temples had far less, although the temples at Heliopolis and Memphis also boasted 12,963 and 3,079 people, respectively. Needless to say, temple high priests wielded considerable power.

In spite of the large temple populations, their personnel could not consume all of the food produced on the grounds, and much of it went to provide part of the rations (salaries) of neighborhood necropolis workers. During frequent and extended festivals, people from the neighboring villages also benefited from the gifts of the gods.

27. Meeks, "Les donations aux temples," 607–8.
28. Janssen, "The Role of the Temple," 508; Shafer, "Temples, Priests, and Rituals," 5.
29. Sauneron, *Les prêtres de l'ancienne Égypte*, 53.
30. Papyrus Harris I, translated into English by Breasted, in *Ancient Records of Egypt*, 4.87–206.

The Structure of the Temple Hierarchy

The Egyptian general term for priest is *wꜥb* 'pure person', or 'purified'.[31] Herodotus states (2.37), "Priests shave all their bodies every other day, that no louse or any unclean thing be engendered in them who serve the gods. For raiment the priests wear only a linen garment and shoes of papyrus; no other cloth is allowed them, nor any other kind of shoes. They wash twice daily in cold water and twice every night." The status of being "clean" is expected of anyone who approaches the god and anyone who approaches the king, because he is also a god. The Victory Stele (ca. 734) of the (Nubian) King Piye (or Piankhy) supports Herodotus:

> At dawn of the next day there came the two rulers of Upper Egypt and the two rulers of Lower Egypt, the *uraeus*-wearers, to kiss the ground to the might of his majesty. Now the kings and counts of Lower Egypt who came to see his majesty's beauty, their legs were the legs of women. They could not enter the palace because they were uncircumcised and were eaters of fish, which is an abomination to the palace. But King Nanmart entered the palace because he was clean and did not eat fish. The three stood there while the one entered the palace.[32]

Priests were divided into two orders: (1) *ḥmw-nṯr*, the higher, called "prophets" by the Greeks, but literally entitled 'Servant of the God'; and (2) the ordinary *wꜥb* priests, the lower order.[33] The title "Servant of God" appears first at the end of the 1st Dynasty. This priest prepared offerings, performed rituals, had access to the divine image, and controlled entrance to the temple. During the New Kingdom, a common priestly title was 'father of the god' *it nṯr*. The holder of this title ranked between the prophets and the *wꜥb* priests in the lists of priests. The appellation originally indicated that the holder was a father-in-law of the king and had one or more daughters in the king's harem. From the time of the New Kingdom on, the fathers-of-the-god belonged to the same class as the prophets, with the title "prophet" or "servant" reserved for the higher members of that class. The titles "first father of the god" and "second father of the god" became synonymous with "First Prophet" and "Second Prophet." At Thebes in the Late Period (Dynasties 22–25), the office of "god's wife" (wife of Amun) held immense power. Often a daughter of the king, she ruled as high priestess and as governor of the Theban region.[34]

31. Blackman, "Priest, Priesthood (Egyptian)," 126; Sauneron, *Les prêtres de l'ancienne Égypte*, 34.

32. Lichtheim, "The Victory Stela of King Piye," 80. The stele commemorates the victory of the Nubian King Piye over the various kings who ruled areas of Egypt.

33. Blackman, "Priest, Priesthood (Egyptian)," 127. The term *wꜥb* signifies both the generic term for 'priest' and the lower-order priesthood.

34. Myśliwiec, *The Twilight of Ancient Egypt*, 94.

The ptolemaic *Decree of Canopus* gives the correspondences of Greek and Egyptian titles for priests: (1) the *mr šn,* called in Greek λεσῶνις, was the high priest, ἀρχιερεύς, and chief administrator of the temple; (2) *ḥmw-nṯr,* the 'servants of the god', were in Greek προφῆται, the 'prophets'; (3) *ḥryw-sšt3,* in Greek στολισταί, were 'those who are over the mysteries'; (4) "the learned scribes of the god's book" were in Greek πτεροφόροι καὶ ἱερογραμματεῖς 'feather-bearers and sacred scribes'; and (5) the *wʿb* priests, were in Greek ὁι ἄλλοι ἱερεῖς 'the rest of the priests'. Priests began their career as an ordinary *wʿb* priest and moved up through the ranks.There was also a class of 'shrine-bearers' *wnw,* or 'shrine-openers'. These were auxiliaries, not really priests at all, who operated below the level of the *wʿb* priests.

The title of the high priest depended on the god he served. In the temple of Amun at Thebes he was simply 'First Prophet in Thebes' *ḥm-ntr tpy.*[35] In Heliopolis he was "he who sees the Great One (i.e., the god)."[36] In the Second Intermediate Period, this title was no longer restricted to the high priests at Heliopolis but was extended to the high priests of the sun-god in Thebes, Amarna, and Thinis.[37] The high priest of the god Ptah at Memphis carried the title "the great one of the chiefs of the artisans."[38] In the huge Temple of Amun at Thebes, there was also the Second Prophet, or the Second Servant of God. He stood in for the First Prophet when the occasion warranted; he was in charge of the workshops and the fields, and of the tribute the god received each day. He had at his control an army of bureaucrats and scribes who assured sound financial control over the temple.

At the Elephantine Temple of Khnum and elsewhere, the high priest was the *mr šn,* the *lesonis,* λεσῶνις. The title first appears in the 21st or 22nd Dynasty but may go back to the Old Kingdom *mr šn-w* 'to examine', 'to inventory', with the hieroglyph determinative of the eye, indicating one in charge of the inventory, responsible for the temple assets.[39] Kees reports that the term *mr šn* existed in 18th Dynasty inscriptions from the mortuary temple of Thutmosis I still with its old meaning of 'infantry commander'.[40] By the time of the 22nd Dynasty, many temple estates were headed by the *mr šn,* the *lesonis.* Kees suggests that it was an elected position. In the Late Period, the *mr šn,* or λεσῶνις, or ἀρχιερεύς (high priest), was sometimes called the προστάτης,

35. Sauneron, *Les prêtres de l'ancienne Égypte,* 59; however, under the 25th Dynasty, the main power at Thebes held the office of Fourth Prophet of Amun (Myśliwiec, *The Twilight of Ancient Egypt,* 111).

36. Moursi, *Die Hohenpriester des Sonnengottes,* 147–54.

37. Ibid.

38. Maystre, *Les grands prêtres de Ptah de Memphis,* 3–13.

39. De Cenival, *Les associations religieuses en Égypte,* 154.

40. Kees, *Probleme der Aegyptologie,* 217 n. 2.

the 'one who stood before'. That is, he was the leading man, the presiding officer, the one in charge.[41]

The high priest, *mr šn*, or First Prophet, or First Servant of God had supreme control of the great wealth of the temple and was responsible for the administration of its estates, for the care of its buildings, and the erection of new ones. In pharaonic times, he had almost autocratic control over the priests and functionaries serving under him.[42] Often he would be assisted by a group of priests called the *knbt nt ḥt-nṯr* 'governing body of the temple'.[43] This board consisted of the various department chiefs—that is, the chief of the herds, the chief of the treasury, the chief of the granary, and so forth.[44]

At the Temple of Amun at Teuzoi, for example, during the time of Psammetichus I, the title "divine father" or "father of god" was reserved for members of the priestly college.[45] These were high-ranking members of the priesthood. Besides this common title, the temple boasted a "prophet" for each of the 16 gods resident there. The temple's holdings were divided into 100 portions: 4 went to the prophet of Amun, one went to each of the prophets of the 16 additional gods, making 20; and one portion was assigned to each of the 80 "divine fathers" who served under them.[46]

The priesthood in each temple was called the 'staff' *wnwt*, literally, 'service of the temple' *wnwt nt ḥt-nṯr.*[47] The temple staff was generally divided into four 'courses or gangs of the service' *sꜣw wnwt.* In Greek these were termed φυλαί. Each phyle served one lunar month and had three months off between rotations. Established under the Old Kingdom, the system continued into Greco-Roman times.[48] The phylarch in charge belonged to the phyle and rotated with it. In the New Kingdom, he was called *ḥr sꜣ* 'over a phyle'.[49] The office of phylarch could be held by a prophet, a *wꜥb*, or even the high priest himself, although the latter's office was permanent and did not rotate with his phyle. The office of chief lector was also permanent.[50] The lector priest, literally, "he who carries the festival text," read the ritual text and

41. De Cenival, *Les associations religieuses*, 155, and references there.

42. Blackman, "Priest, Priesthood (Egyptian)," 130.

43. Ibid., 129.

44. Sauneron, *Les prêtres de l'ancienne Égypte*, 58.

45. Griffith, "Papyri from El Hibeh," number I, Sale of Priesthood, p. 45 nn. 1, 4.

46. Idem, "The Petition of Peteesi," 13:7–8, p. 90. Blackman, "Priest, Priesthood (Egyptian)," 132. Peteesi was a prophet for each of the gods and claimed 1/5 of the endowments of the temple.

47. Blackman, "Priest, Priesthood (Egyptian)," 128.

48. Ibid.

49. Ibid., 128–29.

50. Ibid., 129.

supervised the performance of the rite.[51] Some minor officials, such as door-keepers and temple-sweepers (*k3wty*), also served permanently.[52]

When not serving in their tour of duty, members of the phyle spent their time doing other jobs as employees of the state. They returned from their cultic duties to their regular positions in the government bureaucracy.[53] Tombs reveal that cult functionaries could also serve as viziers, overseers of all the king's works, chiefs of various provinces, inspectors of scribes of the treasury, directors of the palace, overseers of the palace, overseers of messengers, and royal hairdressers.

Temple-Palace Relations

At least beginning in the New Kingdom, and most likely as far back as the end of the Old Kingdom, the high priest was technically appointed by the pharaoh, but the appointment tended to be pro forma. In reality, high-level positions in the temples were hereditary. Among the high priests of Ptah at Memphis whose filiations are known, most were sons of high priests themselves.[54] High priests who were sons of high priests included two in the Middle Kingdom, two in the 19th Dynasty, three at the end of the 21st Dynasty and the beginning of the 22nd Dynasty, four during the 22nd Dynasty, one during the 26th (Saite) Dynasty, and seven during the Ptolemies.[55] Of those that were not sons of high priests, three were the sons of kings, two sons of viziers, one the son of a judge, two sons of prophets, and two sons of a father of the god; only two had fathers with no social standing. The role was likely not hereditary at first, but its hereditary nature became more common during the Late Period. Even then, it was still far from absolute, and the high priest could be recruited from a wide range of social classes. As far as the records show, once appointed, the high priest of Ptah at Memphis continued in his position until his death.

Throughout the period of the Old Kingdom, high priests of the sun-god at Heliopolis were appointed by the king. They were the sons of kings or of viziers.[56] Princes and relatives of the royal house made up most of the high priests and high officials of the temple. A few of these high priests were viziers themselves.[57] By the New Kingdom, most priesthoods were hereditary. A

51. A. M. Roth, "Organization and Functioning of the Royal Mortuary Cults," 137. He may have served only for a year; there is a reference to a "lector priest who is in his year."
52. Blackman, "Priest, Priesthood (Egyptian)," 129.
53. A. M. Roth, "Organization and Functioning of the Royal Mortuary Cults," 136.
54. Maystre, *Les grands prêtres de Ptah de Memphis*, 21.
55. There are no records from the Persian period for this temple.
56. Moursi, *Die Hohenpriester des Sonnengottes*, 154.
57. Ibid., 157.

stele from the Late Period lists a 17-generation genealogy, all high priests of the same god.[58] Even though members expected the priesthood to remain in their family, appointment was still nominally by the king. In the perhaps fictitious "Petition of Peteesi," Pharaoh Psammetichus I rewards Peteesi for services rendered by appointing him to the priesthood in all the temples where Peteesi's father had been priest.[59] That the king's power to appoint was only nominal by this period is revealed in the wording of Pharaoh's command: "And Pharaoh called to the scribe in charge of letters, saying, 'Write a letter to the temples of which Peteesi son of Ieturou shall say "My father was priest in them," saying, "Let Peteesi be priest in them if it were fitting."'"[60] Whether or not the story is fictitious, the phrasing put into the mouth of the king implies that the ultimate decision to appoint remained with the temple. Kings could interfere, but by the Late Period such interference was rare. Sacerdotal families maintained their hold without fear, perhaps because of the many temples and the large number of priests within each.[61] The "Peteesi Petition" also shows that priesthoods overlapped—a man could serve as priest in many temples. Since the king could not hope to monitor them all, the power vacuum was comfortably filled by the priestly college. If no son was born to the reigning high priest, the college of priests would meet in committee to nominate a new one from their ranks. In fact, even a member of a sacerdotal family had to be approved by this council of temple officials.[62]

Papyri from El Hibeh as well as the "Petition of Peteesi" illustrate the autonomy of the priesthood during the Saitic period. Legal contracts from the archive show that priests donated, bought, sold, and bequeathed their offices at will, along with the stipends that went with them. In the "Petition of Peteesi," the Master of the Shipping, who previously owned title to the office of prophet of Amun of Teuzoi and his Ennead of deities, simply signed his title over to Peteesi.[63] Peteesi appointed his son-in-law, Haroudj, to the priest-

58. Sauneron, *Les prêtres de l'ancienne Égypte*, 42. Because Sauneron does not provide footnotes, I am not sure what family he refers to. Kees does provide genealogies of numerous priesthoods and amply demonstrates that temple priesthoods remain in families for countless generations; 17 generations is consistent with the genealogies presented by Kees (Kees, *Das Priestertum*, 224).

59. Griffith, "The Petition of Peteesi," 8:14–20; Sauneron, *Les prêtres de l'ancienne Égypte*, 42. Cf. Kitchen, *Third Intermediate Period*, 234ff. On this petition and its historical veracity, see now Vittmann, "Eine mißlungene Dokumentenfalschung." Vittmann suggests that the petition was created by Peteesi himself to garner favors for him and his progeny.

60. Griffith, "Petition of Peteesi," 8:17–19, p. 83.

61. Cf. Kees, *Probleme der Aegyptologie*.

62. Sauneron, *Les prêtres de l'ancienne Égypte*, 43.

63. Griffith, "Petition of Peteesi," 8:1–3, p. 82. The Peteesi petition has provided a rich source for our knowledge regarding the pharaonic legal system. See, e.g., Seidl, *Aegyptische*

hood of Amun at Teuzoi; he had only to ascertain that Haroudj's father had been a priest there as well.[64] Peteesi then loaned this son-in-law the income of his own shares of the temple income; he also assigned a share permanently to his daughter.[65] In Papyrus I from El Hibeh, the Divine Father, prophet of Harmakhis at Teuzoi, sells three offices at the temple, with their stipends, to the Divine Father Essemteu, son of Peteesi, for an unspecified amount of silver.[66] The document is signed by 16 witnesses. In a separate legal document, dated to the next month, the priests, prophets, and Divine Fathers of the Temple of Amun at Teuzoi guarantee an estate on the property of Amun for Essemteu, son of Peteesi, and his two brothers.[67] This is signed by 11 priests and prophets of the temple. These two legal documents, dated to the 21st year of Psammetichus I, describe the inauguration of the three brothers into the priesthood of Teuzoi. There is no record in these documents of consultation with the king, his vizier, or a member of his court. The temple and its priesthood were autonomous.

No matter how the high priest was selected, royal ideology considered him to be the representative of the king, and cultic ritual included the statement that he had been personally selected by the king for the task. The king was viewed as selecting and installing local priests as part of his role as intermediary between god and man and as part of his care and solicitation for the well-being of the gods. This is illustrated by Tut-ankh-Amun's stele in the Temple of Amun at Karnak. It commemorates the restoration of the old cults after the heresy of the Aten.

> When his Person appeared as king, the temples and the cities of the gods and goddesses, starting from Elephantine [as far] as the Delta marshes . . . were fallen into decay and their shrines were fallen into ruin, having become mere mounds overgrown with grass. Their sanctuaries were like something that had not come into being and their buildings were a footpath—for the land was in rack and ruin. The gods were ignoring this land: if an army [was] sent to Djahy to broaden the boundaries of Egypt, no success of theirs came to pass: if one prayed to a god, to ask something from him, he did not come at all. Their hearts were weak because of their bodies [i.e., images] and they destroyed what was made.

Rechtsgeschichte der Saiten- und Perserzeit. An interesting example of the use of fiction for understanding the operation of pharaonic Egypt's legal system is Shupak's "New Source for the Study of the Judiciary and Law of Ancient Egypt." The writer explores the implications of "The Tale of the Eloquent Peasant" for our understanding of Egyptian legal practices.

64. Griffith, "Petition of Peteesi," 9:1–4, pp. 83–84.

65. Ibid., 9:14–17, p. 84.

66. Griffith, "Papyri from El Hibeh," 44–47.

67. Ibid., 47–48.

> But after some time had passed over this, [His Person] appeared upon the throne of his father and he ruled over the shores of Horus (= Egypt): Black Land and Red Land were under his supervision, and every land was bowing to his power. . . .
>
> This Person took counsel with his heart, investigating every excellent deed, seeking benefactions for his father Amun and fashioning his noble image out of genuine electrum. . . .
>
> He gave more than what had existed before, surpassing what had been done since the time of the ancestors: h*e installed lay priests and higher clergy from among the children of the officials of their cities*, each one being the "son-of-a-man" whose name was known: he multiplied their [offering tables], silver, copper and bronze, there being no limit to [anything]; he filled their workrooms with male and female slaves from the tribute of His Person's capturing. All the [possessions] of the temples and cities [were increased] twice, thrice, fourfold, consisting of silver, gold, lapis lazuli, turquoise, every precious stone, as well as royal linen, white linen, fine linen, moringa oil, gum, fat . . . , incense, aromatics, and myrrh without limit to any good thing.[68]

The stele states that the king inducted priests and prophets from the children of the nobles in their towns. We do not know who these were, but they were evidently scions of local priestly families.

This stele also illustrates the direction of the flow of wealth in pharaonic Egypt. Money and resources went from the king's estates and treasuries to those of the temples and in the Late Period these offerings were enormous.[69] According to another stele (St. Claire JE 36861), Pharaoh Taharqa (690–664) reconstructed a small sanctuary to Amun near the grand Temple of Ptah at Memphis that had fallen into ruins. After building the edifice, the king provided the economic means for it to assume its role in the life of the community. He gave it cult utensils, a provision of fruits and vegetables, oil, and incense. The king made the temple the beneficiary of taxes from Memphis trade and fisheries. He granted it acreage sufficient to produce incense, oil, honey, clothing, geese, and sheep, as well as grain. The Temple of Amun was not unique; its care exemplifies the pharaonic attitude toward every temple in the first half of the first millennium. Not only did the Pharaoh provide for temples at their installation, he and private individuals donated land and goods to temples throughout their existence. Meeks presents a corpus of 130 documents that describe gifts of land to Egyptian temples. The steles fall between the 17th and 26th Dynasties, most between the 22nd and the 26th. These donations abruptly cease at the end of the 26th Dynasty, begin to reappear in the 29th Dynasty under the indigenous kings Nepherites and

68. Murnane, "Restoration Inscription of Tutankhamun," *Texts from the Amarna Period in Eygpt*, 213–14.

69. Meeks, "Les donations aux temples," 607.

Achoris, and appear in full force with the 30th Dynasty and the reign of Nectanebo I.[70] Meeks's findings show that pharaonic and private donations were not a one-time event but an ongoing process of accrual and support.

The Impact of Achaemenid Rule

The Persian King as Pharaoh

When the Persians conquered Egypt, their king became Pharaoh. Udjaḥorresnet, high priest of the Saitic dynasty's main cult center in Sais, handed over to his Persian masters full pharaonic titulary.[71] On his autobiographical stele, Udjaḥorresnet states:

> I composed his [Cambyses'] titulary, to wit his name of King of Upper and Lower Egypt, Mesuti-Re [Offspring of Re].[72]

Udjaḥorresnet calls Cambyses *ḥkꜣ ꜥꜣ n Kmt* 'Great Ruler in Egypt' (line 11), meaning that, whatever he was outside Egypt, he was Pharaoh inside it. His entire title, composed of the usual five names, appears in two epitaphs of Apis bulls. The name includes the typical pharaonic titles plus the throne name composed by Udjaḥorresnet: "The Horus *Smꜣ-tꜣ·wj* (Horus who unites the two lands), King of Upper and Lower Egypt, *Mś·tjw-Rꜥ* (Son of Re), The Good God, Lord of the Two Lands."[73] Like the titulary of previous pharaohs, Cambyses' proclaims him to be the god Horus.

Udjaḥorresnet: A Priestly Collaborator with Cambyses

Why would Udjaḥorresnet bestow pharaonic throne names on Cambyses? He was a collaborator. Lloyd's study of the Inscription of Udjaḥorresnet gives us some insight into the thinking of local priests who collaborated with the invading Persian armies.[74] The inscription is a first-person account of an Egyptian admiral coming to terms with, and finally abetting, Persian conquest. Admiral of the Egyptian fleet under Pharaohs Amasis (570–526) and Psammeticus III (526–525), Udjaḥorresnet retained only civilian titles after the Persian conquest, some no doubt conferred by Cambyses himself. These

70. Ibid., 654.

71. For a recent discussion of Cambyses' invasion of Egypt as well as of Udjaḥorresnet and his titles, see Cruz-Uribe, "The Invasion of Egypt by Cambyses," plus references cited there.

72. Lichtheim, "Statue Inscription of Udjahorrensne," 40 n. 9.

73. Posener, *La première domination perse en Égypte,* 31. For a discussion of regnal names, see Gardiner, *Egypt of the Pharaohs,* 50–52; von Beckerath, *Handbuch der ägyptischen Königsnamen.*

74. Lloyd, "The Inscription of Udjaḥorresnet"; Lichtheim, "Statue Inscription of Udjahorrensne."

titles (which he recounts as the titles of his father) include: "scribe, inspector of council scribes, chief scribe of the great outer hall, and administrator of the palace . . . chief-of-Pe priest, *rnp*-priest, priest of the Horus Eye, prophet of Neith, who presides over the nome of Sais."[75] They indicate that Udjaḥorresnet was high priest of the Temple of Neith and of the entire third nome of Lower Egypt.

> (I am) the one honored by Neith-the-Great, the mother of god,[76] and by the gods of Sais, the prince, count, royal seal-bearer, sole companion, true beloved King's friend, the scribe, inspector of council scribes, chief scribe of the great outer hall, administrator of the palace, commander of the royal navy under the King of Upper and Lower Egypt, Khenemibre,[77] commander of the royal navy under the King of Upper and Lower Egypt, Ankhkare,[78] Udjaḥorresnet.

As Lloyd points out, Udjaḥorresnet's primary motivation for collaborating was very likely self-interest.[79] Udjaḥorresnet lost his military titles with the conquest, but he was able to retain a high-ranking and influential position at court. This was a strong inducement to collaboration. Lloyd also points out a second motivation. Udjaḥorresnet insists on the fact that Cambyses accepted the traditional model of pharaonic kingship and acted in conformity with it.

> The one honored by the gods of Sais, the chief physician, Udjaḥorresnet says:
>
> The King of Upper and Lower Egypt, Cambyses, came to Sais. His majesty went in person to the temple of Neith. He made a great prostration before her majesty, *as every king has done.* He made a great offering of every good thing to Neith-the-Great, the mother of god, and to the great gods who are in Sais, *as every beneficent king has done.*
>
> His majesty did this because I had let his majesty know the greatness of her majesty Neith, that she is the mother of Re himself. [80]

That Cambyses acted in conformity with traditional values of kingship is demonstrated by two epitaphs of an Apis bull who died during Cambyses' reign.[81] Both provide Cambyses' full pharaonic titulary. On one, Cambyses

75. Ibid., 37. The titles are discussed in Posener, *Première domination perse en Égypte,* 7–11.

76. The sun-god, Re.

77. Throne name of King Amasis.

78. Throne name of King Psammeticus III.

79. Lloyd, "The Inscription of Udjaḥorresnet."

80. Lichtheim, "Statue Inscription of Udjahorrensne," 38. Emphases mine.

81. Posener, *La première domination perse en Égypte,* 30–36.

is shown in pharaonic dress kneeling beside an offering table. There, and on the bull's sarcophagus, he is said to perform the appropriate rites to conduct his father, the bull—now Osiris—to the good land of the west.[82]

Cambyses' willingness to adopt the traditional model of kingship seems crucial in Udjaḥorresnet's willingness to collaborate.[83] Udjaḥorresnet portrays Cambyses as overthrowing primeval chaos and causing order to reign. He pictures himself as instrumental in bringing about this order.[84] It must have seemed evident that Cambyses really was Offspring of Re (line 13), as Udjaḥorresnet had entitled him, or Re would not have permitted the Persian conquest of Egypt.

Divine complicity is not expressly stated in Udjaḥorresnet's inscription, but the concept must have operated in Egypt as it did in Mesopotamia. The lamentation literature of conquered Mesopotamian cities bemoans the god's displeasure with his people and his king. It is this displeasure that has caused him to abandon the city, leaving it open to conquest and destruction. The restoration of order, particularly the restoration of the status quo ante, is proof that the local god has participated in the conquest and has negotiated the restoration of order. Cambyses' participation in the Akītu festival, the return of cult statues to their former sanctuaries, and the restoration of these sanctuaries to their former glory are interpreted as divine pleasure in the new ruler. (This is the major theme of the Cyrus Cylinder and the Verse Account as well. Both assert that Marduk has used Cyrus to bring about the status quo ante. In this way, the priests of Marduk, newly installed by Cyrus, were able to see themselves as true to, and in the service of, their god. It was likely in exchange for their collaboration that Cyrus released the newly installed priests of Marduk and the city of Babylon from taxes and corvée labor.)

The Trilingual Statue of Darius

Darius continued the tradition started by Cambyses. Darius's titulary can also be seen on an epitaph for an Apis bull. He too is shown in pharaonic dress, kneeling beside the bull, his father, piously ushering him westward.[85] The remains of three additional steles erected to commemorate Darius's completion of his canal at Suez also exhibit his use of royal pharaonic

82. Ibid., nos. 3 and 4, 30–36, pl. 2.

83. Lloyd, "The Inscription of Udjaḥorresnet," 174. Pace Cruz-Uribe ("The Invasion of Egypt by Cambyses"), who does not think that Cambyses actually did come to the Temple of Neith at Sais.

84. Lloyd, "The Inscription of Udjaḥorresnet," 176–77.

85. Ibid., nos. 5, 36–41, pl. 3. Although Udjaḥorresnet does not mention it, he likely provided Darius's titulary as well.

titulary.[86] A fragment from one of the steles there states in part: ". . . (Darius) . . . born of Neith, mistress of Sais; image of Re; he whom [Re] placed on his (Re's) throne in order to achieve what he (Re) had begun."[87] The inscriptions on these three steles can be compared with those on the statue of Darius recently discovered at Susa.[88] Like the steles found at the canal at Suez, this statue is inscribed on one side in three cuneiform languages (Old Persian, Elamite, and Akkadian) and on the other in hieroglyphs. The material is Egyptian granite. Although the figure of Darius is in Persian dress, the work was clearly done in Egypt by master Egyptian artists.[89] The hieroglypic inscription is as follows:

Text 1 a (on the left side of the belt):

> The King of Upper and Lower Egypt, Master of the accomplishments of the rites, Darius—may he live forever.

Text 1 b (on the right side of the belt):

> The Perfect God, master of the Two Lands, Darius—may he live forever.

Text 2 is written vertically in four columns of unequal length:

> (1) The Perfect God, acting by his own hand, the sovereign, regent of the two crowns of the North and the South, he who inspires fear in the heart of humans, possessor of prestige in the face of whoever sees him, he whose power has conquered each of the two lands, who acts in conformity with the order of God. The son of [Re?], the engendered of the god Atum, the living image of Re, he whom Re has placed on his own throne in order to see to fruition that which he has begun.
>
> The Perfect God rejoices in Truth, (2) he whom Atum Lord of Heliopolis has elected to be the master of all that circumscribes the solar disk, for he knows that he is his son, his guardian. He ordered him to conquer each of the two lands. The goddess Neith gave him the bow that she holds, in order to turn back all her enemies, acting as she had [always] done to the profit of her

86. Posener, *La première domination*, nos. 8–10, 48–87, pls. 4–15. Diodorus claimed that Darius did not finish the canal (1.33.9); however, the second stele, the stele found 3 km south of Kabret, states, "ships filled with . . . arrived in Persia," indicating that it was completed (line 16; Posener, 76). The location of a fourth stele is unknown. See Posener, 48 n. 3; and Tuplin, "Darius' Suez Canal and Persian Imperialism."

87. For further discussion and additional bibliography, see Root, *The King and Kingship in Achaemenid Art*, 61–68; Briant, *HEP*, 494–95, 973–74.

88. Kervran et al., "Une statue de Darius découverte à Suse."

89. Yoyotte, "Les inscriptions hiéroglyphiques: Darius et l'Égypte." See also Perrot et al., "La porte de Darius à Suse"; and Root, *The King and Kingship in Achaemenid Art*, 68–72. The three Suez steles and the Susa statue are probably contemporaneous, but their date is disputed.

> son Re, the First Time from which he is vigorous in order to repulse those who would revolt against him, to reduce (3) those who would rebel against him in each of the Two Lands.
>
> The Strong King, great in prestige, master of Power as He who presides at Letopolis, master of (his own) hand, he who erases the Nine Bows, whose counsel is effective and whose plans succeed; master of his (own) arm, when he penetrates the chaos, drawing exactly his arrow without ever missing (4) his aim, he whose power is as the god Montu.
>
> The King of Upper and Lower Egypt, master of the Two Lands (Dari)us—may he live forever—Great (King), King of Kings, the lord supreme over the earth [in its totality, the son of] the Father of a God, Ushtapa, the Achaemenid, he who appeared as King of Upper and Lower Egypt on the throne on which Horus reigns over the living, as Re at the head of the gods, eternally.

On a ledge of the base, a dedication in five columns, in a framework which conveys the image of the sky:

Text 3:

> The Perfect God, master of the Two Lands, King of Upper and Lower Egypt, Darius, may he live forever.—Image made to the exact resemblance of the (2) perfect god, master of the Two Lands, that His Majesty had made in order that a monument of him might be lastingly established (3) and that one might remember his person, after his father Atum, Heliopolitan Lord of the Two Lands, Re-Harakhte, for the extent of eternity. May the latter accord to him in turn all life and all strength, all health, all joy, as Re commands it.[90]

These are traditional pharaonic epithets.[91] "Perfect God" is the title of every pharaoh; Darius has been chosen by the supreme god, Re, and armed by the mother of this god, Neith. The Egyptian dedication (text 3) also affirms that Darius is Atum in effigy. Both Cambyses and Darius appropriated for themselves the traditional Egyptian royal mythology. They became Pharaoh.

Did the Egyptians accept the Persian king as Pharaoh? A small limestone stele from the Fayyum now in the Berlin Museum suggests that at least one person did. The stele shows a kneeling figure adoring Darius, who is represented simply as a hawk. Beneath this scene runs an inscription expressing the desire that the Horus Darius will give life to his worshiper, Pediosiripre. This is not in an official context but at a relatively humble level of society.[92] It shows that, at least for this one person, Darius as pharaoh had been assimilated to the god Horus.

90. Yoyotte, "Les inscriptions hiéroglyphiques: Darius et l'Égypte," 259.

91. Ibid.

92. Burchardt, "Datierte Denkmäler der Berliner Sammlung aus der Achämenidenzeit," 71ff.; Lloyd, "Nationalist Propaganda in Ptolemaic Egypt"; idem, "The Inscription of Udjaḥorresnet," 174.

The Impact of Cambyses' Conquest

Although Cambyses had arrogated to himself the mythology of the divine pharaoh, his reputation among Egyptian priests was bad.[93] Herodotus reports that Cambyses desecrated the body of Amasis, the previous pharaoh, and that he murdered the Apis bull, incarnation of the god Ptah, in a fit of pique upon his arrival in Memphis (Herodotus 3.27–29). According to Herodotus:

> After Cambyses came to Memphis, that Apis appeared in Egypt whom the Greeks call Epaphus. On his appearance, the Egyptians immediately donned their finest garments and engaged in festival. At the sight of the Egyptians doing this, Cambyses was fully persuaded that these signs of joy were for his misfortunes, and summoned the leaders of Memphis. When they came before him he asked them why the Egyptians acted so at the moment of his coming with so many of his army lost, though they had done nothing like it when he was at Memphis before. The leaders told him that a god, who was wont to appear only at long intervals of time, had now appeared to them; and that all Egypt rejoiced and made holiday whenever he so appeared. At this Cambyses said that they lied, and he punished them with death for their lie.
>
> Having put them to death, he next summoned the priests before him. When they gave him the same account, he said that "if a tame god had come to the Egyptians he would know it"; and with no more words he ordered the priests to bring Apis to him. . . .
>
> When the priests led Apis in, Cambyses—for he was nearly mad—drew his dagger and made to stab the calf in the belly, but struck his thigh. Then laughing he said to the priests: "Oh, evil people, are these your gods, beings of flesh and blood, susceptible to iron weapons? This is a god worthy of the Egyptians. But as for you, you will not go unpunished for making me a laughing stock." Saying this, he commanded those being in charge of such things to scourge the priests severely, and to kill any other Egyptian who participated in the festival. So the Egyptian festival was ended, the priests were punished. The Apis, having been struck on the thigh, died in the sanctuary where he lay. After he died from his wounds, the priests did as they were accustomed to, but in secret from Cambyses.

The account is usually considered fiction, derived from priestly hostility to Cambyses. Herodotus states that Cambyses died from a stab wound to the thigh, "the very place where he had struck the Apis" (3.64). This wonderful tit for tat illustrates the pattern of human hubris and divine revenge that characterizes Herodotus's writings. Although the sarcophagi reveal only two bulls who lived and died in the time of Cambyses, Depuydt suggests that Herodotus's third bull may have died as a calf and, being buried in secret, left no

93. Idem, "Herodotus on Cambyses," esp. p. 65; idem, "Cambyses in Late Tradition."

trace.[94] It seems unlikely, however, that the same person who is portrayed so piously on two bulls' sarcophogai would turn around and slay a third. Herodotus, writing in ca. 450, has very likely tapped into a long literary tradition of priestly hostility to the Achaemenid kings in general, and Cambyses in particular.[95] Two factors may have caused this: one is the desecration of Egyptian temples during the Persian onslaught; the other is Cambyses' severe restriction on temple income.

Cambyses' Desecration of Egyptian Temples

A letter dated to 407 from Jedaniah, the priest of the Jewish Temple of Yhw in Elephantine, to Bagavahya, governor of Judah states, "From the days of the kings of Egypt our fathers built this temple in the citadel of Yeb. When Cambyses [came] to Egypt he found this temple built. The temples of the gods of Egypt, all of them, they overthrew (אגורי אלהי מצרין כל מגרו), but each thing in this temple was not damaged (חבל)" (*TAD* A.4.7, 4.8).[96]

In spite of the Jedaniah letter, there is no archaeological evidence to support a Persian-period destruction layer in Egyptian temple sites.[97] Could Jedaniah have meant something else by מגר than 'overthrow'? The root appears in Ezek 21:17[12]: 'my people shall be cast to the sword' מגורי אל חרב היו את עמי; and in Ps 89:45: 'you have hurled his throne to the ground' וכסאו לארץ מגרתה. In Hebrew, the root means 'to throw, hurl'. As for Aramaic, it appears several times in the Targum as a term for destroying the wicked (e.g., 2 Kgs 9:33; Isa 22:19; Ps 101:5, 8) and in the twelfth benediction of the Amidah.[98] It also occurs in the letter from Darius to the Jewish community in Jerusalem (Ezra 6:12).

ואלהא די שכן שמה תמה ימגר כל־מלך ועם
די ישלח ידה להשניה לחבלה
בית־אלהא דך די בירושלם

94. Depuydt, "Murder in Memphis."

95. See Cruz-Uribe, "The Invasion of Egypt by Cambyses," for a thorough discussion of the issues.

96. Porten, *Archives from Elephantine*, 8–21. Recent excavations show that the Temple of Yhw dates from the Saitic period (von Pilgrim, "Der Tempel des Jahwe").

97. Burkard, "Literarische Tradition und historische Realität," esp. 93–101, and references cited there; Kaiser et al., "Zur Frage persischer Zerstörungen in Elephantine"; Redford, *Pharaonic King-Lists*, 328 n. 192. Prof. Redford reiterates (personal communication) that there is no evidence of destruction of Egyptian temples during the first Persian domination, although there is evidence at Mendes for extensive destruction and demolition in 343 during the second invasion under Artaxerxes III.

98. This was pointed out to me by B. Porten (personal communication).

> May the god who causes his name to dwell there cast down מגר (?) any king or people who sends his hand to change or to harm חבל the house of this god who is in Jerusalem.

This phrase has parallels in the Jedaniah letter (A.4.7:13–14): "When Cambyses [came] to Egypt, he found this temple built, and the temples of the gods of Egypt—all—they cast down (?) (מַגֵּר) but nothing in this temple was harmed (חַבֵּל)." Note the same pair of words חַבֵּל/מַגֵּר.[99]

The inscription of Udjaḥorresnet may indicate what Jedaniah meant by מַגֵּר and חַבֵּל.[100] Udjaḥorresnet states:

> The Great Chief of all foreign lands, Cambyses, came to Egypt, and the foreign peoples of every foreign land were with him. . . . I made a petition to the majesty of the King of Upper and Lower Egypt, Cambyses, about all the foreigners who dwelled in the temple of Neith, in order to have them expelled from it, so as to let the temple of Neith be in all its splendor, as it had been before. His majesty commanded to expel all the foreigners [who] dwelt in the temple of Neith, to demolish all their houses and all their unclean things that were in this temple.
>
> When they had carried [all their] personal [belongings] outside the wall of the temple, his majesty commanded to cleanse the temple of Neith and to return all its personnel to it, the . . . and the hour-priests of the temple. His majesty commanded to give divine offerings to Neith-the-Great, the mother of god, and to the great gods of Sais, as it had been before. His majesty commanded [to perform] all their festivals and all their processions, as had been done before. His majesty did this because I had let his majesty know the greatness of Sais, that it is the city of all the gods, who dwell there on their seats forever.[101]

Troops of Cambyses had evidently installed themselves in the temple compound.[102] They lived there (probably in the houses of the priests who had been expelled) and profaned the temple with their "unclean things." The festivals and the processions had ceased. It may be this that is meant by מגר and חבל. The temple building itself was left standing but could no longer function. It had been desecrated. The Temple of Neith at Sais was restored to its former position because Udjaḥorresnet had collaborated with Cambyses (and then with Darius), but other temples were not so lucky.[103] Data regarding

99. The root חבל denotes 'destroy' and 'harm' in Dan 4:20 and 6:23, as well as in *TAD* C.1.1:44, "The Words of Aḥiqar."

100. Burkard, "Literarische Tradition und historische Realität," 97–99.

101. Lichtheim, "The Statue Inscription of Udjahorresne," lines 11–12, 17–23.

102. Thiers, "Civils et militaires dans les temples: Occupation illicite et expulsion."

103. Cruz-Uribe ("The Invasion of Egypt by Cambyses") suggests that Cambyses moved the troops that had been occupying Sais to Memphis. This would have resulted from Udjaḥorresnet's collaboration with Persia.

the priesthood of the Temple of Ptah of Memphis support this. A complete genealogy of the high priests of Ptah at Memphis can be constructed from the 4th Dynasty up to and including the high priests of the 26th; a separate genealogy can then be constructed from the Ptolemaic period through to the Roman period.[104] The priestly genealogy does not continue across the Persian period but begins anew in Ptolemaic times. There are no names from the Persian period. This is also true for the priests of the sun-gods at Heliopolis, Thebes, Amarna, and Thinis. Priests' names can be tabulated from the early dynastic periods through the 26th Dynasty and again from Ptolemaic times.[105] There are no names from the Persian period. These temples seem to have been closed under the Achaemenids.

Cambyses' Removal of Cult Statues

Additional data suggest that Cambyses removed cult statues from some temples. Devauchelle lists four inscriptions from the period of the Ptolemies that describe the return of cult statues from Syria back to Egypt.[106] The earliest example is Ptolemy I's Stele of the Satrap, dated to the 7th year of the reign of the minor, Alexander IV, son of Alexander the Great, 312 B.C.E. Lines 3–4 state: "He has brought back the statues of the gods found in Syria, as well as all the objects, all the works of the temples of Upper and Lower Egypt, and he has returned them to their place."[107]

The second example is the Stele of Pithom, which dates to the 6th year of the reign of Ptolemy II (279 B.C.E.). Lines 10–11 state:

> The king went in the country of Syria. After he had reached Palestine, he found there the gods of Egypt in great number. He carried them back to Egypt. They went with the king of Upper and Lower Egypt, Master [of the Two Lands], Ptolemy, to Khemty. His Majesty sent them to Egypt. They

104. Maystre, *Les grands prêtres de Ptah de Memphis.* Porten points out (personal communication) that the family letters found at Hermopolis (*TAD* A.2.1–7) all began with blessings by Ptah for the addressees, suggesting the family's connection to Memphis. The letters, dated to the end of the 6th century, are directed to the writer's family now in Syene. It is tempting to speculate that the family fled there after Cambyses' onslaught. There is no mention of a Temple of Ptah in the letters.

105. Moursi, *Die Hohenpriester des Sonnengottes von der Frühzeit Aegyptens bis zum Ende des Neuen Reiches*; see esp. pp. 140–46 for the list of priests from the end of the New Kingdom to the Ptolemaic period. There are no names from the Persian period. This is also noted for Thebes by Tuplin, "Darius' Suez Canal and Persian Imperialism," 267.

106. Devauchelle, "Le sentiment anti-perse chez les anciens Égyptiens," 71–72; Hölbl, *A History of the Ptolemaic Empire*, 81–84.

107. This translation is taken from Devauchelle, "Le sentiment anti-perse chez les anciens Égyptiens," 71–72. The stele is published by Mariette, *Monuments*, 14; Brugsch, "Ein Dekret Ptolemaios"; Sethe, *Urkunden*, 2.11–22.

> were received by the guardians of Egypt in joy according to the order of these gods. . . . They came there to the place of His Majesty, before these gods. They found that it was the statue of the nome of Harpon of the west. They passed there ten days with His Majesty. The gods of Egypt went to Egypt; the gods of Pithom-Tcheku remained there; it is their place for eternity.[108]

A third, the Canopus Decree, is in both hieroglyphics and demotic. It is dated to the 9th year of Ptolemy III (238 B.C.E.). Line 6 says: "The divine images that the vile Persians had carried out of Egypt, after His Majesty had marched against the Asiatic countries, he saved them, he brought them to Egypt and put them in their place in the temples where they had been placed before."[109] Finally, the Decree of Raphia, in demotic, dated to the 6th year of Ptolemy IV (217 B.C.E.), says, in lines 21–23:

> He gave every care to the images carried out of Egypt toward the lands of Syria and Phoenicia at the time when the Persians were damaging the temples of Egypt. He ordered them to be searched for with care. Those which were found were more than those which his father had [already] carried back to Egypt, he had them carried back to Egypt, celebrating the feast, offering sacrifices before them. He had them conducted to the temple from which they had been carried before.[110]

It is clear that this theme had become a literary topos among the Ptolemies. Even so, it is possible that Cambyses had confiscated cult images and taken them with him from Egypt.[111] The capture of foreign gods typically accompanied conquest.[112] The steles' details do not suggest imagined events, since they describe the feasts, the priests who were invited from all over the realm,

108. This is my translation of Devauchelle's French translation. The stele is published by Naville, *The Store-City of Pithom and the Route of the Exodus*, 16–19, pls. 8–10; Sethe, *Urkunden*, 2.81–105; Kamal, *Stelae ptolémaiques et romaines (Catalogue general)*, 1.171–77; 2, pl. 57. The text has been translated by Roeder, *Die ägyptische Götterwelt*, 108. Recently, Lorton has discussed this text and confirmed the reading of Palestine in this text (Lorton, "The Supposed Expedition of Ptolemy II to Persia"). See additional references there.

109. My translation of Devauchelle's French translation. The document is published by Sethe, *Urkunden*, 1.124–54.

110. Again, from Devauchelle. This text has been published by Gauthier and Sottas, *Un décret trilingue en l'honneur de Ptolémée IV*; Spiegelberg, *Die demotischen Denkmäler*, 20–26.

111. Lorton ("The Supposed Expedition of Ptolemy II to Persia," 162) states: "it is difficult to imagine . . . that the Egyptian priests would have invented such lies [simply to praise the Ptolemaic rulers]." Lorton does not attribute the removal of the statues to Cambyses but simply to "the Persians." Winnicki ("Carrying Off and Bringing Home the Statues of the Gods") argues forcefully that the steles depicting the return of the statues do not belong to a "literary topos, but refer to historical events.

112. Cogan, *Imperialism and Religion.*

and other actions taken in regard to the temples.[113] Their confiscation under Cambyses and their retrieval by the Ptolemies would explain the closure of so many Egyptian temples under the Persians and their reopening under the Ptolemies. Cambyses died in Syria on the way from Egypt to Susa (Herodotus 3.64). Thus, the statues may have been taken from his entourage at the time of his death and kept there.[114]

Restriction on Temple Donations

Column 4 of the verso of the so-called Demotic Chronicle partially preserves a decree of Cambyses, according to which all income to the temples of Egypt—income both from property and from donations—was to be drastically reduced.[115] Except for three specifically named temples, all donations were forbidden, and temple land was taken away. Instead of their traditional estates, temples were assigned southern marshland and forced to rely on those lands and their own animals to feed themselves and their gods. The inscription of Udjaḥorresnet has been taken to provide evidence against the historicity of this decree, since Udjaḥorresnet states: "His majesty commanded to give divine offerings to Neith-the-Great, the mother of god, and to the great gods of Sais, as it had been before."[116] Kienitz suggests that, since the temple of Neith at Sais is not mentioned as one of the three temples exempted from the decree, either the decree was not enacted, or it was enacted

113. Winnicki, "Carrying off and Bringing Home the Statues of the Gods," 187.

114. Pace Cruz-Uribe, "The Invasion of Egypt by Cambyses"; and Hölbl, *A History of the Ptolemaic Empire*, 81. Winnicki ("Carrying Off and Bringing Home the Statues of the Gods," 168) argues that because Cambyses was forced to take the most direct route, he would not have gone through Syria but over the desert through Petra. This being the case, he would not have carried cult statues with him over that arduous route. He argues that statues were indeed carried off but that it was Artaxerxes III who did it. Tuplin ("Darius' Suez Canal and Persian Imperialism," 260) also states, "The topos about recovery of images looted by the Persians found in fourth and third century Ptolemaic texts is, of course, a reaction to the events of 343 not of 525." Balcer (*Herodotus and Bisitun*) notes, however, that since anti-Cambyses fervor is strong in Herodotus (484–425), it doubtless stems from the 6th century and probably from Darius. It seems reasonable to assume that either Darius I or Cambyses carried off cult statues, some of which were left in Syria–Palestine and recovered later.

115. Spiegelberg, *Die sogennante demotische Chronik des Pap. 215*, 32ff. The text was brought to Paris by a member of Napoleon's army. Bresciani reports on Italian excavations of the Temple of Tebtynis in the Fayoum led by Carlo Anti. These excavations have brought to light thousands of fragments of papyri, some literary and some judicial. Among the fragments are excerpts that appear to be from a duplicate of Demotic Chronicle no. 215. They are at the Institut Papyrologique G. Vitelli of Florence, and Bresciani has been entrusted with their publication (Bresciani, *Cambyse, Darius I et le droit des temples égyptiens*).

116. Lichtheim, "Statue Inscription of Udjahorrensne," 38.

after the income to the Temple of Neith had been restored.[117] Meeks's data illustrate, however, that an abrupt cessation of gifts under the Achaemenids did take place and could only have been a consequence of Cambyses' order.[118] The apparent exception at the Temple of Neith at Sais is likely due to an agreement, a quid pro quo, made with Udjaḥorresnet, not to a failure to enact the command immediately. One reason for the decree was the large amount of economic power held by the administrators of local temples who styled themselves "heads of priests."[119]

Udjaḥorresnet's inscription makes clear that the Temple of Neith did not receive a continuous supply of resources under Cambyses. The priest states that it was Darius, not Cambyses, who ordered him "to restore the establishment of the House of Life—after it had decayed" (lines 43–44). Whatever Cambyses had provided for the Temple of Neith at Sais evidently did not prevent it from falling into decay (lines 43–44). The text does not explicitly state who provided the funds for the restoration. Darius commanded Udjaḥorresnet to furnish [all the parts of] the House of Life with "every good thing, in order that they may might carry out all their crafts," and Udjaḥorresnet did so, "as they had been before" (line 45).[120] It is not likely that Darius could have ordered Udjaḥorresnet to furnish the temple without supplying the funds for it, and these would have come from the satrapal revenues. Perhaps he did this to honor Cambyses' previous agreement with Udjaḥorresnet or perhaps because of a quid pro quo that he reached with the priest himself.

The general desecration of Egyptian temples by Persian troops during Cambyses' attack, the absence of priestly names from many temples during the Achaemenid period, Cambyses' likely removal of cult statues, and the general cessation of donations illustrate the effect of Cambyses' occupation of Egypt on the priestly caste. All this may have been what Jedaniah referred to as מגר. The hostility toward Cambyses and the impious acts rumored about him that are reported in Herodotus (e.g., he cast the body of Pharaoh Amasis to the flames, and he killed the Apis bull) seem to reflect the influence of temple circles. Even if Cambyses did not commit the particular egregious acts that Herodotus attributes to him,[121] those that he did commit were enough to warrant priestly animosity.[122]

117. Kienitz, *Politische Geschichte Aegyptens*, 59, following Posener, *La première domination perse en Égypte*, 170–71.

118. Meeks, "Les donations aux temples."

119. Ibid., 638–39.

120. Lichtheim, "Statue Inscription of Udjahorrensne," 40, lines 44–45.

121. See Posener, *La première domination perse en Égypte*, 30–41, 164–75.

122. So also Lloyd, "Herodotus on Cambyses"; some scholars assert that Cambyses did not deserve his reputation: for example, Cruz-Uribe, "The Invasion of Egypt by

The Impact of Darius

Nearly every scholar who has broached the subject views the religious policy of Darius as favorable to the gods of subject peoples.[123] Bresciani says, "Darius I displayed tolerance and respect for the Egyptian province, as for the other provinces of the empire, leaving notable traces of . . . a policy aimed at attracting the support of the Egyptian priestly class."[124] Porten describes Darius as "benevolent."[125] Kienitz states that Darius broke with the most unfortunate (*unglücklichsten*) part of Cambyses' Egyptian policy to provide for the temples.[126] The evidence for this is Column C of the so-called Demotic Chronicle #225, which states that Darius ordered the satrap of Egypt to send to him in Susa "wise individuals from the ranks of warriors, priests, and scribes."[127] These men were to compile "the *hp* of Pharaoh, the temples, and the people" that were in force in the country at the time of the Persian conquest. While often translated 'law', the word *hp* has the basic meaning 'legal right', 'customary observance or act' and most often simply denotes tradition, right action, the norm.[128] These norms were to be written in both Aramaic and demotic—the Aramaic presumably for the satrapal chancellery, and the demotic presumably for the people of Egypt. If the story is historical,[129] then Darius collected and codified the customs and traditions (*hpw*) that operated in Egypt prior to the Persian conquest. Frei views this codification of Egyptian law as an example of Persian imperial authorization of local norms.[130]

Since the traditions collected by Darius included those up to the 44th year of Amasis (lines 10–11), and since these traditions certainly included provisions for the temple, Kienitz concludes that "undoubtedly Darius had

---

Cambyses," and Bresciani, *Cambyse, Darius I et le droit des temples égyptiens*, but they have not discussed the issues raised here.

123. This theme as it pertains to Egypt seems to have been initiated among modern scholars by Posener in *La première domination perse*, 178 and has been picked up subsequently by others.

124. Bresciani, "The Persian Occupation of Egypt," 507.

125. Porten, *Archives*, 23.

126. Kienitz, *Politische Geschichte Aegyptens*, 61ff.

127. Spiegelberg, *Die sogenannte demotische Chronik des Pap. 215*, col. C, line 11.

128. Cruz-Uribe, "The Invasion of Egypt by Cambyses." For varying opinions on *hp*, see Nims, "The Term *hp*, 'Law,' 'Right,' in Demotic"; Hughes and Jasnow, *Oriental Institute Hawara Papyri*, 13; Pestman, *Les papyrus démotiques de Tsenhor (P. Tsenhor)*, 86; Bontty, *Conflict Management in Ancient Egypt*. See also Redford, "The So-Called 'Codification' of Egyptian Law under Darius I"; and my "You Shall Appoint Judges."

129. It may not be; see Johnson, "The Demotic Chronicle as an Historical Source"; idem, "Is the Demotic Chronicle Anti-Greek?"

130. Frei, "Zentralgewalt und Lokalautonomie im achämenidischen Kleinasien"; idem, "Die persische Reichsautorisation: Ein Überblick"; idem, "Zentralgewalt und Lokalautonomie im Achämenidenreich"; idem, "Persian Imperial Authorization."

at least restored a part of the income to the temples."[131] Cruz-Uribe also suggests that, in contrast to Cambyses, Darius attempted to gain support from the traditional holders of power in Egypt—that is, the temples, the army, and the bureaucracy—by restoring their perquisites and benefits (their *hp*) to them.[132] This would have consolidated Darius's hold over the main power groups in Egypt and enabled him to become popular with those most useful to him.

Data discussed above show, however, that priestly genealogies at Egyptian temples did not continue during the Achaemenid period but jumped from the 26th Dynasty to the Ptolemaic. Meeks's data illustrate further that gifts to the temples abruptly ceased at the beginning of Cambyses' conquest and were not resumed by Darius or at any time under the Achaemenids. They resumed only in the Hellenistic period.[133] The so-called Demotic Chronicle does not demonstrate that Darius rescinded Cambyses' order or that he supported local temples and local norms.

Scholars cite Darius's temple-building activities to demonstrate his benevolence toward Egyptian religion.[134] The Temple of Hibis at El-Kargeh has been offered as a primary illustration, since it is the only example to survive intact from the Persian period.[135] The temple is assumed to have been built by Darius, and temple reliefs show the king giving gifts to rows of deities who appear in a multitude of guises. One room in the Hibis sanctuary depicts the king making offerings to over 700 different gods in register after register. Cruz-Uribe suggests that the temple may have been dedicated to "a universal deity (Amun, lord of Hibis) who is to be identified in his various aspects, all of which are displayed."[136]

It can no longer be assumed that the temple was built by Darius. Close examination of Darius's cartouches reveals that all but three have been painted or recut over previous ones.[137] Only three are original, and these were cut in empty spaces over door jambs. Two sharply different styles of decoration can also be seen in the rooms. The excavator suggests that the temple was built by a Saite king and partially decorated by him. While in

131. Kienitz, *Politische Geschichte des Aegyptens*, 61.

132. Cruz-Uribe, "The Invasion of Egypt," 33–34.

133. Meeks, "Les donations aux temples."

134. E.g., Posener, *La première domination perse*, 179; Porten, *Archives*, 23; Kienitz, *Politische Geschichte des Aegyptens*, 61; and Bresciani, "The Persian Occupation of Egypt," 508.

135. Winlock et al., *The Temple of Hibis*; N. de G. Davies, *The Temple of Hibis*; Posener, *La première domination perse*, 179; Kienitz, *Politische Geschichte des Aegyptens*, 62; Root, *King and Kingship*, 125–28; Cruz-Uribe, "The Hibis Temple Project."

136. Ibid., 166.

137. Ibid., 164–65.

Egypt, Darius took an interest in the building and painted his own cartouche over those of the previous ruler. Darius's modest and temporary interest was evidently not maintained past his visit to Egypt. The decorations (primarily the outer gateways and portico) were completed finally by Nectanebo, not Darius. The king shown making offerings to hundreds of Egyptian gods is not Darius at all, but an earlier Saite king.[138]

Darius's cartouche is evident in many other temples in Egypt. It has been found, for example, in temples at El-Kab, Hierakonpolis, and Karnak, but in all of these, the indications of Darius's presence are as minimal as at Hibis.[139] There are two temples at El-Kab, a large temple assigned variously to the 18th or 19th Dynasties, and a smaller one assigned to either the 26th or the 29th Dynasty; none is assigned to the Persians.[140] The presence of Darius is indicated only by his cartouche. According to the excavator,

> On the portico which is built against the south wall of the Hypostyle hall [of the smaller temple] we find the cartouches of Darius (Dyn. XXVII) and Achoris (Dyn. XXIX). This portico was an exceedingly thin piece of masonry. I [= Clarke] venture to assert that the south wall of the Hypostyle Hall must needs have existed before the little portico was set up. The Hypostyle Hall is, therefore, older than Darius or Achoris.[141]

Clarke suggests that the masonry was added to the south wall decades after construction, indicating the same process as at Hibis, where Darius's cartouches were also secondary. Clarke reminds his readers, "We must always keep in mind that an inscription or sculpture on the walls of an Egyptian building does not necessarily fix the date of that building."[142]

Similarly, the excavator at Karnak found the minimal traces of architectural activity at Thebes striking, given the presumed "piety of the Persian kings."[143] At Karnak three inscriptions bearing Darius's cartouche have been found. The first, inscribed on a counterweight of faience, reads: "Darius (*Intrywš*), beloved of Haroeris, Lord of Upper Egypt."[144] This object could

138. Arnold, *Temples of the Last Pharaohs*, 88. The table of contents lists tellingly: chap. 4: "The Saite Period (664–525 B.C.)" and chap. 5: "The 28th to 30th Dynasties (404–343 B.C.)." There were no temple-building activities during the Persian periods.

139. Cruz-Uribe, personal communication, Nov. 7, 1999.

140. Clarke, "El-Kab and Its Temples"; Capart, "Les Fouilles d'El Kab"; Aufrère, Golvin, and Goyon, *L'Égypte restituée*, 50; Derchain, *El Kab*, 5–9.

141. Clarke, "El-Kab," 27.

142. Ibid., 27.

143. Traunecker, "Un document nouveau sur Darius Ier à Karnak," 210.

144. Ibid. Found in the court of the "cache," the court facing the Seventh Pylon, in which over 751 stone statues and steles plus over 17,000 bronzes were excavated from beneath the pavement (see also Murnane, *The Penguin Guide to Ancient Egypt*, 298).

have come from Qos, near Coptos, the home of this god. The second, found in the same place, was inscribed on a plaque fragment covered with bronze veneer. Here Darius, labeled by his cartouche (*Trywš*), is shown laden with a plate of offerings for the traditional Nile gods. The mutilated remains of a third inscription were found among blocks stored behind the Temple of Opet that adjoined the Temple of Khonshu in the northwest corner of the Precinct of Amun. A small half-drum from a column carried the words "He who accomplished the rites, the king of Upper and Lower Egypt, Dari[us] (*Try*[*wš*])."[145] In the present state of excavations, the drum cannot be associated with any known column of the temples at Karnak. Its dimensions correspond to those of the temple columns at Opet, but this chapel is dated to the 30th Dynasty at the earliest and cannot be traced to Darius.[146] The excavator thinks that builders of the Temple of Opet used columns from earlier buildings. These are the only indications of Darius at Karnak.

An additional inscription bearing the cartouche of Darius has been found in front of a sheik's house on the banks of the Nile in the city of Abusir.[147] The block is three feet square. On one side is a hole, "probably for a press of some kind."[148] On the other side is the inscription, which includes a representation of a sitting goddess. Above her left hand are the emblems of life, stability, and purity, which she gives to Darius. The vertical column reads, "Lord of the two lands, Darius, you reign over the two lands, you direct [them] like Ra."[149] Over the name of the goddess is the name Menkhetheb. There is no evidence of a building at the site except for the sheik's house. Finally, Posener states: "[Darius's] donations to the temple of Edfu are known."[150] Yet, at the present time, the Temple at Edfu is dated to the Ptolemaic age and cannot have received donations from Darius.[151] These few scattered cartouches do not indicate that Darius supported or contributed to Egyptian temples.

Posener suggests further that inscriptions of Khnemibre carved in the rock at the stone quarries of Wadi Hammamat provide confirmation of Darius's architectural activities.[152] Khnemibre was director of public works of Upper and Lower Egypt, and his father, Ahmose-sa-Neith, had been director

145. Traunecker, "Un document nouveau sur Darius Ier à Karnak," 210.

146. Ibid., 212.

147. Naville, *Mound of the Jew*, 27.

148. Ibid.

149. Ibid.

150. Posener, *La première domination perse*, 179.

151. Cauville, *Edfou*, 62ff.; Sauneron and Stierlin, *Edfou et Philae: Derniers temples d'Égypte*, 34ff.

152. Posener, *La première domination perse*, 179, inscription nos. 11–12, 15, 16, 18–22.

of works under Amasis.[153] The purpose of the numerous trips to the wadi was evidently to oversee the quarrying, but the purpose of the stone is not stated. Posener argues that it was to build the canal from the Nile to the Red Sea.[154] His last inscription is dated to the 30th year of Darius, and since the usual period suggested for the completion of the canal is the last third of Darius's reign, this is a plausible inference.[155]

However, Darius's canal between Suez and the Nile does not bear on his solicitude for Egyptian temples. The point of a Nile–Suez Canal was to create a link between the Mediterranean Sea, the Nile Valley, the Red Sea, the Persian Gulf, and then on to India, with the main thrust being to connect the Nile Valley and the Mediterranean to Persia. As Tuplin points out, the goal of this connection was most likely neither military nor mercantile but simply to increase the number of routes by which tribute could flow to Persia.[156] This very practical purpose cannot be generalized to imply a concern for local temples. Further, the completion of the canal was announced to every passerby through four immense steles. These proclaimed for all to see that it was Darius (Lord of the Two Lands—Life! Prosperity! Health!) who built it. Had any temple been built or refurbished by Darius, statues or steles would have loudly proclaimed it. There would not be an isolated cartouche, here and there, hidden on doorways.

An exception to the general demise of Egyptian temples during Persian occupation appears to be a newly discovered temple to Osiris and Isis at the southern end of the Kharga Oasis, 120 km from the modern Kharga town.[157] The site had been occupied from the end of the Palaeolithic period, but at the end of the 3rd millennium the springs dried up, and the site was abandoned. In the middle of the 5th century B.C.E., during the reign

153. Evidently he was a collaborator with his Persian overlords, like Udjaḥorresnet, and so was able to inherit his father's office.

154. Ibid.

155. These steles were described briefly above in the section "Udjaḥorresnet: A Priestly Collaborator with Cambyses." Hinz ("Darius und der Suezkanal") dates the canal to Darius's 24th year. Yoyotte (in Kervran et al., "Une statue de Darius, 266) suggests the last third of that king's reign. These late dates have been disputed by Root (*King and Kingship*, 65–68), who opts for a date around the 4th or 5th year of Darius. The dispute about the date centers around the orthography of Darius's name and around Darius's visit to Egypt. Root objects that Darius commissioned the Canal Steles while he was in Egypt. There is nothing in the text of the steles to suggest this, as has been shown by Tuplin, "Darius' Suez Canal and Persian Imperialism," 244, 247.

156. Ibid., 278–81.

157. Wuttmann, Gonon, and Thiers, "The Qanats of ʿAyn-Manâwîr (Kharga Oasis, Egypt)"; Wuttmann et al., "Premier rapport préliminaire des travaux sur le site de ʿAyn Manāwīr (oasis de Kharga)"; Wuttmann et al., "ʿAyn Manāwīr (oasis de Kharga): Deuxième rapport préliminaire."

of Artaxerxes I, a network of tunnels (*qanat*s) was built that allowed the underground water reservoir to be tapped. Settlement continued as long as the water lasted, until the first decades of the 4th century C.E., but the temple was abandoned in the Roman period. The system of *qanat*s enabled the desert to bloom: date palms furnished food, material for baskets and mats, as well as wood. Barley was cultivated for bread, beer, and fodder. Olive trees as well as grape vines grew. The demotic documents refer moreover to camels, domestic fowl, and small herd animals.

The excavators suppose that it took at least five years to build one tunnel. The means necessary to build these *qanat*s and to establish a viable settlement in what had been an arid desert zone would have to have come from Memphis. It would have to have been the decision of the satrap, if not of the king himself. No reason is given for the erection of the site, except that perhaps Xenophon (Oec. 4.8) was correct in his assessment that the Persian emperor could not tolerate uncultivated land:

> As for the country (χώρα), he (the emperor) personally examines so much of it as he sees in the course of his progress through it; and he receives reports from his trusted agents on the territories that he does not see for himself. To those governors who are able to show him that their country is densely populated and that the land is in cultivation and well stocked with the trees of the district and with the crops, he assigns more territory and gives presents and rewards them with seats of honor. Those whose territory he finds uncultivated and thinly populated either through harsh administration or through contempt or through carelessness, he punishes, and appoints others to take their office.

Since no city or town could be built without a temple to its gods, the Persians created a temple for Osiris and Isis when the settlement was established.

Official Correspondence

Against the positive portrayal of Darius provided by his inscriptions and the Greek authors (according to whom Darius was loved by both the people and the priests)[158] comes the official correspondence between the priests of Khnum at Elephantine and various officials of the satrapal hierarchy.[159] One letter (P. Berlin 13536) dates to Darius's 24th year.[160]

158. E.g., Diodorus 1.95. This theme is expounded by Kienitz, *Die politische Geschichte des Aegyptens*, 61ff. According to Kienitz, "Egypt experienced under the great Darius three and one-half decades of rest, peace and prosperity" (p. 66).

159. Martin, "The Demotic Texts," 290–95. First published by Spiegelberg, "Drei demotische Schreiben"; cf. Hughes, "The So-Called Pherendates Correspondence"; Zauzich, *Demotische Papyri aus den Staatlichen Muzeen zu Berlin*, vol. 3.

160. Zauzich, ibid., suggests that the sender is the same Khnemibre who is listed as superintendent of works in the Wadi Hammamat inscriptions, but he does not carry the same title, and the name was not uncommon.

P. Berlin 13536

Khnemibre greets the priests of Khnum of Elephantine (Yb), the Lesonis Priest, (and) the temple scribes: Oh, may Neith make your life long! I have earlier written to you that they wrote in my name, namely, the *ḥry-ib-tpy*: Let them bring the priests of Khnum, the Lesonis Priest, and the temple scribe, to the house where I am, on a day within about ten days, about the 16th of Mechir of the 24th year. Until today you have not arrived in the house where I am, in which the *ḥry-ib-tpy* is. When this letter reaches you, come to the house where I am, and let the temple audit be written in your hand, [namely] three books and the invoice of the wealth of the temple of Khnum from years 22, 23, and 24. And go to the house where the *ḥry-ib-tpy* is. Let the date not go by, about which they have written to me, to the *ḥry-ib-tpy*.

Petubastis has written in the 24th year, on the 6th of Phamenoth.

Khnemibre greets the priest of Khnum of Elephantine, the Lesonis Priest, and the temple scribe of Elephantine.[161]

The title *ḥry-ib-tpy* has received much discussion recently.[162] Originating only in the 27th Dynasty, the first Persian period, it is equivalent to another late Egyptian title, *senti,* and to the Greek title, διοιχητής. In the Ptolemaic period, this official was second only to the Ptolemaic ruler; he administered the wealth of Egypt, both divine and private, for the king's benefit. He estimated taxes from temple and from private estates and determined their allocation. This function is apparent in this letter as well. The Lesonis was required to present to the satrapal official, to the *senti,* a report of temple accounts for the previous three years. The purpose would only have been to determine the amount of taxes the temple owed the king. Instead of funds and support allocated by the king to the temples, now funds went the other way. Taxes were paid by the temples to the king. That this title *ḥry-ib-tpy* originated only in the 27th Dynasty, under the first Achaemenid rulers, indicates the tremendous change brought about by Persian domination, a change equivalent to that found in Babylon under the Achaemenids. It illustrates that in Egypt, as in Babylon, temples had become the fiefdoms of the king. That the Lesonis did not respond to the previous requests suggests an attempt to resist imperial domination.

Two other letters (P. Berlin 13539–40) also elucidate satrapal-temple relations under Darius. They are dated to 493, the 29th and 30th year of Darius I, five years after the previous letter.[163] Pherendates is the satrap.

161. Ibid. The text is my translation of Zauzich's German translation.

162. Chauveau, "La Chronologie de la correspondance dite 'de Phérendatès"; Yoyotte, "Le nom égyptien du 'ministre de l'économie'—de Saïs à Méroé"; Quaegebeur, "*Phritob* comme titre d'un haut fonctionnaire ptolémaïque."

163. This dating of the letters, and their corresponding interpretation, reflects the recent reading of Chauveau, "Le chronologie de la correspondance dite 'de Phérendatès.'"

P. Berlin 13539

Recto:

Voice of the servants, the priests of Khnum the Great, Lord of Elephantine, before Pherendates, to whom Egypt is entrusted.

We make the blessings of Pherendates before Khnum, the great god. Oh, may Khnum cause his lifetime to be long.

It happened in the year 29, Pharmouthi [July 22–Aug. 20, 493], the time for selecting a successor to the Lesonis. We replaced Petikhnum, son of Haaibre, who was Lesonis. We caused Eskhnumpemet, son of Horkheb, to follow him as Lesonis. We are in agreement [to make him] Lesonis. He will cause burnt offerings to be carried and made before Khnum.

Wrote Espemet, son of Eshor, the overseer (of) sacred wrappings in year 30, Thoth ⸢2⸣.[164]

This letter was written approximately December 25, 493. It informs the satrap that the priests of Khnum had appointed a new Lesonis more than four months earlier. The letter stresses that it is "we," the priests, who replaced the previous Lesonis when the time arrived; "we," the priests, who caused the new Lesonis to follow the previous one; "we," the priests, who are in agreement. "He" and he alone will cause his duties to be carried out.

The priests of Khnum received the following response to this announcement:

P. Berlin 13540

Recto:

Pherendates, to whom Egypt is entrusted, says to all the priests of Khnum, Lord of Elephantine:

Now, Pherendates (is) the one who says, There are priests[165] whom the *ḥrj-ib-tpj*[166] brought before (me) earlier saying, "Let them be made Lesonis." Yet,

164. This is dated to the 29th year rather than the 30th according to the new reading by Chauveau, "La chronologie."

165. Martin ("Demotic Texts") uses the phrase "*wꜥb*-priests" here and defines this as "the generic term for the multitude of second-tier priests who assisted the prophets in the temples" (p. 290 n. 3). He cites Lloyd, *Herodotus Book II Commentary 1–98*, 170. Because the Lesonis is drawn from the *wꜥb*-priests, Martin concludes that the Lesonis is also a second-order priest, whose responsibilities lay in administration and organization, rather than in cultic matters. I have discussed the term *wꜥb*-priest above. While it also refers to second-level priests, it is primarily the generic term for priest, without regard for rank. This is how Hughes has translated the term (Hughes, "The So-Called Pherendates Correspondence," 78). Briant has concluded that the Lesonis is not a priest, properly speaking, but an administrator of the temple estates (*HEP*, 490). This view cannot be sustained. The final line of the second letter (P. Berlin 13539), states that the Lesonis will "cause burnt-offerings to be made before Khnum." This is the highest cultic act in the temple; as the high priest, he stood in for Pharaoh.

166. This new reading is also suggested by Chauveau, "La chronologie."

one of these priests in question, who had fled, the order was given to seek for him; (another) one of them, he was (a) servant of another man. The like of these is not suitable to make Lesonis.

Now, the priest whom it is suitable to make Lesonis is (a) great man whom, it will happen, I will cause to carry out his functions, there being nothing which he has let fail, one who will be selected in accordance with that which Darius (the) Pharaoh has ordered. The like of this is one whom it is suitable to make Lesonis.

Now, the priest who will be selected to be made Lesonis is like this: The one who will be selected, he is to be brought in accordance with that which Darius (the) Pharaoh has ordered. The priest to whom it will happen that there is (a) thing which he has let fail, or the one who is (a) servant of another man, the like of these, do not let them be brought to be made Lesonis. Let it happen (that) it is known to you.

Satibar knows this order.

Peftuaunet (is) the one who wrote this letter.

Wrote Wahibre in year 30, Choiak, day 29.

Verso:

[A letter to] all the priests of Khnum, [Lord (of) Elep]hantine, from Pherendates, to whom Egypt is entrusted.[167]

In this letter (written April 21, 492) Darius, through his satrap, claims control over the Lesonis of Khnum at Elephantine, the head of the temple. The selected priest will have to be brought before the satrap for his approval. The one in charge of bringing the nominee before the satrap is none other than the *ḥry-ib-tpy,* the one to whom the Lesonis must report his temple's financial affairs. Very likely, he also had to approve the nominee. Even with the prior approval of his *senti*, satrapal approval was not *pro forma*; he had already rejected the first two candidates brought to him. The *senti,* or *ḥry-ib-tpy,* had evidently not yet achieved the status that he had under the Ptolemies. He may have served as the Egyptian liaison between the temple priests and the satrap, perhaps serving as translator as well as the chief accountant over the temples of the satrapy.

The priests of Khnum had submitted two names, and the satrap had rejected both—the first because he had fled. (Why would a man nominated for possibly the most important position in the temple flee?) The second, because he was a servant of another man. Martin suggests that the latter had been "under contractual obligation to and at the service of another, often following failure to repay a loan."[168] Hughes similarly suggests that he was

167. P. Berlin 13540, Martin, "The Demotic Texts (C1)," 290–91; Hughes, "The So-Called Pherendates Correspondence," 78–84.

168. Martin, "The Demotic Texts (C1)," 291 n. 8.

not a free man but had sold himself and his descendants to another.[169] It ought not be thought that the priests of Khnum would nominate someone of an inferior character to be their high priest and to manage the temple's estates. The approach of Zauzich is more likely: the "other man" to whom the second candidate belonged may have been a political adversary of the satrap.[170] If this were true of the first candidate as well, the fear of being found out would explain the flight. Indeed, the third candidate, Eskhnumpemet, who finally became Lesonis, may also have been in service to this other man. We have no indication that he was ever brought before the satrap. That he remained as Lesonis is confirmed by another letter, dated to June of 492.

> P. Berlin 13572
> Naneferibreemakhet blesses Es[khnum]pemet, the [Les]onis: Oh, may Re cause his lifetime to be long. You caused (my) heart to be satisfied with the $\frac{1}{4}$ of the silver concerning which you wrote to Pekhet to give it to me. You gave it to me. (My) heart is satisfied with it. (I) will cause Pekhet to be far from you with respect to it. If I do not cause him to be far, (I) will give to you silver, 5 (*deben*), without taking any legal action in the world against you.
> Wrote Naneferibreemakhet, son of Pakheret, in year 30, Mecheir, day 16.[171]

This letter was written on June 7, 492, 44 days after the letter from Pherendates to the Khnum priesthood. A letter (P. Berlin 23584) dated a month earlier is from Ravakaya, the Persian garrison commander on the island, to Eskhnumpemet, the Lesonis. It is dated to barely a month after the letter from the satrap was written.[172] It is not likely that in the intervening month Pherendates' letter was received at Elephantine and that Eskhnumpemet was marched up to Memphis, presented to the satrap, and confirmed by him. Yet, he is recognized by the Persian garrison commander as the legitimate Lesonis. The Khnum priesthood successfully defied the orders of the satrap and the "intention of the Great King to strictly monitor the appointments and the functioning of the great temples."[173] As Pherendates' letter suggests, such defiance was not normally the case.

Frei interprets the required satrapal approval of the nominated Lesonis as another example of imperial authorization of local norms. The fact that the first two nominees were rejected indicates, rather, Persian abolition of the local custom according to which the priesthoods of local temples selected their own leaders.

169. Hughes, "The So-Called Pherendates Correspondence," 81 note j.
170. Zauzich, "Demotischen Papyri von der Insel Elephantine," 426.
171. Martin, "The Demotic Texts," 292–93.
172. See Zauzich, *Ägyptische Handschriften*, 119ff. (no. 211).
173. Paraphrasing Chauveau, "Chronologie de la correspondance dite 'de Phérendatès,'" 271.

Receipt for Payment for a Priestly Appointment

Required Persian approval of temple offices was not limited to the Lesonis. P. Berlin 13582 records payment of a total of 2 *deben* of silver to Parnu, then commander of the Persian garrison at Syene. Paibes, son of Petiese, paid Parnu to secure the appointment of his son, Djedhor, as second priest of Khnum.[174] The receipt is dated to Pharmouthi (July 21–August 19) of 487, the closing year of Darius I's reign.

> P. Berlin13582
>
> Year 35, Pharmouthi, of Pharaoh Darius.
>
> Payment received for making second priest of Khnum, the Great, Lord of Elephantine. [Djedhor] son of Paibes, 1 silver (*deben*)-*ḥr*, makes . . . in accordance with the . . . , (which) Paibes, son of Petiese, his father, brought to the collection-box of Parnu, [he of Tshet]res, to whom the fortress of Syene is entrusted, amounting to 2 silver (*deben*)-*ḥr*, [makes] in accordance with the . . . (to) the collection-box of Parnu, he of Tshetres, to [whom the] fortress of Syene is entrusted. They were received; they were delivered; their payment which was made for him before was in them.
>
> Wrote Espemet, son of Horoudja.[175]

The position of second-priest of Khnum was not purchased from the satrap. Rather, the fee was paid to the commander of the garrison, here the Iranian Parnu, "of Tshetres." Evidently an earlier payment of one *deben* was supplemented by an additional *deben* of silver. Tshetres, called Patros in the biblical text (Isa 11:11; Jer 44:1, 15, etc.), was the administrative district that stretched from Thebes or even Abydos southward.[176] The letter confirms a requirement to purchase the position of second-priest at Khnum from the local garrison commander.

According to Martin, Parnu was both the governor (*frataraka*) of the district of Tshetres and head of the garrison at Syene.[177] This seems unlikely. The demotic term for the one in charge is "he to whom X is entrusted." For example, Pherendates, the satrap, is the one "to whom Egypt is entrusted"

174. Martin, "The Demotic Texts," C35, pp. 374–75. This interpretation is different from that of Zauzich, *DPB, III.*

175. Martin, "The Demotic Texts," 374–75. Again I substitute "priest" for Martin's phrase "*wʿb*-priest." Martin assumes that this letter refers to a second-tier level of *wʿb*-priests, that is, that *wʿb* priests are ranked (p. 374 n. 3). However, the term *wʿb* is the generic term for all priests. I assume that the appointment is for the second in command of the temple. If Martin is correct, then every priest in the temple, no matter how low his rank, would have had to pay for his appointment.

176. Porten, *Archives from Elephantine,* 42–43. Redford, "Pathros"; Cruz-Uribe, personal communication.

177. Martin, "The Demotic Texts," 375 n. 9; 296 n. 2.

(P. Berlin 13540).[178] Parnu, equivalently, is called "he to whom the fortress of Syene is entrusted." He is not called *frataraka*, but simply "of Tshetres." The Iranian Parnu, as garrison commander, was head of the district of Syene-Elephantine; as such he represented the governor of Tshetres (the southern district), who most likely resided at Thebes.[179]

The Persian garrison commander apparently had veto power over the candidates for the office of second-priest, just as the satrap had over the appointment of Lesonis. In this way, the Persian kings controlled high temple personnel. It seems likely that only the priests of the top echelon—perhaps only those supervising temple funds—required official Persian approval. Two additional contracts from the temple of Khnum at Elephantine show that temple offices of scribe and "ship's scribe" were bought, sold, and bequeathed between priests, seemingly without Persian intervention.[180]

Persian Satrapal Administration

Besides controlling the appointment of the upper echelon of Egyptian temples, Arsames' archive illustrates other ways that the king through his satrap controlled the minutiae of affairs in the empire. The archive consists of 16 letters, all but one written by the satrap himself.[181] Probably the earliest is the letter to Arsames, dated November 6, 427 (*TAD* A.6.1)—that is, toward the end of the reign of Artaxerxes I (464–424 B.C.E.). The remainder of the letters in the collection are from Arsames, and undated. According to letters from the Jewish community of Elephantine (*TAD* A.4.5 and *TAD* A.4.7/8), Arsames left the country during the 14th year of the reign of Darius II (410). Two additional letters from Elephantine, dated to after Darius's 17th year, suggest that he had returned to Egypt by then (*TAD* A.4.9 and A.4.10). The letters from Arsames most likely stem from the time of his absence from Egypt, from the beginning of the 14th year of Darius (April 17, 410) to sometime after Marḥeshvan of Darius's 17th regnal year (November 407).

The early letter to Arsames (*TAD* A.6.1; dated 427) provides titles of some officials in the satrapal hierarchy and hints at their functions. The verso reads:

> [To] our lord Arsames [w]ho is in Egypt, [from] your servants Achaemenes and his colleagues the heralds (אזדכריא), Ba[gadana and his colleagues][182] the

178. Ibid., C1, pp. 290–91.

179. So also Wiesehöfer, "*PRTRK, RB ḤYLʾ, SGN* und *MRʾ*," 305 n. 2.

180. P. Wien D 10150 (C28 in *EPE*, 348–50) and P. Wien D 10151 (C29 in *EPE*, 351–55).

181. Porten, *TAD* A.6.1–16.

182. This phrase has been restored from another part of the letter.

> judges, Peteisi and his colleagues the scribes of the province of Pamunpara/ Nasunpara, Harudj and his colleagues the scribes of the province of. . . .

It should be noted that the herald, Achaemenes, and the judge, Bagadana, are both Iranian, as are probably their colleagues, the rest of the heralds and judges.[183] The provincial scribes, Peteisi and Harudj, are Egyptian. The herald is a high official, well known from Assyrian and Neo-Babylonian administrative texts as the *nāgiru.*[184] As a messenger of the king, his job included traveling from town to town to announce royal and satrapal edicts and to recruit soldiers and workers for the corvée. He likely had a police contingent with him, since he was responsible for ensuring recruitment as well as enforcing edicts. Except for the scribes and the chief accountant, the *ḥry-ib-tpy*, there seem to have been no Egyptians among the officials in the satrapal court. Even the Egyptian Khnemibre, chief of public works of Upper and Lower Egypt, was supervised by the Iranian Atiyvaya, saris of Persia, from the 6th year of Cambyses to the 12th year of Xerxes.[185] The title saris, an interpretation of the Egyptian *srs*, must go back to the Akkadian *ša reši šarri* and refer to a representative of the Persian king at the satrapal court.

The recto of this same letter to Arsames states:

> [To our lord Arsa]mes, your servants Achaemenes and his colleagues, Bagadana and his colleagues, and the scribes of the province.
>
> May [all] the gods abundantly seek after the welfare of our lord [at] all times.
>
> And now an order has been issued to us, saying: "The allotment (מנתא) which is given in the province where . . . separately, each kind, month by month, do send me." Moreover, a rescript (?) was written and given to us. Now. . . .

According to this letter, the heralds, the judges, and the scribes received an order from the satrap to send the מנתא allotment to him monthly.[186] In

183. Every judge named, but one (a Babylonian) in the Elephantine archives is Persian; there are no Egyptian judges.

184. *CAD* N/1 116–18. This office is discussed by Tadmor, "Temple Cities," 187.

185. Posener, *La première domination perse en Égypte*, 117–30; Bongrani Fanfoni and Israel, "Documenti achemenidi nel deserto orientale egiziano (Gebel Abu Queh—Wadi Hammamat)." Due to Atiyavaya's long tenure and to the fact that many of the inscriptions are dual-dated to the reigns of both Darius and Xerxes, the latter authors suggest a co-regency between Xerxes and his father in the last 12 years of Darius's reign.

186. I assume that this allotment, the מנתא, is a tax. If it is a rent on Arsames' private estates, then he is using satrapal officials to collect his rents. This seems unlikely, since other letters refer to an Egyptian *paqîd* in charge of his private estates. In discussing this term, Porten defines it as 'share', as in the "share of the king" from an estate ("The Address Formulae in Aramaic Letters," 409), suggesting a tax in kind. See n. 187 (p. 88).

addition to the usual functions of the herald, he was evidently also charged with collecting the taxes from the various towns of a province and bringing them to the satrap. The judges and scribes assisted. The letter also indicates that the satrap was to be kept informed each month by his heralds, judges, and scribes of the status of every province in the satrapy.

The remaining letters in the archive, all written by the satrap, illustrate the tight control that he exerted over his satrapy. In one letter, Arsames gives orders to permit the repair of a boat owned by the Iranian Mithradates. The letter lists in minute detail the materials that he may purchase, down to the 200 bronze and iron nails (*TAD* A.6.2). In another letter, Arsames writes to permit the punishment of runaway slaves belonging to one of his officials, according to the official's request (*TAD* A.6.3); in another, he permits an official to inherit the post of his father (*TAD* A.6.4); in another, he orders a garrison commander to obey the word of his superior (*TAD* A.6.8); in still another, he orders a man deprived of his estate to receive the estate (*TAD* A.6.11); and in others, he orders rents on land to be brought to the holder of that land (*TAD* A.6.13–14).[187] These letters suggest that nothing happened without the order of the satrap—not a boat repaired, not a slave punished.[188]

The Paschal Letter

That the Persian king exercised tight control over every activity in his empire through his satraps is also exhibited in the so-called Passover Letter (*TAD* A.4.1) found in the archive of Jedaniah, high priest of the temple of Yhw at Elephantine. The letter reads:

> [To my brothers Je]daniah and his colleagues the Jewish ga[rrison,] your brother Ḥanan[i]ah.
>
> May God/the gods [seek after] the welfare of my brothers [at all times.]
>
> And now, this year, year 5 of King Darius (II), it has been sent from the king to Arsa[mes . . .]

187. The word here translated 'rent' is מנדא *manda,* or מנתא *manta* (*TAD* A.6.1:2), and is called *mandatu* or *middattu* in Akkadian and *middâ* in Hebrew (Neh 5:4). If translated 'share', as Porten suggests, it would perhaps more accurately fit the various contexts. The owner of the land in the present case is a Persian prince, Varuvahya, son of the house. Varuvahya is in Babylon and complains that he is not receiving his *mandattu.* The letters indicate that members of the royal house owned land in various satrapies.

188. This was certainly not unique to Egypt. Unpublished letters from Uzbekistan show the local (Iranian) governor requesting permission from the (Iranian) satrap to allow the soldiers building a city wall to stop momentarily in order to kill the locusts that were destroying the crops. The satrap gives permission but demands that the men return to wall-building as soon as the locusts are destroyed. These letters, dated to the reign of Artaxerxes III, are being published by S. Shaked. I thank Prof. Shaked for allowing me to examine the letters.

> . . . Now, you thus count four[teen days in Nisan and on the 14th at twilight ob]serve [the Passover] and from the 15th day until the 21st day of [Nisan observe the Festival of Unleavened Bread. Seven days eat unleavened bread.
>
> Now,] be pure and take heed. [Do] n[ot do] work [on the 15th day and on the 21st day of Nisan.] Do not drink [any fermented drink. And do] not [eat] anything of leaven [nor let it be seen in your houses from the 14th day of Nisan at] sunset until the 21st day of Nisa[n at sunset. And b]ring into your chambers [any leaven which you have in your houses] and seal (it) up during [these] days. [. . .]
>
> [To] my brothers Jedaniah and his colleagues the Jewish garrison, your brother Ḥananiah s[on of PN].

The letter is quite fragmentary; one-half of the scroll is nearly obliterated. Its purpose is still clear: to permit—nay, command—the Jews to obey the Passover traditions and to abstain from work on the first and seventh days of the holiday. Refraining from work could not have been done without the express permission of the king, and his written authorization would have protected the Jews from any who questioned their behavior. Frei sees this as an example of imperial authorization of local norms. Yet the letter makes no mention of the slaughter of the Paschal lamb (sacred to the god Khnum), so that instead of being an authorization of local norms, it may imply their abridgment.

The Role of the Hyparch

The Iranian Artavant, to whom many of Arsames' letters were addressed, was in charge of executing the satrap's orders while the latter was away. This was the role of the hyparch, the second in command, described by Xenophon. In the satrap's absence, he was "to govern the people, to receive the tribute, to pay the militia, and to attend to any other business that needs attention" (Xenophon, *Cyr.* 8.3). When the satrap was at home, the hyparch served as garrison commander at the capital (Herodotus 5.27; 7.106, 194).[189] The hyparch also had a second role. According to Xenophon:

> When [Cyrus the Great] arrived in Babylon, he decided to send out satraps to govern the nations he had subdued. But the commanders of the garrisons in the citadels and the colonels in command of the guards throughout the country, he wished to be responsible to no one but himself. This provision he made with the purpose that if any of the satraps, on the strength of the wealth or the men at their command, should break out into open insolence or attempt to refuse obedience, they might at once find opposition in their province. (*Cyr.* 8.6.1)

189. Tuplin, "Xenophon and the Garrisons," 183–84.

Artavant, then, may have been commander of the garrison located at Memphis and governed Egypt under Arsames' orders while the latter was away. He also would have served as the "eyes and ears" of the king.

Judicial Practices under the Persians

The satrap was the last court of appeal in Egypt, although an appeal to the king in Susa could be made, in principle. This role of the satrap is evident from a badly mutilated document (*TAD* A.4.2) in the archive of Jedaniah, son of Gemariah, leader of the Jewish community at Elephantine. The letter refers to Arsames, residing in Memphis, and to Thebes, the capital of the southern district, or nome, to which Elephantine belonged. The letter illustrates the judicial path that a case could encounter. Unfortunately, only the right-hand side of the letter is preserved.

> To my lords Jedaniah, Mauziah, Uriah and the garrison, [yo]ur servant [PN]. [May all the gods] seek after [the welfare of our lords at all times. It is well with us here. Now, every day which . . . he complained to the investigators. One Zivaka, he complained to the investigator . . . we have, inasmuch as the Egyptians gave them a bribe. And from the (time?) . . . which the Egyptians before Arsames, but they act thievishly. Moreover, . . . the province of Thebes and say thus: Mazdayasna/A Mazdean is an official of the province . . . we are afraid inasmuch as we are fewer by 2. Now, behold, they favored. . . . If only we had revealed our presence to Arsames before, then something like this would not have [happened to us. . . .] He will report our affairs before Arsames. Pisina pacifies us [lit. our presence]. [Whatever] you find—honey, castor oil, string, rope, leather skins, boards [send us, since] they are full of anger at you.
>
> Pasu son of Mannuki came to Memphis and . . . and the investigator. And he gave me silver, 12 staters and [I am] happy with it. . . . Ḥori gave me when they detained him because of the pitcher. Tiri . . . said: ". . . at the order of the king and they detain them. And the damage (caused to) Arsames and the compensation (due to) Djeh[o . . .] and Ḥori whom they detained."
>
> On the 6th day of Phaophi the letters arrived . . . we will do the thing.
>
> To . . . my lords, Jaadaniah, Mauziah, y[our] se[rvant. . . .]

Whatever the difficulty may have been, satisfaction was evidently not achieved at Elephantine, the local level, because the case was taken to Thebes. The judgment went against the letter writer there ("the Egyptians gave them a bribe"), so the case was taken to the next level, the satrap. The letter reveals an almost naïve faith in the latter's justice: "If [only] we had revealed ourselves to Arsames," "if Arsames had known about this, this wouldn't have happened to us." The Iranian, Pisina, was willing to go to Memphis and to Arsames and present their case to him, but goods for the bribes were needed. Pasu, son of Mannuki, a Babylonian, provided the letter writer with 12 staters, presumably for Arsames. Jedaniah and his colleagues at the garrison were asked to send whatever they had, most likely to add to it. If the bribe was not for Arsames, it may have been for the investigators and judges who acted in his court.

The word translated 'investigator' in the above letter is the Iranian word *patifrasa*, meaning 'investigator', 'examiner'. The use of a Persian title for the office implies Persian officials and a Persian judicial process at both the satrapal and provincial levels. In addition to the judge, two other sets of officials were involved in the Persian-period judicial system. The last two lines of a similar judicial request read:

יתעבד מן דיניא תיפתיא גושכיא זי ממנין במדינת תשטרס
יתי[דע] למראן לקבל זנה זי אנחנה אמרן

> If inquiry be made of the judges, police, and hearers who are appointed in the province of Tshetres, it would be [known] to our lord in accordance to this which we say. (*TAD* A.4.5:9, 10)

The word here for 'police' is *typatya'*, from the Old Persian **tipati-*.[190] These officials are also included in Dan 3:2 in a list that begins with the satrap. The Aramaic word for 'hearers' is *goškia'*, from the Old Persian **gaušaka*. These were known in classical sources as the "king's ears," that is, the intelligence officers.[191] The use of Persian loanwords suggests a completely Persian judicial system in the Egyptian satrapy, with provincial judges, police, and intelligence officers appointed by Persian officials. Indeed, in both the Elephantine archives and the Arsames letters, nearly every named judge is Iranian.[192] There were no Egyptian judges for the Egyptians or Jewish judges for the Jews.[193] These judges were either royal appointees (judges of the king, *TAD*

190. Porten, *Elephantine Papyri in English,* 136 n. 20; idem, *Archives from Elephantine,* 50 n. 83.

191. Idem, *EPE,* n. 21; idem, *Archives,* n. 84.

192. Examination of the Aramaic documents from Hermopolis and Elephantine reveals only one Egyptian who gave his son a Persian name: Bagadata, son of Psamshek (*TAD* B.4.3:24; B.4.4:20); one Aramean: Varyzata, son of Bethelzabad (B.3.9:11); and one Jew: Arvaratha, son of Yehonatan (*TAD* B.4.4:21). Also, if Ostanes is the physical brother of an ʿAnani in Judah (*TAD* A.4.7/8:18), then a second Jew had an Iranian name. Lozachmeur, "Un nouveau graffito araméen provenant de Saqqâra," reports a graffiti on a stone block 3.5 m above the pavement of the funerary temple of Queen Mother Ankhesenpépy II, southwest of the monument of her husband, Pépy I. The inscription reads, לבגת בר חורי 'to Bagadāta, son of Ḥori'. Thus, a second Egyptian gave his son a Persian name. This is out of thousands of names, strongly implying that those with Persian names were Persian (B. Porten, personal communication).

193. Most situations that we would consider "legal" did not involve a judge. Sales and inheritances of goods, land, and offices were handled through contracts written by Egyptian or Aramean scribes, writing in Aramaic. See Seidl, *Aegyptische Rechtsgeschichte der Saiten- und Perserzeit*; Muffs, *Studies in the Aramaic Legal Papyri from Elephantine.*

B.5.1:3) or provincial appointees (judges of the province, *TAD* A.5.2:4, 7).[194] As B. Porten points out:

> "Judges" appeared regularly in the contracts as one of the three parties before whom a complainant might bring a suit or register a complaint, the other two being lord and prefect (*TAD* B2.3:13, 24; B3.1:13, 19; B3.2:6; B3.12:28; B4.6:14; B7.1:13). In a case involving an inheritance they are called "judges of the king" [i.e., royal judges] (*TAD* B5.1:3) and in a petition seeking redress of grievances they are "judges of the province" (*TAD* A5.2:4, 7). When named, they were always Persian—Pisina (*TAD* A3.8:2), Bagadana (*TAD* A6.1:5–6), Damidata (*TAD* B2.2:6), Bagafarna and Nafaina (*TAD* A5.2:6)—and once Babylonian—Mannuki.[195]

This is consistent with Cyrus's mode of administration, discussed above. We know that after Cyrus's conquest of Babylon, the king's Iranian agent, Gubarvaya, appointed the local officials. The presence of a Babylonian name among the Iranian judges is also telling. Babylonians seem to have held a central position in the empire. Stolper notes that they operated the central bureaus at Persepolis and produced and transmitted orders in the names of the (Iranian) chief administrators.[196] Of 31 high-ranking officials at Persepolis, fully a third were Babylonian. Since there would be no reason for Iranians to have taken Babylonian names, these names can only indicate their bearers' origins.

The Jewish Garrison at Elephantine

During the first Persian occupation of Egypt (525–404), the Nile island of Elephantine housed a garrison manned by Jewish and Aramean mercenaries.[197] Excavators of the island found three papyrus archives plus numerous unrelated documents and letters, which provide a window into garrison life.

194. The distinction between royal and provincial judges referred to the mechanism of appointment. There is no mention of satrapal judges in the Egyptian archives. According to Herodotus (3.31), "royal judges are a picked body of men among the Persians, who hold office till death or till some injustice is detected in them." The judges for the satrapy were royal judges who were appointed by the king; provincial judges were appointed by the governors. In Babylonia, beginning with Hammurabi's rule, judges for the major Babylonian cities and the areas around them were appointed by the king. They were called "judges of the king," and their seals titled them "servant of King NN." Judges for the smaller cities were appointed by the royally appointed provincial governors. See Harris, "On the Process of Secularization under Hammurapi"; Postgate, *Early Mesopotamia: Society and Economy at the Dawn of History*, 277.

195. Porten, *The Elephantine Papyri in English*, 136 n. 19.

196. Stolper, "The Neo-Babylonian Text from the Persepolis Fortification," 305–6.

197. Porten, *Archives from Elephantine*, still provides the most complete study of the Jewish garrison.

These archives confirm the existence of a Jewish community there and of its temple to Yhw. Of primary importance are the communal archive of Jedaniah, chief priest of Yhw, and Ananiah's family archive.

Recent excavations have confirmed the interpretation of the island's topography that had been derived from the papyri:[198] the temple of Yhw was located directly southwest of the Khnum precinct. The excavator identified a row of domestic houses across from the temple to the southwest as the Jewish and Aramaic quarters of the city.[199] Although the entire southern part of the temple is completely lost today, he did find the remains of its eastern part. According to the excavator:

> [The] location between the Khnum precinct and the Jewish houses on the west, but above the burn layer of building layer 5, can be evaluated there as a further indication that these are the last remains of the Jewish temple. The burn layer there should be seen in direct connection with the destruction of the temple, which is verified for the year 410. There is no doubt the temple stood there continuously from its founding in Saitic times. It must have been linked first to the structures of building layer 5 (26th Dynasty), which corresponds widely to the recognizable stratigraphic findings for that time. The plaster tiles lying directly above the burn layer and the wide exterior wall (334 M) in the west of the area are however to be brought in connection to the younger, rebuilt temple of building layer 4 (between 407 and 402).[200]

The excavator determined that the temple of Yhw was built in Saitic times, destroyed in the year 410, and rebuilt between 407 and 402. He states further: "It has been occasionally doubted whether the temple as a complete construction had been erected again. But actually, it is expressly recorded that it was to be built 'as it was formerly' [כזי הוה לקדמן] (*TAD* B.3.12:8). Speaking in favor of a complete rebuilding is the fact that in later documents it has been designated as a temple [אגורא] (*TAD* A.4.10:8, B.3.12:18)."[201] The temple of Yhw faced toward the northeast and Jerusalem.[202]

Yeb, bîrtāʾ

The documents from Elephantine refer to יב בירתא 'Yeb (= Elephantine), the citadel'. Lemaire and Lozachmeur define a בירתא, a citadel, as the capital

198. Von Pilgrim, "Der Tempel des Jahwe," 142. See the plans that Porten derived from the papyri, figs. 1–6 in *TAD*, vol. 2, and figs. 5–15 in *Archives.* Porten's alternative 1 is consistent with the findings of the excavators.

199. Von Pilgrim, "Der Tempel des Jahwe," 142.

200. Ibid., 143.

201. Ibid., 143 n. 281.

202. Porten, *TAD*, 2.176. Porten informs me that according to von Pilgrim the lay of the land required this orientation (personal communication).

of its province, stating that it housed: (1) the administrative headquarters of the region; (2) the administrative archives; (3) a garrison; (4) a fortress for the populace to retreat to during a siege; and (5) stores to maintain the population during it.[203] The papyri refer to both the island of Elephantine and the city of Syene as *birtāʾ*s and, admittedly, each housed a garrison and a royal storehouse from which disbursements of food and silver were made. It is doubtful, however, that Elephantine/Syene was the capital of its district. The double-town, governed by the garrison commander, רב חילא, was part of the southern province of Tshetres, which was administered from its capital at Thebes (called נא in the papyri). Decisions made at Elephantine could be appealed to a higher court at Thebes, and if satisfaction was still not achieved, they could be appealed directly to the satrap at Memphis. The *frataraka* (*fratara* = 'superior' + *ka* = 'the one who')[204] supervised the garrison commander at Syene/Elephantine, but it is not clear if his seat was at Elephantine and he reported to the governor at Thebes, or if he was the governor at Thebes himself. One text (*TAD* B.2.9) suggests that a *frataraka* sat as judge in a trial at Elephantine, but the nature of the case may have required that it be held there rather than at Thebes. A great deal of material goods appears to have been brought into evidence in the case, which may have made travel to Thebes difficult (line 5).

Besides guarding the southern border of Eygpt, the garrison at Syene/Elephantine was likely used as a military escort for quarrying expeditions (or even to work the nearby quarries themselves) and to escort caravans traveling between Upper and Lower Egypt (*TAD* A.4.3).[205] Members of the garrison guarded goods being loaded or unloaded at the harbor (*TAD* C.4) and collected tariffs on them. The practice of collecting tariffs on goods is demonstrated by a list found at Elephantine of duty imposed on Ionian and Phoenician ships throughout year 475. The record is closely written on both sides of a scroll measuring 7.5 m long and over 30 cm wide.[206] The duty collected was turned over to the treasury of the king.

The members of the garrison at Elephantine/Syene lived there with their wives and children, who grew up to continue the profession of their parents.[207] They were organized into units called *degel*s, identified by the names

203. Lemaire and Lozachmeur, "*Bîrāh/Bîrtāʾ* en araméen."

204. Kent, "Lexicon," *Old Persian*, ad loc.

205. Suggested by Porten, *Archives*, 40–41.

206. Yardeni, "Maritime Trade and Royal Accountancy." The ships referred to on this account list, as well as the goods listed, are Aegean. This suggests to Porten and Yardeni (*TAD* C, xx) that the account was originally written at Migdol, Tahpenes, or Memphis—that is, at a port on the Mediterranean rather than from the south. But why was it at Elephantine?

207. Porten, *Archives*, 29.

of their (Persian or Babylonian) commanders. The papyri testify to four *degels* in the period 464–460: Artabanu, Atroparan, Haumadata, and Varyzazta; and four between 446–420: Varyazata, Iddin-Nabû, Nimasu, and Arpaḥu; later, a Nabu-kudurri is also attested as *degel* leader.[208]

The men were provided monthly rations of food and silver. One account (*TAD* C.3.14) lists the amounts in *ardabs* of barley, which had been allocated to the men of the Syenian garrison in the 4th year of Darius II. Various loan guarantees indicate that loans of silver (*TAD* B.4.2) or grain would be repaid from these monthly rations:

> (In the) Month of Thoth, year 4 of King Artaxerxes, then in Syene the fortress, Anani son of Haggai son of Meshullam, a Jew of the *degel* of Nabukudurri, said to Pakhnum son of Besa, an Aramean of Syene of that *degel* also, saying:
>
> I came to you in your house in Syene the fortress and borrowed from you and you gave me emmer, 2 *peras*, 3 *seahs*. Then I Anani son of Haggai, shall pay and give you that emmer: e(mmer), 2 *p*(*eras*), 3 *seahs* from the ration which will be given me from the treasury of the king. (*TAD* B.3.13)

The Persian Administrative System at Elephantine

The administrative and judicial roles of satrap, governor, and garrison commander as well as the inner workings of garrison life are all revealed in these Aramaic documents from Elephantine. The garrison commander either alone (*TAD* B.2.10), or in conjunction with the provincial governor, served as judge in local disputes. In 420, Menaḥem and Ananiah, Elephantine Jews of the garrison detachment of Iddin-Nabû, brought suit (*TAD* B.2.9) against Jedaniah and Mahseiah, Jews of the same detachment. The suit was brought in Elephantine before Ramnadaina, then the Persian *frataraka* (פרתרך; line 4), or governor, and Vidranga, then the *rab ḥaylāʾ* (רב חילא; line 5), the Persian garrison commander.

As part of his judicial and supervisory activities, the garrison commander also allocated land. This is shown in the following case (*TAD* B.5.1), dated to October 22, 495:

> On the 2nd day of the month of Epiph, year 27 of King Darius, Salluah daughter of Kenaiah and Jethoma her sister said to Jehour daughter of Shelomam: "We gave to you half the share which the royal judges and Ravaka the garrison commander gave us in exchange for half the share which came to you along with Nahabeth."[209]

The document indicates that Salluah and Jethoma had to go before the judges of the Persian king and before Ravaka, the Persian garrison commander, to

208. Ibid., 30–31.
209. As an inherited share.

receive their share.[210] This may have been due to the unanticipated death of their father, Kenaiah. The younger sister's name, *Jethoma,* means 'orphan', suggesting that she had been born after the death of her father. The text shows that the (Persian) garrison commander along with the royally appointed judges settled land disputes and allocated land among the garrison families and, indeed, probably all the families in the area.

The garrison commander seems to have been in charge of the families under his command wherever they were. This is revealed in the following letter from the archive of Jedaniah, the priest of the temple of Yhw at Elephantine (*TAD* A.4.3). The first part of the letter is as follows:

> To my lords Jedaniah, Uriah and the priests of Yhw the God, Mattan son of Jashobiah (and) Berechiah son of . . . , your servant Mauziah.
>
> [May the God of Heaven seek after] the welfare of [my] lords [abundantly at all times and] may you be in favor before the God of Heaven.
>
> And now, when Vidranga, the garrison commander, came to Abydos, he imprisoned me on account of one dyer's stone which they found stolen in the hand of the merchants. Finally, Djeḥo and Ḥor, servants of Anani, intervened with Vidranga and Ḥarnufi, with the protection of the God of Heaven, until they rescued me.

This first part of the letter reveals the garrison commander's power to imprison. Vidranga made the decision at Abydos, about 370 km's traveling distance from Elephantine.[211] Alternatively, if Mauziah, son of Nathan, was guarding the merchants and so was on official garrison business, it might have warranted Vidranga's special attention. It appears that he was held responsible for the theft.

The letter continues as follows:

> And now, behold, they are coming there to you. You, look after them. Whatever desire and thing that Djeḥo (and) Ḥor shall seek from you—you, serve them [lit.: stand before them] so that they shall not find a bad thing about you. It is known to you that Khnum has been against us since Ḥananiah has been in Egypt until now. And whatever you will do for Ḥor, you are doing for your[. . .]. Ḥor is a servant of Ḥananiah. You, lavish from our houses goods. Give him as much as you can. It is not a loss for you. For that (reason) I send

210. Jehour, daughter of Shelomam, inherited her share along with Nahabeth (her sister?), presumably at the death of a parent. It may have been given as a gift prior to the parent's death. Such gifts in anticipation of death were common at Elephantine (e.g., *TAD* B.3.10). These documents, signed by witnesses, prevented disputes over the property after the death of the grantor.

211. Porten, *EPE,* 131 n. 11. Cruz-Uribe (personal communication) suggests the southern district stretched from Elephantine down to Abydos, so this may have been the extent of Vidranga's authority as well.

> (word) to you. He said to me, "Send a letter ahead of me." [. . .] If there is much loss, there is backing for it in the house of Anani. Whatever you do for him shall not be hidden from Anani.

Anani may have been the same Anani who is listed in the Arsames correspondence (*TAD* A.6.2:23) as 'chancellor' *beʿēl ṭeʿēm*, a high official in the satrapy. If so, then Ḥananiah was an official in the satrapal office as well, since Ḥor worked for both of them. Both Anani and Ḥananiah were evidently Jews (since they bore Yahwistic names), indicating that Jews served in highly placed official capacities throughout the Persian Empire.[212] The anger of the priests of Khnum against the priests of Yhw, which had existed since this Ḥananiah had come to Egypt, may explain why there was no mention of the Passover sacrifice in the Passover letter (*TAD* A.4.1). There may have been apprehension about aggravating them still further. The present text indicates the importance of keeping the Jewish community in Elephantine on the good side of Djeḥo and Ḥor, emissaries from the satrapal office. According to the letter, this had become especially important given the antagonism of the priests of Khnum.[213] The reason for the hostility is not known.

Additional letters reveal the worsening situation for the Elephantine Jews and, along with it, the hierarchical structure of the satrapal judiciary system. One letter (*TAD* A.4.4) lists several Jews who were imprisoned in Elephantine (Berechiah, Hosea, Pakhnum).[214] No reason for the arrest is given. The letter also names five women and six men, all Jews, imprisoned at the gate of Thebes. The men included Jedaniah, son of Gemariah, chief priest of Yhw and head of the Jewish community. The letter continues most enigmatically:

> [They left] the houses which they broke into in Yeb [i.e., Elephantine] and the property which they took they surely returned to their owners. However, they mentioned to [their] owners [silver], 120 *karsh*. May another decree not again be [upon] them here.
>
> Greetings to your house and your children until the gods/God show/s me [your face in peace.]

The gate of Thebes was the place of a tribunal. It was the seat of the governor of the southern district, Tshetres, to which Yeb belonged. As such, it was the seat of appeal for those at Elephantine. Jedaniah was chief priest of the Temple of Yhw and leader of the Jewish community. His inclusion among those arrested at Thebes suggests that the Jews had appealed a case affecting

212. Like Nehemiah, they likely came from Persia or Babylon, that is, central areas of the empire.

213. This letter is discussed in Porten, *Archives*, 280–82. Porten argues that Ḥananiah came to Egypt to bring the Passover letter with him.

214. Despite his name, this Pakhnum may have been Jewish. A Ḥanan ben Pakhnum is recorded as a member of the community (*TAD* C.4.6:5); cf. Porten, *EPE*, #B16, 133 n. 8.

the temple and the entire community.[215] It did not avail them; they were seized and imprisoned. It is not known who entered the houses in Elephantine and seized the goods in them or why.[216] It is possible that Jews had broken into the houses [of Khnum?]. If so, then the Jews returned the property and paid the 120 *karsh* as penalty. They may have broken into houses of the Khnum priests to get property taken when the temple was vandalized or simply in revenge. If so, this letter belongs after the following one.[217]

A second letter (*TAD* A.4.5), found in the archive of Jedaniah and dated to 410, indicates the tense state of affairs between the priests of Khnum and Yhw, as well as the power that the *frataraka* had over the cities in his district. The letter reports that Vidranga, then *frataraka*, had permitted the Khnum priests to tear down part of the royal storehouse and to build a wall across the fortress that apparently covered the garrison's well. In the process, they vandalized the temple, taking something (אשרנא 'beams?') from the temple to use in their construction. Several lines of the letter are missing:

> [Several lines missing.]
>
> . . . we grew/increased,[218] detachments of the Egyptians rebelled. We did not leave our posts, and nothing damaging was found among us.
>
> In the 14th year of Darius the [ki]ng, when our lord Arsames went to the king, this is the evil act which the *kōmer*-priests[219] of Khnum, the god, did in

215. The appellate process suggested in this and the following letters is consistent with that portrayed in the Petition of Peteesi (Griffith, Rylands IX). That petition was written during the time of Darius I, and though it is set in the Saitic period, it describes equally well the judicial process under the Achaemenids. One could be beaten or imprisoned for bringing a false accusation: for example, Petition of Peteesi I 14, II 6–9. See also Seidl, *Aegyptische Rechtsgeschichte der Saiten- und Perserzeit*, for a discussion of the legal system under the Achaemenids. Seidl brings out the civil nature of every case. The judge attempts only to bring a reconciliation between the parties. The return of the stolen property and the 120 *karsh* of silver effected this reconciliation.

216. Porten (*Archives*, 288–89) and Grelot, *Documents* (#100, pp. 396–98) posit that the priests of Khnum had invaded the Jewish houses and stolen their goods. If so, the Khnum priests returned the goods to their owners and paid them 120 *karsh* in silver for damages. Grelot follows Porten's *Archives* in suggesting that this letter and the sack of the houses in Elephantine followed the destruction of the temple. Porten now (*EPE*, #B16, pp. 133–34) places this letter prior to the temple's destruction and considers the Jews guilty of invading private property, stealing from it, and paying the penalty. He conjectures that it was while the Jewish leadership was imprisoned in Thebes that the attack on the temple occurred.

217. Or the arrests in Elephantine and at Thebes may have had nothing to do with the conflict between the priests of Khnum and the priests of Yhw. There is no way to know.

218. Proposed by Porten and Yardeni as a probable restoration. Grelot, *DAE*, reads: "we cry out our anguish," #101, p. 401.

219. As in the Bible, the priests of other gods are called *kōmer*-priests, *komārîm*, or in

the capital of Yeb (i.e., Elephantine) in league with Vidranga who was *frataraka* here. They gave him silver and goods. There is part of the king's storehouse which is in Yeb the *bîrtāʾ*, they demolished it and built a wall in the middle of the *bîrtāʾ* of Yeb.

[About 3 lines missing.]

And now that wall [stands] built in the midst of the *bîrtāʾ*. There is a well which was built in the midst of the *bîrtāʾ*, which did not fail to give the garrison drink. Whenever they would be [garrisoned?] there, they would drink water from [th]at well. The *kōmer*-priests of Khnub the god stopped up that well.

If inquiry be made of the judges, police, and hearers who are appointed in the province of Tshetres, it will be kno[wn] to our lord in accordance with this which we say.

Moreover we are separated . . .

[Three lines missing.]

(d/r)ḥpnyʾ which are in Yeb the *bîrtāʾ* . . . we grew/increased . . . was not found in . . . to bring meal-offer[ing] . . . to offer there to Yhw the g[od] . . . in which . . . but a brazier . . . the אשרנא they took [to make them their] own. . . .

If it please our lord . . . much . . . we from the garrison. . . . [If it] please our lord, may an order be issued . . . we. If it please our lord, . . . they protect the things which . . . to [build] our . . . which they demolished.

The letter, written perhaps to an official at the satrapal level, states that information on behalf of the Jews is known to "the judges, police, and hearers who are appointed in the province of Tshetres." If Vidranga was the governor of Tshetres at Thebes, then this suggests that the provincial judges, police, and so on, operated independently of the governor and were likely not appointed by him but by the satrap or the king. They would have served as eyes and ears of the satrap or king in the provincial court. This is consistent with what we know from Xenophon's writings and with Cyrus's mode of administration as well.[220]

In Tammuz of that same year, year 14 of Darius II, a few months after Khnum's initial building acivities, Vidranga ordered the temple of Yhw completely destroyed. In a desperate appeal for help, the Jews sent the following petition (*TAD* A.4.7/8) to Bagavahya, the Persian governor (*peḥāh*) of Judah.[221]

Aramaic *kûmarayyāʾ*. This is in contradistinction to the priests of Yhw, called both here and in the Bible *kôhănîm*, or in Aramaic *kôhĕnayyāʾ*.

220. See above, chap. 2, pp. 31–32; Nabonidus Chronicle III:20.

221. Two drafts of the letter (*TAD* A.4.7 and A.4.8) were found at Elephantine. The letter quoted is from the first draft.

To our lord Bagavahya, governor of Yeḥud, your servants Jedaniah and his colleagues the priests who are in Elephantine the citadel.

May the God of Heaven seek after the welfare of our lord abundantly at all times, and grant you favor before King Darius (II) and the princes a thousand times more than now, and give you long life, and may you be happy and strong at all times.

Now, your servant Jedaniah and his colleagues say thus: In the month of Tammuz, year 14 of King Darius, when Arsames had departed and gone to the king, the priests of Khnum, the god, who are in Yeb the citadel, in agreement with Vidranga, who was *frataraka* here, (said), saying, "Let them remove from there the Temple of Yhw the god which is in Yeb the citadel." Then, that Vidranga, the wicked, sent a letter to Naphaina his son, who was garrison commander in Syene the citadel saying, "Let them demolish the temple which is in Yeb the citadel."

Then Naphaina led the Egyptians and other troops. They came to the citadel of Yeb with their weapons, broke into that temple, demolished it to the ground, and the pillars of stone which were there—they smashed them. Moreover, it happened [that the] 5 gateways of stone, built of hewn stone, which were in that temple, they demolished. And their standing doors, and the hinges of those doors, bronze, and the roof of wood of cedar—all which, with the rest of the אשרנא and other (things) which were there—all with fire they burned. But the basins of gold and silver and the things which were in that temple—all they took and made them their own.

And from the days of the kings of Egypt our fathers had built that temple in Yeb the citadel and when Cambyses entered Egypt he found that temple built. And they overthrew the temples of the gods of Egypt, all, but one did not damage anything in that temple.

[And when this had been done, we with our wives and our children were wearing sackcloth and fasting and praying to Yhw the Lord of Heaven that he may let us see our revenge on that Vidranga. (May the dogs tear his guts out from between his legs! May all the goods which he acquired be lost! May all the men who plotted evil for that temple—all of them—be killed, and may we watch them!)][222]

Moreover, before this—at the time that this evil was done to us—we sent a letter (to) our lord, and to Yehoḥanan the high priest and his colleagues the priests who are in Jerusalem, and to Ostanes the brother of Anani, and the nobles of the Jews. They did not send us a single letter.

Moreover, from the month of Tammuz, year 14 of King Darius and until this day, we are wearing sackcloth and fasting; our wives are made as widow(s); (we) do not anoint (ourselves) with oil and do not drink wine.

222. Pace Porten and Yardeni, *TAD* A.4.7 and 4.8. The translation of the words in brackets is suggested by Lindenberger, "What Ever Happened to Vidranga?: A Jewish Liturgy of Cursing from Elephantine." My thanks to Prof. Lindenberger for sending me his article. See also idem, "Razing of Temple."

Moreover, from that (time) and until (this) day, year 17 of King Darius they did not make meal-offering and incense and holocaust in that temple.

Now your servants Jedaniah and his colleagues and the Jews, all citizens of Yeb, say thus: "If it please our lord, take thought of that temple to rebuild it. Regard your well-wishers and your friends who are here in Egypt. Let a letter be sent from you to them about the temple of Yhw the god to rebuild it in Yeb the citadel just as it was formerly built. And they will offer the meal-offering and the incense, and the holocaust on the altar of Yhw the God in your name and we shall pray for you at all times—we and our wives and our children and the Jews, all who are here. If they do thus until that temple be rebuilt, you will have a merit before Yhw the God of Heaven more than a person who offers him holocaust and sacrifices whose worth is as the worth of silver, 1 thousand talents, and gold. Because of this we have sent and informed (you).

Moreover, we sent in our name all these words in one letter to Delaiah and Shemiah sons of Sanballat governor of Samaria.

Moreover, Arsames did not know about this which was done to us.

On the 20th of Marḥeshvan, year 17 of King Darius.

The lines in square brackets reflect Lindenberger's interpretation. Porten (*TAD* A.4.7:16, 17) translates the paragraph thus:

> And when this had been done (to us), we with our wives and our children were wearing sackcloth and fasting and praying to Yhw the Lord of Heaven who let us gloat over that Vidranga. The dogs removed the fetter from his feet and all goods which he had acquired were lost. And all persons who sought evil for that Temple, all (of them), were killed and we gazed upon them.[223]

To Porten, the verbs are in the simple narrative perfect. Lindberger argues, however, that the narrative portion of the letter ended prior to the present paragraph. The Vidranga passage is included in the part of the text detailing the community's response to the destruction, which was to put on sackcloth, to fast, and to pray. The passage is the prayer itself. Lindberger considers the verbs to be precative perfects, or perfectives of prayer and imprecation, rather than narrative perfects.[224] He also finds a correspondence between the Aramaic *kblʾ* (usually translated 'fetter') and Akkadian *qablû* 'innards'.

If Lindenberger's translation is correct, the passage does not assign either death or punishment to Vidranga; it is only the Jewish community's prayer for his demise. If Porten's translation is correct, then Vidranga was executed for his actions.

223. Porten discusses this passage and the reasoning behind his translation in his *Archives*, 288 n. 19.

224. Lindenberger (p. 12 n. 44) cites Waltke and O'Connor, *An Introduction to Biblical Hebrew Syntax*, 494ff., and the references cited there.

A written reply to the petition was not found among the papers of Jedaniah's archive. Only the following memorandum (*TAD* A.4.9) was found:

> Memorandum of what Bagavahya and Delaiah said to me: Memorandum: Saying: "Let it be for you in Egypt to say before Arsames about the altar-house of the God of Heaven which was built in Yeb the citadel formerly before Cambyses, which the wicked Vidranga demolished in the year 14 of Darius the king: to rebuild it on its site as it was before, and the meal offering and the incense offering, let them be offered on that altar just as formerly was done."

As in the Passover letter, Bagavahya and Delaiah mention only meal and incense to be offered if the temple is to be rebuilt, no animal sacrifice, no holocaust. Was this to pacify the priests of Khnum, to whom the ram was sacred? Or was it imposed by the priests of YHWH in Jerusalem who thought animals should be offered only there? The Jews must have agreed to the condition, for the following letter (*TAD* A.4.10) offers to forego animal sacrifice and to content themselves with meal and incense only. It also offers the addressee silver and barley. The addressee is probably Arsames himself. This is a draft of a letter that was sent.

> Your servants—Jedaniah son of Gemariah by name, 1
> Mauzi son of Nathan by name, 1
> Shemiah son of Haggai by name, 1
> Hosea son of Jathom by name, 1
> Hosea son of Nattum by name, 1
> all told 5 persons, men of Syene, who are in Yeb the citadel—thus say:
> If our lord . . . and our temple, the one of Yhw the god, be rebuilt in Yeb the citadel as formerly it was built—and sheep, ox, and goat (as) burnt offering are (n)ot made there, but (only) incense (and) meal-offering—and should our lord make a statement [about this, afterwards] we shall give to the house of our lord si[lver . . . and] barley, a thousa[nd] *ardab*s.

As noted above, recent archaeological data confirm that the temple was rebuilt on its site, as it was formerly. The appeal of Bagavahya and Delaiah, the agreement not to conduct animal sacrifice, the silver and barley—all may have had an impact. Or, Bagavahya and Delaiah may have been able to produce evidence of Cambyses' confirmation of the temple's right to exist on that land.

How should this attack on the Jewish temple be understood? Briant has reviewed the various explanations that scholars have put forth.[225] The primary understanding sees Vidranga as an Egyptophile who acquiesced to the desires of the Khnum priests, who wished to destroy the temple of the Persian garrison at Elephantine and to tear down part of the royal storehouse as well. If so, such acts of defiance would have resulted in the latter's death, as

225. Briant, "Une curieuse affaire à Elephantine en 410 av. n.e.," 118–20.

Porten's translation requires. However, a much broken letter (*TAD* A.3.9) has been used to suggest that Vidranga was still alive ten years later, in 399:

> [To my lord Islaḥ, your servant] Shewa. May all the gods [seek after] the welfare of my lord abundantly at all times. No[w] . . . in the matter of Apuḥas . . . saying: [It/He rea]ched me. When [this] le[tter] will reach you . . . they [will] bring (to) Memphis the king, Amyrtae[us, . . .] the king Nepherites sat (upon the throne) [in] Epiph [. . . . . . .until the gods show me] your face in peace . . .[. .]. . . the king Nephe[rites.] The silver which you sent me by the hand of [. . .] . . . these things/words. Menahem bought/sold it [. . .] above . . . [. .]. . . bronze which . . .
>
> Greetings to Anani son of Neriah. Greetings to all the sons of [. . .] here. Do not be [concerned about us. In] the matter of [. . .] each word/thing [. . .] the boat has [re]ached/will reach us here, they will release [me in the matt]er of Vidranga [. . .] force [. . .] . . . . . .
>
> On 5 Epiph th[is] letter was written.
>
> To. . . . My lord Islaḥ son of [PN,] your servant Shewa son of Zechariah.

When Upper Egypt fell to native Egyptians, those jailed by Persian officials may have been released.[226] This seems to be the case here; Islaḥ was released in the matter of Vidranga when Nepherites conquered Egypt.[227] It is possible that Vidranga was still alive, and in a position of power, when Nepherites seized the throne, 11 years after the temple's destruction.[228]

The fact that the order to tear down the temple was put in writing suggests to Briant that the act was legal and that Vidranga would not have been punished for it.[229] Briant, building on previous work by Porten, puts the entire affair into a cadastral framework. The temples of Khnum and Yhw bordered each other, and when the temple of Khnum began to expand, conflicts developed. This is visible in the Ananiah archive. The various contracts in which Ananiah buys and then sells portions of his house provide a history of the area.

On September 14, 437, Ananiah, a servitor (לחן) of Yhw,[230] acquired a house in Elephantine whose property lines are described as follows (*TAD* B.3.4:7ff.):

226. The dating formulas in the Elephantine archives indicate that Amyrtaeus did not achieve control in the south; letters and contracts are still dated to the years of Artaxerxes III.

227. Diodorus reports (16.41.5) that the Phoenicians arrested local Persian officials when they revolted against Persia. The Egyptians may have done the same in Egypt and released those whom the Persians had imprisoned.

228. Although the letter is too broken to come to any sort of conclusion (Porten, *Archives*, 288 n. 19).

229. Briant, "Une curieuse affaire à Elephantine en 410 av. n.e."; Porten, *Archives*, 284ff.

230. The cultic term לחן is discussed by Porten, ibid., 200.

> Above it is the house of Shatibar, below it is the district[?] of Khnum the god, and the street of the king is between them. To the east is the royal treasury adjoining it, and to the west of it is the temple of Yhw the god, and the street of the king is between them.

Shatibar's house adjoined Ananiah's house to the north. East of Ananiah's house, and adjoining it, was the royal treasury. West, but across the street, was the temple of Yhw. South of it, but across the street, was the district of Khnum. These were Ananiah's boundaries in 434, but by 420 they had changed—the temple of Khnum had expanded (*TAD* B.3.7). By 420, the temple of Khnum had built a house for Ḥor, gardener of Khnum, in front of Ananiah's house. Ananiah's house was no longer on the street but separated from it by Ḥor's house and by a small courtyard that lay between them. The courtyard opened onto a side street. By 404, Khnum had expanded still further. This is apparent from the contract (*TAD* B.3.10:8) in which Ananiah gave part of his house to his daughter, Jehoishma:

> East of it is the protecting wall which the Egyptians built, that is the way of the god.[231] Above it, the house of the shrine of the god adjoins it wall to wall. Below it is the wall of the stairway; and the house of Ḥor son of Peteesi, a gardener of Khnum the god, adjoins that stairway. West of it is the wall of the (i.e., Ananiah's) large room.

Thus, sometime between 420 and 404, but probably before 410, the Egyptian priests had taken over Shatibar's house and converted it into a shrine for Khnum. This meant that a shrine for Khnum stood behind Ananiah's house, and the district of Khnum stood in front of it. Probably in the summer of 410, the 14th year of Darius II, when Arsames had left the country, the priests of Khnum built a protecting wall (*TAD* A.4.5), the way of the god, to cover the walkway that connected the district of Khnum in front of Ananiah's house to the shrine behind it.[232] In the process of building the walkway and the wall, they tore down part of the royal treasury and stopped up the well, now under the wall. Ananiah's house became surrounded on three sides by property of Khnum.

It may have been these expansions to Khnum's property that led to the conflict with the temple. In 410, when the "way of the god" between the shrine and the district of Khnum was built, part of the temple of Yhw was torn down (*TAD* A.4.5). A few months later the temple was completely dismantled (*TAD* A.4.7/8). That Vidranga ordered his son, the garrison com-

231. For the translation of this line, see Porten, *EPE,* 239 nn. 18–19; idem, *Archives,* 284–85.

232. Site plans for the areas of Yhw, Khnum, and Ananiah's house based on the contracts are presented in figs. 1–6 of *TAD* B, pp. 176–82.

mander, *in writing*, to tear down the temple (line 7) suggests that it was an official act. If an official act, the decision would have been approved by the satrap and probably the king as a result of a judicial suit. Briant suggests that Khnum may have claimed prior ownership to the land on which the temple of Yhw stood.[233]

The walkway that connected the temple of Khnum and its chapel skirted Ananiah's house to the east. It would have been much easier for the priests of Khnum to tear down Ananiah's house and build their walkway straight across. But Ananiah held title to his house. That they went around and not through it reveals that they were concerned about the law. This suggests that neither the Jews nor the royal treasury had been able to prove title to their property, and the Khnum priesthood may have been able to convince Vidranga that the land was theirs. Because Arsames was out of the country, appeal to him was delayed.[234] The priests of Khnum most likely planned to build a walkway on both sides of Ananiah's house but were prevented from building on temple property on the west while its status was under appeal. Had this been a rebellion against Persian occupation by an Egyptophile *frataraka*, the priests of Khnum would have torn down the royal treasury building completely. They would not have left it standing to collect taxes and tribute.

Unwilling to make room for a walkway, and probably as a result of a judicial decision (i.e., by Vidranga), the priests of Yhw had to stand aside while the temple was torn down. Had it been a revolt against Persian occupation, the Jewish garrison would have resisted with force. The Jews state that Arsames did not know (line 30), but this is hardly likely, given Arsames' close control over events in his satrapy. It is more likely that Vidranga acted with satrapal approval and that this is what led to the appeal to the Persian governors of Yehud and Samaria and to the priests of YHWH in Jerusalem. The intercession of the two governors was evidently effective. There is no mention of the temple of Yhw in a contract of 404; but by 402, the temple of Yhw is again mentioned as one of the boundaries of Ananiah's house (*TAD* B.3.12). Indeed, archaeology confirms that the temple was built on its site, "as it had been before."

As is evident, Persian control over affairs at Syene/Elephantine was not restricted by local assemblies. Tuplin suggests that the Jewish community assembly at Elephantine was a judicial body that acted to adjudicate land disputes.[235] Yet the land disputes mentioned in the papyri were all resolved by

233. Briant, "Une curieuse affaire à Elephantine en 410 av. n.e.," 124; Porten, *Archives*, 289.

234. So Briant, "Une curieuse affaire à Elephantine en 410 av. n.e."

235. Tuplin, "The Administration of the Achaemenid Empire," 111.

judicial proceedings involving Persian garrison commanders, judges, governors, and finally the satrap. The cases that he cites in reference to local assemblies (*TAD* B.2.6, B.3.3, and B.3.8) are marriage and divorce proceedings in which a party proclaims in front of the assembly that the couple is divorced, or in which one party agrees to fulfill an obligation if a divorce does occur. As in Babylon, the assembly served as witness only.

Conclusion

Egyptian data support conclusions derived from Babylonia. Districts were ruled by Persian (non-Egyptian) governors (*frataraka*s) and cities by Persian garrison commanders. High officials in the satrapal court, including judges and heralds, were ethnic Persians; lower officials included Babylonians and (probably Babylonian) Jews. Local Egyptians served only as scribes, accountants, and assistants. References to royal judges indicate that the king appointed satrapal officials who operated independently of the governor, serving as the eyes and ears of the king. The satrap similarly may have appointed the provincial judges. The satrap also appointed the top officials of the few temples that remained in operation, and the local garrison commander appointed second-level temple priests. This is not consistent with a model of self-governance or even a model of imperial authorization of local norms. Rather, these data are consistent with the model of bureaucratic empires put forth by Eisenstadt. The temples—and the entire satrapy—were run by the Persian rulers as a fiefdom for the king.

Persian rule had a strongly negative impact on the growth, development, and autonomy of Egyptian temples. Before the Achaemenids, temples were the beneficiaries of pharaonic largess. Meeks's donation steles reveal the huge amounts that Egyptian kings poured into temple estates. These ended with Cambyses' decree and were not reinstated—not by Darius nor by any Persian ruler. Pharaonic donations to temple estates began again only with Nepherites and then again with the Ptolemies. The lack of priestly genealogies for many temples during the Achaemenid period suggests that they did not function under the Persians, resuming operations only under the Greeks. Moreover, under the pharaohs, temples had been largely autonomous. The pharaoh appointed high priests, but these were most often the sons of previous high priests or other high officials. If no heir was available, the priestly college would select their leader by a vote. Pharaonic approval was *pro forma.* Data from Elephantine show that under the Achaemenids this was no longer the case. Letters from the temple of Khnum indicate that appointment of the Lesonis required satrapal approval; secondary temple officials required approval of the garrison commander. These were not *pro forma.* Fees to purchase these positions were necessary and went into the king's coffers. A local priest struggled for autonomy, if he dared, only in opposition to the Persian ruler. These letters reveal moreover that every three years, at least, the Lesonis had to bring the temple account books to the *ḥry-ib-tpy*, the *senti*, at the satrapal office. This official used these accounts to determine the temple's taxes to the royal and satrapal coffers. Instead of the pharaohs donating to the temples, under the Persians the temples sent tribute to the Great King. The office of *senti*, appearing for the first time in the 27th Dynasty, confirms that in Egypt, as in Babylon, Egyptian temples had become simply another source of revenue for the Great King.

Events surrounding the destruction and rebuilding of the temple of Yhw at Elephantine illustrate the judicial system under the Achaemenids. Cases were heard initially in the city of Syene/Yeb and could be appealed to Thebes if necessary, and all the way to Memphis if desired. Decrees were carried out as ordered by the judges. Those acting as arbiters included the Iranian garrison commander, the Iranian *frataraka,* or governor, and the Iranian satrap, along with royal and provincial judges—Iranian and Babylonian. There were no Egyptian judges or Egyptian judicial officials; this was an entirely Persian judicial system.

Relief might be provided by intercession from the governors of neighboring provinces, however. Involvement of governors and satraps in the affairs of their neighbors is especially apparent among the provinces and satrapies of Persian period Asia Minor, to which I now turn.

Chapter 4

Temple-Palace Relations in Asia Minor

Data from Asia Minor are meager relative to those from Babylonia and Egypt. There are no individual or temple archives; only a few isolated inscriptions permit a window into Persian administration and temple-palace relations there. A representative sample of such inscriptions includes Darius's Letter to Gadatas; a border dispute between two cities, Miletus and Myus; an inscription from Sardis; a decree of Mylasa; and the Trilingual Inscription from Xanthus.

Darius's Letter to Gadatas

Darius's letter to Gadatas has been cited as proof of the Persian rulers' solicitude and support for non-Zoroastrian cults and their priests. It has even been dubbed "an edict of tolerance for foreign gods."[1] Now in the Louvre, it was found inscribed on a marble corner-block of a wall of a Turkish house in Deirmendjik, on the road linking Magnesia on the Maeander to Tralles.[2] The shape of the letters dates the engraving firmly to the time of Hadrian (117–38 C.E.).[3] An adjacent side contains two other inscriptions, also dated to the period of imperial Rome. The first makes connection with the letter from Darius by naming the sanctuary of Apollo at Magnesia, but the letters on this second side of the stone have almost entirely disappeared.[4] The editors suggest that the three inscriptions together comprise letters of kings and decrees of consuls that preserved the privileges of the temple.[5]

Author's note: This chapter benefited immensely from Gerda Seligson's (ז"ל) help in translating the Greek. For a map of the sites discussed in this chapter, see p. 236.

1. Von Hüttenbach, "Brief des Königs Darius," 93.
2. Meiggs and Lewis, *Selection of Greek Historical Inscriptions*, 20; Brandenstein and Mayrhofer, *Handbuch des Altpersischen*, 92; the *editio princeps* is Cousin and Deschamps, "Lettre de Darius." The amount of literature on this inscription is immense. See now Briant, "Histoire et archéologie d'un texte: La *Lettre de Darius à Gadatas* entre Perses, Grecs et Romains," and literature cited there.
3. Kern, *Inscriptiones*, 102; Boffo, "La lettera di Dario I a Gadata," 268–69, and literature cited there.
4. Cousin, "Correction"; Boffo, "La lettera di Dario I a Gadata," 268–69.
5. Cousin and Deschamps, "Lettre de Darius," 532, 541–42.

Darius begins the letter by praising his subordinate for planting fruit trees on the coast of Asia Minor. He ends by chastising him for levying a tax (φόρον) on the priests of Apollo and for forcing them to engage in corvée labor on land belonging to the king. Darius states that this is unjust (ἠδικημένου) to the god "who spoke only truth to the Persians." The inscription is as follows:

1.	King of Kings	[β]ασιλεὺς [βα]σιλέ-
2.	Darius, son of	ων Δαρεῖος ὁ Ὑσ-
3.	Hystapes, to Gadatas	τάσπεω Γαδάται
4.	Servant, says thus:	δούλωι τάδε λέγε[ι]:
5.	I learn that you	Πυνθάνομαί σε τῶν
6.	my orders	ἐμῶν ἐπιταγμάτων
7.	in all things do not	οὐ κατὰ πάντα πει-
8.	obey. Because on the one hand	[θ]αρχεῖν. Ὅτι μὲν γὰ[ρ]
9.	you work my	[τ]ὴν ἐμὴν ἐκπονεῖ[ς]
10.	land, planting the produce from	[γ]ῆν τοὺς πέραν Εὐ-
11.	Beyond (the) Euphrates as far as	[φ]ράτου καρποὺς ἐπ[ὶ]
12.	the coast of the region of Asia,	τὰ κάτω τῆς Ἀσίας μέ-
13.	I commend	[ρ]η καταφυτεύων, ἐπαι-
14.	your goal and	[ν]ῶ σὴν πρόθεσιν καὶ
15.	on account of all these things there will be established for you	[δ]ιὰ ταῦτά σοι κείσεται
16.	great gratitude in the King's	μεγάλη χάρις ἐμ βασι-
17.	house. On the other hand, because	λέως οἴκωι ὅτι δε τὴν
18.	my will on behalf of the gods	ὑπερ θεῶν μου διάθε-
19.	you lose sight of, I will give	σιν ἀφανίζεις δώσω
20.	to you, if you do not change,	σοι μὲ μεταβαλομένωι
21.	a proof of my offended an-	πεῖραν ἠδικη[μέ]νου θυ-
22.	ger. Indeed, from the gardener	μοῦ φυτουργοὺς γὰρ
23.	priests of Apollo, tribute	[ἱ]εροὺς Ἀπόλλ[ω]νος φό
24.	you have exacted, and profane land	ρον ἔπρασσες καὶ χώραν
25.	to dig you assigned [them],	[σ]καπανεύειν βέβηλον ἐπ[έ]-
26.	not recognizing my	τασσες ἀγνοῶν ἐμῶν
27.	ancestors' purpose on behalf of the god	προγόνων εἰς τὸν θεὸν
28.	who spoke to the Persians	[ν]οῦν ὅς Πέρσαις εἶπε
29.	only truth, and to the . . .	[πᾶ]σαν ἀτρέκε[ι]αν καὶ τη

The Letter's Authenticity

At the time of the Roman conquest, cities and temples were required to produce proof of their privileges and immunities in order to retain them.[6]

6. Briant, *HEP*, 507.

This may have been the reason for the letter's being engraved on the temple walls. According to Tacitus (*Annals* 3.60–62):

> Tiberius [14–37 C.E.] meantime, while securing to himself the substance of imperial power, allowed the Senate some shadow of its old constitution by referring to its investigation certain demands of the provinces. In the Greek cities license and impunity in establishing sanctuaries were on the increase. . . .
>
> It was accordingly decided that the different states were to send their charters and envoys to Rome. Some voluntarily relinquished privileges which they had groundlessly usurped; many trusted to old superstitions, or to their services to the Roman people. It was a grand spectacle on that day, when the Senate examined grants made by our ancestors, treaties with allies, even decrees of kings who had flourished before Rome's ascendancy, and the forms of worship of the very deities, with full liberty as in former days, to ratify or to alter.
>
> First of all came the people of Ephesus. They declared that Diana and Apollo were not born at Delos as was the vulgar belief. They had in their own country a river Cenchrius, a grove Ortygia, where Latona . . . gave birth to those two deities, whereupon the grove at the divine intimation was consecrated . . . during the Persian rule its privileges were not curtailed. They had afterwards been maintained by the Macedonians, then by ourselves.

Tacitus's statement demonstrates that privileges were confirmed periodically, so that although he refers to Tiberius and our inscription was engraved a century later in the time of Hadrian, it need not be doubted that temple immunities would have been an issue then as well. The inscription states that Darius I exempted the priests of Apollo of Aulai from taxes and from the requirement to do corvée labor on non-temple land.[7] It may be a later copy of an archival letter or of a stone that had become weathered.

Because the letter constitutes proof of ancient privilege, it has aroused a suspicion of forgery among modern scholars.[8] The original editors argue that its authenticity need not be questioned in spite of the five centuries between the date of the letter and its engraving. Even Hansen, who concludes the letter is a forgery, puts the forgery in the time of Darius I.[9] Hansen, citing Strabo (14.1, 5; 17.1, 43), suggests the letter is a forgery because "during Darius's reign the greatest sanctuary of Apollo in Asia Minor, the temple at Didyma, was burnt down by [his son] Xerxes."[10] However, Xerxes had noth-

7. Kern, *Inscriptiones*, 102. The location of the temple and the local name of the god worshiped there have been demonstrated by L. Robert, "Documents d'Asie Mineure," 40–46.

8. Most recently, Briant, "Histoire et archéologie d'un texte."

9. Hansen, "The Purported Letter of Darius," 95–96.

10. Ibid.

ing to do with the destruction of the Temple of Apollo at Didyma (Herodotus 6.19, against Strabo).[11] That he was not co-regent or even crown prince at this time has been carefully argued by Root.[12] Hansen sees the comment about the god "who spoke only truth to the Persians" as deeply ironic, since in her view the Persians had just destroyed the Temple of Apollo at Didyma. She dates the inscription to the reign of Darius, after the destruction of the temple, arguing that a date before that is possible "if other crimes against sanctuaries of Apollo had taken place before the destruction of the temple at Didyma."[13] Hansen interprets the inscription as a backlash against Darius (and Xerxes) for their destruction of Apollo temples, but use of irony in the text cannot be proved.[14] Further, as Wiesehöfer notes, the letter includes praise of Gadatas for planting fruit trees in Beyond the River up to the coast of Asia Minor. This has nothing to do with the sanctuary of Apollo and is unlikely to have been included by a forger interested only in demonstrating the priesthood's rights.

Briant has recently raised some objections to the letter's authenticity that were first offered by van den Hout.[15] To begin with, Briant finds difficulties with the expression Πέραν Εὐφράτου (Beyond [the] Euphrates) in the letter, since it appears without the intervening article. To Briant, an authentic Persian period document would have had the article Πέραν τοῦ Ποταμοῦ 'Beyond the River' or Πέραν τοῦ Εὐφράτου. Von Hüttenbach uses the fact that Old Persian has no article, however, to argue that the Greek is a calque from the Persian and to argue for a Persian original.[16] It could also be an Aramaic original. The term replicates directly the Akkadian name of the satrapy, *Ebir Nari,* which has no article. If this were an actual letter from the king to his official, the original would most certainly have been in Aramaic, not Persian. The letters from Arsames to his Persian officials were not in Persian but Aramaic. Letters recently found in Afghanistan from the local Persian satrap to his Persian governor are also entirely in Aramaic,[17] and the name can be found

11. So also Wiesehöfer, "Zur Frage der Echtheit des Dareios-Briefes," 396–97.

12. Root, *King and Kingship,* 83–85. See, however, Bongrani Fanfoni and Israel ("Documenti achemenidi nel deserto orientale egiziano"), who suggest a co-regency in the last 12 years of Darius's reign.

13. Hansen, "The Purported Letter of Darius," 96.

14. In agreement with Wiesehöfer ("Zur Frage der Echtheit des Dareios-Briefes," 397), I think that the irony is not conspicuous.

15. Briant, "Histoire et archéologie d'un texte: La *Lettre de Darius à Gadatas* entre Perses, Grecs et Romains"; van den Hout, "Studies in Early Greek Letter-Writing."

16. Von Hüttenbach, "Brief des Königs Darius," 93–98.

17. S. Shaked, personal communication. I thank B. Porten for acquainting me with this correspondence.

without the article in the Aramaic letters of Ezra as עבר נהרה (Ezra 4:11; 7:21, 25).[18]

Briant argues, secondly, that if authentic, the name of the satrapy would have been 'Beyond the River' Πέραν τοῦ Ποτάμου, not 'Beyond the Euphrates' Πέραν τοῦ Ευφράτου. Van den Hout suggests, however, that the name of the river would have been substituted for the actual name of the satrapy, "Beyond the River," at the time of the engraving, because 2nd-century Greeks would not have known which river was meant.[19] Briant argues that the phrase "Beyond (the) Euphrates" indicates that the entire letter is based on Greek literary sources and is not authentic. Yet nowhere among any of the Greek writers does the phrase Πέραν (τοῦ) Ποτάμου ('Beyond the River') or Πέραν (τοῦ) Ευφράτου ('Beyond the Euphrates')—with or without the article—appear as a designation for a particular satrapy or administrative district.[20] In Greek literature, the phrase is used only to designate an area of land on the opposite side of a river from the speaker. This term for a particular satrapy could not have been gleaned from any extant Greek historical or literary text.

Briant also questions the term δοῦλος 'servant' as a reference to Gadatas. The original editors suggest that it translates the Persian *manā badaka*, found in the Behistun inscription (DB 5:8).[21] Briant argues, however, that such a comparison cannot be made when the term *badaka* is so rare in Achaemenid texts. The Aramaic terms עבד and עלים are ubiquitous in the Arsames correspondence, however, and either one could be translated δοῦλος. *TAD* A.6.1 begins, "[To our lord Arsa]mes, your servants (עבדיך) Achaemenes and his colleagues, Bagadana and his colleagues, and the scribes of the province." Another well-known letter (*TAD* A.4.7, 8) begins, "To our lord Bagavahya, governor of Yehud, your servants (עבדיך) Jedaniah and his colleagues the priests who are in Elephantine, the citadel." *HALOT* translates עלים as "youth, servant"; Porten and Yardeni translate it by the Hebrew term נער.[22] Yet it is clear that an important official, clearly an adult, is meant (e.g., *TAD* A.6.4). From Arsames to Artavant:

> [And now, the grant] was given [b]y the king and by me to Aḥḥapi my servant (עלימא זילי) who was an offic[ial], פקיד, in my domains which are in Up[per and Lower Egypt. . . .]

18. Unless the *he* at the end of נהר is an orthographic variant for the *ʾalep*.

19. So also Porciani, *La forma proemiale*, 27, "ma bisogna tener conto della traduzione greca, che avrà operato un compromesso tra la formulazione del testo persiano e le competenze geografiche di un pubblico greco."

20. I thank Beau Case, Jeffrey Gibson, and Ann Nyland for their help in searching the databases.

21. The phrase *manā badaka* 'my servant' refers to a Gubarvaya, whom Darius sent to be satrap over Elam (DB 5:1–14).

22. *HALOT*, 835. Porten and Yardeni, *TAD* A, ad loc.

Greek δοῦλος would be the normal translation for these terms.[23]

Briant also sees a problem in the name Gadatas, when the Persian ought to be Bagadatès or Megadatès, both well attested. But Briant himself recognizes, citing Schmitt, that the same name, spelled *Ka-da-da*, is known at Persepolis.[24]

Van den Hout argues that the form of the letter is not original, but reflects the missives in Revelation 2 and 3.[25] He points out that in the New Testament book, there is also first praise, then a reproof, and then an exhortation to improve. Yet, as Boffo notes, one of the Arsames letters (*TAD* A.6.10) exhibits this same pattern.[26] First the satrap commends former officials for their behavior and states that he has heard that his officials in Lower Egypt are performing just as well. Then there is a warning to the recipient that if he does not do as these others he "will be interrogated by force and a word of rebuke given to [him]."

> From Arsames to Nakhṭor. And now, formerly, when the Egyptians rebelled, then Samshek, the former official, strictly guarded our domestic staff and goods in Egypt so that there was not any decrease in my estate. Moreover, from elsewhere he sought domestic staff of craftsmen of all kinds and other go[o]ds in sufficient numbers and made (them over) to my estate.
>
> And now, thus have I heard here, that the officials who are [in Low]er (Egypt) are being diligent during the troubles (?). They are strictly guarding the domestic staff and goods of their lords. Moreover, they are seek[ing] others from elsewhere and add[ing (them) t]o the estate of their lords. But you are not doing so.
>
> Now, even formerly I sent (word) to you about this: "You, [be] diligent. Strictly guard m[y] domestic staff and good[s] so that there will not be a[n]y decrease in my estate. Moreover, from elsewhere seek domestic staff of craftsmen of all kinds in sufficient numbers and bring them into my court, and mark them with my brand, and make (them over) to my estate just as the [for]mer officials had been doing."
>
> Thus let it be known to you: if there be any decrease in the domestic staff or in my other goods and from elsewhere you do not seek and you do not add to my estate, you will be strictly called to account and a harsh word will be directed at you.
>
> [Ar]taḥaya knows this order. Rashta is the scribe.

This pattern of first praise, then a command, and then a threat observed in the Gadatas letter is not surprising for official correspondence between a superior and his officials.

23. Δοῦλος translates עבד throughout the LXX.

24. Briant, "Histoire et archéologie d'un texte," 11 n. 52; Schmitt, "Bemerkungen zu dem sog. Gadatas-Brief," 96.

25. Van den Hout, "Studies in Early Greek Letter-Writing."

26. Boffo, "La lettera di Dario I a Gadata," 278–79.

A further problem to Briant is the inclusion of Darius's patronym, which appears elsewhere only in Persian royal inscriptions. Because the sender's patronym is not used in the opening salutation either in the letters of Arsames or in the Aramaic letters of the Bible, Schmitt suggests that it is a later addition to the text.[27] Yet, how can this be argued when we have no letters from a king to his satrap with which to compare it? The closest parallel is the Trilingual Inscription of Xanthus, to be discussed below. The inscription, in Aramaic, Greek, and Lycian, describes the establishment of a temple in Xanthus. In this inscription, Pixadarus, the satrap, gives his patronym.

In the month of Sivan, in the first year	1. בירח סיון שנת חד
of Artaxerxes the King,	2. ארתחשסש מלכא
in the citadel (*birta*ʾ) of Arna, Pixodarus,	3. באורן בירתא פגסוד[ר]
son of Hecatomnos, satrap	4. בר כתמנו חשתרפנא
who is over Caria and Lycia, s[ays]:	5. זי בכרך ותרמיל א⟨מר⟩

Other examples are the Arsames letters to his officials. The outside of these often read: מן ארשם ברביתא 'from Arsames, the son of the house [= the prince]'. This identification is completely equivalent to Δαρεῖος ὁ Ὑστάσπεω 'Darius, son of Hystaspes'. This suggests that the prescript on the inscription may have come from the identification on the outside of the parchment. The salutation, without the customary wishes for welfare and strength, is reminiscent of Arsames' many letters to his officials in which such a benediction is lacking (e.g., *TAD* A.6.8; 6.9; 6.10).

Van den Hout and now Briant also object that the phrase τάδε λέγει 'thus (he) says' is out of place. They argue that in Persian and Aramaic letters, this phrase would occur at the beginning of the prescript, not at its end. Yet, as the Arsames letters show, the phrase may appear anywhere in the letter (e.g., *TAD* A.6.8):

Inside:

From Arsames to Armapiya. And now, Psamshek my official (פקידא) sent (word) to me *saying thus*: "Armapiya with the troop which is at his command do not obey me in the affair of my lord (about) which I am telling them."

Now Arsames says thus כעת ארשם כן אמר, "(In) the affair of my estate (about) which Psamshek will tell you and the troop which is at your command—(in) that, obey him and do (it). Thus [let] it be kn[ow]n to you: If Psamshe[k] later sends me a complaint against you, you will be strictly called to account and a harsh word will be directed at you."

Bagasrava knows this order. Aḥpepi is the scribe.

Outside:

From [Ar]sames to Armapiya
Concerning (the fact that) Psamshe[k] said: "They do not ob[e]y me."

27. Schmitt, "Bemerkungen zu dem sog. Gadatas-Brief," 99.

The phrase "Now Arsames (son of the house) says thus" is parallel to "King of Kings, Darius, son of Hystaspes, to Gadatas Servant, says thus" (τάδε λέγε[ι]). This placement of the phrase "says thus" is normal in the Arsames letters. Porciani supplies examples of Greek translations of Aramaic letters in which the phrase τάδε λέγει, τάδε γράφει, or χαίρειν ('Greetings!') appears at the end of the prescript (LXX: Esth 3:13; Ezra 7:12; Esth 8:12; Jos., *Ant.* 11.273; Hdt. 3.122; 5.24; 7.150; 8.140).[28] He concludes that in Greek translations the pattern is not fixed and is independent of the original word order.[29] This variation is abundantly clear from the Trilingual Inscription of Xanthus, as shown above. The Aramic version has the word אמר 'says' at the end of the prescript, exactly as in the letter to Gadatas. More telling, however, is that this sentence does not appear in the Greek inscription on the stele. The Greek is not a translation of the Aramaic but is an independent rendition of the edict.[30]

The arguments put forth to suggest that the letter is a forgery, created in the Roman period, do not convince. If the priests of Apollo were to have invented a forgery, it seems more likely that they would have simply created a decree from Darius, rather than this letter in which privileges are conferred only obliquely. The letter seems an odd thing to offer as proof, unless there was nothing better to use than this, Gadatas's reprimand.

The issue of Greek translations of Aramaic texts, or even later Greek transcriptions of earlier Greek documents, affects the present understanding of many inscriptions. Knowing that the Greek and Aramaic texts on the Xanthus Stele are not identical is helpful. If we only had the Greek, we would not suppose that an Aramaic version also existed. This point is brought out clearly by Habicht's study of a Greek forgery.[31] The text purports to be the exact words of Themistocles' decree in 480 B.C.E., although it was inscribed much later, probably during the time of Alexander. Habicht has shown that the text could not represent the actual decree and so cannot be used as a historical source. According to the inscription, only Athenians with legitimate sons could serve as trierarchs (commander of a trireme) in the navy. However, this makes sense only after the law of Pericles in 451; prior to that time, every child of an Athenian citizen was considered legitimate. Habicht argues further that the allocation of a ship to a trierarch by lot could only be a development of the democratic ideal, an ideal that belongs to the fourth century, not the fifth. These and other anachronisms (e.g., the list of gods) date

28. Porciani, *La Forma Proemiale,* 27–29.

29. Ibid., 30.

30. Or a translation of the Lycian. For an interesting discussion of the issues, see Lemaire and Lozachmeur, "Remarques sur le plurilinguisme en Asie Mineure."

31. Habicht, "Falsche Urkunden zur Geschichte Athens im Zeitalter der Perserkriege"; Jameson, "A Decree of Themistocles from Troizen."

the text to the mid–4th century. Yet Habicht does not suggest that the document is fictive. Rather, he argues that it is a 4th-century reconstruction of a genuine 5th-century decree. It is not a historical source but an example of the process of historiography. It describes the decree as it "must have been." Thucydides (*Hist.* 1.22) states the problems of creating an accurate recounting of even contemporaneous events:

> As to the speeches that were made by different men, either when they were about to begin the war or when they were already engaged therein, it has been difficult to recall with strict accuracy the words actually spoken, both for me as regards that which I myself heard, and for those who from various sources brought me reports. Therefore the speeches are given in the language in which, as it seemed to me, the several speakers would express, on the subjects under consideration, the sentiments most befitting the occasion, though at the same time I have adhered as closely as possible to the general sense of what was actually said. But as to the facts of the occurrences of the war, I have thought it my duty to give them, not as ascertained from any chance informant nor as seemed to me probable, but only after investigating with the greatest possible accuracy each detail, in the case both of the events in which I myself participated and of those regarding which I got my information from others. And the endeavor to ascertain these facts was a laborious task, because those who were eye-witnesses of the several events did not give the same reports about the same things, but reports varying according to their championship of one side or the other, or according to their recollection.

The remarks by Thucydides, the rewriting of Themistocles' decree, plus the disparity between the Greek and Aramaic texts on the Xanthus Stele force the conclusion that even contemporaneous Greek documents are not literal renditions of events. Yet neither are they fictive. They are historiography; they report occurrences as they "must have been." This is most likely the situation of the Gadatas letter. Rather than assume that it is a literal translation of an Aramaic or Persian original, I think that it may represent the Apollo priests' tradition of Darius's reprimand to Gadatas inscribed as it "must have been."

Who Was Gadatas?

Assuming then that the inscription reconstructs a historical event, we may ask who Gadatas was: satrap of Lydia or keeper of a *paradeisos* (one of those famous Persian gardens) near Magnesia on the Meander in Asia Minor. Because Darius praises Gadatas for cultivating royal land by transplanting fruit trees from Beyond the River Euphrates into Asia Minor, Dandamayev suggests that he was a keeper of a *paradeisos.*[32] Briant (in an earlier work)

32. Dandamayev, "Royal *Paradeisoi*," 114. For an interesting discussion of *paradeisoi* in the Achaemenid Empire, see Heltzer, "Some Questions about Royal Property."

concurs, since those gardens traditionally included a section devoted to experimentation with rare species.[33] He compares Gadatas to Asaph, "keeper of the king's *pardēs*," in Lebanon during the period of Artaxerxes I (Neh 2:8).

The Date of the Letter

If one assumes a late reconstruction of an actual letter, the location and date of its original writing can be fixed. Written by Darius I, the letter must be dated to his reign (522–486). The year must be after 518, when the series of rebellions that rocked the empire at his ascension ended.[34] The date can be narrowed further. Darius traversed Asia Minor in 513 in his attempt to conquer the Scythians.[35] He crossed the Bosphorus, reached the Danube, and was back in Sardis by 512 or 511; by 510 he had returned to Susa.[36] Briant suggests that, if authentic, the letter to Gadatas would have been composed while Darius was in Sardis, 512–511.[37] He bases this suggestion on the hint in Herodotus 5.12 that Darius received delegations there. A delegation from the priests of Apollo may have petitioned the king and received a favorable response.

Although Darius may have heard the petition while in Sardis, he may not have written his letter there. He likely waited until he returned to Susa or Ecbatana before writing it. If the letter were based on agreements made by Cyrus, Darius would have needed to examine the archives to verify the claims. The earliest date then would have been 510 when Darius returned to Susa. It is unlikely that Darius would have written it after the Ionian revolt in 499.[38] The destruction of the Apollo Temple at Didyma (Herodotus 6.19) demonstrates that the Apollo priesthood participated in the revolt. Darius could not have written that the god spoke "only truth to the Persians" after that revolt. According to this reasoning, the original letter must have been written between 510 (when Darius had returned to Susa) and 499 (the Ionian revolt and the destruction of the Temple of Apollo at Didyma). It was probably written shortly after his return.

A Divine Quid Pro Quo?

As discussed in chap. 2, superintendents of *paradeisoi* had the power to compel corvée labor from local priesthoods. Records from Eanna and Ebabbar reveal that it was common practice in Babylonia for both Nabonidus and

33. Briant, *HEP*, 508.
34. Kent, *Old Persian*, "Behistun Inscription," 116–34.
35. Hdt. 4.1, 83–144; for the date, see Briant, *HEP*, 154; cf. notes on p. 931.
36. Ibid., 154–58, 931–32.
37. Ibid., 507.
38. Following Briant's dating (ibid., 160).

the Achaemenid rulers to plant their *pardēsus* near temples in order to have laborers nearby to prepare and till the gardens. Darius's letter suggests that this was the practice in Asia Minor as well. Whether or not he was the keeper of a *pardēsu*, until the letter arrived from Darius, Gadatas had the authority to command local priests to perform corvée labor on royal land. The temples in Asia Minor, like the temples in Babylonia, were subject to the demands and requirements of the empire. The priests in Asia Minor, like their counterparts in Babylonia, formed a labor pool that could be freely drawn upon by the palace.

If tribute and corvée labor were the rule, why were these priests of Apollo exempted?[39] In lines 25–29, Darius chastises Gadatas for not recognizing "my ancestors' purpose on behalf of the god who spoke to the Persians only truth." Who were these ancestors of Darius? Neither the Behistun Inscription nor the Greek authors record a relationship between Darius's father or grandfather and the god Apollo. Nor do they record that Darius's father or grandfather were in Asia Minor. Yet, both facts are recorded for Cyrus. According to Herodotus, Croesus, a Lydian by birth, was king of all the peoples west of the Halys River when Cyrus began his march westward in 548.[40] Before engaging Cyrus in war, Croesus set about to propitiate the gods and to inquire of them. He sent messengers to Apollo at Delphi, to the Branchidae priests of Apollo at Didyma, and to many others, asking if he should make war on the Persians.[41] The responses of the oracle at Delphi and at Amphiaraus were the same: "If Croesus were to make war against the Persians, he would destroy a mighty empire." This may have been the first truth the god spoke concerning Cyrus. After his conquest of Lydia and the fall of Sardis, Cyrus ordered the Lydian Pactyes to raise tribute from the conquered territories (Hdt. 1.153). As soon as Cyrus left the area, Pactyes induced the Lydians to revolt, and he himself ran off with "all the gold of Sardis" (Hdt. 1.154). Hearing this, Cyrus sent an army back toward Lydia to bring Pactyes to Ecbatana. Pactyes fled to Cyme, whereupon the Persian general Mazares sent to Cyme to command them to surrender the betrayer (Hdt. 1.157). The men of Cyme inquired of the god Apollo at the sanctuary of the Branchidae.[42] The oracle told the Cymeans to surrender Pactyes to the Persians (Hdt. 1.158). A second inquiry brought a second identical response. This would have been the second truth the god Apollo spoke concerning Cyrus.

39. Pace Blenkinsopp ("Did the Second Jerusalemite Temple Possess Land?"), who argues from this inscription that priests were automatically free from taxation.

40. Herodotus 1.6; for the date, see Briant, *HEP*, 44–45.

41. Hdt. 1.46–55.

42. Parke, "The Massacre of the Branchidae," 59.

Mention of these "truths" suggests that an agreement, a quid pro quo, existed between Cyrus and the priests of Apollo like the one that existed between Cyrus and the Marduk priesthood and between Cambyses and the priest Udjaḥorresnet. In return for their collaboration, Cyrus agreed to grant priests of all the Apollo Temples permanent immunity from tribute and corvée labor. This arrangement would have resulted from a specific quid pro quo; there is no evidence of a blanket exemption for priests in the Persian Empire. The reference to past "truths to the ancestors" suggests that the Apollo priests at Aulai appealed to Darius for redress of grievances based on past favors. The letter to Gadatas would have been Darius's response to this appeal, or at least, a reconstruction of that response. Even if historical, the letter cannot provide evidence for a universal positive attitude toward foreign cults. This was generally not the case, not in Egypt and not in Asia Minor. Indeed, according to Diodorus (5.63):

> The greatest thing is that the Persians, when they ruled Asia and were plundering all the temples of the Greeks, held off from the precinct of Hemithea . . . , and the pirates, who were seizing everything, left this one quite unviolated, even though it was unwalled and plundering was free of risk.[43]

Rather, the letter provides further evidence for the Persian practice of granting exemptions to specific temples in return for their collaboration. As Briant puts it, "the attention accorded to local sanctuaries found its limit in the subjects' loyalties."[44] Herodotus reports the fate of Miletus after it participated in the Ionian revolt against Persia:

> Most of the men were killed . . . ; the women and children were made slaves, and the temple at Didyma, both shrine and oracle, was plundered and burnt. . . . The Persians themselves occupied the land in the immediate neighborhood of the town, and the rest of the cultivated region which belonged to it, and made over the mountainous parts of the interior to the Carians of Pedasus. . . . In this way Miletus was emptied of its inhabitants. (Hdt. 6.19–20, 22)

Border Dispute between Miletus and Myus

A second Greek inscription (Tod 113) consists of two noncontiguous fragments of a stele of bluish marble.[45] The first is complete on the right, with a vacant space above. The second is complete on both the right and the left sides but broken at the top and bottom. It describes a territorial dispute between two cities, Miletus and Myus, which lay on opposite sides of the Latmic Gulf, into which the Maeander River flowed. The inscription shows

43. Quoted from Rigsby, *Asylia: Territorial Inviolability in the Hellenistic World*, 6.
44. Briant, *HEP*, 510.
45. Tod, *A Selection of Greek Historical Inscriptions*, 2.36–39, #113.

that the cities turned to the Great King, who handed the problem over to Struses, his satrap, for resolution. The text has been reconstructed by L. Piccirilli.[46]

Fragment A

1	Διονυσ	
2	πέ]μπων, ἃ χ-	. . . se]nding, the ones whom
3	[αρίζονται ὁ βασιλεὺς καὶ ὁ] ἐξαιτρ-	[the king and the] sat[rap
4	[απεύσας τῆς Ἰωνίης Στρού]σης· διεφ-	of the Ionians, Str]uses, a[ccepted]. They diff[ered
5	[έροντο περὶ τῆς γῆς τῆς] ἐμ Μαιάνδρ-	about the land] in the Maeander
6	[ο πεδίωι, ὥστε παμπόλλα]ς γενέσθαι	[plain, so that] there were
7	[ταῖς πόλεσι περὶ αὐτῆς] ἀμφισβητή-	[around its cities numerous]
8	[σεις· νῦν δὲ καὶ ἑκατέρ]ας τῆς πόλεω-	disput[es. So each of the tw]o
9	[ς ἐπιτρεψαμένης τῶι β]ασιλεῖ, καὶ σ-	citie[s submitted[47] to the k]ing, and
10	[τείλαντος βασιλέως Στ]ροούσην, ὅπ-	[the king dispatched St]rouses,
11	[ως οἵ τε τῶν Ἰώνων δικασταὶ συ]νελθό......	[in order that the jurors[48] of the Ionians may]
12	[ντες.....................................]ντ	meet . . .

Fragment B

[many lines missing, followed by a list of the names of the jurors and their cities]

19	. . . . καὶ τ[ε]θείσης τῆς δίκη-	and when the proceedings were established
20	ς ὑπὸ Μιλησίων καὶ Μυησίων καὶ τῶμ	by the ones from Miletus and from Myus and by the
21	[μ]αρτύρωμ μαρτυρησάντων ἀμφοτέρ-	witnesses on both sides giving testimony,
22	[ο]ις καὶ τῶν οὔρων ἀποδεχθέντων τῆ-	and statements were accepted regarding the boundaries of the
23	[ς] γῆς, ἐπεὶ ἔμελλον οἱ δικασταὶ δικ-	areas, [but] when the jurors were about to
24	ἃν τὴν δίκην, ἔλιπον τὴν δίκημ Μυή[σ]-	render a decision, the Myusians left the proceedings.
25	[ι]οι. Οἱ δὲ προδικασταὶ ταῦτα γραψ[α]-	Then the advocates writing these things
26	[ν]τες ἔδοσαν ἐς τὰς πόλεις αἵτινε[ς]	gave [the documents?] to the cities which
27	τὴν δίκην ἐδίκαζομ, μαρτυρίας εἶν-	had judged the case, to serve as

46. Piccirilli, *Gli arbitrati interstatali greci,* 1.155–59. His restoration is emended by Ann Nyland, personal communication.

47. The word ἐπιτρέπω came to be a technical term meaning 'to submit to arbitration'.

48. 'Jurors' is used here to render Greek δικασταὶ; others translate it 'judges' or simply transliterate it as *dikasts.* I discuss the term below. Here it is supplied by Piccirilli.

αι. ἐπεὶ δὲ Μυήσιοι τὴν δίκην ἔλιπο-	a witness. After the Myusians
ν, Στρούσης ἀκούσας τῶν Ἰωνων τῶν [δ]	left, Struses hearing from the Ionian jurors
[ι]καστέων, εξαιτράπης ἐὼν Ἰωνίης, [τ]	—being satrap of Ionia —
έλος ἐποίησε τὴν γῆν εἶναι Μιλησ[ί]-	finally assigned the land to Miletus.
ων, προδικασταὶ Μιλησίων Νυμφ . . .	The Milesian advocates were . . .
. . . ελλεονίο, Βάτων Διοκλ[ε . . .	

Imperial Authorization of Local Norms?

Frei argues that the Miletus-Myus inscription demonstrates his theory of imperial authorization of local norms.[49] According to him, the Ionian League came to an independent decision and the satrap authorized it. Frei sees its background in the decree of Artaphernes, hyparch of Ionia during the Ionian Revolt of 493. The Ionians had been thoroughly crushed by the Persians in that war. According to Herodotus (6.42–43),

> In this year (493) no further deed of enmity was done by the Persians against the Ionians; but at this same time certain things happened which greatly benefited them. Artaphernes, viceroy (ὕπαρχος) of Sardis, summoned to him ambassadors from the cities and compelled the Ionians to make agreements among themselves that they might submit to redress at law and not harry and plunder each other. This he compelled them to do; and he measured their lands by parasangs, . . . and appointed that each people should according to this measurement pay a tribute which has remained fixed ever since that time to this day.[50]

Most scholars assume that it was in accordance with this agreement that five representatives from each of the cities of the Ionian League (except the disputing cities) were called in to serve as judges and to arbitrate.[51] However, it is also possible that Artaphernes' reorganization meant the end of the Ionian League.[52] Neither the Persian nor the Athenian Empires would have easily tolerated an unregulated political entity within their boundaries. Briant cites the present inscription as proof of Herodotus's claim that Artaphernes had imposed an agreement on the cities that they would submit to binding arbitration. However, he argues for the continued existence of the League as it was before. According to Briant,

> This document [of Struses] confirms the quality of information that Herodotus received. It testifies admirably to the relationship that the satrap

49. E.g., Frei, "Persian Imperial Authorization," 18–19.

50. Translation is that of A. D. Godley, Loeb Classical Library.

51. Frei, "Persian Imperial Authorization"; Tod, *Greek Historical Inscriptions*, 2.38; Piccirilli, *Gli arbitrati interstatali greci*, 158; Briant, *HEP*, 510–11.

52. Hornblower, *Mausolus*, 58–59.

> established with the cities. The administration officially recognized their autonomy, inasmuch as Struses did not act on his authority alone but delegated responsibility to a local authority traced back to the old Ionian League (which had never officially disbanded). At the same time, the proceeding makes clear that the power resided at Sardis.[53]

Briant continues:

> The arbitration forced on the Ionian states by Artaphernes was in full harmony with Achaemenid methods, which aimed less at directly governing the cities than at controlling them. . . . The autonomy of the cities was . . . kept in check by higher orders, since recourse to arbitration no longer relied on their good will but instead on a policy advocated by the satrap, who kept a close watch over its application. As soon as a judgment was handed down, no city could evade it without risking being considered a rebel. It was up to the satrap to enforce the judgment, if necessary by force of arms.[54]

If Briant's assessment is correct, then this inscription provides evidence in support of Frei's theory of imperial authorization. Is it correct however? Did Struses act on his authority as satrap, or did he delegate his authority to the Ionian League and then validate their decision?

Historical Background

To answer this question, it is necessary to examine the impact of the Achaemenid regime on city governments. The primary effect of Persian rule in Asia Minor was the installation of tyrants in the cities conquered, if they had been democracies, or a propping up of the tyrants who were there before. The word *tyrant* was not originally Greek but "borrowed from some eastern language, perhaps in western Asia Minor."[55] Hornblower suggests the word is Lydian.[56] The first written appearance of the term is in a poem by Archilochus describing Gyges of Lydia. This implies the institution of tyranny is Lydian and that it existed in Asia Minor well before the advent of Cyrus.[57] Herodotus lists the cities of Ionia who fought with Darius against the Scythians in ca. 513 (4.137–38). The cities standing with Darius, according to Herodotus, were: Abydos, Lampsacus, Parium, Proconnesus, Cyzicus, Byzantium, all from the Hellespont; and from Ionia: Chios, Samos, Phocaea, Miletus; and from Aeolia: Cyme (4.138). Each was headed by a tyrant (τύραννος). Tyrants thus ruled these cities of Asia Minor at the very beginning of Darius's reign, if not before.

53. Briant, *From Cyrus to Alexander* (English ed.), 495.
54. Ibid.
55. Austin, "Greek Tyrants and the Persians," 289.
56. Hornblower, *Mausolus*, 18.
57. Austin, "Greek Tyrants and the Persians," 294.

More indicative of the effect of Achaemenid rule is Herodotus's opinion of the relationship between Darius and the Greek despots. He puts this speech in the mouth of Histiaeus of Miletus:

> "Now," said he, "it is by help of Darius that each of us rules (τυραννεύει) his city; if Darius's power be overthrown, we shall no longer be able to rule (τυραννεύεσθαι), neither I in Miletus nor any of you elsewhere; for all the cities will choose democracy rather than despotism." (4.137)

Histiaeus's speech reveals Herodotus's opinion that the Persian Empire supported tyrannies in the cities of Asia Minor and was in turn supported by them. The converse is implied: the Persian Empire did not support democracies in these cities; in turn, democratic factions did not support Persia.

The pattern of tyrannies supporting Persia and being supported by them is shown in the Ionian Revolt. This revolt began in ca. 500–499, when "certain men of substance" were banished from the island of Naxos by the δῆμος, the community (Hdt. 5.30). These men sought help from Aristagoras, then tyrant of Miletus. Aristagoras offered to speak on their behalf to Artaphernes, brother of Darius, satrap of Sardis, and governor of all the seacoast peoples of Asia Minor. With approval from Darius, Aristagoras besieged Naxos. The subsequent siege lasted more than four months, and Aristagoras, fearing impoverishment, revolted against Persia (Hdt. 5.37). In order to gain support for his revolt, he gave up his tyranny and converted the government of his city to a democracy (ἰσονομία). According to Herodotus:

> Aristagoras revolted openly, devising all he could to Darius's hurt. And first he made a pretense of giving up his tyranny and gave Miletus equality of government, that so the Milesians might readily join in his revolt; then he did likewise in the rest of Ionia; some of the tyrants he banished; as for those tyrants whom he had taken out of the ships that sailed with him against Naxos, he gave them over and delivered them each and all to their own cities severally, for he wished to please the cities.
>
> So Coes, when the Mytilenaeans received him, was taken out by them and stoned; but the Cymeans let their man go, and so did most of the others. Thus, an end was made of tyrants in the cities. (Hdt. 5.37–38)

Conscious of his inferior numbers, Aristagoras sought and received the aid of the *dēmos* of Athens in his revolt against Persia but could not enlist the aid of the despot of Sparta (Hdt. 5.97). With the support of Athens, Aristagoras attacked Sardis in 499 and burned it (5.97). Hearing of the attack and burning of Sardis, other provinces of Asia Minor came to Sardis's aid. They pursued the Ionians to Ephesus and defeated them there. In spite of the defeat, by 497 the revolt had spread northward as far as Byzantium and southward as far as Caunus. Probably this was the only city of Caria to join in the revolt, for afterward, Persia gave to the Carians of Pedasa half the island of

Miletus (6.20). Northern and inland Caria must have fought on the side of the Persians.

Among the cities within the Greek orbit, alliance with Persia implied a tyranny; revolt against Persia implied democracy. Despots ruled the cities of Asia Minor before the Persian conquest in the 6th century. At the same time, they had democratic factions in them waiting and able to take the helm when the opportunity arose. In the Ionian Revolt, displaced tyrants fled to the Persians, where they formed, as Briant says, a "fifth column" (Hdt. 6.9–10).[58] According to Herodotus, the cities siding with Sardis were ruled by tyrants, not by the *dḗmos.*

The same pattern existed in the Ionian cities half a century later, during the Samian revolution of 440–439: democratic cities supported Athens, while tyrannies supported Persia.[59] During the war between Samos and Miletus over possession of Priene, Miletus sent to Athens for aid (Thucydides 1.115). Citizens from Samos who wanted to set up a democracy there accompanied the envoys. The Athenians sailed to Samos with 40 ships and established a democracy, enforced by an Athenian garrison. Samian oligarchs fled to Sardis and to Pissuthnes, the Persian satrap.[60] The democratic faction of Samos had sought Athenian help, while the oligarchic faction sought aid from Persia. This pattern obtained until the advent of Alexander. If an Ionian city-state allied with the Athenian imperial system, the ruling faction in the city would be democratic. Oligarchs and others who supported either a tyrant or an oligarchy lived in forced exile in rural districts outside the urban center. These oligarchs turned to Persia to regain control of their cities.[61] Sometimes the reverse was true; pro-Persian tyrants (appointed and installed with Persian aid) and supportive oligarchs controlled the central city while pro-Athenian democrats lived in exile in country villages. The names of these villages appear in Athenian tribute lists.

This historical background puts the present inscription in context. If the Struses in the inscription named as satrap of the Ionians is the Struthas of Xenophon (*Hell.* 4.8.17–19), then the year is 392–391. The king is Artaxerxes II, who had defeated his brother Cyrus the Younger a few years earlier (400). Sparta and Athens were vying with each other and with Persia for control of the Greek cities on the west coast of Asia Minor, which had sided with the defeated Cyrus. Tissaphernes, who had led the battle against the rebel, was wreaking vengeance on cities that had sided with Cyrus and that had appealed to Sparta for help. Artaxerxes responded to the appeal to Sparta by

58. Briant, *HEP,* 163.
59. Balcer, "Fifth Century B.C. Ionia."
60. Ibid., 32.
61. Ibid. Balcer cites numerous examples.

giving Conon, the Athenian admiral, as much money as was required to destroy Spartan naval power (Diod. 14.81.5). Conon's first success (396) was to incite the Rhodians to rise up against Sparta (Diod. 14.79.6–8). David suggests that the Diagorean ruling family must have collaborated with Conon and defected from the Spartan cause.[62] He bases this on the Spartan execution of Dorieus, a prominent member of the family, and by the family's survival in power after the Athenian conquest. This family of oligarchs was overthrown only in the summer of 395, when the Diagoreans and eleven of their oligarchic class were murdered. The Athenian Conon returned to Rhodes later in 395 to help set up a democracy and to expel the rest of the oligarchic faction.[63]

Sparta, panicking after Conon's early victories, sent King Agesilaus to Asia Minor to secure the other islands of the Aegean and Asia Minor's coastal cities. He reached Ephesus in the spring of 396 (Xen., *Hell.* 3.4) and assembled Carian, Aeolian, Ionian, and Hellespontine Greek military contingents there (*Hell.* 3.11). Tissaphernes, general of the Persian armies of western Anatolia, attempted to push the Lacedaemonians out of Asia, but by 395, Agesilaus had managed to establish favorable garrisons in most of the coastal cities. Ephesus, where Agesilaus was camped, became a "workshop of war," engaging carpenters, smiths, leather-cutters, and painters—all busy with the production of weapons. By 394, however, Conon and Pharnabazus, the satrap of Phrygia, inflicted a crushing defeat on the Spartan fleet off Cnidus, effectively destroying Sparta as a maritime power. Persia—and Athens—now controlling the sea, drove the Spartan garrisons out of the islands (Cos, Nisyros, Teos, Mytilene, and Chios) and then out of western Asia Minor. Ephesus, Erythrae, and other coastal cities switched sides to join the Persians; Agesilaus fled to Delphi (Diod. 14.84.3; Xen., *Hell.* 4.8.1–2).

Xenophon suggests that Conon had been advising Pharnabazus to promise each of the cities that he would not establish garrisons in their midst and to leave them independent, so that the cities would remain friendly. Conon warned that if he wanted to enslave them, he would have trouble not only from them but from the people of Greece as well. Pharnabazus evidently accepted his advice (*Hell.* 4.8.4). The cities newly conquered by Conon established democratic assemblies. Xenophon states that Sparta knew that if the oligarchs gained mastery of a city, it would be theirs; but if the *dêmos,* then it would be in the hands of the Athenians (*Hell.* 4.8.20).

Dercylidas alone resisted the Athenian/Persian onslaught. He was in Abydos at the time of the naval battle, and instead of fleeing like the other Lacedaemonian governors, kept the city for himself (*Hell.* 4.8.3). Hearing

62. David, "The Oligarchic Revolution at Rhodes, 391–89 B.C."
63. Ibid., 272.

this, the governors and oligarchs who had been expelled from their cities fled to Abydos, and by 393 had taken nearby Sestos as well. Pharnabazus and Conon attacked the Spartan cities of Greece proper, and the Persian gave Conon funds to repair the long walls of Athens and the wall around Piraeus, destroyed at the close of the Peloponnesian War (*Hell.* 4.8.7–8).

Seeing that Pharnabazus and Tissaphernes were aiding the Athenians, the Spartans sought out the Persian general, Tiribazus, who responded by secretly giving Sparta funds to rebuild her fleet to equal Athens', imprisoning Conon for good measure. Then, fearful that Artaxerxes would hear it from someone else, Tiribazus rushed to the king to tell him what he had done. With Tiribazus at the capital in the interior of the empire, the king sent Struthas to take charge of affairs on the coast in his absence (Στρούθαν καταπέμπει ἐπιμελησόμενον τῶν κατὰ θάλατταν). Tiribazus evidently did not persuade the king, for Struthas favored Athens. According to Xenophon,

> Struthas devoted himself assiduously to the Athenians and their allies, remembering all the harm which the King's country had suffered at the hands of Agesilaus (the Spartan general). The Lacedaemonians accordingly, when they saw that Struthas was hostile to them and friendly to the Athenians, sent Thibron to make war upon him. And Thibron, crossing over to Asia and employing as a base of operations not only Ephesus, but also the cities of the plain of the Maeander—Priene, Leucophrys, and Achilleum—proceeded to plunder the territory of the king. (*Hell.* 4.8.17)

In 392, Struthas (Struses) sent a large force to attack Thibron's Spartan army, and among the first to be killed was Thibron himself. When Thibron fell, the rest fled.

Arbitration in the Greek Cities of Asia Minor

This is the historical context in which the inscription must be understood. The cities listed as participating in the arbitration (Ephesus, Erythrae, Chios, Clazomenae, Lebedos, Miletus, and Myus) were important cities on the Aegean coast. They had spent the previous four years succumbing to first Persian (and Athenian) and then Spartan dominance. At the time of the inscription, Struses had just ousted the recent Spartan incursion by dramatically killing their leader.

According to the theory of imperial authorization of local norms, the mechanism used to resolve this intercity dispute should be typically Greek and its decision simply validated by the satrap. According to a theory of central control, the system used should be Persian, with the satrap alone issuing the verdict. The matter ought to be simple to decide. Contrary to the cities of Mesopotamia and Egypt, the legal system of democratic Athens employed no judges.[64] Rather, two disputing litigants addressed several hundred jurors (*dikasts*), ordinary citizens, who appeared each morning for jury duty and who were assigned to the case by lot. The jurors voted at the end of the proceedings and decided in favor of one or the other litigant by majority rule. The trial was presided over by an archon who served to keep order but who had no judicial capacity. This is quite different from Mesopotamian courts, discussed above, where the judge(s) determined the outcome, and the assembly that witnessed the proceedings neither voted nor expressed an opinion.

The procedure in Greek interstate disputes differed, however, from the normal Greek trial.[65] Treaties between warring parties often included a clause that future disputes would be settled through arbitration; that is, the two parties would submit them to a third party. (Myus and Miletus may have had such an agreement forced upon them by Artaphernes, 100 years earlier.) Even without such a treaty arrangement, states could still refer their problem to a third party. In this case, one of the parties would send an embassy to the other, requesting that they submit to arbitration. The agreement to submit acted as a signed statement from both parties to abide by the decision. The agreement stated the nature of the dispute and specified the identity and limits of the arbitrator. The two sides would choose a neutral city, which would then select an individual or a committee by lot. A committee could include up to several hundred individuals. When disputes involved land boundaries, smaller numbers were usually selected, however, since it was too cumbersome to show such a large group around the disputed area.

According to the present inscription, the two parties requested arbitration from the Persian king. This indicates above all that they accepted his sovereignty. The king then turned the problem over to his satrap, who then apparently convened jurors (*dikast*s) from several cities nearby. These jurors were ones whom Struses and the king approved (lines 2–4); contrary to normal practice, they were not chosen by lot by the cities themselves. They heard evidence from the litigants and their witnesses, but again contrary to the usual practice, they did not vote. Instead, the statements of the litigants and the witnesses were drawn up, and copies were given to the participating cities and to the satrap. The satrap then issued his verdict. He did not validate the decision of the *dikast*s. Because they never voted, there was no decision to validate. Admittedly, the satrap heard from the jurors (line 41). But what did he hear? He could not have heard their decision because the text explicitly states that they never made one. What Struses heard was a summary of the proceedings as drawn up by the scribes.

64. Johnstone, *Disputes and Democracy*, 1; Roebuck, *Ancient Greek Arbitration*, 36–47.
65. The following discussion relies on Ager, *Interstate Arbitrations*, 3–33.

The procedure may be compared to a decision discussed above regarding a conflict between a Babylonian temple on the one hand and three cousins on the other, who claimed ownership of a house.

> Nabû-aḫḫē-bulliṭ, the provincial governor (*šākin māti*), sent PN_1, PN_2 and PN_3 [the three cousins] along with Nidintum-Bēl, the *šatammu* Eanna . . . , Nabû-aḫḫē-iddin, the *ša rēši šarri bēl piqitti* Eanna . . . , and temple scribes (*ṭupšarru*^{meš}) to stand before Imbiya, the mayor of Uruk (*šākin ṭēmi Uruk*), . . . and the judges (*dayyānu*^{meš}) of Nabû-aḫḫē-bulliṭ, the governor, so they may make a decision regarding them.

This case is similar to an interstate property dispute, since the cousins did not fall under the temple's jurisdiction. The *šākin māti,* probably equivalent to the hyparch at this time, selected judges, including the mayor of Uruk, to adjudicate. Even if an assembly of citizens also participated (i.e., the *mār bāni* meeting in *puḫaru*), they would not have voted but simply would have witnessed that the case was transcribed as it had occurred. This is the role that Struses intended for the *dikast*s from the several cities. Had he intended them to vote, they would have voted. The fact that Myus abandoned the proceedings before their completion would not ordinarily have stopped them from voting.

Herodotus gives his opinion on the difference between arbitration among democratic Greek cities and arbitration among cities under Persian rule:

> Among the Medians there was a clever man whose name was Deioces, son of Phraortes. And this Deioces loved power and set about getting it like this. Already being well regarded in his own place, one of the many country towns in which the Medes had settled, he began to offer more ambitiously his services in resolving disputes justly. . . .
>
> The Medes of his own town, noticing this development, chose him to be their *dikast.* Because he had his eye on power, he was straight and just and by acting in this way won not a little approval from his fellow citizens. So that, when the people of other towns, who had previously had to put up with unjust decisions, heard about Deioces and found out that he was the only man who made straight ones, enthusiastically they pestered him with their pleas. Eventually they would submit (ἐπετράποντο)[66] their disputes to no one else.
>
> The numbers who came with their disputes grew and grew, because they found out that all his judgments accorded with the reality. When Deioces knew that everything was entrusted to him, he refused to sit and hear disputes and said he would not adjudicate as he had done. He said it was of no advantage to him to spend all day adjudicating for his neighbors.
>
> Robbery and crime increased in the towns, to more than it had been before. . . . It was most likely Deioces' friends who said: "Since, as a result of

66. This is an early use of the term επιτρέπω in its technical sense of submitting to arbitration.

> recent developments we cannot live in our place like we used to, come on, let's establish a *basileus* for ourselves." . . .
>
> Forthwith they were faced with the question of whom they should appoint *basileus.* Every man was full of praise and support for Deioces and so they came to appoint him *basileus.* He told them to build him houses worthy of his position as *basileus* and to arm him with a bodyguard.
>
> (And so the Medes exchanged their *dikasts* for a professional *basileus.* But Deioces exploited his power, built the mighty palace of Ekbatana, encircled it with seven walls, and would let none of his old acquaintances near him.)
>
> Deioces built these walls round his own palace and told the rest of the people to live round the outside. When all the buildings were finished, it was Deioces who first established the convention that nobody was allowed to come into the presence of the *basileus.* All business had to be done through messengers. The *basileus* should be seen by nobody. It was a particular outrage for anybody to laugh or spit in his presence. . . .
>
> When he had sorted all these things out, and protected himself with tyrannical power, he became severe in his dispensation of justice. Everyone had to write down their pleas and send them in to him. Then he would take them all in, make his decisions (*diakrinōn*) and send them out again. That is how he made his judgments. (Hdt. 1.96–100)[67]

Herodotus describes here the difference between arbitration in a free democracy and that under the tyranny of the Persian monarchy. Instead of an ad hoc mediator, chosen freely by the parties, the state intervenes. The decision no longer has to be viewed as just by all the parties concerned because the state has the power both to enforce attendance at the arbitration and to enforce obedience to whatever decision it makes. This aptly describes Struses' role: he sat in his palace, received a written summary of events, and rendered his decision. It did not have to be viewed as just. The judicial procedure was Persian through and through; there was no validation of local norms.

The Donation of Droaphernes

The third inscription to be studied memorializes the gift of a statue to a Temple of Zeus by Droaphernes, hyparch of Lydia, in the 39th year of Artaxerxes. It was found in 1974 in Sardis, the capital of the Persian satrapy of Lydia, on a stone reused as a building block in a late Roman building.[68] The inscribed face of the block is 45.5 cm high and 58 cm wide.[69] L. Robert, who published the text, assigns the paleography to the Roman period, most likely the middle of the 2nd century of our era.[70] Like Darius's letter to Gadatas,

67. The translation is by Roebuck, *Ancient Greek Arbitration,* 150–51.
68. Robert, "Une nouvelle inscription grèque de Sardes," 306.
69. Ibid., 306.
70. Ibid., 307–8.

this inscription too has been used to argue that Achaemenid rulers were supportive of foreign cults. It is complete in 13 lines:

1. Ἐτέων τριήκοντα ἐννέα Ἀρτα-	In the thirty-ninth year of Arta-
2. ξέρξεω βασιλεύοντος, τὸν ἀν-	Xerxes' being king, Droaphernes
3. δριάντα Δροαφέρνης (vac.)	son of Barakes, hyparch of Lydia
4. Βαρ[ά]κεω,[71] Λυδίης ὕπαρχος, Βαρα-	[is donating] a statue
5. δάτεω Διί. (leaf) Προστάσσει τοῖς	to Baradates Zeus. (leaf) He commands
6. εἰσπορευομένοις εἰς τὸ ἄδυ-	the ones entering into the adyton,
7. τον νεωκόροις θεραπευ- (vac.)	the temple custodians, the ones tend-
8. ταῖς αὐτοῦ καὶ στεφανοῦσι τὸν θε-	ing him and crowning the god,
9. ὸν μὴ μετέχειν μυστηρίων Σαβα-	not to partake of the mysteries of Saba-
10. ζίου τῶν τὰ ἔνπυρα βασταζόν-	zios, of the ones carrying the burnt offer-
11. των καὶ Ἀνγδίστεως καὶ Μᾶς. Προσ-	ing, of Angdistis or of Ma. They com-
12. τάσσουσι δὲ Δοράτῃ τῷ νεωκόρῳ τού-	mand Dorates, the temple custodian,
13. των τῶν μυστηρίων ἀπέχεσθαι. (leaf)	to keep apart from these mysteries. (leaf)

The inscription has been divided into three parts:

Part I, lines 1–5, refers to the dedication of a statue to a temple. These lines name the donor as Droaphernes, the hyparch of Lydia; the donation as a statue; and the recipient as the Temple of Zeus. Both the name of the donor, Droaphernes, and the name of his father, Barakes, are Greek renderings of Iranian names (Droaphernes is Druva-farnah 'solid-prosperity').

Part II, lines 5–11, entails a command to the temple custodians (the ones privileged to enter the adyton and serve the god) to avoid three proscribed mystery cults. A leaf in the center of line 5 separates Parts I and II.

Part III, lines 12 and 13, refers to a command by at least two unnamed persons ("they command") to a certain Dorates, a custodian of Zeus like the others, to hold himself apart from these same mysteries. A second leaf concludes the inscription.[72]

Robert suggests that part I was translated into Greek from an Aramaic original at the time of composition (the Persian period), not at the time of engraving (the Roman period). He deduces this from the Ionisms of the language apparent in part I, lines 1–5.[73] As for part II, Robert says it is not a word-for-word translation of an original, but a summary only. He gives no reason for this. Robert judges that part III (lines 12 and 13) was added at the time of

71. The stone has ΒΑΡΛΚΕΩ.
72. Briant, "Droaphernes et la statue de Sardes," 211.
73. Robert, "Une nouvelle inscription grèque de Sardes," 310.

engraving and does not belong to the original inscription. This is because the subject of the verb switches to the plural and selects one individual, Dorates, for a command previously directed to the entire group.[74]

The Date of the Inscription

If authentic, the date of Droaphernes' donation is fixed to the 39th year of either Artaxerxes I Longhand (465–424) or Artaxerxes II Memnon (404–358). Only these two Artaxerxes had reigns long enough to qualify. If the first, the date of the donation is 426; if the second, 365. Robert opts for the second, later date.[75] He assumes that the Persian, Droaphernes, who donated the statue, worshiped at this temple; that the god worshiped was Ahura Mazda; and that the statue donated was a statue of the god. These three assumptions, plus a statement of Berossos, who lived toward the end of the 4th century B.C.E., combine to produce a dating of 365. Berossos is paraphrased in Clement of Alexandria, *Protrepticus* (*Exhortation*) 5.65.2–3, as follows:

> The Persians, Medes, and Magoi do not make statues of their gods from wood or stone but honor fire and water as the philosophers do. . . . Berossos, however, says in the third book of his Chaldean history that later, after the passage of many years, the Persians did have statues of human figures. This began under Artaxerxes Ochus, son of Darius, who first set up the statue of Aphrodite Anaitis (Anahita) and showed respect to it at Babylon, Susa, and Ecbatana, in Persia and Bactria, and at Damascus and Sardis.[76]

Berossos must mean Artaxerxes II Memnon, the son of Darius, rather than Artaxerxes III Ochus, the son of Artaxerxes II. According to Berossos, this Artaxerxes set up a cult statue of Anahita and worshiped it, contrary to Persian custom. That Artaxerxes II was devoted to Anahita is known from his inscriptions. An inscription from Ecbatana reads: "Thanks to Ahura Mazda, Anahita and Mithra, I have made this Apadana. May Ahura Mazda, Anahita and Mithra protect me from every evil and may they not destroy nor damage anything which I have made."[77] Although Xerxes and Darius II do mention unnamed "other great gods," this is the first mention of any god but Ahura Mazda by name. This confirmation of part of Berossos's statement (that Artaxerxes II worshiped Anahita) lends credibility to the rest (Artaxerxes II inaugurated cult statues). Because Robert assumes that the statue donated was the god Ahura Mazda, he dates the inscription to Artaxerxes II.

74. Ibid., 326.
75. Ibid., 310.
76. Verbrugghe and Wickersham, *Berossos and Manetho*, 62.
77. Lecoq, *Les inscriptions de la perse achéménide*, 269.

Reliance on Berossos's statement to date the text requires that the statue be a god. If it is of a man, either date is possible. The Persian kings had always made statues of men: a statue of Darius I was found at Susa. The word in our inscription is ἀνδριάς, which Liddell and Scott define as the statue of a man or woman.[78] They oppose it to ἄγαλμα, the statue of a god. But Robert notes that the term ἀνδριάς has been applied to statues of gods in Greek inscriptions from Egypt.[79] The word also refers to a statue of the god Apollo in an inscription from Phrygia of the 2nd century of our era.[80] An older inscription of a colossal Apollo of the Naxians at Delos refers to the god and his pedestal, ἀνδριάς καὶ τό σφέλας. Debord asks why a statue of a man would be dedicated to a god.[81] The temple at Sardis from which this inscription apparently came had a double cella, one for Zeus and another for Artemis. (An earlier bilingual inscription [Lydian-Greek], from the mid–fourth century, is dedicated to Artemis.[82]) Debord suggests that Droaphernes installed a statue of Zeus in a temple previously dedicated to Artemis.

Robert suggests that the god was the Zoroastrian Ahura Mazda, although, according to the inscription, the resident god was Baradates Zeus. He argues that the word *Βαραδατεω (from which he posits Baradates is derived) combines two Persian words *dāta* 'law' and *bara* 'one who carries'. This epithet, while novel, would be an Iranian word, according to G. Dumezil and M. Mayrhofer, with whom Robert consulted.[83] It would denote Zeus who bears the law, Zeus Legislator.[84] Since Zeus himself was never considered a lawgiver, and since Zeus is the traditional Greek interpretation of Ahura Mazda, Robert argues that the god to whom the temple is dedicated is not Zeus but Ahura Mazda. Unfortunately, the word **baradāta* is not as well-formed an epithet as it appears. Dandamayev reports that *dātabara* is a common title in Babylonian documents.[85] *Dātabara* is Old Persian, meaning 'bearer of law' or 'judge'. The term **baradāta* as a noun or title never occurs. It is not a Persian epithet.

Gschnitzer finds only two interpretations of Βαραδατεω linguistically possible: (1) a dative of an adjective derived from a name with an ε(ι)ος ending, such as κύρειος; or (2) the much simpler regular Ionic genitive of the name Βαραδάτης.[86] Both assume a personal or family name, not an epithet.

78. Debord (*L'Asie Mineure au IVe Siècle*, 370 n. 20) notes that the majority of epigraphic occurrences of the term come from the Roman period.

79. Robert, "Une nouvelle inscription grèque de Sardes," 313.

80. Ibid., 313 n. 19.

81. Debord, *L'Asie Mineure au IVe Siècle*, 370 n. 72.

82. Ibid., 369.

83. Robert, "Une nouvelle inscription grèque de Sardes," 314.

84. Ibid., 314.

85. Dandamayev, *Iranians in Achaemenid Babylonia*, 9.

86. Gschnitzer, "Eine persische Kultstiftung in Sardeis," 47.

The association of a god with the genitive of a personal or family name is frequent in western Asia Minor, and especially in Lydia.[87] According to Gschnitzer, the inscription should be read "Zeus of Baradates," referring to a place or family. How these family names become attached to the god is not understood, but the name may go back to the founder of the cult, and he may have been a Persian. *Bard* means 'high' or 'exalted' in Old Persian. The root is found in Bardiya (Smerdis). The suffix *a:ta* is the Persian patronymic ('son of'); it is found in the Persian name Mithradates, son of Mithra. Baradates may have been a Persian, living in Sardis, who helped found the temple. Or he may have been Lydian. A great many of the Lydian nobility took Iranian names in the Achaemenid period.[88] If Baradates was the cult founder, Droaphernes was probably not descended from him. There should be some similarity among the three names, Droaphernes, Barakes (his father), and Baradates (the name of the founder of the cult), if they all stem from the same family.[89] Nor does this suggest the identity of the god. There is a little evidence that Persian nobility worshiped at temples dedicated to Artemis.[90] If so, they may have syncretized her with the Persian goddess Anahita. There is no evidence yet of Persian worship in Lydia at temples to Mithra or Ahura Mazda—that is, to male gods capable of being given the Greek title Zeus. Nor is one likely to find Ahura Mazda worshiped in temples; Zoroastrian sacrifices were held outdoors, and temples were not used. Any flat space could be marked out as a sacred precinct, usually at the house of the sacrificer.[91]

If the statue is not Ahura Mazda, it cannot serve to date the text. But the existence of the inscription itself may date it. Traditionally, residents of Greece or the Greek cities of Asia Minor did not memorialize their donations.[92] When Hecatomnos of Caria (392–376) inscribed his name on his donations (an offering table to the ancient sanctuary at Sinuri and a statue-base to Zeus Labraundeus at Labraunda), he broke with tradition.[93] The number and assertiveness of the dedications increased with his son, Mausolus (377–353). This self-advertising spirit of the Hecatomnids was imitated, but none preceded it. One imitator may have been the hyparch of Lydia, Droaphernes, son of Barakes. The custom initiated by the Hecatomnids in Caria may have spread to neighboring satrapies and have been imitated there. If so,

87. Ibid., 47–48.

88. Sekunda, "Achaemenid Colonization in Lydia," 15. He cites Zgusta, "Iranian Names in Lydian Inscriptions."

89. Gschnitzer, "Eine persische Kultstiftung in Sardeis."

90. Sekunda, "Achaemenid Colonization in Lydia," 18. The only evidence is a few passages among the Greek authors (primarily Berossos) that Persians worshiped Artemis Anaitis, but there is no direct evidence to indicate such worship in the satrapies.

91. Boyce, *A History of Zoroastrianism*, 1.166.

92. Hornblower, *Mausolus*, 274.

93. Ibid., 278.

this would date the first part of the inscription, the part that memorializes the donation of the statue, to 365, the later date.

What about the rest of the inscription? Robert believes part II (lines 5–11) was composed at the time of the original inscription, in 365. He believes part III (lines 12–13) to be a later addition, composed in the Roman period. Robert interprets the second part as belonging naturally to the first since he interprets Droaphernes as the subject of the verb 'he commands' that heads part II. Since he sees no subject for the plural verb at the end of line 11, he believes that the last two lines were added later.

The presence of a leaf in the middle of line 5, at the beginning of part II and again at the end of the document, suggests to Briant that parts II and III are a single section enclosed between the leaves.[94] (Robert did not notice this second leaf.) Briant argues that this entire section was added in the Roman period to summarize Roman cult regulations.[95] Citing Hermann, Briant argues that caretakers (*neokoroi*) and *therapeutae* were more at home in the Hellenistic–Roman periods than in the Persian.[96] However, both were common to classical Greek religion.[97] *Neokoroi* were required to organize the sacrifices, from the purchase of the animals to the sale of the skins; and they are referred to from the beginnings of permanent sanctuaries and cult images, that is, from the 7th century onward. Burkert notes that the *therapon*, or 'servant/attendant', is common to epic poetry: for example, Patroclus is Achilles' *therapon.* He is the one who cares for him. The term stems from the verb *therapeuein* 'to take care of' in relation to parents, children, the sick, public favor, and especially the gods. Plato refers often to the *therapeutai*, always in relation to the care of the gods.[98] Use of these terms cannot suggest a date for the inscription.

Furthermore, the section enclosed by the two leaves must be considered one section. Not only is it bracketed by the two leaves, but the two parts use identical vocabulary. The major words in lines 12 and 13, προστάσσουσι, νεωκόρῳ, and μυστερίων, are identical to those of the preceding lines, lines 5–11. The plural subject undoubtedly refers to the custodians, the ones tending the gods. Droaphernes commands the custodians, and in turn, they command Dorates, whose behavior likely brought about the order. The verb-first construction of all three sentences in parts II and III suggests an Aramaic or (to Gschnitzer) even a Lydian original.[99]

94. Briant, "Droaphernes et la statue de Sardes," 211.

95. Ibid., 211–13.

96. Ibid., 225, citing Hermann, "Mystenvereine in Sardeis."

97. Burkert, *Greek Religion,* 88–96, 272–73. See also Debord, *L'Asie Mineure,* 371, for numerous references to the *neokoros* and the *theropeutai* in the epigraphy of the 4th century.

98. Plato, *Phaedrus* 252c; *Laws* 740c.

99. Gschnitzer, "Eine persisch Kultstiftung in Sardeis."

The single second section (parts II and III) must also date to 365, the date of part I. As Debord points out, a *neokoros* of the Roman period, whose responsibilities were largely honorific, would have been a Roman citizen.[100] It is unlikely that he would have had only one name (Dorates), whereas an individual with one name only would have been usual in the 4th century. Moreover, Gschnitzer's work shows that this second section does contain an Ionism, since Βαραδατεω is a simple, regular Ionic genitive of the name Βαραδάτης.[101] There does not seem to be any reason to dissociate the second part from the first, and the entire inscription can be dated to 365.

Historical Background

The date 365, if correct, provides the key to the text's historical background. The year 366–365 was the beginning of the so-called "Great Satraps' Revolt" (366–360) in the western satrapies of Anatolia.[102] Its seeds were sown decades before. In 387, Ariobarzanes became satrap of Dascylium, replacing his father, Pharnabazus, grandson of Darius I. As satrap, Ariobarzanes built up his territories, and by 367 he controlled both sides of the Hellespont, the major cities of Abydos and Sestus.

In adjoining Lydia, Autophradates was satrap. Tension arose between the two satraps as Ariobarzanes spread out into territory that Autophradates considered his. Autophradates finally sent emissaries to the Great King to denounce Ariobarzanes as a traitor. By the end of the year 367, the king had declared Ariobarzanes a rebel and ordered neighboring satraps to attack him. In 366–365, Autophradates (by land) and Mausolus (by sea) laid siege to the cities of Dascylium.[103]

The inscription places Droaphernes, Hyparch of Lydia, in Sardis, the capital of the satrapy, while the satrap was away at war.[104] Herodotus reveals that Sardis contained an acropolis (Hdt. 5.100). Acropolises contained Persian garrisons:

> We allow that [the king] pays close attention to warfare, because he has given a standing order to every governor of the nations from which he receives tribute, to supply maintenance for a specified number of horsemen and archers and slingers and light infantry, that they may be strong enough to control his subjects and to protect the country in the event of an invasion; and, apart

100. Debord, *L'Asie Mineure*, 372.

101. Gschnitzer, "Eine persisch Kultstiftung in Sardeis," 47.

102. The following discussion is based on Weiskopf, "The So-Called 'Great Satraps' Revolt," 26ff.

103. Contra Diodorus 15.93.1.

104. Also pointed out by Debord, *L'Asie Mineure*, 373.

> from these, he maintains garrisons in the citadels (ἀκρόπολισι). (Xenophon, *Oec.* 4.5)

Autophradates would have taken his horsemen, archers, slingers, and light infantry with him to subdue the rebel Ariobarzanes. He left his hyparch, Droaphernes, in charge of the satrapy, aided by any garrison troops remaining in the citadel.[105] As discussed above in the chapter on Egypt, the role of the hyparch is described by Xenophon. When the satrap was at home he served as garrison commander and as the "eyes and ears" of the king (Xen., *Cyr.* 8.6.1). When away, he carried out the satrap's responsibilities: "To govern the people, to receive the tribute, to pay the militia, and to attend to any other business that needs attention" (*Cyr.* 8.3).

The Purpose of the Inscription

Why did Droaphernes donate the statue, and why *then*, with his master away? The donation and the inscription could have served many purposes. Primary among them was no doubt to memorialize Droaphernes' official patronage of the cult. Temple dedications express the ruler's role in the care of the god's residence. As Kapelrud points out, "in the ancient Middle Eastern world temple building was the task and the privilege of victorious gods and kings."[106] The temple was necessarily rebuilt and embellished by the king but only with the advice and consent of the god. The god's presence in the temple was the physical sign of the god's affirmation of the ruler's authority.[107] Droaphernes' donation of a statue to the Temple of Zeus and the god's acceptance of that statue affirmed and publicized the god's acceptance of Persian hegemony and the Persian satrapal system. The first purpose would have been to suggest Zeus's endorsement of the Achaemenid Empire in general, and of Droaphernes, in particular, as hyparch.

A second purpose may have been to remind those who worshiped at the temple of Persian presence while the satrap was away. Third, a quid pro quo may have been expected. Persian support and patronage of the temple demanded and assumed its support and allegiance in exchange. This may have been crucial while Anatolia was beset with a series of satrapal revolts.

This does not explain why cult regulations were added to the inscription. Why would the Persian hyparch forbid the temple *neokoroi* from participating in the mysteries of Sabazios, Angdistis, and Ma? Was it to support self-

105. So also Chaumont, "Un nouveau gouverneur de Sardes," 608.

106. Kapelrud, "Temple Building, a Task for Gods and Kings."

107. Ibid.; Fried, "The Land Lay Desolate: Conquest and Restoration in the Ancient Near East"; Halpern, *The Constitution of the Monarchy in Israel*; Hurowitz, *I Have Built You an Exalted House*; Lundquist, *Studies on the Temple in the Ancient Near East*; Petersen, "Zerubbabel and Jerusalem Temple Reconstruction," 366–72.

governance, that is, the autonomy of the local temple? Or was it to exert central control, the control of the Persian Empire? Frei asks who may have had a special interest in seeing that the decree in question was carried out.[108] He answers that it must be the cult founder, Baradates, or his descendants, or other influential worshipers. In fact, it was most likely only Droaphernes—and the King—who wanted the decree enforced. As Briant and others point out, there was no fear of the mystery religions or of new gods in 4th-century Greek cities.[109] Moreover, according to present knowledge, the three gods were not common in Lydia.[110] Sabazios and Angdistis were Phrygian, or Myso-Phrygian, and Ma was the war god of Cappadocia.[111] To whom were these gods a threat? As Debord points out, Phrygia was then under the control of Ariobarzanes (Diod. 15.90.3), Mysia was subject to Orontes (15.90.3), and Cappodocia was under Datames (15.91.2–6), all indicted by Artaxerxes as participants in the Great Satrapal Revolt.[112] The gods from these provinces and the priests who spoke for them could not be trusted to conform to the dictates of the Great King and to refrain from fomenting rebellion in areas where they might be worshiped. This is not an instance of imperial authorization of a local norm but, rather, a restriction of previous liberties. Rather than supporting local cults, the inscription testifies to the use of religion as an instrument of political control.

A Decree of Mylasa against the Opponents of Mausolus

A fourth text, a decree from Mylasa, inscribed on the same stele as two later decrees from that city, is also dated to the 39th year (365) of Artaxerxes II, the same year as the Droaphernes inscription. At this time Mausollus was participating with Autophradates in an attack against the rebel Ariobarzanes. The second and third inscriptions on the stele are dated, respectively, to the 45th year (359) of Artaxerxes II and to the 5th year (354) of his son Artaxerxes III.[113] In all three inscriptions the regnal year date is followed by the phrase 'being the satrapy of Mausolus's (Μαυσσώλλου ἐξαιθραπεύοντος). Since Mausolus was likely satrap from 377/6 to 353/2, these stem from the second half of his tenure. The first of the three is illustrative.

Ἔτει τριηκοστῶι καὶ ἐνάτωι Ἀρταξέρξευς Βασιλεύ-	In the 39th year of Artaxerxes,

108. Frei, "Persian Imperial Authorization," 34.
109. Briant, "Droaphernès et la statue de Sardes"; Garland, *Introducing New Gods*, 1–4.
110. Debord, *L'Asie Mineure au IVe Siècle*, 373.
111. See ibid., 373 nn. 46–50, for references.
112. Ibid., 373. Weiskopf, "The So-Called 'Great Satraps' Revolt."
113. Tod, *Greek Historical Inscriptions*, 2.112–16.

οντος, Μαυσσώλλου ἐξαιθραπεύοντος· ἔδοξε	Mausolus being satrap,
Μυλασεῦσιν, ἐκκλησίης κυρίης γενομένης, καὶ ἐπε-	the Mylasians determined, meeting in an authorized assembly, and
κύρωσαν αἱ πρεῖς φυλαί· ἐπειδὴ Ἄρλισσις Θύσσώλλου	the three tribes ratified, that Arlissis son of Thyssolos,
ἀποσταλεὶς ὑπὸ Καρῶν πρὸς βασιλέα παρεπρέσ-	sent by the Carians to the king, acted
βευσε καὶ ἐπεβούλευσε Μαυσσώλλωι, ὄντι εὐεργέτηι	dishonestly and plotted against Mausolus, who is a benefactor
τε͂ς πόλεως τῆς Μυλασέων καὶ αὐτῶι καὶ τῶι πατρὶ	of the city of the Mylasians—himself and his father
Ἑκατόμνωι καὶ τοῖς προγόνοις τοῖς τούτων. Καὶ βασιλεὺς	Hekatomnos and all his ancestors. The king,
ἀδικεῖν καταγνοὺς Ἄρλισσιν ἐζημίωσε θανάτωι.	knowing Arlissis's crime, has sentenced him with death.
Πρᾶξαι καὶ τὴν πόλιν τὴν Μυλασέων περὶ τῶν	According to the practices of the city of the Mylasians,
κτημάτων ἐκείνου κατὰ τοὺς νόμος τοὺς πατρίους·	his possessions according to the ancestral laws
καὶ πρόσθετα ποιήσαντες Μαυσσώλλωι. Ἐπαρὰς	are handed over to Mausolus. Curses
ἐποιήσαντο περὶ τούτων μήτε προτιθέναι ἔτι	they shall make about these things, neither to propose hereafter
παρὰ ταῦτα μηδένα μήτε ἐπιψηφίζειν· εἰ δέ τις	anything against these things nor to put [them] to the vote. If anyone
ταῦτα παραβαίνοι, ἐξώλη γίνεσθαι καὶ αὐτὸν	transgresses these things, let him be utterly destroyed, himself
καὶ τοὺς ἐκείνου πάντας.	and everything that is his.

According to this decree, an envoy sent to Artaxerxes was accused of betraying Mausolus and sentenced by the king to death. The city responded by consigning the traitor's estate to the satrap, "according to its ancestral laws." Briant suggests that this inscription illustrates quite well the relationship between king, satrap, and city.[114] Clearly, the king alone has jurisdiction to judge an individual and sentence him to death. Yet, what is the relationship revealed here between the satrap and the populace? Briant suggests that the city, in free assembly, has the power to turn the traitor's possessions over to the satrap. Certainly. But did it have the power *not* to?

Mausolus's Rule

Several inscriptions from Erythrae (a town on the coast of Lydia, across from the island of Chios) reveal the effect of Mausolus's rule on a coastal

114. Briant, *HEP*, 688.

city's internal government. In a 4th-century inscription (M14), the *dēmos* of Erythrae asks the *dēmos* of Athens not to hand her over to the Barbarians.[115] This most likely dates to the time of the King's Peace between Athens and Persia in 386. According to the terms of the treaty, Erythrae (on the mainland) would fall to Persia. The use of the term *dēmos* in the inscription indicates that Erythrae was a democracy. It appealed to Athens for aid.[116] A later inscription from Erythrae reveals the impact of Persian rule. This inscription, dated between 380 and 353, praises Mausolus, satrap of Caria, and Artemisia, his sister-wife, as benefactors of Erythrae in war and peace; the inscription states that Mausolus and his sister were to be honored with citizenship, proxeny, and statues.[117] This second inscription does not mention a *dēmos*; rather, it speaks of the *boulē*.[118] It appears that Erythrae was no longer democratic, but oligarchic. Mausolus controlled Chios at the time, and evidently was influential in Erythrae, across the strait. That there were still Erythraen democrats is clear from a third inscription—dated to the year of Mausolus's death—according to which several Erythraens dedicated a crown on the Athenian acropolis.[119] A renegade band of democrats may have been seeking help to return democracy to Erythrae. The pattern is clear: Citizens of democratic Erythrae had appealed to Athens for help in 386 before the King's Peace. The city fell to the Barbarians. Shortly thereafter, it became oligarchic and honored Mausolus, the Persian satrap, as hero and benefactor. Under Persian and Hecatomnid occupation, a democratic city became an oligarchy.

The switch from democracy to oligarchy in Erythrae is indicated in the above inscriptions by the switch from *dēmos* to *boulē*. Yet the decree from Mylasa mentions neither. The text states simply that the Mylasians decided while meeting in an authorized assembly (εκκλησίης κυρίης) and that their decision was ratified by the three phyles. Doubtless, there was no democracy; at the very least there was an oligarchy committed to the Hecatomnid's continued rule. Erythrae had had a tradition of democracy before an oligarchy was installed; but Mylasa, the capital of Caria, had no such tradition. Hornblower notes a good many inscriptions from Caria that mention a *dēmos* and a *boulē*. However, all these are from the end of the 4th or the beginning of the 3rd centuries, after Alexander's conquest; none dates to the time of the Hekatomnids.[120] The Mylasians who met in assembly, who decided to turn

115. Hornblower, *Mausolus,* 108, 369 (M14).

116. S. Sahin, "Ein attisches Dekret für Erythrai."

117. Hornblower, *Mausolus,* 107–8; Engelmann and Merkelbach, *Erythrai,* no. 8, pp. 53–56.

118. So also Hornblower, *Mausolus,* 108–9.

119. Ibid., 110; see reference note 28.

120. Ibid., 86 n. 60.

over the entire estate of one disloyal to Mausolus to the satrap himself, acted not in the interest of the city but in Mausolus's own interest, and undoubtedly at his behest. The role of the assembly here seems to be that of the assembly in Babylon and other Persian provinces: to meet and witness the proceedings and certify the decisions of those in power. There is no indication it had the power to decide contrary to the wishes of the satrap.

The Trilingual Inscription of Xanthus

The final inscription to be studied is the Trilingual Inscription of Xanthus. Scholars consider it crucial for understanding the mechanisms of satrapal organization and the relationship between the satrap and the local community.[121] To most scholars, the text suggests that the Persian Empire was lax and nondirective, supporting and encouraging local cults and institutions. Dupont-Sommer sees in this inscription evidence of the Persian concern for local cults.[122] Frei sees the inscription as paradigmatic of the mechanism of imperial authorization he proposes: a local community issues a decree; the satrap makes it his own by registering it on a stele in Aramaic, the official language of the empire.[123] Briant concurs. The satrap involved himself in the cult only to guarantee their rules and regulations.[124] "The satrap of Caria and Lycia is neither directly nor personally concerned with a new cultic foundation at Xanthus: it is the community itself which asked the imperial authority to play a role."[125]

The Trilingual Inscription of Xanthus was found during excavations of a sanctuary of Leto in the Lycian peninsula of southwest Asia Minor. The sanctuary was situated about 4 km to the southwest of the city of Xanthus, on the Xanthus River, 3 km from where the Xanthus flows into the sea.[126] In 1973, excavations brought to light a stele of local limestone 1.35 m high, 0.575 m wide, and 0.3 m deep.[127] Forty-one lines of Lycian cover one of the faces; 35 lines of Greek are engraved on the opposite side. The Greek appears to be a translation of the Lycian. On an edge are 27 lines of Aramaic. The fourth side is not engraved. Based on the epigraphy, the stele is dated to the middle of the 4th century. It is contemporaneous with the Lycian buildings, which preceded the Doric temple.

121. Briant, *HEP*, 727.
122. Dupont-Sommer, "La stèle trilingue," 168.
123. Frei, "Persian Imperial Authorization," 19.
124. Briant, "Cités et satrapes dans l'empire achéménide: Xanthos et Pixôdaros," 334.
125. Ibid.
126. Metzger, "Le sanctuaire de Leto," 9.
127. Idem, "L'inscription grèque," 31.

The Aramaic text is doubtless the official chancellery version; it is original—that is, it is not a translation of the Greek or Lycian.[128] The other two versions are in the autochthonous language of the Lycians and in that of their Greek colonists. Lemaire and Lozachmeur suggest that these two versions coexist because neither population could understand or read the language of the other, implying two separate ethnic groups, living side by side.[129]

The Texts

The Aramaic Text

(The Aramaic text is based on the editio princeps of Dupont-Sommer.[130])

In the month of Sivan in the first year	1. בירח סיון שנת חד
of Artaxerxes the King	2. ארתחשסש מלכא
in the capital (*birta'*) of Arna, Pixodarus,	3. באורן בירתא פגסוד[ר]
son of Hecatomnos, satrap	4. בר כתמנו חשתרפנא
who is over Caria and Lycia, s[aid]:	5. זי בכרך ותרמיל א⟨מר⟩
"The citizens of Arna propose	6. אתעשתו בעלי אורן
to build a temple[131] to Kandawats	7. כרפא למעבד לכנדוץ
Caunian, the god, and his companion.	8. אלהא כבידשי וכנותה
They have installed as priest Simias	9. ועבדו כמרא לסימין
son of Koddorasi. There is an estate	10. בר כדורס ואיתי בי[ת]
that the citizens of Arna have given	11. זי בעלי ⟨א⟩ורן יהבו
to the god Kandawats. Year by year	12. לכנדוץ אלהא ושנה בש-
from the area they will give silver—	13. נה מן מתא יהיבן כסף
one mina and one-half. This priest	14. [מ]נה חד ופלג כמר⟨א⟩ זנה
will sacrifice each new moon a sheep	15. זבח לר⟨א⟩ש ירחא נקוה
to the god Kandawats, and he will sacrifice[132]	16. לכנדוץ אלהא ודבח
every year a bull. This property	17. שנה בשנה תור ודמא
is released. It is his.	18. זנה שביק זי לה

128. So Lemaire and Lozachmeur, "Remarques sur le plurilinguisme en Asie Mineure," 111; pace Briant ("Xanthos et Pixôdaros," 335), who argues unaccountably that in case of conflict it would be the Lycian version to which the satrapal authority would turn.

129. Lemaire and Lozachmeur, "Remarques sur le plurilinguisme en Asie Mineure," 114.

130. Dupont-Sommer, "La stèle trilingue," 136–37.

131. This translation, based on New Persian *kulba* (= 'hut') → **kalpa'* → *krp'*, is suggested by G. Windfuhr, personal communication.

132. The last word of line 16 is difficult. The first and last letters are unclear. According to Dupont-Sommer ("La stèle trilingue," 150), the first letter after the *waw* could be either a D, R, K, or even an M. The second is a B; the third is indistinct, but Dupont-Sommer suggests a *ṣade* and *rbṣ*. Lemaire ("The Xanthos Trilingual Revisited," 427) suggests *dbḥ* 'to sacrifice'.

This law he [Pixodarus] has inscribed and retains it also.	19. דתה דך כתב זי מה⟨ח⟩סן אף
If a man ever removes	20. הן איש מתום יהנצל
from Kandawats, the god, or from	21. מן כנדוץ אלהא או מן
his priest, then let him be removed[133] from Kandawats,	22. כמרא ויהוי מן כנדוץ
the god and his companion,	23. אלהא וכנותה מהנצל
and from the god[s] Leto, Artemis,	24. ומן אלהא לאתו ארתמוש
Ḥšatrapati, and the others. Anyone	25. חשתרפתי ואחורן ⟨א⟩ש
who removes [anything], these gods	26. מהנצל ו⟨א⟩לה אלהיא
will seek [it] from him."	27. יבעון מנה

The Greek Text[134]

1. When Pixodarus, son of Hecatomnos,	Ἐπεὶ Λυκίας ξαδράπης ἐγένετο Π-
2. had become satrap of Lycia, and had appointed Hieron and Apollodotos	ιξώδαρος Ἑκατόμνω ὑός, κατέστη-
3. as archons of Lycia, and	σε ἄρχοντας Λυκίας Ἱέρωνα καὶ Ἀ
4. named as epimeletes over Xanthus	πολλόδοτον καὶ Ξάνθου επιμελη-
5. Artemelis, the people of Xanthus	τήν Ἀρτεμηλιν. Ἔδοξε δὴ Ξανθίοι-
6. and of the neighboring towns resolved to establish	ς καὶ τοῖς περιοίκοις ἱδρύσασθ-
7. an altar for King Kaunios and	αι βωμὸν Βασιλεῖ Καυνίωι καὶ Ἀρ-
8. Arkesima, and they selected as priest	κέσιμᾳ, καὶ εἵλοντο ἱερέα Σιμί-
9. Simias, son of Kondorasis, and whoever	αν Κονδορασιος ὑὸν καὶ ὃς ἂν Σιμ-
10. may be most akin to Simias for all time,	ίαι ἐγγύτατος ἦι τὸν ἅπαντα χρό-
11. and they gave him exemption from public burdens	νον, καὶ ἔδοσαν αὐτῶι ἀτέλειαν τ-
12. on his property, and the city gave the fields	ῶν ὄντων, και ἔδωκαν ἡ πόλις ἀγρὸ-
13. that Kesindelis and Pigres had cultivated	ν ὅγ Κεσινδηλις καὶ Πιγρης κατη-
14. and all that adjoins the fields	ργάσατα καὶ ὅσον προς τῶι αγρῶι
15. and the buildings [on them] to King	καὶ τὰ οἰκήματα εἶναι Βασιλέως
16. Kaunios and Arkesima, and	Καυνίου καὶ Ἀρκέσιμᾳ, καὶ δίδοτ-

133. According to the reconstruction of Lemaire, "The Xanthos Trilingual Revisited," 429.

134. Metzger, "L'inscription grèque," 32–33; Briant, "Xanthos et Pixôdarus," 322–25.

17.	every year three half-minas	αι κατ᾽ ἕκαστον ἐνιαυτὸν τρία ἡμ-
18.	were given from the city, and all those	ιμναῖα παρὰ τῆς πόλεως, καὶ ὅσοι
19.	who would become free shall pay	ἄν ἀπελεύθεροι γένωνται ἀποτί-
20.	to the god two drachmas, and all that	νειν τῶι θεῶι δύο δραχμάς, καὶ ὅσ-
21.	had been written on this stele	α ἐν τῆι στήληι ἐγγέγραπται κατ-
22.	shall be dedicated, all of it, to King	ιερώθη πάντα εἶναι Βασιλέως Κα-
23.	Kaunios and Arkesimas, and from any	υνίου καὶ Ἀρκεσιμα, καὶ ὅ τι ἄν ἐχ-
24.	yield that may come out of these things	φόριον ἐκ τούτων γίνηται θύειν
25.	each new moon, a sheep,	κατ᾽ ἑκάστην νουμηνίαν ἱερεῖον
26.	and every year an ox shall be offered, and the Xanthians and those from their	καὶ κατ᾽ ἐνιαυτὸν βοῦν, καὶ ἐποιή-
27.	neighboring towns made oaths	σαντο ὅρκους Ξάνθιοι καὶ οἱ περ-
28.	to fulfill all the things that had been	ίοικοι ὅσα ἐν τῆι στήληι ἐγγέγρ-
29.	written on the stele for these gods	απται ποιήσειν ἐντελῆ τοῖς θεο-
30.	and for the priests, and not	ὶς τούτοις καὶ τῶι ἱερεῖ, καὶ μὴ μ-
31.	to alter in any way or to permit	ετακινήσειν μηδαμὰ μηδ᾽ ἄλλωι ἐ-
32.	anyone else to do it. If anyone alters [it],	πιτρέψειν· ἄν δέ τις μετακινήση-
33.	he shall be a sinner against these gods	ι, ἁμαρτωλὸς [ἔ]στω τῶν θεῶν τούτω-
34.	and against Leto and against her kinsmen and against the Nymphs, and	ν καὶ Λητοῦς καὶ ἐγγόνων καὶ Νυμ-
35.	Pixodarus shall be in charge.	φῶν. Πιξώταρος δὲ κύριος ἔστω.

The Lycian Text[135]

1. When Pigesere, son of Katamia, became satrap of Termis (= Lycia)
2.–3. and when he had commissioned (as) officers for the Termilites
4. Iyeru and Natrbbiyemi
5. and for Arna (as) governor Ertimeli.
6.–7. The citizens and the neighbors of Arna decreed (?) to establish this (?) sanctuary (?)
8. to Khantawati Khbideñni and to Arkazuma, king.
9.–10. And they made Simiya, son of Kondurahi, priest for these gods

135. Laroche, "L'inscription lycienne," 60ff.; the translation is that of Laroche (my translation of his French translation). This should not be considered an independent translation of the Lycian. Much of the translation of the Lycian is interpreted from the Greek and Aramaic.

11. and the one who would follow Simiya.
12. And they gave him emancipation over all that was his.
13. And the city and the neighboring villages added to it
14.–15. some fields from the city. Now, Khesentedi . . . and Pigres had irrigated them.
16. And all that was added to it—and that which was built on it—
17–18. would belong to the King Kaunios and to Arkazuma.
18.–19. And Arna gives him yearly (?) *adas* for a salary.
20. And he demands that the slaves (?)—
21. all those who would be free from then on—
22. would give him two (?) shekels. And they dedicated
23. everything inscribed on this stele
24. to King Kaunios and to Arkazuma.
25. And that which is returned as a benefit,
26. they shall sacrifice it month by month
27. ritually with a sheep and yearly
28. with a steer to King Kaunios and to Arka-
29. zuma. It is Simias who sacrifices, and he
30. who will be near to Simias. And the city
31. of Arna and the neighbors of Arna made their oath
32. to him regarding this law; thus, they
33. established this law that everything which is
34. inscribed on this stele,
35. nothing will be removed from it, neither that under the regard of these gods
36. nor that under the regard of the priest. That if
37. someone removes it, they demand amends from these gods
38. and from the mother of the one enclosed here,
39. *Pentrenni*, her children, and
40. Eliyana. From Pigesere, if one . . . then. . . .

Date of the Inscription

The Aramaic text dates the inscription to the first year of a King Artaxerxes. Three Artaxerxes had been known prior to this inscription: Artaxerxes I Longhand (465–425), Artaxerxes II Memnon (405–358), and Artaxerxes III Ochus (358–338). The epigraphy alone rules out Artaxerxes I. Both the Greek and Aramaic texts date the inscription to the time when Pixodarus was satrap of Lycia. The choice of king depends on the dates of Pixodarus's tenure. Mausolus, son of Hecatomnos and oldest brother of Pixodarus, was satrap and dynast of Caria and Lycia at his death in 353/352 (Diodorus 16.36).[136] His wife and sister, Artemisia, succeeded him, but it is not known if she was officially confirmed as satrap. Artemisia lived only two years after

136. Ruzicka, *Politics of a Persian Dynasty*, 100.

Mausolus's death; Idrieus, Hecatomnos's second son, succeeded her. Idrieus, with his sister-wife Ada, ruled as satrap and dynast in Mausolus's territory of Caria and Lycia.[137] After Idrieus's death in 344/343, Ada succeeded him, perhaps as satrap, at least as dynast. In 341 Pixodarus, the youngest of the Hecatomnid brothers, ousted Ada and held the satrapy until Alexander crossed into Asia (Diodorus 16.74). The stele must be dated to 341 or later and so cannot refer to the first year of any of the three known Artaxerxes listed above. Arses (338–336) must have taken the throne name of Artaxerxes IV, and the stele should be dated to 338/337.[138] This is simpler and more reasonable than suggesting that Pixodarus ruled twice, once in the first year of Artaxerxes III and once again after he overthrew his sister Ada.[139]

The events described on the stele do not date to 341, the first year of Pixodarus's tenure as satrap, but a few years later. In 341/340, Philip II of Macedon had besieged Perinthos in the Hellespont and then Byzantium.[140] Persian coastal satraps were ordered to aid Perinthos in the face of Philip's attack. In the next year (340/339), Chios, Cos, and Rhodes—all Carian islands—sent aid to Byzantium.[141] Pixodarus, as Carian satrap, would have been heavily involved in these arenas. Only in 338, the first year of Artaxerxes IV, when Pixodarus was back from the war against Philip, could he have attended to domestic matters.

Place of the Inscription

The inscription was found at the sanctuary of Leto just outside the Lycian city of Arna *birta'* (line 3 in the Aramaic inscription). The city is known primarily by its Greek name, Xanthus (line 5 in the Greek). The Aramaic inscription names Pixodarus as satrap of Carach and Tarmil, the Lycian names for the provinces of Caria and Lycia.[142]

The city of Arna is called a *bîrtā'* (בירתא) in the Aramaic inscription (line 3). As discussed in the section on Yeb, during the Persian period this term refers to the capital city of a satrapy or province (*medinta*).[143] The city of Xanthus/Arna was the capital of Lycia and housed the administrative head of the province (*archontes*) and a garrison, headed by the *epimeletes.*

137. Ibid., 102, and references there.

138. Hornblower, *Mausolus,* 47–48, and references there.

139. Contra Dupont-Sommer, "La stèle trilingue," 166–67.

140. Hornblower, *Mausolus,* 45.

141. Ibid., 46.

142. Dupont-Sommer, "La stèle trilingue," 141. See also line 1 of the Lycian inscription.

143. Lemaire and Lozachmeur, "*Bîrāh/Bîrtā'* en araméen."

Archaeological data support this description of Xanthus as the satrapal capital. It was naturally well defended, lying in the valley of the Xanthus River, at the tip of a low spur that extended from Mt. Massikytos and overlooked the river below it.[144] The city had two acropolises, one Lycian and one Hellenistic and Roman. The Lycian lay near the center of the city; its encircling walls dated to the 5th century.[145] Inside the acropolis were storehouses and a large fortress contained in four archaeological strata, two of them Persian. The buildings of the first Persian period were probably built around 540 and destroyed in a huge conflagration around 470.[146] The acropolis was rebuilt almost immediately. The buildings in it and the surrounding wall were enlarged, and a new town outside the acropolis wall arose.[147] This marked the beginning of the second Persian period—the city's most prosperous. This stage lasted until Alexander. The presence at Xanthus of a mint and of the Lycian dynasts' tombs testifies to the importance of the city as a provincial center. Literary data also testify to Xanthus as the capital of Lycia. To Herodotus, the fall of Lycia in 540 resulted from the fall of Xanthus (1.176).[148] He uses the names Xanthus and Lycia interchangeably.[149]

The Greek inscription also indicates that Xanthus was the satrapal capital. Pixodarus appointed two archontes over Lycia and an epimeletes over Xanthus. Presumably, one of the archontes had his seat at Xanthus and the other at Lycia's second-most important city, Limyra, the two locations where dynasts minted coins during the Persian period.[150] The ἐπιμελετής, described in the stele as being *over* Xanthus, would have been in charge of the city and the garrison in the acropolis there.[151]

Purpose of the Inscription

The inscription commemorates the creation of a cult or sanctuary (כרפא in Aramaic, βωμός in Greek) to the god Basileus Kaunios at Xanthus (Arna). It also sets forth the fiscal regulations that would govern the estate of the newly installed god and his priest.[152] It outlines the material and economic responsibilities and prerogatives of the priest and of the citizens of Xanthus

144. Keen, *Dynastic Lycia*, 56.
145. Metzger, *FdX*, 2.1–2.
146. Ibid., 2.20–28, 80–81.
147. Ibid., 2.82.
148. Keen, *Dynastic Lycia*, 58.
149. Ibid.; e.g., Hdt. 1.176.
150. Borchhardt, "Eine Doppelaxtstele aus Limyra," 184 n. 7.
151. Hornblower, *Mausolus*, 147 and references there. Cf. LS, ad loc. It appears that at least by the last half of the 4th century, the king was no longer appointing garrison leaders for every ἄκρα, as stated by Xenophon (*Cyr.* 8.6.9), and this task devolved upon the satrap. Cf. discussion in C. Tuplin, "Xenophon and the Garrisons," 167–88.
152. For a discussion, see Briant, "Xanthos et Pixôdaros," 313–15.

and its neighboring villages. According to the inscription, the villagers exempted the priest from public burdens, implying that they took these burdens upon themselves. The exemption is not granted by the satrap; he simply authorizes the substitution.[153]

Who is this god? Who decided to build him a sanctuary, and what role did the satrap have in this decision?

The God

Who is the god of this cult site? The Lycian inscription refers to him (line 8) as χῆτawατι, a term designating 'rulership' or 'king'.[154] Lycian inscriptions refer to local dynasts as χῆτawατι; for example, "under the χῆτawατα of X." The Lycian text of the present inscription (line 8) qualifies the term χῆτawατι with the Lycian ethnic Khbideñni, or Caunus.[155] The name KNDWṢ, כנדוץ in the Aramaic inscription, transliterates the Lycian name of the god. The ethnic that qualifies it is also transliterated: KBYDŠY (כבידשי is KBYD, plus the designation for an ethnic group, -ŠY). Two Roman period Greek inscriptions from Caunus mention this god.[156] In both, he is simply called King, Basileus, or Βασιλεύς ὁ Θεός 'King, the god'. An inscription from Cos mentions the god as Βασιλέως Καυνίου τοῦ θεοῦ 'King of Caunus, the god'.[157] Basileus Kaunios is the local god of the Carian city of Caunus. In Caunus he is simply King; outside of Caunus, this Carian god is King Caunus (or Kaunios), or King of Caunus, or Caunian King.[158]

The Greek inscription translates rather than transliterates the Lycian divine name. It calls the god βασιλεύς Καυνίος, king of Caunus, or Caunian king. The reverse is true for the name of the god's companion. There the Greek transliterates the name of the second god, Arkazuma, while the Aramaic translates it, KNWTH 'his companions'.[159] The Lycian name includes a letter rare in its language, implying that this god too is Carian.

In addition to King Kaunios and his companion, several gods have been brought in to defend the sanctuary and to curse any who would harm it. The Lycian inscription understandably names the mother goddess of the enclosure, *Pentrenni* (i.e., Leto), her children (presumably her twins Artemis and Apollo by Zeus), and Elyana. The Greek inscription also identifies the gods

153. Pace Blenkinsopp, "Did the Second Jerusalemite Temple Possess Land?" This was commonly done by towns to ensure that someone would take responsibility for an area. See the discussion of the Lagina inscription below.

154. Laroche, "L'inscription lycienne," 104–6.

155. Ibid., 64.

156. Bean, "Notes and Inscriptions from Caunus," 95–105. These are inscriptions 37 and 38.

157. Ibid., 96 n. 19.

158. See also Lemaire and Lozachmeur, "Plurilinguisme en Asie Mineure," 116–17.

159. Ibid., 117.

Leto and her offspring, plus the nymphs. In the Aramaic version, on the other hand, the gods are Leto and Artemis, but instead of the expected Apollo, we read "Ḫšatrapati, the god Satrap, Lord of Power," who is to be identified with both Apollo and Mithra.[160] Artemis may have also been assimilated to Anahita by this time.

Purpose of the Cult

The inscription commemorates the installation of a Carian god and his companion in Xanthus, the capital of Lycia. Who initiated the act and why? According to the Greek text, the people of Xanthus and their neighboring villages decided it (ἔδοξε Ξανθίοις καῖ τοῖς περιοίκοις); according to the Aramaic text, the citizens or perhaps the landowners of Arna intended it (אתעשתו בעלי אורן). Why would the citizens of Xanthus want to introduce a Carian god into their sanctuary for Leto? Why at the very moment of Pixodarus's return from battle against Philip? Was this the voice of the *démos* meeting in assembly? Did an oligarchy of landowners meet in a *boulē* to decide? Or did Pixodarus's hand-picked *epimeletes* simply carry out his master's orders?

Historical Background

The earliest evidence[161] we have of Lycia is of a large, strongly fortified building on the acropolis of Xanthus, dated to the 8th century.[162] It must have served as a palace, housing a king. Pillar tombs in many central cities of Lycia go back to the mid– to late sixth century and indicate a small elite class. The burial type seems to have been indigenous to Lycia and suggests a native Lycian monarchical system; but it does not appear before the Persian occupation. In 540, the Persians conquered Lycia, destroyed the palace, and wiped out the town.[163] Reconstruction and repopulation occurred shortly thereafter, under Persian auspices. Persian conquest left no Xanthian dynast alive—the onslaught killed all the leaders of Xanthus. According to Herodotus, only 80 Xanthian families survived—not the elite but only families herding their sheep and goats on the mountainside who escaped the battle. The ruling dynasty at Xanthus from 540 onward, though Lycian, came from outside Xanthus and was installed by Persia.

160. Ibid., 118; Dupont-Sommer, "L'énigme du dieu Satrape et le dieu Mithra"; Lipiński, "Shadday, Shadrapha et le dieu Satrape." If Apollo was syncretized with Mithra at this time, was he also at the time of Darius I? Was it Mithra who spoke only truth to Darius?

161. This section is based primarily on the work of Keen, *Dynastic Lycia*.

162. Metzger, *L'Acropole lycienne*, 2.16–19.

163. Hdt. 1.176.

Information on the dynastic structure of Persian Lycia comes from tomb inscriptions and coins. The earliest tomb inscription belonged to a man named Kheziga. Buried in the next-oldest tomb was Kheziga's son, Kubernis, who probably reigned next. Evidence for this ruler of Xanthus comes from some coins, minted in Lycia, bearing the Greek inscription KYB. These coins are to be dated from 525 to 500. Kubernis is undoubtedly the same Kuberniskos, son of Sikas, who is mentioned by Herodotus (Hdt. 7.98) as leader of the Lycians during the expedition of Xerxes (481–479). Keen concludes that the phrase normally read Κυβερνισκος Σικα should be emended to Κύβερνις Κοσσίκα 'Kubernis, son of Kossika'. He suggests that Kossika is the Greek phonetic spelling of Xeziga, the first dynast of Lycia. Kubernis, his son, would have ruled from about 525 to at least 480 and Xerxes' expedition to Greece.

Evidence for a third king, Kuprlli, stems from this name in Lycian on a hoard of coins, dating from 480 to about 440. These were minted at Xanthus and at Limyra, the western and eastern capitals of Lycia. The next ruler may have been Arppakhu, son-in-law of Kuprlli. His tomb inscription includes the dating formula "during the reign of Arppakhu," and so he erected his tomb while he was yet alive. He issued no coins and may not have ruled at all. Keen dates the reign of Arppakhu's son, Kheriga (440–410), immediately after Kuprlli.

These dynasts, installed and supported by the Persian satrap of Lydia, would have ruled Lycia as despots, perhaps with oligarchic support. The Athenian tribute lists of the mid–fifth century indicate the dearth of democracies among Lycian cities. The tribute lists do not name any city from the central Xanthus Valley, and only five cities from Lycia: four from the western- and southernmost extreme, and one from the easternmost border. The democratic factions were evidently forced to occupy villages on the outskirts, while the central valley supported Persia. After 430, no Lycian city is recorded in the tribute lists. Kheriga was able to expand his zone of control throughout Lycia. This is certainly because Kherei, Kheriga's younger brother, defeated the Athenian general Melesandros in Lycia in 430/429. The statement about this (taken from the Pillar Tomb Inscription) finds support in a comment by Thucydides (2.69): "the Athenian general Melesandros died in battle at Lycia." Athens may have attacked Lycia in an attempt to convince those five outlying cities to pay the tribute for which they were in arrears.

After the defeat of Melesandros, Kheriga played an important role in Persian foreign affairs. Kheriga acted as arbiter between the Spartans and Tissaphernes, satrap of Lydia, in concluding the Spartan-Achaemenid treaty so favorable to Persia. A sizable proportion of Tissaphernes' force was Lycian in the joint Spartan-Persian attack against Athenian forces at Miletus.

The reign of Kheriga marked a strong increase in the Lycian dynasty's ties to Persia. The dynasty began to ape Persian culture. Kheriga's father, Arppakhu (Harpagos) had an Iranian name, as did Kheriga's son, Erbbina. Kheriga's younger brother and successor, Kherei (410–390), depicted himself on his coins clad in a Persian tiara, a practice followed by other dynasts in Lycia.

The loss of Lycia's independence as a separate satrapy began with Erbbina, son of Kheriga, and nephew to Kherei. Based on coins and tomb inscriptions, Erbbina most likely ruled from 390 to 380. Six other dynasts minted coins in various cities throughout Lycia during Erbbina's reign, and his authority may have been restricted to the Xanthus Valley alone. After Erbbina's death, events become even more confused. Epigraphic and numismatic evidence reveal several "kings" of Lycia in the years 380–360. Coins and inscriptions name two men in particular, Trbbenimi and Perikle, as rulers. Their coins, dating to the 370s, were minted in several eastern cities of Lycia. Trbbenimi and Perikle may have been brothers; their parents may have named the latter after the great Pericles of Athens, implying his family was pro-Greek.

The end of Lycia as an independent satrapy culminated with Perikle. According to Lycian inscriptions, Perikle attacked a certain Arttumpara, known from coins and inscriptions. Called "the Mede" in the inscriptions, Arttumpara too was named ruler of Lycia. His coins were minted at Xanthus in the same years as Perikle's, 380–360. A certain Mithrapata (also Persian) is also known from Lycian coinage and from inscriptions. His coins were minted in eastern cities and were of the heavier eastern standard. Arttumpara's coins, dated to the same period, were minted in the west and were of the lighter western Lycian standard. The Persians must not have looked too kindly on the rise of Perikle, with his possible Greek associations. After the death of Erbbina, Persia may have sent in these two Persian officials to control Lycia: Arttumpara (the Mede) in the west and Mithrapata in the east. Perikle reacted by attacking Arttumpara. Diodorus includes Perikle in his list of those participating in the so-called Great Satraps' Revolt of 362 (15.90.3). Whether Perikle had official status as satrap is doubtful, but he did rebel against Persian authority. Perikle is not mentioned after 360; his revolt must have been crushed, and he must have been executed.

Lycia was probably handed over to Mausolus at this time. It was after this that Mausolus's hyparch, Kondalos, is recorded as raising money from the Lycians (Pseudo-Aristotle, *Oec.* 2.2.14).[164] It would have been then that she lost her independence: coinage and minting disappeared; garrisons were es-

164. It is tempting to think that Kondolos is a misunderstanding of Kondorasias, the father of Simias, the priest, with an *r*/*l* confusion. It would suggest that Simias's father, if not the hyparch, would have been Carian.

tablished at strategic points. In addition to Xanthus, Alexander encountered mercenary citadels on the Lycian borders.[165]

This abbreviated history reveals that a local dynasty ruled Lycia before the advent of Perikle—a dynasty certainly installed and supported by Persia. When the Lycian dynasty could no longer control events, Persian generals moved in to take control, and the province was ceded to neighboring Caria.

Xanthus's Form of Government

Although Perikle may have represented a democratic faction, Lycia itself was likely not democratized, given the evidence from the Athenian tribute lists. Nor would it have been possible for Xanthus—ruled by a Persian satrap, two *archons*, and an *epimeletes* (commanding a Persian garrison)—to have been a democracy. The Greek text does not speak of a *dēmos* or even a *boulē*. The Aramaic says it was the בעלי אורן 'the landowners' who planned it. This implies an oligarchy at least, not a democracy.

Relations between Satrap and Town

Who would have wanted a cult to a Carian god established in the capital city of Lycia? Would it have been local Lycians? According to the Aramaic text, the cult to Basileus Kaunios was established when Pixodarus returned from the wars against Philip II. His first public acts on his arrival were to install two *archons* in Lycia and an *epimeletes* over Xanthus and in charge of the garrison there. These acts brought Lycia tightly under Pixodarus's control. The introduction of a Carian god may have been part of this program.[166] Indeed, King Kaunios was not the only Carian god installed in Lycia, and his introduction was not the only indication of Carianization. In Limyra, the second-most-important city of Lycia, an altar was found with a rectangular base.[167] On all four sides of this base, a double-headed ax was engraved. This double-headed ax is the symbol of Zeus Labraundos, the great high god of the Hecatomnid dynasty.

Briant disagrees with the view that these Carian gods were introduced into Lycia as part of a deliberate policy of Carianization.[168] To Briant, the introduction of a Carian god in Xanthus was the free and independent decision of its citizens, not the satrap. The satrap strove only to maintain peace and tranquility within his province, to recognize the customs, languages, and institutions of the local communities, and to act as their guarantor. He did not

165. See Keen, *Dynastic Lycia*, 174, for the list of sites and discussion.
166. So also Teixidor, "The Aramaic Text in the Trilingual Stele from Xanthos," 182.
167. Borchhardt, "Eine Doppelaxtstele aus Limyra."
168. Briant, "Xanthos et Pixôdaros."

introduce new customs, laws, or institutions. Briant objects to any interpretation of the last line of the Greek text (Πιξώταρος δὲ κύριος ἔστω 'Pixodarus shall be in charge') that conveys the idea that Pixodarus had the right to impose a legally binding decision on the people of Xanthus.[169]

Briant bases his argument on the phrase κύριος ἔστω, which he points out is banal and well known in Greek inscriptions. He provides several examples: In one, taken from Athens, the κύριος carries out the decisions of a magistrate or assembly.[170] In another, also from Athens, an entire assembly is declared κύριος in a judicial domain.[171] According to a third, taken from the Temple of Oropus in Attica, a priest is declared to have full authority (κυρίως, an adverb) to fine by five drachmas anyone who commits a crime within the shrine.[172] In another inscription found near Corinth, five leaders of a group sent to consult the oracle at Delphi were empowered to lay a fine of five drachmas on whoever caused a disorder, 'by reason of their charge' (οἰδὲ κύριοι ἔστων).[173] All these examples, taken from the Greek mainland, exhibit a mundane use of the phrase κύριος ἔστω. As Briant suggests, it is reasonable to conclude from them that the comment regarding Pixodarus simply guarantees a freely taken decision of the Xanthian people. Briant suggests that the present inscription intends κύριος in its customary Greek usage: the delegation of power over a limited area of jurisdiction.[174] Indeed this is the definition of the term in the Decree of Mylasa discussed above. There the assembly was κύριος, that is, described as authorized to make a decision.

Although the expression κύριος ἔστω may be banal and commonplace in mainland Greece, is mainland Greece the best place to look for appropriate parallels? Those inscriptions originated in cities with democratic traditions. Lycia and other areas of Persian-controlled Asia Minor were not democratic. To state that someone was κύριος had an entirely different connotation when that someone was the Persian satrap than when someone simply headed a delegation to a Delphic shrine or even when the referent was an entire assembly in a Carian city.

If the mention of Pixodarus in this inscription is a routine guarantee of cultic regulations, why is satrapal authority not invoked whenever new cultic regulations are pronounced? In 1971, two steles were found in the necropolis of Lagina, in inland Caria. One dates to the middle of the 4th century, the time of Mausolus. It is broken at the top, but the rest is in good condition:

169. Ibid., 330–31.
170. Ibid., 332 n. 93.
171. Ibid., n. 95.
172. Petropoulou, "The *Eparche* Documents and the Early Oracle at Oropus."
173. Rougemont, *Corpus des inscriptions de Delphes*, 19–23.
174. Briant, "Xanthos et Pixôdaros," 333.

> .... Koranzeis to Apollo and Artemis. Skoaranos and his wife Te.......... dedicated the wooded land, which is called the olive-tree field at Koarbonda, to Apollo and Artemis to be always theirs: this field borders on the sacred land of Artemis, has forty trees on it and holds twenty medimnoi of seeds. Oborka's son Hecatomnos and Artaos' son Yssollos, both from Ythybira, Arimas' son Manes and Paktyes' son Paos, both from Patarousa, Manes' son Paktyes and Thyssos' son Dersomanes, both from Angora, Hecatomnos' son Hekataios and Hecatomnos' son Manes, both from Lagina, and Mys' son Idbelas and Yssaldomnos' son Yrgossos, both from Ondra, should see to it (ἐπιμελῆθηναι) that this decision is written on a stone stele and erected in the temenos of Apollo and Artemis. The Koranzeis approved this (ἔδωκαν δὲ Κωρανζεῖς). And whoever looks after the tomb of Skoranos should be exempt from slave tax and all other taxes except the royal ones.[175]

The situation described here is completely analogous to the one described in the inscription from Xanthus. A man and his wife donated land to found a cult site to Apollo and Artemis; a law is established to provide for the permanent care of the donors' tomb: whoever cares for the tomb shall be exempt in perpetuity from all taxes except royal ones (πλὴν φόρων βασιλικῶν). Although no new god is introduced, the provisions of this and the Xanthus inscription are identical. However, the Lagina inscription declares no one κύριος; neither does it call upon the name and power of the satrap. The decision in Lagina is made by a man and his wife; it is approved by representatives (of the oligarchy?) from various parts of the city. The absence of satrapal authority suggests that the satrap did not routinely involve himself in cultic affairs. The involvement of Pixodarus in the cultic regulations at Xanthus was unusual.

There had to have been a reason for Pixodarus to take responsibility for this particular cult in Xanthus, a cult to a Carian god. This reason could only have been to tighten his control over Lycia.[176] The Greek inscription states that the Xanthians decided, but it mentions neither *dēmos* nor *boulē*. The Aramaic text says that the בעלי אורן 'the landowners' had this in mind. Who were these landowners and why would they have wanted this cult? Debord asks how great the margin of maneuverability would have been for a people under a Carian satrap, at least one of the *archon*s, and the *epimeletes,* with his (Carian?) garrison.[177] A. H. M. Jones describes the relationship between

175. M. C. Sahin, "Two New Inscriptions from Lagina (Koranza)," 189–95.

176. A Carian god, linked to the Hecatomnids, would increase attachment to Caria. Similarly, Droaphernes prohibited the *neokoroi* of the cult to Zeus Baradates from frequenting the cults of Phrygian and Cappadocian gods. He did not want them influenced by the gods of rebel satraps.

177. Debord, *L'Asie Mineure,* 67.

kings and cities in the Hellenistic period.[178] He finds it is often expressed in the type of language present in the Xanthus inscription. The king controlled the cities, yet the cities took care to behave as if they were free and independent. Decrees of the king were invariably couched as if they were made by the sovereign *poleis.*

Who would have worshiped at temples to Carian gods in Lycia? It is likely that the Carian cults installed in Lymra and Xanthus were to serve the men of the garrisons there and their families. The *epimeletes,* Artemelis, had a Carian name.[179] The Greek oligarchy, the landowners, very likely the ones who required the Greek version of the inscription, may also have been Carian. At least Pigres, one of the landowners, was Carian and may even have been related to the Hecatomnid family.[180] The erection of a cult to a Carian god when Lycia had just been embedded in the Persian satrapy of Caria cannot indicate Persian support for local gods. The Temples to King Kaunios at Xanthus and to Zeus Labraunda at Lymra were undoubtedly built for the new landowners of the Carian bureaucracy and for the members of the Carian garrison and their families, much as the Temple of Yhw at Elephantine was erected for the Jewish garrison there.

Conclusion

The conclusions derived from these five inscriptions are consistent with those derived from archives of the Babylonian temples and from the Egyptian material. There was no universal concern for foreign cults in the Achaemenid Empire. Priestly exemptions from taxes and corvée labor were an exception to the rule. Darius's letter to Gadatas (if genuine) suggests that, as in Babylon, the exemptions to the priests of Apollo likely resulted from a quid pro quo between them and Cyrus, a quid pro quo that Darius upheld. Droaphernes' command to the *neokoroi* of the Temple to Zeus Baradates in Sardis to avoid the mystery cults did not stem from the *neokoroi* themselves. Rather, it was likely to prevent them from worshiping Phrygian and Cappadocian gods, gods from areas with which the Empire was at war. Similarly, the installation of a cult to the Carian god King Kaunios at Xanthus (and to Zeus Labraunda at Lymra) was not a routine guarantee of local decisions or of foreign cults. Rather, the inscription exhibits Pixodarus's special concern to install Carian gods in the Lycian areas of his satrapy. These gods served to

178. Jones, *The Greek City,* 95ff.

179. Debord, *L'Asie Mineure,* 405.

180. Pigres, son of Hyssaldomos, related to the Hecatomnid family, was a Carian dynast (Hornblower, *Mausolus,* 22). Kondaules was also a Carian dynast (ibid.), and this could be simple metathesis for Kondorasis. Kesindelis was likely a fellow Carian as well.

draw the Lycians more tightly into the Carian sphere of influence and to benefit the Carian colonists and militiamen there.

The goal of this study is to determine whether local temple elites lost, maintained, or accrued power during Persian hegemony. These inscriptions do not indicate any increase in local power. Although the Apollo priests may have regained their lost freedoms, those of the *neokoroi* in Sardis were restricted. The inclusion of a Carian god in the sanctuary to Leto (and the inclusion, doubtless, of a Carian priest) would not have increased the power of the local cult. The power of local priesthoods and of local elites in general declined in Asia Minor under Persian rule, as it did in Babylon and Egypt. All five inscriptions studied here are consistent with Eisenstadt's model of bureaucratic empires. The models of local control are not supported by these data.

Would it have been possible for the Judean priesthood to achieve any secular power at all while the Achaemenids ruled the earth? Did a theocracy form in Judah during the Persian period? The next chapter will address these questions.

Chapter 5

Temple-Palace Relations in Yehud

A Model of Achaemenid Rule

The image of Achaemenid rule derived from a study of the western satrapies of Babylon, Egypt, and Asia Minor provides a consistent picture that can be applied to Judah and tested against the biblical data. According to this image, Persian governors ruled provinces; Persian garrison commanders ruled cities. There is no evidence of self-rule in any of the provinces studied; no city was self-governing. Achaemenid rulers legislated by royal edict, not by legislative assemblies. If assemblies met, they did so to certify the wishes of the decision-maker, not to express their own desires. As Dandamayev points out, the centuries-old rivalry in Babylon between the royal court and the popular assembly of the temple communities had already ended under the Chaldaean kings with the defeat of the assembly.[1] Power was in the hands of the Persian rulers and the men they appointed. There was no vehicle for local control. Data from Egypt and Asia Minor are consistent with this description. The only reference to assemblies in the evidence from Egypt (*TAD* B.2.6, 3.3, 3.8) is from marriage or divorce proceedings. In one case, it was proclaimed in front of an assembly that a couple was divorced; in another, the husband agreed to fulfill a certain obligation if a divorce did occur. Evidence from Asia Minor is inconclusive, yet there is no indication that citizens could meet in an assembly to decide an issue contrary to the wishes of the satrap. Inscriptions suggest that in Asia Minor, too, communities rubber-stamped satrapal orders. Democracy is not evident in cities that were under Persian rule.

Nor were temples self-governing. Babylonian and Egyptian evidence shows that Persian satraps appointed a temple's chief priests; governors appointed lesser officials. Temples were sources of satrapal income, and except in special cases priests were available as corvée labor anywhere in the realm. These data are consistent with Eisenstadt's model of bureaucratic empires.

Does this image apply to Yehud?

1. Dandamayev, "State and Temple in Babylonia," 591.

To answer this question, I investigate first the role of the Persian kings in the restoration of YHWH's Temple in Jerusalem and then the techniques by which they administered the Jewish province. I conclude that, like other provinces in the Persian Empire, Judah too was held tightly at all times under the thumb of Persian imperial control. Eisenstadt's model of bureaucratic empires is found to be a better predictor of events even in Persian-period Judah than is the theory of self-governance or the theory of imperial authorization of local norms.

Sources and Problems for the Study of Judah

Relative to the huge archives from Babylon and Egypt, the material from Judah is sparse. There are no archival data. In contrast to the few inscriptions from Persian period Asia Minor, however, the written material relevant to Judah is extensive. Material pertinent to temple-palace relations in Yehud includes the biblical books of Ezra–Nehemiah, Haggai–Zechariah, and Second Isaiah.[2] The writings of Josephus supplement our knowledge. In addition to the literary material, settlement patterns and the corpus of coins, jar-handle seals, papyri, and bullas contribute to the understanding of Persian period Yehud.

A major problem exists in the interpretation of the historical books of the Bible, however. They are literary texts, not archival, and must be used with caution. History-writing (then as now) is not simply a chronicling of facts but the past encoded in a narrative framework.[3] This framework is determined by the world view of the narrator. To read ancient historiography is to make contact not only with the events the narrator selects but with the ideology that enables him to understand these events. Younger defines ideology as

> a schematic image of social order, a pattern of beliefs and concepts (both factual and normative) which purport to explain complex social phenomena.[4]

Younger has shown that the biblical account of Joshua's conquest of Canaan is based on the same schematic pattern, the same ideology as Assyrian conquest narratives. I found that this was also true for Nebuchadnezzar's conquest of Judah as described in the book of Kings.[5] The biblical writers tell the story of their defeat according to the same structure that Assyrians use to tell

2. Malachi, Esther, Chronicles, and perhaps the Torah literature also date from this period, as might the book of Joel and parts of Ezekiel.

3. Van de Mieroop, "Government of an Ancient Mesopotamian City"; Younger, *Ancient Conquest Accounts.*

4. Ibid., 51.

5. Fried, "The Land Lay Desolate."

the story of their victories. The biblical writers share the ideology of history and history-writing that was common to the ancient Near East. Biblical narratives therefore ought to be read in the same manner and with the same caveats as the Mesopotamian ones.[6]

The Restoration of the Temple of YHWH *in Jerusalem*

C. C. Torrey provides a general theory of the course of events from the date of the Jerusalem temple's destruction by Nebuchadnezzar until its restoration under Darius I.[7] Shortly after the Babylonian armies withdrew from Judah, fugitives began to return and to bring life back to the ruined city. One of their first undertakings was a temporary house for the worship of YHWH on some part of the original site. Jerusalem grew by slow degrees, and by the beginning of the Persian period, fifty years after its destruction, the city had prospered. During the time of Darius I, the prophets Haggai, Zechariah, and perhaps others chastised the people and encouraged them to build a permanent structure worthy of the deity. Work on the temple began in the second year of Darius and was completed sometime thereafter. According to Torrey, there was a modest deportation of citizens from Jerusalem to Babylon, but there was no period in which Jerusalem or Judah remained uninhabited. Life went on as normal. Cyrus's conquest did not bring about a return of the exiles, who had settled down and become part of the citizenry of Babylon. There is no dividing line between the pre- and postexilic periods; it was all one. There was no gap.

Barstad takes up Torrey's cudgel.[8] True, the temple was destroyed; true, there were deportations; but in the main, life went on normally. More specifically, Barstad takes issue with the widespread belief perpetrated by the Chronicler and by the author of Ezra–Nehemiah that the impetus for rebuilding the temple did not come from the local population left in the land but from the putative returnees. To Barstad, the society left in the land comprised agricultural workers, but also artisans, traders, village and town elders, scribes, priests, and prophets. It was a functioning society with many of its political institutions still intact. The destruction of the temple, the removal of the high priests, the royal family, and so on did not change the infrastructure that made society possible. The people even worshiped as they did before. Both Torrey and Barstad take issue with the claim that economic, cultural, and religious activity came to a standstill during Babylonian occupation.

6. See also in this regard Halpern's comparison of 2 Samuel 8 and the Annals of the Assyrian kings (*David's Secret Demons,* 124–43).

7. Torrey, *Ezra Studies,* 285–314. Portions of the following are taken from my article "The Land Lay Desolate."

8. Barstad, *The Myth of the Empty Land,* 19, 42–43, 79.

However, the notion that life went on as before, unchanged, greatly underestimates the role of both temple and palace—the primary institutions in ancient society. J. N. Postgate writes:

> We cannot any longer maintain that because the temple collected commodities and distributed them to its dependants the entire economy operated through "redistribution," or that the priests controlled all agricultural production and commercial activity. Nevertheless, we must not overcompensate, and so underrate the importance of the temple's role. In a sense it represents the communal identity of each city: it symbolizes it, but it also concentrates wealth and offers services to the community which are . . . critical to the growth of an urban civilization.[9]

Postgate describes the role of the great Bronze Age temples in Mesopotamia, but the temple was no less a factor during the Neo-Babylonian and Persian periods. Its economic role in ancient societies was crucial, but its psychological impact was even greater. A letter (*TAD* A.4.7) from the Jews at Elephantine, writing after their temple was destroyed, reveals the enormity of the loss:

> from the month of Tammuz, year 14 of King Darius [when the temple was destroyed] and until this day [the 20th of Marḥešvan, year 17 of King Darius] we are wearing sackcloth and fasting; our wives are made as widow(s); (we) do not anoint (ourselves) with oil and do not drink wine. Moreover, from that (time) and until this day they did not make meal-offering and incense and holocaust in that Temple.

After the destruction of the Elephantine temple, life did not continue as before; normal life was aborted. The impetus to rebuild was immediate, and it stemmed from the residents themselves. This seems the appropriate and typical reaction. If so, why was the pressure to build the Jerusalem temple delayed until the time of Cyrus or Darius? Was it a matter of prosperity becoming great enough, as Torrey suggests? Was rebuilding begun only at the exhortations of the prophets Haggai and Zechariah as Bedford assumes?[10] If so, why was their urging necessary? What accounts for the difference in response between the Jerusalem and Elephantine communities? Was there a difference in the response of the two communities to the destruction of their temples?

The Typology of Temple-Building

Temple-building accounts in the ancient Near East exhibit a common pattern; they are based on a common template.[11] This template, or typology,

9. Postgate, *Early Mesopotamia,* 109.

10. Bedford, *Temple Restoration.*

11. Albrektson, *History and the Gods*; Cogan, *Imperialism and Religion*; Holloway, *The Case for Assyrian Religious Influence*; Hurowitz, *I Have Built You an Exalted House*; Kutsko, *Ezekiel.*

reveals not only the way in which temple restoration is described in ancient Near Eastern historiography, but also the ideology by which it is understood. If biblical writers based their account of temple rebuilding on the same template as was used throughout the ancient Near East, then it ought to be possible to uncover that building story from the biblical text. If so, we ought to accord it the same respect that we accord other building narratives. The disclosed story ought to reveal the source of the impetus for temple-building, the date in which building was begun, the role of the Persian kings, and the dynamic of temple-palace relations in Judah in the first decades of the Persian Empire.

Based on a comprehensive study of Mesopotamian and Northwest Semitic inscriptions, Hurowitz is able to delineate the typology of temple-building in the ancient Near East.[12] His work agrees with Ellis's previous effort on foundation deposits and ceremonies.[13] These authors have found eight components that underlie the building stories of all ancient Near Eastern temple-building inscriptions. As Younger's study has shown, the fixed components in ancient Near Eastern narratives are more than a series of episodes; they represent an *ideology*, a world view. They encode a grammar that enables a particular temple-building project to be understood. These fixed components are as follows:

- A. A brief history of the temple—why it was in ruins[14]
- B. The decision to build
    1. The king receives a divine command to build a temple, usually in his first year. Temples that had been destroyed through conquest were not rebuilt without this ingredient.
    2. Additional aspects may be included:
        - a. The god is reconciled to his city or temple.
        - b. A specified, preordained period of time is concluded.
        - c. The king clarifies the divine will—through extispicy, divination, prophetic visions, etc. Rarely, the initiative comes from the king himself, in which case this last step is doubly important.
- C. The acquisition and preparation of building materials
    1. Building materials are brought from the ends of the earth. Foreign peoples contribute (involuntarily during the Assyrian period, voluntarily in the Persian period).

12. Hurowitz, *I Have Built You an Exalted House*, 131–310.
13. Ellis, *Foundation Deposits*.
14. The following schema is based on Hurowitz, *I Have Built You an Exalted House*, with expansions from Ellis, *Foundation Deposits*.

    2. Wood is brought from Lebanon and floated down the river to the building site.
- D. Laying the foundations and preparation of the site
    1. The ruler participates in the foundation rites, and they are often performed according to the prescription of a diviner or prophet.
    2. If a new temple is built near the site of an old one, lamentations are sung by lamentation priests to placate the gods and bridge the gap between the old temple and the new. A stone taken from the old temple is placed in the new one during construction. Lamentations are made for the old temple until the new one is completed.
- E. A ceremony for later building stages (e.g., the dedication of the altar or the anointing of doors and sockets in preparation for the god's entrance)
- F. The description of the completed temple and its furnishings
    1. A description of the temple
    2. A statement that the king has built the temple as he was commanded
- G. The dedication ceremony of the finished building
    1. The god is installed in the temple and takes up residence.
    2. Celebration
    3. Presentation of gifts and appointment of temple personnel
- H. Prayer or curses

The Typology of Temple-Building in Jerusalem

The Jerusalem temple's restoration is described in Ezra 1–6. These chapters begin with a notice of the decision to build under Cyrus (Ezra 1:1–2) and end with the statement that the temple was finished, a description of its dedication, and the subsequent celebration under Darius I (Ezra 6:13b–22). It is clear, however, that these chapters do not constitute a building story. It is not possible to go through the intervening verses and place them in the schema outlined above. These initial chapters in Ezra are a hodgepodge: they are in both Hebrew and Aramaic, they include letters to and from a series of different Persian kings, and they include a narrative segment about squabbles between various groups of residents. Williamson has suggested that the historian who compiled Ezra 1–6 wrote his narrative long after the events described, based on a set of independent sources that he had at his disposal.[15] Indeed, these chapters could not have been completed before 465 and the beginning of the reign of Artaxerxes I, because they include letters to and from that king

15. Williamson, "The Composition of Ezra I–VI"; idem, *Ezra, Nehemiah*, xxiii–xxiv.

(Ezra 4:7–22). Williamson considers the historian's sources to be: (a) the decree of Cyrus (Ezra 1:2–4); (b) the inventory of temple vessels (Ezra 1:9–11); (c) the list of those returning (Ezra 2); (d) two letters, which the historian summarizes (Ezra 4:6 and 7); (e) a letter in Aramaic from Reḥum and others to Artaxerxes (Ezra 4:8–16); (f) Artaxerxes' reply (Ezra 4:17–22); (g) a letter from Tattenai to Darius (Ezra 5:6–17); and (h) Darius's reply (6:3–12), which includes the transcript of a separate decree of Cyrus (Ezra 6:3–5). To Williamson, the remaining material was composed freely by the historian based on the prophetic books of Haggai and Zechariah and on events from his own day. In addition to sources b–h, but instead of Cyrus's decree, I suggest that the historian had the Second Temple's actual building inscription available to him as a separate source. If so, we ought to be able to uncover it and use it to clarify the conditions under which the Temple of YHWH was built.

If the sources available to the historian of Ezra 1–6 included a building inscription, it should be possible to weed out the extraneous narrative portions, lists, and letters that he added. The result should be a building story that corresponds to the schema outlined above.

A. Brief History of the Temple

This section is not present in Ezra 1–6 except in Tattenai's letter to Darius, a separate source. Of course, the book of Chronicles is the history of the Jerusalem temple. If the author of Ezra 1–6 had Chronicles at his disposal, and if he considered his work to be read as an addition to that history, then he would not have needed to include the temple's history again.

B. The Decision to Build

The king receives a divine command, usually in his first year. A specified, preordained period of time is concluded.

> And in the first year of Cyrus, king of Persia, in order to complete the word of YHWH by the mouth of Jeremiah, YHWH stirred up the spirit of Cyrus, king of Persia, and he sent a herald throughout all his kingdom and also by writing, saying: Thus says Cyrus, king of Persia, "All the kingdoms of the earth YHWH, god of heaven, has given me, and he charged me to build a temple for him in Jerusalem which is in Judah." (Ezra 1:1, 2)

The passage that opens the book of Ezra is often assumed either to quote a genuine decree of Cyrus the Great or to mimic such a decree.[16] However, these statements contain the requisite ingredients of a typical ancient Near

16. See Schaper, *Priester und Leviten,* 67–75, for a review of the extensive literature on the topic and a lengthy discussion of the issues. Schaper concludes that it does go back to an authentic decree. That the first word is the copulative *waw* suggests that this continues a history, however.

Eastern temple-building inscription. They name the king, they state his year in office (the appropriate first year), they state the god whose temple it is, and most importantly they state that the impetus for the temple-building came by a divine command from the god to the king. Hurowitz makes clear that only kings built temples. The divine command to the king is paramount, for it implies the god's willingness to return to his temple. Hurowitz discusses the great length to which kings went to ascertain the mood of the god:[17]

> The king who builds a temple without permission [of the god] is courting disaster—either he will not complete the project successfully, or the completed building will not stand, and may collapse after completion.[18]

Consistent with a building inscription for a Temple of YHWH in Jerusalem, the passage is written by and for Jews. The language is Hebrew; the reference to Jeremiah is relevant only to Jews and indicates that the specified preordained period of time has passed (Jer 25:11, 12; 29:10). The phrase "to stir up the spirit" is a Hebrew idiom indicating that the command has indeed come from YHWH. These words are strange if interpreted—as they usually are—as a genuine edict of Cyrus (or even if interpreted as Cyrus's response to an official Jewish request).[19] They are entirely appropriate, however, in a building inscription for a Jerusalem temple. There is no need for building inscriptions of local temples to use the language or idioms of the Achaemenid bureaucracy. For example, the inscription of Udjaḥorresnet describes the restoration of the Temple of Neith in Sais, Egypt, which was begun under Cambyses and completed under Darius. It is written completely in hieroglyphs using expressions and idioms peculiar to Egyptian culture and, while naming the Persian emperors, gives due credit to Neith, the mother of God.[20] As another example, the Cyrus Cylinder has been shown to be a foundation document for the restoration of the Esagil, the Temple of Marduk in Babylon.[21] This too employs the language and idioms of the Babylonian priesthood, not the Achaemenids.

Halpern objects that there is no narrative statement that the Judean exiles actually decided to build the temple.[22] This is true and conforms completely to the building-story genre. According to the ideology of temple-building, it

17. Hurowitz, *I Have Built You an Exalted House,* 135–63.

18. Ibid, 137.

19. This has been a major problem in accepting the authenticity of the so-called Cyrus Edict (Ezra 1:2–4; Bedford, *Temple Restoration,* 114–81).

20. Lichtheim, "Statue Inscription of Udjahorrensne."

21. Kuhrt, "Nabonidus and the Babylonian Priesthood"; Harmatta, "Modèles littéraires."

22. Halpern, "A Historiographic Commentary on Ezra 1–6."

is not the exiles who decide to build. The decision to build must come from the god to the king who has the power to build it.

Some have argued that all of Ezra 1 is "a free creation of the editor."[23] They point to the numerous discrepancies between it and Cyrus's command to Sheshbazzar described in Tattenai's letter to Darius (Ezra 6:3–5). If it is a free composition of the historian, it is odd that the king named is no native king, neither Sheshbazzar nor Zerubbabel, but the Persian emperor. Naming Cyrus as the king to whom YHWH gives his command is a recognition that he, not the Davidic heir, is YHWH's choice as interlocutor. This is unlikely to have come from the historian himself. Moreover, it recognizes that it is Cyrus alone who has the power to make the decision to rebuild.

It has been argued that Cyrus's title, "King of Persia," is anachronistic.[24] The title is never used in any of Cyrus's inscriptions; it is not used for Achaemenid kings before Darius I.[25] Yet this is precisely when a building inscription would have been written, the 6th year of Darius I, the date of the building's dedication (Ezra 6:15). Bedford also argues that the term "god of heaven" is anachronistic—it does not appear until the time of Darius.[26] The term is sometimes applied to local gods by non-Persians in an attempt to equate their god with Ahura Mazda, but only after the time of Darius.[27] The phrase may be anachronistic if the text is offered as a genuine edict of Cyrus but not if it is a building inscription from Darius's 6th year. It has also been thought odd that Cyrus, the Persian emperor, would use the term "god of Israel" when the Achaemenid bureaucracy customarily referred to the area as Yehud. *Yehud* and *Shomron* are the terms used on official seals—never Israel.[28] The term *Israel* seems to have been used only by the Judean exiles in Babylon.[29] Both Deutero-Isaiah and Ezekiel refer to the exiles as the People Israel, or the House of Israel. Deutero-Isaiah may have created YHWH's title as the Holy One of Israel.[30] The term is not used in the Elephantine papyri.

23. For example, Bedford, *Temple Restoration*, 128, 180; Blenkinsopp, *Ezra–Nehemiah*, 74.

24. Bedford, *Temple Restoration*, 120–22; Halpern, "Historiographic Commentary on Ezra 1–6," 91.

25. Kent, *Old Persian*; Lecoq, *Les inscriptions*; Schaudig, *Die Inschriften.*

26. Bedford, *Temple Restoration*, 122–28; Lecoq, *Les inscriptions*; Schaudig, *Die Inschriften.*

27. Herodotus equates Zeus with Ahura Mazda (1.131) and implies that the Babylonians equated Marduk with him (1.183). The Elephantine Jews also refer to YHW as the God of Heaven (*TAD* A.4.7; Bolin, "The Temple of Yhw").

28. Avigad, *Bullae and Seals*; Carter, *The Emergence of Yehud*, 259–83; E. Stern, *Material Culture.*

29. Bedford, *Temple Restoration*, 116; Williamson, *The Book Called Isaiah*, 41–42.

30. Williamson, ibid.

If it originated among the exiles in Babylon, it points to the Babylonian origin of the author of the underlying building account. None of these supposed anachronisms is a problem if these verses are understood to stem from a building inscription written in the 6th year of Darius I by a Jewish returnee from Babylon rather than from a supposed Edict of Cyrus.

According to Ezra 1:1–2, a herald announced throughout the kingdom the decision to rebuild the temple, and there was also a written document, this last remark added almost as an afterthought (1:1). A written document disseminated throughout the kingdom is not likely. Had there been one, the Jews would have been able to present it to Tattenai when he requested it (5:3).[31] It was lack of a written edict that necessitated Tattenai's letter to Darius (Ezra 5:6–17, assuming that letter to be authentic). Nor is it likely that a herald was sent throughout the Empire without a written edict. As one of Arsames' letters makes clear (*TAD* A.6.1), and as was true throughout history, heralds were high court officials, who read the edicts they proclaimed; they did not recite official proclamations from memory.[32] More likely the situation was as described in Tattenai's letter to Darius: Cyrus gave an order to Sheshbazzar, whom he had appointed governor, to take YHWH's vessels from the Esagil to Jerusalem, to rebuild the temple there, and to install the vessels in it. Presumably Sheshbazzar did not go alone but took with him a contingent of Jews. The phrase שם טעם used of Cyrus in Tattenai's letter (Ezra 5:13) is employed throughout Arsames' letters (*TAD* A.6.1, A.6.3, A.6.7, etc.) to indicate a simple command to a subordinate. There is no mention in either Tattenai's letter to Darius or in Darius's response of an order to anyone but Sheshbazzar. Had there been a general edict, it would have been written, and the Jews would have retained a copy of it.

The language of these two verses fits the language of a building inscription; it does not fit the language or idioms of an official Persian edict.

C. The Acquisition and Preparation of Building Materials

1. *Contributions come from all over the world, from foreign peoples and kings.*

> "Anyone among you from all his people—let his god be with him. Let him go up to Jerusalem that is in Judah and rebuild the house of YHWH the god of Israel, that is, the god that is in Jerusalem. And all who remain in the places where he had sojourned, the men of his place, they shall assist him with silver,

31. Halpern, "A Historiographic Commentary," 91.

32. Postgate, *Early Mesopotamian Society*, 285–86. A text (KAJ 310:20) affirms that proclamations were physical tablets read by the herald:

> 1 *quppu ša sasu nagiri ša bītāti ša* GN
> 1 chest containing the proclamations of heralds concerning the (purchase of) houses in the city of Assur.

> gold, cattle, and animals, along with the freewill contributions to the house of the god in Jerusalem."
>
> The heads of the clans of Judah and Benjamin, the priests, and the Levites, all whom the god stirred up his spirit to go up and build the house of YHWH that is in Jerusalem, got up. And all around them freely strengthened their hand with vessels of silver, of gold, with cattle, and animals. (Ezra 1:3–6)

This idea is common to building inscriptions in the ancient Near East.

Commentators explain the "despoliation of the neighbors" as the historian's "direct concern to present the return as a second Exodus."[33] It may point instead to Persian period embellishments of the earlier Exodus story. That men and kings have come from all over the world to contribute their wealth to the new temple is a common component of temple-building inscriptions. If those in this passage who are described as "left behind" are considered to be non-Jews making free-will offerings to the Jews who return, then this is reminiscent of Persian-period building stories.[34] At that time, the description of free-will donations from foreigners was common. As Hurowitz notes, although this practice is not unique to the Persian period and goes back to Gudea, it is still quite different from that of Assyrian and Neo-Babylonian building inscriptions. In those accounts, materials are also brought from all over the world, but they are from vassals subject to the Assyrian and Babylonian kings; they are not portrayed as free-will offerings. It is by the mighty strength of the Assyrian or Babylonian gods that the material is brought, rather than because of a spontaneous desire to honor the temple and the god, as is portrayed in building inscriptions from the time of Darius.

The text continues with a reference to the temple vessels:

> King Cyrus brought out the vessels of the house of YHWH that Nebuchadnezzar had brought out from Jerusalem and deposited in the house of his god. Cyrus, king of Persia, had them brought out by Mithradates the *ganzabara*, who counted them out to Sheshbazzar, the *naśi'* of Judah. (Ezra 1:7–8)

Halpern objects that Sheshbazzar's return is referred to obliquely here but not directly reported.[35] Yet, according to the literary genre of the building story suggested here, the goal is not to report a history of the return but to portray the wealth of nations pouring in from all over the world to contribute to the temple's construction. Sheshbazzar is named here because he is part of that portrayal. He has no independent significance. Halpern argues further that the original decree provided for the vessels' return (6:3–5), so the notice of

33. E.g., Blenkinsopp *Ezra–Nehemiah*, 75–76; Williamson *Ezra, Nehemiah*, 16.

34. Hurowitz, "The Priestly Account of Building the Tabernacle"; idem, *I Have Built You an Exalted House*, 207–10; Root, *King and Kingship*, 17–23.

35. Halpern, "A Historiographic Commentary," 89.

their return should have been included as part of the edict quoted in 1:2–4. However, its inclusion here belongs to the component that treats the wealth flowing to the temple. Its exclusion from the description of the decision to build is consistent with the format and ideology of a building inscription.

The vessels are then listed (Ezra 1:9–11).

> These [vessels] that were counted out were:

ăgarṭĕlê	gold	30
ăgarṭĕlê	silver	1,000
maḥălāpîm		29
kĕpôrê	gold	30
kĕpôrê	silver	90
Other vessels		1,000
All the vessels of gold and silver		5,400

> All these Sheshbazzar brought up with the ones who went up of the exiles from Babylon to Jerusalem. (Ezra 1:9–11)

The form of the list is identical to accounts in the Elephantine Papyri and in the Persepolis tablets. The names of the items are obscure and may be Persian. The amounts do not total correctly; the list has become corrupt in transmission. This inventory is not likely to have been part of the original building inscription and stems from a separate source. Commentators agree that it goes back to a genuine list of vessels returned to the Temple of YHWH in Jerusalem.[36] In its present position in the building story, the list of temple vessels simply represents another aspect of building materials flowing in from all over the world—including from Cyrus.

In his discussion of the temple vessels, Ackroyd argues that the intent of the final redactor of 2 Kings 24 and 25 was to stress that these vessels were brought to an end.[37] To Ackroyd, the list in Ezra 1 is fictitious; the account in 2 Kings leaves "no room for restoration."[38] It is not necessary to translate the Hebrew of 2 Kgs 25:15 to imply that all the vessels were destroyed, however, and many commentators do not.[39] Moreover, Nebuchadnezzar is known to have deposited captured booty in the Esagil. The following text is representative of Nebuchadnezzar's inscriptions:

36. For example, Blenkinsopp, *Ezra–Nehemiah,* 78–79; Williamson, *Ezra, Nehemiah,* 7–8.

37. Ackroyd, "The Temple Vessels."

38. Ibid., 53.

39. For example, Cogan and Tadmor (*II Kings,* 316) translate 25:15, the critical verse, as "the chief cook took the fire pans and the sprinkling bowls, those of gold and silver" (cf. Gesenius, 123e), rather than "those of gold, as gold; those of silver, as silver."

> Gold, silver, exceedingly valuable gemstones, thick cedars, heavy tribute, expensive presents, the produce of all countries, goods from all inhabited regions, before Marduk the great lord, the god who created me, and Nabû his lofty heir who loves my kingship, I transported and brought into Esagil and Ezida.[40]

Gold and silver vessels from the temple in Jerusalem were likely among the goods contributed to Marduk's store. Ackroyd stresses that the vessels' return is a continuity theme for the writer, whom he considers to be the Chronicler.[41] But their return is more than a literary topos. As Williamson notes, "the deposit [of temple vessels] in the temple of the victor's god was intended to underline to the devotees [of the conquered god] the inability of their god to save."[42] It also exhibits the decision of the conquered god to leave his own temple (and his own people) and reside in the temple of the conqueror. The return of the vessels denotes the return of the conquered god and his reconciliation with his people.

The text of Ezra continues in chap. 2 with a list of the returnees. This is not likely to have been part of an original building inscription but was inserted by the historian. It is a natural place to insert the list. A list of people returning from Babylon to Judah follows naturally on the heels of the list of vessels also returning from Babylon to Judah.

Following the list of returnees, the text jumps to "the seventh month when the people Israel are in their cities" (3:1). This phrase is repeated in Nehemiah 7:72b[ET 73b], so it is difficult to know its origin. Here in Ezra 3:1 it is followed by a reference to Zerubbabel, the governor of Judah, and Yeshua, the high priest, implying a jump to the seventh month of a year in the reign of Darius. (The writings of Haggai and Zechariah firmly fix Zerubbabel and Yeshua in Darius's reign rather than Cyrus's.) The text continues to describe the erection and the dedication of the altar (3:2–3) and adds that all the traditional holidays were celebrated—the Feast of Sukkot as well as the daily and monthly offerings (3:3b–6a). Compared with traditional building accounts, the placement of the dedication of the altar here is out of order. The text states that the temple foundations had not yet been laid (3:6b). This clause suggests that the writer knows that an expected passage about laying the temple foundations is not here. He seems to have rearranged his material to convey the zealousness of the returnees and to imply that all the offerings were performed according to the prescribed law from their first arrival in Jerusalem. The erection of the altar typically belongs to one of the last stages

40. Cited in Vanderhooft, *The Neo-Babylonian Empire*, 46.
41. Ackroyd, "The Temple Vessels," 57.
42. Williamson, *Ezra, Nehemiah*, 16.

of temple construction.[43] The altar will be discussed below in the context of its likely original position in the Second Temple's building account.

2. *Wood is brought from Lebanon and floated down a river to the site.*

> And they gave silver to the stonemasons and woodcutters as well as food and drink and oil to the Sidonians and the Tyrians to bring cedar wood from Lebanon to the sea at Yaffo, according to the grant that Cyrus, king of Persia, gave us. (Ezra 3:7)

This statement is common to temple building inscriptions, even to the point of floating wood from Lebanon down to its destination. Commentators uniformly note the similarities between this and the building account of the First Temple in 1 Kings 8. They assert that, because there is no reference to timber in either Tattenai's letter to Darius or the return letter from him, that its mention here is simply to recall the First Temple. More likely, the references in both building accounts are aspects common to building inscriptions in the ancient Near East. They are part of the genre. This does not make it fictitious. The roof of the Temple of YHW in Elephantine was of cedar beams (*TAD* A.4.7); they must have been shipped from Lebanon by sea in the manner described here. Further, the items paid to the Sidonians and Tyrians are typical of allocations to workers reported in the Persepolis tablets.[44]

Following the statement about purchasing wood from Lebanon, the historian inserts another comment about Zerubbabel and Yeshua, the priest:

> In the second year of their coming to the house of god in Jerusalem in the second month, Zerubbabel, son of Shealtiel, and Yeshua, son of Yoẓadak, and the rest of their brothers, the priests and the Levites, and all who came from the captivity to Jerusalem began, and they appointed Levites from twenty years old and up to supervise the work of the house of YHWH. And Yeshua appointed his sons and brothers, Qadmiel and his sons, the sons of Judah, to supervise the carrying out of the work on the house of God. (Ezra 3:8–9)

This passage is either an insertion from a later point in the building story or a free creation of the historian. Temple personnel are usually appointed after the temple is constructed and after the god is brought into it, not before.[45] The reference to Zerubbabel and Yeshua, the priest, in the second year of their coming to Jerusalem is intended to give the impression that they came to Jerusalem in the first year of Cyrus, under Sheshbazzar. The historian has compressed the entire temple-building process into a few years in order to convey the zeal of the founding community. If this passage does indeed

43. Ellis, *Foundation Deposits*, 32–33.

44. Hallock, *Persepolis Fortification Tablets.*

45. Hurowitz, *I Have Built You an Exalted House*, 56.

belong to the original building inscription, it may be that Zerubbabel and Yeshua came to Jerusalem in the second year of Darius (as implied by the writings of Haggai and Zechariah), and in the fourth year, the second year of their coming, they installed a priesthood. Installation of temple personnel at this later stage would be consistent with traditional building accounts in the ancient Near East.

Next comes the text that describes the actual foundation-laying and the ceremonies surrounding it.

D. Laying the Foundations

1. *Mesopotamian rulers usually participated in the foundation rites, and they were often performed according to the prescription of a prophet or diviner.*

> And the builders laid the foundations of the temple of YHWH. (Ezra 3:10a)

There is no mention here of Sheshbazzar, or any other ruler, leading the ceremonies. Because of this, Williamson argues that Sheshbazzar did not lay the foundations and that the work did not go on continuously from then until the first year of Darius, as reported in Tattenai's letter to that king (Ezra 5:16).[46] However, Sheshbazzar's participation is corroborated by Tattenai's own assessment of the situation in 5:8, to which Williamson has no adverse reaction. Blenkinsopp also contends that Sheshbazzar was not part of the temple-building.[47] According to him, the statement in Tattenai's letter to Darius regarding Sheshbazzar was fabricated by the Jewish community in Jerusalem to gain prestige for the temple. He also suggests that the way in which Sheshbazzar is referred to (e.g., "one Sheshbazzar by name," 5:14) is not complimentary and that the man had become *persona non grata* to the Persians. If so, it is difficult to see how mention of his name would add prestige in Darius's eyes. Furthermore, it is not likely that the Jewish community would risk falsifying the facts; Darius did not look kindly upon the lie (*drauga*).[48] It is more likely that Sheshbazzar's name was omitted from the building account just because he had become *persona non grata*, and that in fact he had laid the foundations, as is reported in the letter.[49]

46. Williamson *Ezra, Nehemiah*, 79.

47. Blenkinsopp, *Ezra–Nehemiah*, 122–23.

48. If these letters are historical (Hensley, *The Official Persian Documents in the Book of Ezra*; Porten, *The Documents in the Book of Ezra*; but see Schwiderski, *Handbuch*). Bedford (*Temple Restoration*, 181) concludes that the letters are genuine but that they are an "unreliable witness when compared to the writings of Haggai and Zechariah 1–8."

49. The installation of a new Persian king was invariably accompanied by the appointment of new officials throughout the Empire. This was especially true of Darius, who came to the throne under dubious circumstances. Cyrus's and Cambyses' appointees could not be trusted to remain loyal to the new king.

Ceremonies are conducted when the foundations are laid.

> The priests attended in their vestments, with their trumpets, and the Levites, the sons of Asaph, with their cymbals, to praise YHWH. . . . And they answered in praise and thanksgiving to YHWH, because he is good and his steadfast love is forever over Israel. And all the people gave a great shout in praise to YHWH because of the foundations of the temple of YHWH. (Ezra 3:10b–11)

This type of statement is typical of temple-building inscriptions.

2. *If a new temple is built near the site of an old one, lamentations are sung by lamentation priests to placate the gods and to bridge the gap between the old temple and the new.*

> And many of the priests, the Levites, the heads of the clans, and the elders who saw (ראו) the first temple on its foundations (this is the temple in their eyes) wept with a loud voice. (Ezra 3:12)

The verb ראו is usually translated 'had seen' and interpreted as referring to elderly people who had seen the original temple, perhaps fifty years earlier. This may not be the intent of the verse. Thureau-Dangin has published the Mesopotamian *kalû* ritual, the ritual prescribed for building new temples while the old temple lies in ruins.[50] The only text extant is from the Seleucid period, but it likely goes back to an older practice, certainly to the Persian period, if not before. The following are the instructions for the *kalû,* or lamentation priest:

> When the wall of a temple falls into ruin, in order to demolish and then rebuild[51] that temple, . . . the builder of that temple shall put on clean clothes and put a tin bracelet on his arm; he shall take an ax of lead, remove the *maḫritu* brick, and shall put it in a restricted place. You set up an offering table in front of the brick for the god of foundations, and you offer sacrifices; you shall sprinkle every type of (aromatic?) grain; you will pour beer, wine, and milk (over the brick?); you will prostrate yourself (before the brick?). As long as you [they?] demolish and (re)build [the temple] you will offer water. Then the *kalû* priest will make a libation of honey, cream, milk, beer, wine, and [good] oil (over the brick?). The *kalû* priest [shall recite] the (composition called) "*Enūma anu ibnū šamē.*" . . . [A]s long as the demolishing and (re)building

50. Thureau-Dangin, *Rituels accadiens,* 35–59.

51. Thureau-Dangin (ibid.; followed by *ANET,* 339–42; and Ellis, *Foundation Deposits,* 184) translates the verb 'to lay the foundations', interpreting *uš-šu-ši* from *uššu* 'foundation'. Von Soden (AHw 1442) suggests, however, that the verb is the D stem of *edēšu* 'to renew' (AHw, *uššušu*[*m*]). It is clear from the final section of the ritual, quoted here, that the rites continue during the entire construction of the building, not only when the foundations of the new temple are laid.

> (are going on), offerings and lamentations shall be made and the *kalû* priest shall not cease strewing (aromatic?) flour and making libations and recitations.[52]

In his discussion of the enigmatic term *libbitu maḫritu* ('the *maḫritu* brick') in this text, Ellis concludes it does not mean "first brick," as it is often translated, but any previous brick from the former temple.[53] It cannot be the first brick that was laid when the original temple was built. Bricks cannot be recognized by their inscriptions, because they are usually laid face down. In the *kalû* ritual, the one designated the builder removes a brick or stone from the old temple. He sets it aside. A *kalû* priest makes offerings and sings lamentations over it while the old temple is demolished and the new temple is constructed. He continues to sing lamentations until the new temple is finished.

Rather than referring to the weeping of very old men who remembered the first temple from almost fifty years before, the crying may refer to prescribed lamentation rites for the old temple, whose ruins they still saw before their eyes. Jacobsen suggests that city laments, or *balag*s, were composed after the destruction of a city for just such a purpose. Its recitation by *kalû* priests was an indispensable part of the *kalû* ritual accompanying the restoration of the destroyed city's temples.[54] The *balag* lament includes a vivid description of the city lying desolate and of the attack that devastated it.[55] Whether the city has been rebuilt or not, it is lamented as though in ruins and empty until the new temple is finished and dedicated.[56]

The weeping described in Ezra 3:12 may have been part of such a lamentation ritual, perhaps over a building stone that had been set aside from the ruins of the First Temple. Indeed, the אבן הראשה that Zerubbabel brings out (Zech 4:7) may have been such a stone, a stone that had been set aside by the "builder" during the foundation ceremony (Ezra 3:10a).[57] The phrase אבן הראשה has been translated 'head stone', 'premier stone', 'first stone', and

52. Thureau-Dangin, *Rituels accadiens*, 40–43.

53. Ellis, *Foundation Deposits*, 26–29.

54. Jacobsen, "Review of *Lamentation over the Destruction of Ur*," 219–24.

55. Ibid., 222–23.

56. This is reminiscent of the current Jewish lamentation rite for the temple on Tisha b'Av, the anniversary of the temple's destruction. Jews will continue to wear mourning garb, fast, and recite the book of Lamentations on Tisha b'Av until the temple is rebuilt. The book of Lamentations, describing the devastation and desolation of Jerusalem in the present tense, is read, even though the city is now a bustling metropolis.

57. See Halpern, "The Ritual Background of Zechariah's Temple Song," and the references cited there. The ritual proposed here is slightly different from the one proposed by Halpern. Rather than Zerubbabel's removing the stone from the ruins or from the mountain (where it was quarried?), I suggest that he simply brought it out from the restricted place where it had been kept during the years of the *kalû*.

'top stone'.[58] However, there is reason to think it ought to be translated 'former-times stone', as is also appropriate for the *libbitu maḫritu.* BDB defines ראשה, vocalized *ri'šâ,* the singular of *ri'šôt,* as 'beginning time, early time'. I suggest 'former time'. This translation is based on Ezekiel 36:11, "I will increase upon you man and beast; they will greatly multiply, and I will cause you to dwell as in your early times (כקדמותיכם), and I will cause more good than your former times (מראשותיכם), and you will know that I am YHWH."

At some point, the *libbitu maḫritu* is incorporated into the new building. It is difficult to know when this occurs. The *kalû* ritual suggests it occurs very late in the construction process—perhaps when the building is near completion but before the walls are paneled. It may be only then that the new temple becomes the temple in actuality; the act of inserting the brick may be what makes the transference complete. (Ezra 3:12 suggests that the old temple lying in ruins was still the temple in the eyes of the people.) When Zerubbabel brought out the "former-times" stone (Zech 4:7), he is said to have laid the foundations of the temple (יסד, Zech 4:9). However, the *kalû* ritual prescribes that laments be sung for the old temple as long as demolishing and rebuilding continue, presumably until the new temple is dedicated, even after the *libbitu maḫritu* is installed. Laments for the temple in Jerusalem continued still into the fourth year of Darius (Zech 7:1–3), even though Zerubbabel had laid the אבן הראשה in the second year. In the light of the *balag* and the *kalû* ritual, Haggai and Zechariah's references to the temple still in ruins and to the city still devastated does not demonstrate that temple-building had not begun or had stopped under Sheshbazzar. Ritual laments were prescribed throughout the building process until the new temple was dedicated.

E. Ceremonies are held to honor later stages of building, for example, the dedication of the altar or the anointing of doors and sockets.

> In the seventh month . . . Yeshua, son of Yoẓadak, and his brothers, the priests, and Zerubbabel, son of Shealtiel, and his brothers arose and built the altar of the god of Israel and sacrificed burnt offerings upon it, as is prescribed. . . . And they erected the altar on its place. . . . And they offered burnt offerings upon it to YHWH morning and evening. (Ezra 3:1–3)

The reference to Yeshua, the priest, and to Zerubbabel suggest that the dedication of the altar took place during the reign of Darius; the writings of Haggai and Zechariah place these men securely in this period. Although the

58. 'Top stone', NRSV; 'premier stone', Meyers and Meyers, *Haggai, Zechariah,* 228, 248. Meyers and Meyers consider it to be a stone from the First Temple, as does Peterson, *Haggai and Zechariah,* 237–42, who translates it 'the former stone'.

location of these verses in the book of Ezra implies that the altar was dedicated prior to laying the foundations, this is not likely. As stated above, altars are routinely built during later stages of construction, not before the foundations are laid.[59] It is impossible to know when this occurred. The reference to "the seventh month" is not reliable; such an auspicious month may have been inserted to suit the theological goals of the historian. Halpern suggests that the four horns that symbolize the four enemies of Judah and Israel mentioned in Zechariah 1:18 are the four horns of the altar.[60] If so, the altar dedication would have occurred on the 24th day of the 11th month of Darius's 2nd year (Zech 1:7).

Placing the building-story components according to their order in typical building accounts may provide the historical order of the Second Temple's construction: The foundations were laid under Sheshbazzar, the altar much later, during the reign of Darius. At the foundation ceremony under Sheshbazzar and Cyrus, one designated "the builder" removed the "former-times" stone from the ruins of the old temple. Later, during the reign of Darius, Zerubbabel installed it in the walls of the new temple (Zech 4:7). No date is given in Zechariah, but Haggai refers to a foundation ceremony in the 24th day of the 9th month of Darius's 2nd year (Hag 2:18). It is likely that this is the date when the אבן הראשה, the "former-times" stone, was brought out and incorporated into the new building (Zech 4:7–9).

After the statement of the dedication of the altar, the usual building account in the ancient Near East would have a description of the building and its furnishings. Instead, there is an account of a struggle between two groups (Ezra 4:1–5), an aborted letter to King Xerxes (4:6), and some letters to and from the kings Artaxerxes (4:7–22) and Darius (5:6–6:12). These were added by the historian to an original building account. The conflict between the Judeans and their "adversaries" may have been drawn from the historian's own time and reflected his own world view. As has been pointed out, Haggai and Zechariah, writing in the time of Darius, gave no indication of conflicts between various groups of people.[61]

F. *The Description of the Temple and Its Furnishings*

1. *A description of the completed temple*

This component is unaccountably missing.

59. Ellis, *Foundation Deposits*, 32–33.

60. Halpern, "Ritual Background," 177–78.

61. Bedford, *Temple Restoration*, 172–80; Halpern, "A Hisoriographic Commentary," 104.

2. *A statement that the king has built the temple according to the command of the god*

> Then Tattenai, governor of Beyond the River, Shatar-bozenai, and their colleagues did diligently just as Darius, the king, ordered. And the elders of the Jews built successfully by means of the prophesying of Haggai, the prophet, and Zechariah, son of Iddo, and they finished according to the command of the god of Israel and the command of Cyrus and Darius . . .[62] king of Persia. They completed this house on the third day of the month of Adar that was [in] the sixth year of the reign of Darius, the king. (Ezra 6:13–15, Aramaic)

Although in Aramaic, this statement is typical of building inscriptions in the ancient Near East. The switch to Aramaic in the building account is worth noting. The original building inscription may have been bilingual, Hebrew and Aramaic, as was common. Hebrew would have served the populace and Aramaic the chancellery. The historian began by using the Hebrew version and switched to the Aramaic when he inserted the Aramaic letters into his narrative. As appropriate for the Aramaic version, the credit for the temple is given to Tattenai, the satrap, and to Shatar-bozenai and his colleagues, satrapal officials. The reference to "the elders of the Jews" may have been added by the historian, or taken from the Hebrew version of the inscription.

G. The Dedication Ceremony

1. *The god takes up residence in the temple.*

This component is noticeably missing. The reference above to Zechariah and Haggai's prophecies may reflect their prophetic assurances that YHWH had reconciled himself to his people and had entered the temple.

2. *Celebration*

> And the people Israel, the priests, and the Levites and the rest of the exiles dedicated this house of God with joy. And they offered at the dedication of the house of God one hundred bulls, two hundred rams, four hundred lambs, and he-goats as a sin offering on behalf of all Israel, twelve for the twelve tribes of Israel. (Ezra 6:16–17, Aramaic)

This statement is typical of building inscriptions.

3. *Presentation of gifts and appointment of temple personnel*

> And they established priests according to their orders, and Levites according to their courses for the service of the god that is in Jerusalem [as has been prescribed]. (Ezra 6:18, Aramaic)

62. I have omitted the name of King Artaxerxes here. It was undoubtedly added by the historian who added the letters to and from that king (Ezra 4). For a discussion of this verse, see my "ʿAm Hāʾāretz in Ezra 4:4."

It is more likely that this passage is original to the building inscription than the earlier passage of Ezra 3:8–9. That one may have been a free composition of the historian based on events from his own day. Zechariah 3 seems to refer to a ceremony for the installation of the high priest. If so, it may have occurred at this point after the dedication, in the 6th year of Darius. Or the high priest could have been installed in a separate ceremony earlier, perhaps when the altar was dedicated, and the rest of the temple personnel installed after the dedication.

The source seems to end here. The historian himself added the celebration of the Passover (6:19–22), which is in Hebrew.

H. Prayer or Curses

The building account proper does not include a curse or prayer, although Darius places a very lovely one at the end of his letter. Perhaps his curse was included in the original building inscription and not repeated by the historian:

> I issue an order that anyone who changes a word of this edict—a beam shall be torn out of his house, he will be beaten and impaled upon it and his house will be made into a dunghill on account of this. May the god who [causes his name to] dwell(s) there overthrow any king or people who sends his hand to change or to harm the house of this god that is in Jerusalem. I Darius issue an order; let it be done with all diligence. (Ezra 6:11–12)

The historian seems to have doctored Darius's curse a bit to make it conform to Deuteronomistic theology.

Conclusion

The above analysis suggests that the historian who wrote Ezra 1–6 built his narrative around a typical ancient Near Eastern building story. It may even have been around the Second Temple's authentic bilingual building inscription. Nearly every component of the structure that marks the typical building account is here. The historian simply rearranged some components to suit his theological motives; the only items out of order are the notice of the altar dedication and the early notice of the priestly inauguration, both in Ezra 3. He supplemented his building account with narrative, letters, a list of returnees, and a list of temple vessels.

To interpret the basic genre of Ezra 1–6 as a building story radically restructures the understanding of the history of this period. When the components are rearranged into the order typical of building stories, it may reveal their actual historical order. The *kalû* ceremony for the demolition and rebuilding of new temples provides ideological background for events not fully explained by the building account itself. As reconstructed here, the temple was begun under Cyrus and the foundations laid by Sheshbazzar, when the "former-times" stone, the אבן הראשה, was removed by one called "the builder." It was brought out decades later by Zerubbabel and installed when the temple neared completion, probably in the 9th month of Darius's 2nd year. (The altar was dedicated in a separate ceremony two months later.) The act of incorporating the stone from the First Temple into a wall of the Second functioned as a second foundation ceremony, with the actual foundations being laid many years before. Prior to the new temple's dedication, and so long as there was building activity going on, the temple was spoken of as being in ruins, and laments were recited for it. According to this scenario, the temple was continuously under construction from the time that Sheshbazzar arrived in the reign of Cyrus until the 6th year of Darius, when it was dedicated.

Having extracted an ancient Near Eastern building story lying behind Ezra 1–6, what ought we to do with it? Can a history of the period be written on the basis of this piece of historiography? Had we before us the actual 6th-century building inscription along the lines suggested here, no one would doubt the historicity of the events described. No one doubts that Gudea built his temple or that Sennarcherib built his, for example, although, as Hurowitz has shown, their building inscriptions are just as stylized.[63] To refrain from treating the biblical text differently from other ancient historiography, I conclude (1) that Cyrus ordered Sheshbazzar to take some exiled Jews and some of YHWH's vessels that had been stored in the Esagil, to go to Jerusalem, and to build a Temple to YHWH there, (2) that he did so, and (3) that the temple was dedicated in Adar of Darius I's 6th year as a result.

Cyrus the Messiah and a Divine Quid Pro Quo

Why would Cyrus have returned the temple vessels and have allowed the Jews to rebuild the temple?[64] Temples were not built without the approval of the king.[65] Indeed, as has been seen, the Achaemenids did not automatically rebuild destroyed temples or support indigenous cults. There was a quid pro quo behind every case—and likely behind the Jerusalem temple as well. The quid behind Cyrus's quo may have been provided by Deutero-Isaiah when he handed over to Cyrus the Davidic title of "YHWH's Anointed."

According to Isa 45:1, Cyrus was YHWH's Anointed, his Messiah:

כֹּה־אָמַר יְהוָה לִמְשִׁיחוֹ לְכוֹרֶשׁ אֲשֶׁר־הֶחֱזַקְתִּי בִימִינוֹ

Thus says YHWH to his anointed, to Cyrus whom I took by his right hand.

63. This point is brought out eloquently by H. Barstad, "History and the Hebrew Bible," 60.

64. This section is taken from my article "Cyrus the Messiah?"

65. Hurowitz, *I Have Built You an Exalted House*; Kapelrud, "Temple Building"; Lundquist, *Studies on the Temple.*

What would Deutero-Isaiah have meant by this title? The process of anointing can describe a mechanism of divine selection for a specific task.[66] In the priestly writings, the high priest is described as the 'anointed priest' הכהן המשיח (Lev 4:3, 5, 16; 6:15). In the Deuteronomic history, Elijah is told by God to anoint Hazael as king of Aram (1 Kgs 19:15), Jehu son of Nimshi as king over Israel, and Elisha son of Shaphat as prophet in Elijah's place (1 Kgs 19:16).

The phrase "YHWH's anointed" has a much different connotation, however. This term refers only to the one selected by YHWH to be the legitimate ruler of the Judean people, either under the United Monarchy or in Judah alone.[67] The phrase occurs 30 times in the Hebrew Bible, half from the pen of the Deuteronomic historian. It refers to Saul 10 times (1 Sam 12:3, 5; 24:6 [twice], 10; 26:9, 11, 16, 23; 2 Sam 1:16); to David 3 times (1 Sam 16:6; 2 Sam 19:22; 23:1), and to an unnamed king of either the United Monarchy or Judah twice (1 Sam 2:35). To the historian, "YHWH's anointed" is the legitimate king, appointed and protected by YHWH (1 Sam 24:7, 11; 26:9, 11, 16, 23).[68] Outside the Deuteronomic history, the term is used in Lamentations (4:20) to refer to the last Judean king. It also appears in eight of the Psalms, in Habakkuk's prayer (3:13), and in the prayer of Hannah (1 Sam 2:10).

In the Psalms, "YHWH's anointed" is idealized, mythical. Psalm 2 opens Book I of the Psalter with a presentation of the preexilic royal Judean court theology surrounding YHWH's anointed. The decree (חק) in v. 7 legitimates the king as YHWH's son and vassal (vv. 6–7).[69] As suzerain of all the earth, YHWH gives to his anointed son all the nations as his inheritance (v. 8). This theme of sovereignty over the nations is echoed in Psalms 18 and 20. YHWH gives his anointed Davidic king victory in battle. He has placed him at the head of nations (18:44); peoples who do not know him serve him (v. 44);

66. Anointing was used to mark selection throughout the ancient Near East, most notably in the context of selection of wives and appointment of vassal kings: Dalley, "Anointing in Ancient Mesopotamia"; Kutsch, "Salbung as Rechtsakt"; de Vaux, "Le roi d'Israël, vassal de Yahvé"; Thompson, "The Anointing of Officials in Ancient Egypt"; Fleming, "The Biblical Tradition of Anointing Priests"; Viganò, "Rituals at Ebla II, ì-giš sag: A Purification Ritual or Anointing of the Head?"

67. So also Mowinckel, *He That Cometh*, 5, 7.

68. Cross, "The Judaean Royal Theology," in *Canaanite Myth and Hebrew Epic: Essays in the History of the Religion of Israel*, 241–73.

69. So Mowinckel, *The Psalms in Israel's Worship*, 62–63. Mowinckel argues this is a written document expressing YHWH's covenanted relationship with the Davidic scion. I doubt that such a written document existed; but certainly there would have been an enthronement ceremony, and this ceremony would have involved anointing. For a discussion of anointing practices in the ancient Near East and Emar in particular, see Fleming, "Biblical Tradition of Anointing Priests," and references cited there.

they come cringing as soon as he calls (v. 45). He strikes down his enemies (v. 38); they fall under his feet (v. 39). YHWH gives victory to his anointed, to his king, to David and his seed forever (v. 51).

Psalm 89 also reveals the preexilic theology of the Davidic king. It most likely stems from the exile. There is no hope of a return or restoration in it; the exile itself is readily apparent (vv. 39ff.).[70] As a whole, the psalm describes the pain of being abandoned by God after the fall of Jerusalem. It suggests that prior to the fall, an eternal Davidic dynasty was expected. The Davidic king is YHWH's anointed (vv. 21, 39, 52), YHWH's servant (vv. 4, 21, 51), but his hand has not been upheld in battle, his sword has been turned back, and all his fortified cities have been breached. If it is correct to date this psalm to the exile at the latest, then an exilic Isaianic writer and his audience would have known the Davidic myth, they would have known of an eternal Davidic covenant (v. 29), and they would have experienced the disappointment and rejection of its apparent collapse.

Persian Rulers and Local Royal Court Theology

How then, knowing the full theology associated with the term YHWH's Anointed, could Deutero-Isaiah have applied it to Cyrus, a Persian? This needs to be understood against the background of the initial years of the Achaemenid Empire. During the reigns of Cyrus, Cambyses, and Darius, priests of powerful temples delivered up to their Persian conquerors the titles and theologies surrounding their local kings. Udjaḥorrsnet gave to the Persian victors Cambyses and Darius the title "Pharaoh" (see p. 63) and the Marduk priesthood styled Cambyses "King of Babylon" and Cyrus "King of Lands" (see p. 30). In return, the Temple of Neith in Sais was spared ends meted out to other Egyptian temples, and the Babylonians were relieved of taxes and corvée labor. So it was with Isaiah and the Jerusalem temple.

Cyrus, משיח יהוה

An examination of the undisputed Cyrus songs in the book of Isaiah (Isa 41:1–4; 41:25, 26; 44:24–28; 45:1–8, 9–13; 46:8–11; 48:14–16a) reveals

70. Schniedewind, *Society and the Promise to David,* 111ff. For other opinions, see Sarna, "Psalm 89: A Study in Inner Biblical Exegesis"; and Fishbane, *Biblical Interpretation in Ancient Israel,* 466–67. Schniedewind dates the first third of the psalm (vv. 2–19) to the 10th century and the emerging monarchy, the second third (20–38) to the period of Josiah, and the final third to the fall of Judea. Verses 6–15 may have been adapted from an ancient Ugaritic hymn, but I find it difficult to assign vv. 2–5 (which speak of the Davidic covenant) and vv. 16–19 (which refer to God as קְדוֹשׁ יִשְׂרָאֵל 'the Holy One of Israel') to the 10th century. The latter phrase occurs 25 times in the book of Isaiah and 6 times in the rest of the *Tanak.* Williamson (*The Book Called Isaiah,* 41–45) concludes that the title originates with the 8th-century Isaianic writer and is not earlier.

that, like Udjaḥorresnet in Egypt and the priests of Marduk in Babylon, Deutero-Isaiah handed over to Cyrus the royal Judean title of "YHWH's Anointed," as well as the entire royal Judean court theology associated with it. The Davidic themes of victory for the anointed king, of nations falling under his feet are now applied to Cyrus. Instead of the Davidic monarch, as in Psalms 2, 18, and 20, it is Cyrus, the newly anointed king (Isa 45:1ff.) who subdues nations.[71] The following Cyrus songs illustrate the application of the Davidic theology to Cyrus:

> 2. Who has stirred up one from the east?
> Righteousness calls his every step.
> He places nations before him, he subdues kings.
> He makes their swords dust;
> Like chaff, their bows are driven.
> 3. He pursues them and passes on safely,
> The path does not touch his feet.
> 4. Who performed and did [this],
> calling generations from the beginning?
> I, YHWH, am first, and with the last, I am He. (Isa 41:2–4a)
>
> 25. I stirred up one from the north, and he has come,
> From the rising of the sun, he is mine.[72]
> 26a. He shall trample on rulers as on mortar,
> as the potter treads clay. (Isa 41:25–26a)
>
> 1. Thus says YHWH to his Anointed: "To Cyrus, whose right hand I have grasped
> To subdue nations before him and strip kings of their robes,
> To open doors before him—the gates shall not be closed:
> 2. I will go before you and give access to their cities.
> I will break in pieces the doors of bronze and cut through the bars of iron." (Isa 45:1, 2)

Instead of the Davidic monarch, it is now Cyrus for whom YHWH subdues kings (41:2), for whom he make their swords dust, their bows like chaff (41:2). He causes Cyrus to trample on rulers like mortar, like the potter treads the clay (41:25); he causes Cyrus to subdue nations and humiliate kings (45:1).

71. So also Motyer (*The Prophecy of Isaiah*, 357), who cites Psalms 1 and 110.

72. Vocalized with the Greek to the *Niphal*, "He is called by my name." However, if the prophet described Cyrus as calling upon YHWH by name, it would not be a problem. The Egyptians also described Cambyses and Darius as calling upon the Egyptian gods, and the priests of Marduk described Cyrus as calling upon the Babylonian god. These poems do not present Cyrus as he really was but only as he was perceived.

Along with the title "Anointed," Cyrus is called My Shepherd, the one whom YHWH loves, both epithets of the Davidic king:

24b. I am YHWH, who does anything.
26b. Who says to Jerusalem, Be inhabited!
And to the cities of Judah, Be built!
And to her ruins, I set them up.
28. who says to Cyrus, "My Shepherd."
All my purpose, he will fulfill.
Saying to Jerusalem: Be built!
And to the temple: Be re-founded! (Isa 44:24b, 26b, 28)

14b. YHWH loves him
He performs his purpose against Babylon;
His arm is against the Chaldeans.
15. I, even I, I have spoken,
I even I called him.
I have brought him,
and made his way a success. (Isa 48:14b, 15)

It is now Cyrus as YHWH's shepherd—not the Davidic king—who fulfills YHWH's purposes (46:11; 48:14, 15). YHWH's purpose is clear:

13. I have aroused him (Cyrus) in righteousness,
I have made all his paths straight
He shall rebuild my cities,
And send out my exiled ones,
And not for a price or a bribe,
Says YHWH of Hosts. (Isa 45:13)

In these poems, Cyrus is YHWH's Anointed, his Shepherd, his Beloved, and the one who fulfills all his purposes. YHWH takes Cyrus by the hand, and him alone he calls in righteousness (or in legitimacy). These are the titles of the Davidic monarch. By so labeling him, the writer proclaims Cyrus and his descendants to be the legitimate Davidic kings, rightful heirs of David's line.

His audience understood this and was aghast. How could the prophet imply that God had handed over to a foreigner a theology that belonged to the Davidic ruler? The prophet rebukes them; YHWH has made heaven and earth; he has made them, and he will do as he pleases.

9. Woe to the one who strives with his Maker,
earthen vessel with the potter!
Does the clay say to the one who fashions it,
"What are you making?" or "Your work has no handles"?
10. Woe to anyone who says to a father,
"What are you begetting?"

or to a woman, "With what are you in labor?"
11. Thus says YHWH, the Holy One of Israel, and its
Maker: Will you question me about my children,[73]
or command me concerning the work of my hands?
12. I made the earth, and created humankind upon it;
it was my hands that stretched out the skies;
I commanded all their host.
13. I have aroused him in righteousness,
and I will make all his paths straight;
he shall build my city,
and send out my exiles.
Not for a price and not for a bribe,
Says YHWH *Ṣebāʾôt.* (Isa 45:9–13)

As did Udjaḥorresnet and the priests of Marduk, Deutero-Isaiah helped to install the Persian conqueror as the legitimate Judean king. The reasons that motivated those priests would have motivated Deutero-Isaiah as well. Self-interest was likely one important reason. Yet, like these others, a second reason would have been crucial for him: Isaiah would have been convinced that Cyrus was YHWH's Anointed because Cyrus was restoring the *status quo ante.* Cyrus had agreed to rebuild the temple, to replace the temple vessels in it, and to enable the Jews to return to worship YHWH in Zion restored. Bedford recognizes that the Persian conquerors stressed their legitimacy by appropriating local norms in Egypt and Babylon but adds that they did not adopt the role and titulary of smaller states such as Judah.[74] It appears, however, that they did.

This quid pro quo was, of course, not the only reason that Cyrus permitted the Jews to return to Judah and to rebuild their temple in Jerusalem. Primary may have been the Persian emperor's abhorrence of uncultivated land (Xenophon, *Oec.* 4.8). The Temple to Osiris and Isis at the southern end of the Kharga Oasis was an exception to the general demise of Egyptian temples during Persian occupation.[75] This oasis was dotted with tunnels (*qanat*s), each taking five years to construct. The permission and the means to build and to establish a viable settlement in what had been an arid desert zone would have to have come from the king himself. Because no city or town could exist without its temple, one was necessarily built for Osiris and Isis when the settlement was established.

73. Emending הָאֹתִיּוֹת שְׁאָלוּנִי to הָאֹתִי תְשְׁאָלוּנִי with BHS.
74. Bedford, *Temple Restoration*, 141.
75. See p. 79 and n. 157 there.

The Jewish settlement in Yehud and their temple in Jerusalem would not have warranted less attention.[76] It is likely that the initial cost of the building and its maintenance came from the satrapal treasury (Ezra 1:2; 6:4, 8) and was funneled through the bureaucracy, as would have been the case at the Kharga Oasis.[77] The response of the Jews of Judah to the destruction was, in the end, no different from the response of the Jews of Elephantine. Jews in Babylon, likely under the leadership of Second Isaiah, appealed to the Persian authorities to rebuild the temple. In the Persian Empire, only the king held the power to make these decisions. For YHWH's Temple in Jerusalem, it was Cyrus who made the initial decree and Darius who honored it. This is the pattern in the Udjaḥoressnet and Gadatas inscriptions as well.

The Political Organization of Persian Period Yehud

According to Wellhausen, the old institutions of prophet and king had perished in the conflagration of 586. Because foreign rule did not permit the reinstatement of the monarchy, and because prophetic ideas did not suffice to build a state, the temple priesthood rose to fill the vacuum.[78] The priesthood had the power and the freedom, and felt themselves to have the obligation, to direct a new Israel ruled by God alone—that is, by themselves, in a self-governing theocracy. But was there a power vacuum?

Was There a Power Vacuum in Yehud?

Data from Babylon, Egypt, and Asia Minor suggest that a power vacuum would not have been possible during the Persian period. Every province had an imperial governor, every satrapy a satrap. When the governor or satrap was absent (called to Susa, for example, or to war), the imperially appointed head of the garrison ruled the province or satrapy and implemented his master's orders. The Arsames letters show that even when away from the province the satrap remained completely in charge. This would have been true in Yehud as well.

As elsewhere, Persian governors continuously ruled Yehud, and we know their names. Most informative is a hoard of 67 bullas and 2 seals, purchased on the antiquities market and published by Nachmun Avigad.[79] This collection of bullas is homogenous and appears to come from a single archive. The presence in it of several bullas stamped with the name of the province, plus

76. Pace Bedford (*Temple Restoration,* 305), who views temple construction as a political act, a first step to the creation of an independent kingdom.

77. Blenkinsopp, "Did the Second Jerusalemite Temple Possess Land?"

78. Wellhausen, *Prolegomena,* 420.

79. Avigad, *Bullae and Seals from a Post-exilic Judean Archive.*

personal names with their titles, reveals an official archive. Joined with literary data, papyri, and coins, the bullas enable us to form a list of Judean governors for the Persian period.

Governors of Judah

1. Sheshbazzar ("a certain Šešbaṣar, whom he [Cyrus] had made governor [פחה]," Ezra 5:14), 538–522 B.C.E.[80] It is not likely that he was a Davidide.[81]
2. Zerubbabel, son of Shealtiel ('governor of Judah' פחת יהודה, Hag 1:1, 14), 522–516 (?). Zerubbabel was the grandson of Jehoiakin, the king of Judah who was exiled to Babylon in 597 (1 Chr 3:17, 18).[82]
3. Elnatan ('belonging to Elnatan the governor' לאלנתן פחוא, in Aramaic on a bulla and on a seal from Avigad's hoard of bullas and seals), end of 6th century (515[?]–495?).

A seal inscribed "Belonging to Shelomith, maidservant of Elnatan [the] gov[ernor]" was also part of this archive. The word אמת 'maidservant' is the feminine equivalent of 'servant' עבד, a high official of either the king or the governor. This Shelomith may have been the daughter of Zerubbabel. A Shelomith is listed among Zerubbabel's children (1 Chr 3:19); it would be unlikely for her to be listed unless she were an important personage in her own right, important enough to have her own seal.[83] She may have been married to Elnatan, the governor, since אמת also connotes a wife.

The following names have been found stamped on the handles of storage jars, rarely on the bodies. The stamps are in Aramaic script, and their paleography places the names generally between 500 and 450 B.C.E.[84] Most have the word *yhwd*, a personal name, and the Aramaic word for governor, *pḥwʾ*. Unfortunately, the paleography cannot provide an order for the names.

80. Some scholars who do not agree that Sheshbazzar and Zerubbabel were governors base this opinion on their view that Judah was part of Samaria (cf. Weinberg, "Central and Local Administration in the Achaemenid Empire"). This is discussed below. Others argue that Judah was autonomous and ruled by local assemblies. This too is discussed below.

81. Berger, "Zu den Namen *ššbṣr*."

82. In Haggai, Zerubbabel is called son of Shealtiel. In 1 Chronicles he is said to be the son of Pedaiah, Shealtiel's brother; in either case he is the grandson of Johoiakin, king of Judah.

83. E. M. Meyers, "The Shelomith Seal."

84. Avigad, *Bullae*, 23–28; Carter, *The Emergence of Yehud*; Christophe, *The Yehud Stamped Jar Handle Corpus*; E. Stern, *Material Culture*, 202–13. Stern disagrees with this assessment. He follows the view of Alt (*Die Rolle Samarias*) that there were no governors in Yehud between Zerubbabel and Nehemiah. Christophe's statistical tests disprove this hypothesis (*The Yehud Stamped Jar Handle Corpus*, 187–89).

4. *Yehoʿezer* (ca. 495–445). Four stamps from Ramat Raḥel and one from Jerusalem's City of David are inscribed יהוד / יהועזר / פחוא 'Judah / Yehoʿezer / Governor'. Eight from Ramat Raḥel and one from Jericho are simply inscribed ליהעזר 'Belonging to Yehoʿezer'.
5. *Aḥaziya* (ca. 495–445). Nine stamps from Jerusalem's City of David, five from Ramat Raḥel, and one from Jericho are inscribed לאחזי / פחוא 'Belonging to Aḥaziya, the governor'.
6. *Uriah* (ca. 495–445). One stamp from Jericho reads יהוד / אוריו 'Yehud/Uriah'. Uriah may not have been a governor, since the word פחוא does not appear on his seal. However, given the fact that Yehoʿezer has nine seals that simply say "Belonging to Yehoʿezer," he may have been.
7. *Ḥananah* (ca. 495–445). Two stamps from Ramat Raḥel and two from the city of David read יהוד / חננה 'Yehud / Ḥananah'. This may be the seal of Ḥanani / Ḥananiah, whom Nehemiah appointed over Jerusalem, or it may be the seal of the governor directly preceding Nehemiah, who informed him about Jerusalem (Neh 1:1). Lemaire makes the intriguing suggestion, however, that he may have been the second son of Zerubbabel (1 Chr 3:19).[85]

The following governors appear in the literary and papyrus sources.

8. *Nehemiah* (445–410?). Neh 5:14, "From the time he commanded me to be their governor in the land of Judah, from the 20th to the 32nd year of King Artaxerxes [I]. . . ." The total length of Nehemiah's tenure is not given. In the 32nd year of Artaxerxes he was recalled (Neh 13:6). "After some time" he returned to Jerusalem (13:7), where he remained at least until the high priesthood of Yehoiada, son of Eliashib (Neh 13:28).
9. *Bagavahya* (ca. 410–370?). In 407, the Elephantine Jews sent a letter (*TAD* A.4.7), "To our lord, Bagavahya, governor of Judah (פחת יהוד)." The letter states that they had written to Bagavahya three years before (lines 17–18). Thus, Bagavahya had been governor at least between 410 and 407, and probably much longer. He most likely directly followed Nehemiah. If 410 marked the beginning of Bagavahya's reign, then Nehemiah would have been governor for 35 years.[86]

The following is based on numismatic data.

10. *Yeḥizqiyah* (370?–333?). Several minute silver coins bearing the legend יחזקיה הפחה 'Yeḥizqiyah (Hezekiah), the governor' in paleo-Hebrew

85. Lemaire, "Zorobabel et la Judée," 56.
86. These dates are discussed more fully below.

have been found, but not in a controlled excavation. The date is therefore disputed. One coin has his name, title, and the name of the province, [יה[ד.[87] Most are without the name of the province; some exist without his title. Numismatists have dated these coins from the end of the Persian period into the Macedonian.[88] Avigad suggests the late date based on association with a high priest Ezikias, mentioned by Josephus (*Ag. Ap.* 1.187–89), who would have been 66 years old in 312 under Ptolemy.[89] This identification is not necessary, however, since the name was quite common.[90] Meshorer dates these coins to the middle of the 4th century and later. Yeḥizqiyah's tenure as governor probably began after Bagavahya's ended. He was most likely the last governor of Yehud before the Macedonian conquest and may have continued as governor under Alexander.[91] If the two governors served an equal amount of time, Bagavahya would have governed from 410 to 370, and Yeḥizqiyah from 370 to 330. These are reigns of 40 years each. These lengths are realistic but remain guesses.[92] Barag

87. Deutsch, "Six Unrecorded 'Yehud' Silver Coins," 6.

88. Machinist ("The First Coins of Judah and Samaria," 369–71) argues for a Macedonian date on the basis of the lack of title on some of these coins. This indicates to him a change in status of the province. He also argues for the late date on the basis of the spelling יהודה, which differs from the spelling found in other clearly Achaemenid coins (יהד, יהוד). It also differs from later Ptolemaic spellings (*yhdh*). If Machinist is correct, Yeḥizqiyah continued as governor under Alexander. See now my article "A Silver Coin of Yoḥanan Hakkôhēn," and n. 91 below.

89. Avigad, *Bullae and Seals*, 29.

90. Meshorer, *Ancient Jewish Coinage*, 1.33. Thackeray (trans. of Josephus, *Against Apion*, 238) points out that Ezekias was not the *high* priest. The high priest during this period was Onias (*Ant.* 11.347).

91. Meshorer, *Ancient Jewish Coinage*, 1.34. Meshorer compares this coin to the Samarian coins from a cave at the Wadi Daliyeh, which have a clear provenience. A similar coin from Samaria is in paleo-Hebrew and inscribed שמרין 'Shomron', "Samaria." Five coins are inscribed with the name ירבעם 'Jeroboam'. The coins from the cave were minted between 350 and 333. Meshorer places the Yeḥezqiyah coin in the same period as the Jeroboam coin, around 350. The absence of a title in the Jeroboam coin indicates that the lack of title in the Yeḥezqiyah coin cannot imply a Macedonian date. Mildenberg ("Yehud: A Preliminary Study of the Provincial Coinage of Judea," 188) dates the coin with a title to the end of the Persian period and the one without a title to the Macedonian. Yet, he points out that the coin is an imitation of "one of the most popular Greek designs, a type created about 406 by the Syracusan engraver Kimon and widely copied in Sicily, Magna Graecia, continental Greece, Asia Minor and Syria–Palestine around the turn of the fifth and throughout the fourth century." See Meshorer and Qedar, *The Coinage of Samaria*, 14, 49.

92. Mazday probably became satrap of Cilicia in 361 and as a general "almost defeated Alexander." He surrendered the city of Babylon to him in 333. Alexander appointed him satrap of Babylon, and he served in this capacity until his death in 328 (Mildenberg,

suggests that the beardless male on the coin is Yeḥizqiyah.[93] If so, then Yeḥizqiyah was a eunuch and could not have been a priest.

If the suppositions are correct, this constitutes a complete list of Persian-period governors.[94]

Was Judah Originally Part of Samaria?

This list of governors suggests that Judah had been a separate province in the Persian satrapy Ebar Nahara from the time of the first return under Cyrus. Alt argues that, when Judah fell to the Babylonians, Cyrus appointed Gedalia in charge of Judah, but under Samaria's supervision—a status it retained under the first Persian emperors.[95] Nehemiah's visit marked a change in Achaemenid policy: only then did Judah achieve provincial status with its own governor. This renewal of Judean independence caused the conflict between Judah and its neighbors, especially Samaria, because it meant a real diminution of Samarian power.

Several arguments against Alt's theory have been put forward. Smith brings to bear Neh 5:15:

> The first governors (הפחות) who were before me oppressed the people; they took food and wine from them plus forty shekels of silver from each.[96] Even their servants ruled over the people. But I did not do such a thing, because of the fear of God.

The point in Neh 5:15 would be lost if Nehemiah had not been preceded by men of his own rank, the rank of governor of Judah.[97] McEvenue contends

"Notes on the Coin Issues of Mazday," 9–10). Presumably, he was not a young man when he was appointed satrap of Cilicia and must have served in high-level positions for at least ten years before.

93. Barag, "A Silver Coin of Yoḥanan and the High Priest," 9. Caution is advised, however, in seeing known personages on coins (Harrison, *Coins of the Persian Satraps*).

94. Even if this is not a complete list and some names are missing, a governor would have been assigned by Persia to the province at all times. Carter (*The Emergence of Yehud*, 280) assumes that the existence of a complete line of governors from Zerubbabel to Yeḥizqiyah "indicates a substantial level of autonomy [in Judah] in carrying out *internal* provincial affairs [emphasis his]." By internal, he means that Judah had no foreign policy or army. He views the relationship between the state of New York and the United States as analogous. This is not the conclusion I would draw from this list of Persian governors of Yehud. For one thing, New York elects its own governors; they are not appointed by Washington.

95. Alt, "Die Rolle Samarias bei der Entstehung des Judentums."

96. Changing *ʾaḥar* to *ʾeḥad*.

97. M. Smith, "Appendix: Alt's Account of the Samaritans," *Palestinian Parties and Politics That Shaped the Old Testament*, 196. For a discussion of Judah's relationship to Samaria, see my "ʿAm Hāʾāretz in Ezra 4:4."

that the term פחה in postexilic Biblical Hebrew could have more than one meaning and that Smith's argument is not valid.[98] More telling is Avigad's work on coins and bullas referred to above.[99] Avigad points out that the term יהוד/יהד in Aramaic on coins, bullas, and jar handles marks Judah as a separate administrative unit beginning in the 6th century and that the term פחוא ('governor') on them indicates that it was a province with a separate provincial governor.[100] Stern argues that these bullas and coins are later than Nehemiah and that a change in Judah's status took effect then.[101] Neither Stern nor McEvenue discusses the epigraphy. The shape of the *waw* in פחו places the bullas in the generation immediately after Zerubbabel, however: the late 6th or the beginning of the 5th century.[102] The work of Avigad and of Meyers[103] indicates that the term פחה on these 6th-century bullas refers to the office of the Judean provincial governor. Nehemiah was not Judah's first governor, and we know the names of those who preceded him. Although all but one had Yahwistic names, these governors must be considered Persian. They ruled at the discretion of satrap and king.[104]

Did Local Elites Participate in Governing Yehud?

Although there may have been Persian governors over the province of Yehud beginning from the time of Cyrus, the theory of self-governance assumes that they had no real power and that the province was self-governing.

The role of the governor is suggested by Widengren:

> When the interests of the Persian government were not directly involved, the province was a self-governing body. It was the task of the governor to pass judgments and collect taxes in order to have the sums handed over to the royal treasury. In other affairs, the governor collaborated with the assembly representing the population. This assembly was composed exclusively of Jews, the sons of the exiles, as they are called (Ezra 10:7).[105]

98. McEvenue, "The Political Structure in Judah from Cyrus to Nehemiah."

99. Avigad, *Bullae and Seals.*

100. Ibid., 6.

101. Stern, "Seal-Impressions in the Achaemenid Style in the Province of Judah"; idem, "The Archeology of Persian Palestine," 113; idem, *Material Culture of the Land of the Bible in the Persian Period 538–332,* 206. Stern reiterated his position recently in his *Archaeology of the Land of the Bible,* 2.355, 545–50.

102. Williamson, "The Governors of Judah under the Persians," 64; Avigad, *Bullae and Seals,* 6. Machinist states emphatically that, if Avigad's dating of the bullas is correct, then "Alt's celebrated theory . . . would have to fall" (Machinist, "The First Coins of Judah and Samaria," 373).

103. E. M. Meyers, "The Shelomith Seal."

104. That the satrap could appoint governors is evident from the Xanthus inscription.

105. Widengren, "The Persian Period," 522.

Meyer also argues that, "when the interests of the Persian empire were not under consideration, the subject peoples had free hand in their own affairs. So we find in Judah an extensive self-administration."[106] Meyer suggests that Persian period Yehud was governed by 150 family leaders (ראשי בית האבות), who formed a "Collegium der 'Obersten' oder 'Vorsteher.'"[107] Presumably, as the predecessor to the Sanhedrin, it represented the people, advised on community matters, and supervised the execution of community decisions.[108] Men from this college would have formed the nation's law courts, either as one body in Jerusalem or individually in their separate villages. According to Meyer, this was the same constitution as in preexilic times, except that the Persian governor had taken the place of the king. According to Blenkinsopp, these men even filled "the leading role when the office of governor may have been vacant."[109] Real power, the power to control and direct the resources of the state, lay in the hands of Jewish governing bodies.

The only evidence offered for this legislative body of 150 family leaders is Neh 5:17.[110] There it reads: "One hundred fifty Jews and officials plus those coming to us from the nations round about came to my table." Meyer correctly notes that this was one way in which officials were paid. The large amount of food consumed daily (one ox, six sheep, plus fowl) suggests that the men who ate at Nehemiah's table took food home for their families and servants, as was the custom.[111] Xenophon states that an obligation of each satrap (and presumably each provincial governor) was to model his own court on the court of the king (*Cyr.* 8.6.10–13). The Greek authors describe the lavish table of the Great King as well as that of the satrapal courts at Sardis, Samos, Daskyleion, and Kelainai.[112] The description given by Nehemiah is comparable, considering that his was a provincial, not a satrapal court.

106. Meyer, *Die Entstehung des Judentums,* 131.

107. Ibid., 134.

108. Ibid. The historicity of the Sanhedrin has been debated recently. After a careful study of rabbinic, Christian, and historical sources, Sanders (*Judaism: Practice and Belief, 63 BCE–66 CE,* 475) concludes, "there was no body that combined judicial and legislative powers" in the Roman period. Sanders continues, "there were of course both judicial and advisory bodies. (There were no legislative assemblies. This is not even in the Misnah.) Every ruler had councillors and everyone believed that accused criminals should be formally tried according to some legal system. . . . There is no good evidence for the existence of 'the Sanhedrin.'"

109. Blenkinsopp, *Ezra–Nehemiah,* 66–67.

110. Meyer, *Die Entstehung des Judentums,* 132.

111. I have been told that the amount of meat from one ox and six sheep is 800 pounds.

112. For an overview, see Briant, *HEP,* 357–58.

As Meyer correctly notes, the men who ate at Nehemiah's table served in his government. Whether or not they were Jews, they were Persian officials, סגנים and חורים (Neh 5:17).[113] Egyptian parchments and papyri reveal that, except for scribes and translators who were necessarily local, officials in satrapal courts were Iranian and secondarily Babylonian. This was true even of the men in charge of the דגל, the military unit of the Jewish garrison at Elephantine.

Iranians and Babylonians officiated in the satrapy Beyond the River as well. Ezra 4:9 refers to:

> רחום בעל־טעם ושמשי ספרא ושאר כנותהון דיניא ואפרסתכיא טרפליא אפרסיא ארכוי בבליא שושנכיא דהוא עלמיא:
>
> Reḥum the Chancellor and Šimšai the scribe and the rest of their colleagues: the judges, the investigators, the officials—men from Persia, Uruk, Babylon, Susa, that is, Elam.

Reḥum was the chancellor of Ebar Nahara. He was likely a Babylonian Jew; Riḫim son of Baniah appears among the Murašu documents.[114] He is accompanied by a scribe, judges, envoys, and officials. As in Egypt, the officials of Beyond the River came from central cities of the Persian empire: Uruk, Babylon, and Susa itself.[115] Like the satrapal court, a provincial court also needed heralds, scribes, judges, and accountants. All these would have eaten at Nehemiah's table. They may have been Jewish, but they would not have been local heads of family houses. The presence of Jews in Arsames' administration in Egypt indicates that Jews participated as imperial officials in various satrapal organizations around the empire. This was so in Judah as well. Nehemiah, a Jew, grew up in Susa. He served not as a Jew, but as a Persian governor. The Jews who ate at Nehemiah's table did so not as Jews, but—like Nehemiah himself—as imperial appointees of the Achaemenid king.

Was There a Popular Legislative Assembly or a Council of Elders?

According to Meyer and those who follow him, below the college of 150 heads of fathers' houses, was the popular assembly, or *qāhāl* (קהל), which formed the lower house of the provincial government.[116] Albertz, for ex-

113. The word חורים should be substituted for יהודים here, with the versions. The word יהודים may have been a misreading of חורים.

114. Zadok, *The Jews of Babylonia*, 48.

115. These are Persian officials, not people deported into Samaria by Ashurbanipal (Ezra 4:10), as is glossed by the redactor. See my "ʿAm Hāʾāretz in Ezra 4:4 and Persian Imperial Administration."

116. Meyer, *Die Entstehung des Judentums*, 132; Albertz, *History of Israelite Religion*, 2.446ff.; Widengren, "The Persian Period," 522–23.

ample, posits not one but three legislative houses: The first, a lay body, was composed of men called חורים ('prominent men, nobles') in the Nehemiah memoir but called שבי יהודיא ('elders of Judah') or ראשי האבות ('heads of the fathers' houses') by the redactor of the Ezra–Nehemiah books. The second was the priestly college. It was composed of priests, Levites, and other temple personnel and headed by the high priest. This body was organized like the first by 'fathers' houses' בית אבות. Below these two governing bodies stood the popular assembly, קהל, summoned every now and then when important decisions were due.[117]

Ezra 9 and 10 provide the only evidence for the power of the קהל: Ezra 9:1–2 states: "After these things were completed, the authorities שרים (*śārîm*) met with me and said that 'the people Israel, the priests, and the Levites have not separated themselves from the peoples of the lands. . . . and the authorities שרים, and the magistrates סגנים, are the first in this treachery.'"[118] The instigation for separation came not from the people or the קהל but from the authorities, the שרים. When Ezra heard this he tore his garment and his cloak, pulled the hair from his head and beard, and sat desolate (9:3). As he wept and prayed before the temple, a "very great assembly (קהל) of men, women, and children gathered to him, weeping" (10:1). This statement provides the evidence for the קהל; yet, if the assembly included women and children, it was not a legislative body, but a gathering.[119]

The passage continues:

> [They] sent out a herald (קול) throughout all Judah and Jerusalem—to all the members of the גולה community[120]—to gather in Jerusalem. All who would not come in three days according to the direction (עצת) of the authorities (השרים) and elders (הזקנים) would have their [movable] property utterly destroyed (יחרם) and would be separated from the assembly of the גולה community. (Ezra 10:7–8)

The verse does not say who the "they" were who sent out the herald. It has been assumed that it was the assembly, the קהל, and that it had the power to send out heralds, order attendance, confiscate property, and order divorces.[121]

117. Albertz, *A History of Israelite Religion*, 2.446–48.

118. These verses include what must surely be a later elaboration (if any of this is historical), ". . . whose abominations are like those of the Canaanites, the Hittites, Perizzites, the Jebusites, the Ammonites, the Moabites, the Egyptians, and the Amorites, for they have taken wives from among their daughters for themselves and their sons and have mixed the holy seed with the peoples of the lands."

119. The Akkadian word *puḫru* also has this double connotation. It can refer to a casual gathering or to a group of men called for a specific purpose (*CAD* P, unpublished manuscript).

120. That is, the exiles and their descendants.

121. Meyer, *Die Entstehung des Judentums*, 132; Blenkinsopp, *Ezra–Nehemiah*, 175.

This would give it quite a bit of authority, suggesting a type of self-rule. However, it was not the קהל (consisting, as noted above, of men, women, and children) that had the judicial power to give such orders, but the שרים, the imperially appointed official magistrates.

Kaufmann suggests that the real power in the province was the council of "princes" and elders (עצת השרים והזקנים) mentioned in the present verse.[122] All references to these "elders" are in Ezra, none in Nehemiah. The term occurs in Aramaic (שביא) in Tattenai's letter (5:9) and the letter's introduction (5:5); in Darius's response to it (6:7, 8); and in the result of the response, the dedication of the temple (6:14). It occurs in Hebrew in the passage quoted above (10:8), and the elders are paired with the judges of every town (10:14) to hear divorce cases.[123] Except perhaps for Tattenai's letter and Darius's response, all these passages stem from the hand of the historian—not his sources. Darius's response repeats the words in the letter he received, but would the historical Tattenai have used such a term, and what would he have meant by it?[124]

Dandamayev has studied the role of the *šibū* 'elders' from Neo-Babylonian and Persian-period Babylonian texts.[125] By this period, a city's elders were the citizens who possessed land within the city's districts. They were entitled to sit as witnesses in the *puḫru.* The cases they heard were cases of property disputes and private cases of a local nature. They did not speak or otherwise participate in the proceedings but served as witnesses only.

The situation displayed in the book of Ezra agrees with this picture. Japhet asks how likely it would have been for Tattenai, Darius's newly appointed under-satrap of Beyond the River, to negotiate directly with the elders of the Jews. Would he not have turned to his own subordinate, Zerubbabel, the governor of Yehud?[126] Indeed, it is not likely; however, negotiation is not portrayed here but only an interrogation. Dandamayev points out that "sometimes important instructions from high ranking officials were announced in the presence of the elders."[127] This is the situation here. Second, the reference to "the governor" may have dropped out of the

122. Kaufmann, *History,* 4.206–7.

123. It also occurs in Hebrew in Ezra 3:12, but it is customarily translated there as "old men."

124. Tattenai is known from a cuneiform text to have been governor of Ebar Nahra during the reign of Darius under Ushtanni, satrap of Babylon and Across the River (Olmstead, "Tattenai, Governor of 'Across the River' "; Ungnad, "Keilinschriftliche Beiträge zum Buch Esra und Ester"). In a clean sweep, Darius likely expelled the governors and satraps in office under Cyrus and Cambyses.

125. Dandamayev, "The Neo-Babylonian Elders."

126. Japhet, "Sheshbazzar and Zerubbabel," 82.

127. Dandamayev, "Neo-Babylonian Elders," 40. This is also seen in Nehemiah 5.

text. The entire phrase "the governor and the elders" is present in Darius's response.

Additional references to the elders occur in Ezra 10:8, 14. They are involved there in their normal role as witnesses in cases of confiscation of property and divorce proceedings. The reference to them does not imply an active participation. Both the instigation for the divorces and the sanctions imposed for those failing to comply were by order of the שרים, not the elders (9:1; 10:7). The divorce cases were tried by provincial judges; the elders served as witnesses in the assembly (10:14). As in Mesopotamia, decisions may be stated as having been made in the name of the officials and the elders, but the elders did not speak during the proceedings.[128] As elsewhere, there were no legislative assemblies; there was no self-government.

Nehemiah's Mission and the Ensuing Political Struggle

The Power of the Provincial Governor

Theories of self-governance assume that the legislative assembly or the council of elders held the real power in Judah because the governor had no ability to enforce his orders.[129] According to Widengren:

> The governor had no Persian troops under his command. For the defense of Jerusalem, he had to rely on the clans and families. . . . The clans and their chiefs were called up to defend the people in critical situations (Neh 4:13).[130]

Data from Babylon, Egypt, and Asia Minor demonstrate, however, that every governor had garrisons of soldiers under him, installed in the various cities of his povince. This was also true of Judah. Nehemiah went to Jerusalem to rebuild the gates of the citadel (בירה) and the wall (חומה) of the city (Neh 2:8):[131]

> ואגרת אל־אסף שמר הפרדס אשר למלך אשר יתן־לי עצים לקרות את־שערי
> הבירה אשר־לבית ולחומת העיר ולבית אשר־אבוא אליו ויתן־לי המלך
> כיד־אלהי הטובה עלי׃

128. This role for the elders is also exhibited in Ruth 4:1–6. Elders were called to serve as witnesses to the transaction, but they did not participate directly in it.

129. This section is based on my article "The Political Struggle of Fifth-Century Judah."

130. Widengren, "The Persian Period," 523.

131. The existence of a Nehemiah and his actual memoir within the book of Nehemiah has been accepted by even the so-called "minimalist" scholar Grabbe (*Ezra–Nehemiah*, 155). The scholarly consensus includes in it Neh 1:1–7:5, portions of 12:27–43, and 13:4–31. This is the view taken here. Some few do not include the portion from Nehemiah 13, but the section seems entirely consistent with the rest of his memoir.

> . . . A letter to Asaph, director of the royal *pardes*, that he may give me wood to cut for the gates of the temple citadel (בירה), for the city wall (חומה), and for the house that I shall occupy, the king granted me, for the good hand of my God was upon me.

The term בירה is a loanword from Akkadian *birtu*. It is a fortress or citadel for garrisoning soldiers.[132] The term is well attested throughout the Achaemenid Empire, appearing extensively in the Egyptian papyri to refer to the garrison cities of Elephantine and Syene. The city of Xanthus was also a בירה housing a garrison, and so was Jerusalem.

Xenophon distinguishes two types of citadels: those with ἄκρα garrisons that guarded urban centers, and those with χώρα garrisons to guard the countryside (*Cyr.* 8.6ff., *Oec.* 4.5–11).[133] Nehemiah came to Judah to rebuild the ἄκρα in Jerusalem.[134] Did he bring foreign imperial troops with him to man the ἄκρα, or did he staff it with local Judean soldiers? Hints in these passages of Xenophon suggest that ἄκρα garrisons were manned by "King's Men" in a way that χώρα garrisons were not.[135] Since Nehemiah was fortifying an ἄκρα, not a χώρα garrison, he fortified it with "King's Men." A similar unit of "King's Men" formed part of the Assyrian army, and descriptions of it are available in cuneiform sources.[136] "King's Men" included three types of personnel: (1) cavalry and chariot troops, consisting of elite imperial forces, (2) officials and domestic staff including scribes, and (3) foot soldiers from various parts of the empire.[137] The king sent with Nehemiah שרי חייל ופרשים ('commanders of the army and cavalry', Neh 2:9); these could only be the elite imperial Persian forces of the unit known as "King's Men." Nehemiah

132. BDB, 108. Cf. *CAD* B 261–63. Lemaire and Lozachmeur, "La *Bîrtā*ʾ en Méditerranée orientale." For a discussion of the history and the role of these citadels in the ancient Near East and Egypt, see now Bodi, "La citadelle de Jérusalem: Réalité linguistique et stratégie militaire," *Jérusalem à l'époque perse*, 37–56.

133. Tuplin, "Persian Garrisons in Xenophon and Other Sources"; idem, "The Administration of the Achaemenid Empire," 110ff.

134. As Goldstein points out (*I Maccabees*, 214ff.), the Greek word ἄκρα (or ἀκρόπολις) refers to "a citadel (or fort) on a high hill dominating a town." The fort is entirely within the city. The gates of the בירה in need of repair were not the gates of the city wall (also in need of repair). Nor does the term בירה refer to the watch towers, the מגדלים built along the city walls at various points (Neh 3:1).

135. Tuplin, "Persian Garrisons," 67–68; idem, "The Administration of the Achaemenid Empire," 110.

136. Saggs, "Assyrian Warfare in the Sargonic Period." Ephʿal ("On Warfare and Military Control in the Ancient Near Eastern Empires," 99–100) has shown that the description given by Saggs of the armies of Assyria also holds true for the armies of the Achaemenid Empire.

137. Postgate, *Taxation and Conscription in the Assyrian Empire*, 220.

exhibited the behavior of every other governor throughout the Persian Empire: he brought troops with him.

Scholars have assumed that soldiers accompanied Nehemiah for his protection, not to man the citadel.[138] According to Blenkinsopp, "provision of an armed escort, together with guides and travel rations, was standard procedure. . . . The absence of such an escort for Ezra's caravan (Ezra 8:22) was meant to emphasize his faith in divine providence. . . ."[139] Blenkinsopp cites Hallock as his source that the provision of an armed guard was standard practice for wayfarers.[140] Hallock lists the travel rations for travelers stopping at a way-station for the night; they received a day's ration to supply them until the next night at the next way-station. That there were very few large parties, however, suggests that, contrary to Blenkinsopp, it was not the custom to travel with guards.

Herodotus is the basic source for our knowledge about the common occurrence of travelers and the safety of the roads. His portrayal of the Royal Road describes any main thoroughfare throughout the Persian Empire.[141] To quote Herodotus: "For this, indeed, is what the road is like. All along it are Royal Stages and excellent places to put up; and, as it is all through inhabited country, the whole road is safe" (Hdt. 5.52). This is consistent with the evidence from the Persepolis tablets. Xenophon also testifies to the safety of the roads: "In Cyrus's provinces anyone, whether Greek or native, who was doing no harm could travel without fear wherever he liked and could take with him whatever he wanted" (*Anab.* 1.9.13). Thus, travel was safe and the most that the traveler had to fear was unwanted police surveillance (Hdt. 5.35, 7.239). The cavalry accompanying Nehemiah came not to provide an armed escort for him but to man the citadel at Jerusalem.[142]

Like Blenkinsopp, Grabbe also misunderstands Ezra's unwillingness to ask for guards (Ezra 8:21–23). Ezra fasted and prayed before setting out from Babylon to Jerusalem because, as he says, "I was ashamed to ask from the king soldiers and horsemen to protect us from enemies on the road." To Grabbe, the lack of a personal guard for the large entourage—with all the women, children, and wealth that Ezra had—proves the inauthenticity of the

138. Myers, *Ezra–Nehemiah,* 98, 100; Fensham, *The Books of Ezra and Nehemiah,* 163; Blenkinsopp, *Ezra–Nehemiah,* 216. This is also implied in Williamson's translation (*Ezra, Nehemiah,* ad loc.): "The king had sent army officers and cavalry to accompany me." The Hebrew says: "The king sent army officers and cavalry with me."

139. Blenkinsopp, *Ezra–Nehemiah,* 216.

140. Hallock, *Persepolis Fortification Tablets*; idem, "The Evidence of the Persepolis Tablets."

141. Tuplin, "The Administration of the Achaemenid Empire," 110 n. 6.

142. This is also Hoglund's conclusion (*Achaemenid Imperial Administration,* 210).

text.[143] However, it was not *God* whom Ezra lacked faith in, but the *king*! Ezra was embarrassed to admit to the king that he lacked faith in his ability to ensure the safety of the roads.

Why did Nehemiah establish a citadel, a בירה in Jerusalem? The Greek texts have three other terms for fortresses: πέτρα, βᾶρις, and τεῖχος.[144] The word βᾶρις is used by Josephus to translate the Aramaic term בירתא; the term τεῖχος is used in the LXX to translate חומה in Neh 2:8. The goals of these three types of fortresses were the same. First, they provided a place of refuge for the peasants of the countryside, or χώρα, in case of war or raids from nomads. For this purpose, the fort maintained stores of goods necessary to support the population during a long siege. A second goal was to manage the inhabitants under its jurisdiction; a third, to collect and distribute taxes. These roles can be summed up as *protection* and *control*.[145] According to Xenophon:

> [The emperor] has given a standing order to every governor of the nations from which he receives tribute, to supply maintenance for a specified number of horsemen and archers and slingers and light infantry, that they may be strong enough to *control* his subjects and to *protect* the countryside (χώρα) in the event of an invasion; and apart from these, he maintains garrisons in the citadels (ἀκροπόλεσι). (*Oec.* 4.5)

The main purpose of the citadel (בירה/ἄκρα) and the city walls (τεῖχος) was for the increased protection, management, and control of the populace. This was why Nehemiah came to Jerusalem: to repair the ἄκρα, the בירה that was in Jerusalem, and to furnish it with imperial troops.

In disagreement with this thesis, Hoglund sees the rebuilding of the citadel as implying a new and higher status for the city. According to Hoglund, "the presence of urban fortifications allowed a city to consider itself independent of the empire, capable of determining its own destiny."[146] "The district of Yehud was now to attain a new importance in the imperial system as the empire sought to gain a stronger grip on the Levant."[147] For Hoglund, permission to build the city walls (τεῖχος) indicated an increased status for Yehud. He states:

> Urban fortification systems were rarely encouraged by the imperial officials. As far as can be determined, Samaria never had an urban wall system in the Persian period, despite its certain status as a provincial capital.[148]

143. Grabbe, *Ezra–Nehemiah*, 141.

144. Briant, "Contrainte militaire, dépendance rurale et exploitation des territoires en Asie achéménide," 65.

145. Ibid.

146. Hoglund, *Achaemenid Imperial Administration*, 210.

147. Ibid.

148. Ibid., 210–11.

As evidence, Hoglund cites Kenyon's *Royal Cities of the Old Testament* (pp. 132–34).[149] There Kenyon states that a middle terrace wall "is probably the last structure which can be associated with Israelite Samaria. . . . My own inclination is to regard it as a final stage in Israelite building."[150] One ought not conclude from Kenyon's assertion, however, that Samaria had no walls during the Persian period. Kenyon only meant that the Israelite wall was the last stage of *building*, not the last stage in which the city had walls. Kenyon states repeatedly in her excavation report of Samaria that the Israelite exterior casement defense wall continued in use into the Hellenistic periods, and was certainly in use during the Persian period. According to the excavation report, "the two main walls of defense which were executed in this [casement] style remained in being throughout the Israelite period and for some centuries later."[151] Further, when describing Samaria during the Persian period, the report states again: "Enclosure Walls: As will be seen, it is probably that the Israelite defensive and enclosure walls remained in use with repairs and additions down to the second century B.C."[152] Again, with reference to the lower enclosure defensive walls, the report states that

> within this period [i.e., just before the Hellenistic period] the earliest building operations were devoted to strengthening the Israelite defensive walls by the construction of a number of massive towers along it. [One of these towers] was built astride the Israelite middle terrace wall 573, and this wall apparently continued in use with it. . . . It is obvious that such very strong towers must have been built in connection with an important defensive system.[153]

A major part of this "important defensive system" was wall 573, the Israelite wall mentioned above. The report states further that "the first major alteration (as far as the excavations have ascertained) to the defenses of the city took place in the second century B.C."[154] The Israelite defensive wall system continued to be the defensive wall system of Samaria without alteration, and with only minor repairs, up until late in the Hellenistic period. Samaria had strong casement defensive walls throughout the Persian period.

Hoglund also cites E. Stern's *Material Culture of the Land of the Bible* (pp. 50–51) as evidence for the fact that Samaria did not have walls in the Persian period and for the lack of cities in general with walls.[155] Yet, Stern does not refer in his report to the number of cities with *walls*, he refers simply

149. Ibid., 211 n. 13.

150. Kenyon, *Royal Cities of the Old Testament*, 133.

151. Crowfoot, Kenyon, and Sukenik, *Samaria–Sebaste*, 7. I thank R. Tappy for drawing my attention to this site report.

152. Ibid., 116.

153. Ibid., 117.

154. Ibid., 118.

155. Hoglund, *Achaemenid Imperial Administration*, 211 n. 13.

to those cities whose walls were built during the Persian period and thus would evince Persian period architecture.[156] Even so, quite a number of towns are mentioned. According to Stern,

> defensive walls assigned by their excavators to the Persian period have been uncovered at the following sites: Tell Abu-Hawam, Gilʾam, Tel Megadim, Tel Mevorakh, Tell Abu Zeitun, Jaffa, Tell el-Hesi, and Sheikh Zuweid, all of them towns on the coast and in the Shephelah. Remains of other walls [assigned to this period] have been cleared at Jerusalem, Tell en-Nasbeh and Lachish, and also recently at Heshbon in Transjordan.

It is thus a complete misunderstanding to infer that no other cities had walls during this period.[157]

Both archaeological and literary data demonstrate that it is a misconception to assume that "urban fortification systems were rarely encouraged by the imperial officials." Jerusalem was not the only site in Judah with a garrison. Within the small province of Persian Yehud (50 km × 60 km), there were 15 Persian garrisons and administration centers.[158] Rather, both archaeological and literary data attest to the extreme importance that imperial officials put on the construction of urban fortifications. City defensive systems were part of what it meant to be a city. I cannot agree that "the rarity of such urban fortification systems in the mid–fifth century should serve to highlight the unusual nature of Nehemiah's request and the imperial court's willingness to permit the refortification of Jerusalem."[159] Nor can I conclude that "the combination of a new imperial garrison in Jerusalem and a refortified city suggest . . . [that] the district of Yehud was now to attain a new importance in the imperial system."[160] Nor can I accept Ackroyd's conclusion that "the commissioning of Nehemiah . . . and the Persian policy associated with this . . . [indicate] the subsequent apparent emergence of a greater degree of autonomy for Judah."[161]

Rather than indicating a situation of *more* autonomy for Judah, Nehemiah's appearance signaled a period of *less* autonomy. Beyond the protection and control of the populace provided by the Nehemiah's garrison troops, Xenophon suggests an additional purpose for Nehemiah's visit:

> [The emperor] personally inspects the [governors] who are near his residence, and sends trusted agents to review those who live far away. . . . Those officers

156. E. Stern, *Material Culture of the Land of the Bible*, 50–51.
157. Hoglund accepts this now (personal communication).
158. Carter, *The Emergence of Yehud*, 284. Cf. E. Stern, "Between Persia and Greece," 432.
159. Hoglund, *Achaemenid Imperial Administration*, 211.
160. Ibid., 224.
161. Ackroyd, "Archaeology, Politics and Religion," 17.

> whom he finds to be neglecting the garrisons or making profit out of them he punishes severely, and appoints others to take their office. (*Oec.* 4.6–8)

Nehemiah was one such trusted agent sent to take the place of previous governors who had neglected the garrisons (Neh 2:8) or profited from them (Neh 5:14, 15).

As in every ἄκρα, the garrison commander was in charge of the city, while the provincial governor (who may have resided there) was over the province. This pattern is evident in the Xanthus inscription and in the Elephantine data. It was the pattern throughout the Persian Empire, including Judah and Jerusalem. Neh 7:2 reads:

> I placed Ḥanani, my brother, that is, Ḥananiah, the garrison commander (שר הבירה), over Jerusalem.

Nehemiah, the provincial governor, the *frataraka*, was over the province; Ḥanani, the garrison commander, רב חילא, was over the city. Judah and Jerusalem were no different from any other city and province in the Persian Empire. The situation was comparable to that in Elephantine. In Elephantine, a father and son took these roles. In Jerusalem, it was evidently two brothers.

Nehemiah does not relate the thoughts of the populace when he repaired the city walls and set up an Achaemenid garrison in their city. The reaction may have been similar to that expressed in 1 Maccabees when Antiochus IV Epiphanes refortified the city and established an imperial garrison there:

> They fortified the City of David with a high strong wall (τεῖχος) and strong towers so as to have a citadel (ἄκρα). They stationed in it a breed of sinners, wicked men, who grew strong there. The garrison (ὅπλα) was provided with a store of arms and provisions and they kept there under their hands the spoils of Jerusalem which they had collected, and they became a dangerous menace. It was an ambush against the temple, a wicked adversary against Israel. (1 Macc 1:33–36)[162]

The presence of foreign imperial troops was described with mourning, lamentation, and despair by the author of 1 Maccabees. This seems to be the predictable and appropriate response. It is only because it was Nehemiah, the trusted imperial agent, who described the installation during the Persian period that this reaction is absent from our text. Although Nehemiah was a Jew, this would not have alleviated the situation. The "sinners" in the acropolis were so called, not because of their moral peccadilloes, but because they were Jews who sided with the enemy against their own people.

162. The translation is that of J. Goldstein, *I Maccabees*, ad loc.

E. Meyer and his followers conclude that Nehemiah had no Persian troops at his command, based on their reading of Nehemiah 4.[163] In this passage, Nehemiah states that Sanballat and Tobiah the Ammonite were planning to use force to stop him from fortifying Jerusalem. To protect himself from these enemies, Nehemiah had half of his 'boys' נערים who worked on the wall hold spears, shields, bows, and body-armor, while the other half built the wall (Neh 4:10 [4:16 ET]).[164] Meyer assumes that, if Nehemiah had had Persian troops at his disposal, the builders would not have had to defend themselves. However, the "boys with the weapons," the נערים, were members of the garrison whom Nehemiah had brought with him. These soldiers carried rubble in one hand and a weapon in the other; each had his sword strapped to his side while he worked (4:11, 12 [ET 4:17, 18]). Nehemiah states that "neither I, nor my brothers, nor my 'boys' נערים, nor the men of the guard (משמר), who were under me, none of us took off our clothes or even went to the bathroom" (!) (4:17 [ET 23]).[165] Nehemiah's "brothers" are his fellow officials from Persia. His "boys" are the common soldiers; the "men" of the guard are the leaders of the garrison. They posted guard duty all night. The populace itself was not armed.

The work on the wall was corvée labor—labor commanded and paid for by the state. As elsewhere in the Persian Empire, building the wall was under the jurisdiction of the satrap of Ebar Hannahar himself, לכסא פחת עבר הנהר 'belonging to the throne of the satrap of Beyond the River' (Neh 3:7).[166] Even the priests, even the high priest, had to do the work (Neh 3:1).[167] Like most priests in the Persian Empire, those of the Jerusalem temple were not exempt but were available for corvée labor anywhere in the realm.

163. Meyer, *Die Entstehung des Judentums*; Albertz, *History of Israelite Religion*, vol. 2; Widengren, "The Persian Period."

164. This is also the understanding of Rashi and his followers. Rashi paraphrases 4:7: "I stationed soldiers from below that place around Jerusalem, from behind the wall of the city and on the bare rocks with their weapons according to the families of the soldiers among them." Malbim explains that the two cases of stationing refer to two distinct components of the army: one group that would stay in hiding and one group that would appear in the open. Neh 4:7 is usually translated "I stationed the people according to families with their swords, their spears and their bows." It should be translated "I stationed *troops* according to families. . . ." The use of עם to refer to army troops is frequent in the MT.

165. Literally, "sent out water," repointing from שִׁלְחוֹ to שָׁלְחוּ. Commentators tend to translate it with the Greek ("each kept his weapon in his right hand"), which was probably influenced by השלח 'the weapon' in v. 11.

166. The word used is פחת, usually translated 'governor'. In this case it must refer to the satrap.

167. So alsoEphʿal, "Syria–Palestine," 159.

Nehemiah's Adversaries

The installation of Persian soldiers set off a political struggle in Judah. As Eisenstadt has argued, local elites respond to imperial rule by attempting to impede the aims of the ruler and to create independent dynasties of their own.[168] From the beginning of his appearance in Jerusalem, Nehemiah suspected that the local power structure would oppose his rebuilding the ἄκρα. His arrival initiated political infighting so fierce that he had to inspect the walls under cover of darkness. He could not risk letting "the Jews, the priests, the nobles (חורים), the officials (סגנים), and the rest of those who were to do the work" know of his activities (Neh 2:16).

Who were these men whom Nehemiah expected to oppose him? It is obvious who the priests were, but who were the סגנים and the חורים? The Hebrew term סגן is derived from the Akkadian *šākin.* In the early Persian period, the *šākin ṭēmi* was in charge of urban bureaucracies and the *šākin māti* was directly under the satrap in charge of larger provincial districts.[169] The high rank of the *sgn* is shown in the Elephantine Papyri. He appears numerous times in conjunction with the *dyn*, the judge. He was an important bureaucratic official to whom one complained for redress of grievances.[170] Like the judges, these 'prefects', as Porten and Yardeni translate *seganayyāʾ*, were official employees of the Persian satrapal government.

Judean סגנים would have been Persian employees as well. The Aramaic term סגניא and the Hebrew term סגנים appear 22 times in the Hebrew Bible. These are all in late texts. The term occurs 5 times in the book of Daniel, 4 in conjunction with the words אחשדרפניא and פחותא 'satraps' and 'governors'. It occurs 3 times in the book of Jeremiah and 3 in the book of Ezekiel. In each of these, the term appears in conjunction with the noun פחות 'governors'. Except for once in Isaiah 41, where it refers to local rulers, the remaining occurrences are all in Ezra (1×) and Nehemiah (9×).[171] In 6 of the Nehemiah passages, the סגנים appear in conjunction with חורים. Both groups were wealthy landowners who took the sons and daughters of marginal Judean farmers on pledge for loans (Neh 5:7). Both groups were high-ranking officials of the Persian provincial government, supported by the Persians, who ate at the governor's table (Neh 5:17).

168. Eisenstadt, *The Political Systems of Empire*; see pp. 4–5 above.

169. Petit, "L'évolution sémantique des termes hébreux et araméens *pḥh* et *sgn* et accadiens *pāḫatu* et *šaknu.*" See pp. 11–13 above.

170. *TAD* B.2.3:13; 3.1:13, 18; 3.10:19; 3.11:13; 3.12:28; 4.6:14; 5.4:2, 5.

171. Ezra 9:2; Neh 2:16 (2×); 4:8, 13; 5:7, 17; 7:5; 12:40; 13:11. Of the occurrences in Nehemiah, all but 3 occur in conjunction with חורים. I include 5:17, where יהודים is probably an error for חורים. See n. 113 (p. 190).

The men whom Nehemiah feared, the חורים and סגנים, as well as the priests, were members of the local bureaucracy. In the Persian period, these tended to be members or friends of the Persian royal family, who depended on the latter for land and tokens of wealth and prestige. Even so, Eisenstadt's model suggests that, as aspiring members of the aristocracy, they would have competed with the ruler for power, attempted to reduce his available resources, and to control these resources for themselves.[172] The activities of Nehemiah's adversaries (Sanballat, Tobiah, and Geshem/Gashmu the Arab) reveal this political struggle. Nehemiah's major antagonist was Sanballat the Horonite (Neh 2:10, 19; 3:33–4:17; 6:1–19; 13:28). Although he is not called a governor in the book of Nehemiah, Sanballat is described in the Aramaic Papyri from Elephantine (*TAD* A.4.7, 8, 9), the Wadi ed-Daliyeh Papyri, and by Josephus (*Ant.* 11) as the governor of Samaria.[173] These texts indicate he established a ruling dynasty in Samaria that lasted several centuries. He would have originally been appointed governor by a Persian king and ordered to fulfill a bureaucratic function, yet he was able to make his office hereditary and to maintain powerful dynastic rights in Samaria for his descendants.

Nehemiah's second antagonist was Tobiah, the Servant, the Ammonite (תוביה העבד העמני; Neh 2:10, 19; 3:33–4:17; 6:1–19; 13:4–9). The Tobiad family name is well known in Palestinian history.[174] The Tobiads owned large estates in the Transjordan area. They either retained these during their captivity in Babylon or were able to return to them after the exile.[175] This wealthy family was influential in the politics of Judea, Samaria, Ammon, and Egypt well into the Ptolemaic period. Tobiah, the Servant, the Ammonite, as servant to the Persian king, was most likely governor of Ammon. He, too, originally appointed by the emperor, created a powerful dynasty in Ammon that lasted several centuries.

The third enemy of Nehemiah was Geshem, the Arab (Neh 2:19; 4:1; 6:1–9). His name appears on a silver vessel dated to about 400 B.C.E.[176] The

172. Eisenstadt, *The Political Systems of Empires,* 175–77; see pp. 4–5 above.

173. Cross, "The Papyri and Their Historical Implications"; idem, "A Report on the Samaria Papyri"; Porten, *Archives from Elephantine,* 290.

174. Tcherikover and Fuks, *Corpus Papyrorum Judaicarum,* 1.115–30, esp. letters nos. 4 and 5; Tcherikover, "Palestine under the Ptolemies," esp. p. 3.

175. Gera, "On the Credibility of the History of the Tobiads"; P. W. Lapp, "ʿIraq el-Emir"; N. L. Lapp, "Introduction," *The Excavations at Araq el-Emir,*" 1.1–11; Mazar, "The Tobiads." Photographs of the two Tobiah inscriptions may be seen in Cowan, "The ʿAraq el-Emir and the Tobiads." Gera concludes that the creation of the Tobiad estate in Ammon that Josephus assigns to Hyrcanus was built much earlier, at least in the 4th century, if not earlier than that.

176. Rabinowitz, "Aramaic Inscriptions of the Fifth Century B.C.E." The vessel was found at Tell el-Maskhuta, about twelve miles west of Ismailia, in Lower Egypt; Dumbrell,

inscription reads: זי קינו בר גשם מלך קדר קרב להנאלת 'that which Qainu bar Geshem, king of Qedar, brought-in-offering to Han-ʾIlat'. The inscription places Geshem, the father of the donor, at 440, the period of Nehemiah. It reveals a Qedarite Arabic kingdom to the south of Judah during the Persian period and Geshem or Gashmu, the Arab, Qedar's king. The fact that Geshem's son, Qainu, also became king indicates that Geshem, like Sanballat and Tobiah, strove to perpetuate and maintain his dynastic rights in his own area.[177] These three families were among the חורים and סגנים of the satrapy Beyond the River. They were wealthy public officials of the Persian satrapal organization. Originally appointed by Persia, they had become part of the landed aristocracy.

Nehemiah included the priests among those whom he was afraid would oppose his rebuilding of the ἄκρα (Neh 2:12). The aims of the high priestly family were the same as those of Sanballat, Tobiah, and Geshem the Arab. They also attempted to create a fiefdom in Judah independent of imperial control and to seize for themselves and their descendants political power and authority.

Allusions to a power struggle between the Persian governor and the high priest go back to the 2nd year of Darius. Especially suggestive is the statement that there will be "a council of peace" between צמח 'Branch', Zerubbabel (on his throne as both the Davidic heir and the Persian governor), and the high priest, Joshua, who also sits on a throne (Zech 6:13).[178] This reference to a future "council of peace" between them suggests a present "council of war."[179]

The visions of the prophet/priest Zechariah[180] delineate priestly goals for the governor and the high priest in postexilic Judah. In one, Zechariah sees Joshua, the high priest, standing before YHWH, before the angel of YHWH, and before the Satan (Zech 3:1). They are evidently in the temple but before the divine court as well. The angel tells those standing before him to "put a pure turban (צניף) on [Joshua's] head, so they put a pure turban (צניף) on his head and they put his vestments on him." These are the ceremonial garments of the high priest, and the vision denotes the priest's investiture. In another

"The Tell El-Maskhuta Bowls"; Lemaire, "Un nouveau roi arabe de Qedar"; Porten and Yardeni, *TAD* D.15.4. The latter authors date it to the second half of the 5th century B.C.E.

177. Lemaire, "Populations et territoires de la Palestine à l'époque perse," esp. pp. 47–48 n. 77.

178. Zerubbabel's Hebrew name may have been 'Branch' צמח, as intriguingly suggested by Lemaire, "Zorobabel et la Judée."

179. Pace Ackroyd, *Exile and Restoration*, 199; C. L. Meyers and E. M. Meyers, *Haggai, Zechariah 1–8*, 362. Petersen, *Haggai and Zechariah 1–8*, 278.

180. Assuming, as is likely, that Zechariah ben Berechiah ben Iddo (Zech 1:1) is the same as Zechariah ben Iddo (Neh 12:16). Many of Zechariah's visions seem to occur in the temple, which would imply that he was a member of the priestly caste.

vision, Joshua is given a second headdress. In the so-called crowning scene (Zech 6:9–11, 14), the prophet is told to

> take from the community of the exile, from Heldai, from Tobiah, from Yedaiah, and you yourself come on that day, and come to the house of Josiah ben Zephaniah, who came from Babylon. And take silver and gold and make crowns, and put [one] on the head of Joshua ben Jehozadak, the High Priest. . . . [The other] crown will be for Helem, Tobiah, Yediah, and for Hen ben Zephaniah as a remembrance in the Temple of YHWH.

There has been much discussion over the translation of this passage. In the MT and the LXX, the first occurrence of the term עטרות 'crowns' is clearly plural; whereas, in the Lucianic, the Peshitta, and the Targum, it is singular. It has been suggested by some who favor the plural that the second crown was for Zerubbabel and that his name had been erased out of fear of the Persian authorities.[181] The text states exactly what was done with the other crown, however. It was kept in the temple as a remembrance. There is a problem with the second appearance of the word (6:14). The MT has העטרֹת, vocalized as a plural, but the versions have the singular, consistent with its singular verb. A simple revocalization would render the MT in the singular as well. Thus it is possible to read that one crown is placed on the head of Joshua, the high priest, while the other is placed in the temple as a remembrance. Joshua was to wear both the priestly turban and a crown.[182]

This fulfills a goal of Ezekiel. He had prophesied that the kings of Judah would take off their 'turban' מיצנפת and their 'crown' עטרה and that these would not be put on again until someone came who had Judgment (Ezekiel 21:31–32 [ET 26–27]). Both the מיצנפת and the עטרה would be worn by the same person, as is the case in Zechariah's vision. The two headpieces symbolize that both priestly and secular authority should now be localized in the person of Joshua, the high priest. The second crown made by Zechariah is put away in the temple as a remembrance. It is not to be held in safekeeping for a future Davidic king, as suggested by most commentators;[183] rather, it is

181. E.g., Waterman, "The Camouflaged Purge."

182. Pace Rose (*Zemah and Zerubbabel*, 58), who argues that placing the crown on Joshua's head is a symbolic act guaranteeing that the promise concerning the Zemah will be fulfilled. He derives this from Zech 3:8, where he argues that Joshua's fellow priests, the אנשי מופת 'men of portent', are a sign that Zemah will come. Instead, I read it that the priesthood along with Joshua has been admitted into the divine court (they have walking rights, the right of access, among those standing there—namely, the angel of YHWH and the Satan). The priesthood is given access to the divine council, thus obtaining prophetic abilities. They are not a sign of Branch's arrival; rather, they now have the ability to see it.

183. Ackroyd, *Exile and Restoration*, 196; Meyers and Meyers, *Haggai, Zechariah 1–8*, 363. Petersen, *Haggai and Zechariah 1–8*, 277–79.

put in the temple as a reminder that the true king is YHWH.[184] This is an assertion of a theocracy and the denial of a meaningful role for Zerubbabel, the Davidic scion and the Persian governor.

The role that the priests envisioned for Zerubbabel in a restored Jerusalem is revealed by the specific references to him in the oracles of Zechariah. These are limited to Zech 3:8–10, 4:6–10, 4:11–14, and 6:9–14. In the first passage, YHWH states that he is bringing "my servant, Branch," a reference to Zerubbabel, the Davidic heir (Jer 23:5, 33:15). Yet there is no mention here of Branch's task or role. In the second passage, Zerubbabel brings out the "former-times" stone and with his own hands installs it in the unfinished temple. It is further stated that his hands will also complete the building project.

The third passage, which is usually assumed to refer to the two anointed of YHWH, Zerubbabel and Joshua, does not refer to them at all. The 'two sons of oil', the two בני יצהר mentioned here are not people but olive trees. If people were meant, the word for oil would be שמן, the word used in anointing ceremonies, whereas this oil is יצהר, the oil of the firstfruits, the first pressing, which, like the first of the grain and the wine, is reserved for the priests (e.g., Num 18:12). Rather than people, the בני יצהר are the olive trees that stand on the right and on the left of the candelabra. They serve (עמדים על) the Lord of all the earth; that is, they serve the candelabra (whose seven bowls are YHWH's eyes that range over all the earth, Zech 4:10). The two trees represent the two seraphim who stand in attendance on YHWH when he is in his temple (Isa 6:2); at the same time they provide the pure oil for the eternal flame, which represents YHWH's presence.

The final reference to Zerubbabel is in Zech 6:12–13. In addition to an initial statement that Branch shall build the Temple of YHWH, there is a second statement that "he who builds the Temple of YHWH shall bear royal majesty (הוד), he shall sit (ישב) and rule (משל) upon his throne (על כסאו), and there will be a priest on his throne, and a council of peace will exist between the two of them." This is a reference to Zerubbabel, since Zerubbabel is the one who has laid the "former-times stone" (4:7). It is explicitly stated that Zerubbabel's hands have founded this temple and that his hands shall complete it (4:9). Zerubbabel is the only temple-builder mentioned in Zechariah.[185]

184. Rose (*Zemah and Zerubbabel*, 50–56) makes an interesting case for the existence of only one crown. If this was so, then the one crown that was placed on Joshua's head was to be kept in the temple as a remembrance. This does not change the conclusion.

185. Pace Rose (ibid., 123–24, 130–41), who argues that Zemah is the proper name of a future ruler—not Zerubbabel—and that Zemah will build the temple. His arguments are not convincing. Rose insists on translating הנני מביא את עבדי צמח 'Look, I bring my

The word that is translated 'rule' is not מלך, however, but משל. The root משל 'to rule', while often used as a synonym for 'reign', is also used to suggest the chief bureaucratic administrator of a superior power—that is, a vizier. For example, Abraham's servant, Eliezar, is described as המושל בכל אשר־לו 'in charge of all that belonged to him [i.e., to Abraham]' (Gen 24:2). Further, Joseph is described as

> לאב לפרעה ולאדון לכל־ביתו ומשל בכל־ארץ מצרים:
>
> a father to Pharaoh, lord of all his household, in charge of all the land of Egypt. (Gen 45:8)

Additionally, we have,

> ויקח את־שרי המאות ואת־האדירים ואת־המושלים בעם ואת כל־עם הארץ ויורד את־המלך מבית יהוה ויבאו בתוך־שער העליון בית המלך ויושיבו את־המלך על כסא הממלכה:
>
> And he took the captains of hundreds, the mighty men, the administrators of the people, and all the people of the land, and he took the king down from the house of YHWH, and they entered the high gate into the king's house, and set the king upon the throne of the kingdom. (2 Chr 23:20)

The מושלים are clearly bureaucratic administrators who rule as governors in the name of the king. It seems that the verb מלך was avoided intentionally in Zech 6:13 and משל employed to suggest that Zerubbabel, the governor, ruled simply as a vizier, perhaps under Darius I, but perhaps under YHWH, the true king. In priestly thought, Zerubbabel had been enlisted for the specific task of building the temple but little beyond that. He is not to reign, מלך, even in the future but will only be a מושל, and he will not receive the crown. This priestly vision suggests a rivalry at least between the priesthood and the local Persian governor, even if that governor is the Davidic heir.

A final vision of Zechariah further reveals the situation desired by the priesthood in restored Jerusalem. This is the vision of the flying scroll of the covenantal oath, the *ʾālâ* (אלה), which goes out over the whole land (Zech 5:3). The אלה denotes a curse elicited by a broken oath or covenant. It goes out from YHWH to the thief and to the one who swears falsely by YHWH's name (5:4), suggesting a law scroll, with its corresponding set of sanctions and curses. That it goes out from YHWH, from the temple, signifies that the priests saw themselves as the ones in charge of disseminating and enforcing law, not the Persian governor. The struggle for independence from the Per-

---

Servant, Branch', as referring to a future ruler who has not yet appeared, who will then build a third, more-glorious temple. I find this view far removed from the plain sense of the text. See also Lemaire, "Zorobabel et la Judée."

sian governor hinted at here is similar to the struggle observed between the priests of Khnum at Elephantine and the Persian satrap.

The Political Struggle

This power struggle continued throughout the period of Persian hegemony. Nehemiah's memoir describes relations typical of a local high priest and a Persian governor. The following occurred after 433, after Nehemiah returned from his trip to the king in Babylon (Neh 13:4–9):

> Eliashib, the priest who was appointed over the chambers of the temple, a relative of Tobiah, turned over to the latter a large chamber where before this were put the grain offering, the incense, the vessels, the tithe of grain, new wine, and oil (ordered for the Levites, the singers, the gatekeepers), as well as the contribution due the priests.
>
> During all this, I was not in Jerusalem, because in the thirty-second year of Artaxerxes the king, I had gone to the king in Babylon. After some time, I asked permission from the king, and I came to Jerusalem, and I understood the evil that Eliashib had done with Tobiah, to make for him a room in the courts of the temple. I was greatly angered, and I threw all of Tobiah's things out of the room. Then I gave orders, and they cleaned the rooms, and I returned there the temple furnishings, namely, the grain and incense offerings.

Eliashib took the opportunity provided by Nehemiah's absence to cement ties with the governor of Ammon.[186] This Eliashib may not have been Eliashib the high priest, but rooms in the temple could not have been assigned without the high priest's knowledge and consent.[187] Nehemiah's ejection of Tobiah (Neh 13:4–9) indicates a power struggle, not only between the two of them, but also between Nehemiah and the high priest. Nehemiah's support for the Levites also reveals this power struggle (13:10). The priests had not given the required portions to the Levites while Nehemiah was away; consequently, the Levites and the singers had to return to their fields (13:10). The Levites may have represented a rival faction opposed to the powers of the priests, a faction that Nehemiah could exploit. To aid and abet the lower-level Levites was to attack the high priestly echelon.[188]

Nehemiah's concern for the Sabbath also reveals the power struggle between himself and the high priestly family. As governor, he ordered the gates

186. Pace Williamson, *Ezra, Nehemiah*, 183.

187. Blenkinsopp, *Ezra–Nehemiah*, 354, ad loc. The high priest at the time of Nehmiah's return was likely Jehoiada, Eliashib's son (Neh 13:28).

188. The scholarly literature on Levitical-priestly relations in the Persian Period is vast, and its subject is beyond the scope of the present study. For recent discussions, see Schaper, *Priester und Leviten*; Rooke, *Zadok's Heirs*; Nurmela, *The Levites*; and Boccaccini, *The Roots of Rabbinic Judaism.*

of Jerusalem closed just before Sabbath and not opened again till after the Sabbath the next evening (13:19a). He even stationed his own servants at the gates to prevent anyone from entering (or leaving) on the Sabbath day (13:19b). The 'servants' (lit., 'boys' נערים) whom Nehemiah set to guard the gates were certainly men from the garrison. This is a direct attack on the prerogatives of the high priest. Compare this with Josephus's statement that the high priest Jaddua had the power to decide whether to open the gates of the city to Alexander (*Ant.* 11.326ff.). Under Nehemiah, the high priest could not even decide to open the gates to the Sabbath.

Nehemiah's anger at Eliashib's grandson (for marrying a daughter of Sanballat) also reveals the political struggle between Nehemiah and the high priestly family. Members of the priesthood had intermarried with the families of Sanballat and Tobiah, other governors within the satrapy of Ebar Hannahar. These gubernatorial and high priestly families were on the same side of the political struggle, a struggle in opposition to Nehemiah, the cupbearer of the king.

The aristocratic families of Sanballat, Tobiah, and Eliashib, the high priest, intermarried among themselves and with other members of the nobility. Nehemiah and Josephus report marriages between the families of Sanballat and Eliashib (Neh 13:28; *Ant.* 11.2); between the Tobiads and the high priestly family (Neh 13:4; *Ant.* 12.4.160); and between Tobiah and the nobility of Judah (Neh 6:18).

Wealth accompanied the power and influence of these men, and, as de Ste. Croix makes abundantly clear, wealth is wealth in land.[189] The intermarriages among these families suggest that each owned land throughout the satrapy. The Murašu business tablets demonstrate that the Great King seized lands and other properties belonging to the conquered peoples and distributed them in large estates as inalienable and hereditary property to friends, benefactors, table companions, and relatives—to whoever had rendered the king a service.[190] Provincial governors were also in a position to acquire wealth in this manner. Nehemiah contrasts himself favorably to the previous governors in Judah because he alone did not acquire land in the province (Neh 5:16). Apparently most governors did use their position to aggrandize wealth and power for themselves. Xenophon (*Hell.* 3.1.27–28) reveals the vast amounts of land held by Zenis of Dardanus, a provincial governor of the satrap Pharnabazus, in the years around 400. The personal wealth of this provincial governor was enough to provide nearly a year's pay to an army of

189. De Ste. Croix, *The Class Struggle in the Ancient Greek World.*

190. Cardascia, *Les archives des Murašû*; idem, "Le fief dans la Babylonie achéménide"; idem, "Ḫaṭru"; idem, "Armée et fiscalité dans la Babylonie achéménide"; Dandamayev, "Achaemenid Babylonia"; Stolper, *Entrepreneurs and Empire,* 52–69.

8,000 men! Gifts of land to Persian period dynasts were not always in their own provinces (Arsames, Satrap of Egypt, held landed estates in Syria and Babylon).[191] This fact and the extensive intermarriages among them suggest that the holdings of the families of Sanballat, Tobiah, and the high priest were spread throughout the satrapy. Governors previous (and possibly subsequent) to Nehemiah very likely also participated. Although they may have begun as local officials appointed by the Persian king, the land granted to them propelled them into the aristocracy. Then, as dynasts and as members of the aristocratic class, they "attempted to deny the ruler resources and support, and plotted and worked against [him] either in open political warfare [Neh 3:33; 4:1, 2] or by sleight of hand, infiltration, and intrigues [Ezra 4:7–23; Neh 6:10–14, 17–19]."[192] This was no less true for the high priests. Their goal would also have been to deny power to the imperial representative, to support local opposition, and to establish an independent dynasty in Judah (Neh 13:4–9).[193]

191. In one letter (*TAD* A.6.9), Arsames orders the superintendents at way-stations along the route from Susa to Egypt to supply his servants with rations *mn btʾ zyly zy bmdyntkm* ('from my estate which is in your province[s]'). Stolper (*Entrepreneurs and Empire*, 53) states that "Whitehead has shown convincingly [in his dissertation *Early Aramaic Epistolography*, 60–64] that . . . the letter authorizes superintendents of estates held by other members of the nobility to supply the travelers and to debit Aršam's own estates; debits are to be transferred and cleared through a system of accounting operated by the imperial government." Based on his examination of the Persepolis archives, Whitehead concludes that Arsames did not hold lands in Syria. This is not the plain meaning of Arsames' letter. The Persepolis tablets (Hallock, *Persepolis Fortification Tablets*; idem, "The Evidence of the Persepolis Tablets") portray the accounting situation at Persepolis: provincial governors were required to provide way-stations at a day's interval on the main roads throughout the empire. Those traveling under the king's aegis were provided with a letter from the king authorizing officials at the way-stations to provide the traveler with a day's rations. The provincial governors were then reimbursed from stores in Persepolis. Arsames' letter implies that this accounting system extended to satraps as well. Those traveling under the satraps' aegis were reimbursed, not from Persepolis, but from the satraps' own estates. These exchanges did not involve the imperial government. Arsames' letter states that, in this case, instead of sums borrowed against a central estate in Egypt, they were to be borrowed against his estates that were in "your province," that is, in Syria. The Murašu tablets also indicate that Arsames owned land in the vicinity of Nippur (Stolper, *Entrepreneurs and Empire*, 64). The Murašu archives show further that a great many absentee nobles held landed estates in Nippur (ibid., 52–69). They also held land around Uruk, as is clear from the Eanna archives (Cocquerillat, *Palmeraies et Cultures de l'Eanna d'Uruk [559–520]*). One governor of Byblos held land in Sippar (Fried, "A Governor of Byblos").

192. Eisenstadt, *The Political System of Empires*, 14.

193. This was feasible for the high priest, since the Judean governors seem to have been eunuchs. Nehemiah served the king in the presence of the queen (Neh 2:6), so he was likely a eunuch—the royal women were kept under tight restrictions. Yeḥizqiyah, the last

Nehemiah's adversaries—Sanballat, Tobiah, Geshem, and Eliashib—were hereditary rulers in their own provinces, able to bequeath their offices to their descendants. As argued by Eisenstadt, it was the goal of any satrap, provincial governor, clereuch,[194] or priest to make his office dynastic. It was in the Emperor's interest to prevent this. Within every province were garrisons, agricultural land, and workers who paid tribute on the land and its produce. The provincial governor collected the tribute and funneled it to the ruler; but the very system that the ruler imposed eventually became a problem to him. The local governors (appointed to their office by the ruler) soon became hereditary monarchs of their own small fiefdoms, threatening centralized sovereignty.

The ruler strove to limit the power of this aristocratic bureaucracy.[195] He had many ways to do this. A common way was to "create and maintain an independent free peasantry with small holdings, and to restrict land-owners' encroachments on these small holdings."[196] A free peasant class was essential; it constituted the backbone of the national army or militia. The reform described in Nehemiah 5 illustrates the political struggle. Small landholders and free peasants mortgaged their property and sold their children to pay the king's tax. If they could not pay their debts, their land and their children fell into the hands of those from whom they had borrowed the money. In this way, those with money to lend increased their land holdings; the peasantry became serfs or slaves to the aristocracy, removed from imperial control.[197] Nehemiah endeavored to reduce the power of these large landholders by abrogating the debts of the peasants and returning to them the ownership of their land. The reforms of Nehemiah were an attempt to create a strong peasant class, dependent upon the Persian representative, in opposition to the landed aristocracy.[198]

---

governor of Judah, was beardless if he is the one pictured on his coins, so he too would have been a eunuch. Bagavahya's (Bagoses') presence in the temple defiled it, according to Josephus (*Ant.* 11.297), so he too was likely a castrate. It may have been for this reason that Nehemiah did not attempt to set up a dynasty for himself in Judah, as Sanballat did in Samaria.

194. A clereuch (κληροῦχος) was an individual who held an allotment of land in a foreign country. This was usually land obtained by conquest and divided by the conqueror among his friends and retainers. The allottee differed from a colonist in that he was still a citizen of the motherland and did not become a citizen of the new state (LS ad loc.).

195. Eisenstadt, *The Political Systems of Empires*, 144.

196. Ibid., 136.

197. De Ste. Croix, *The Class Struggle*, 162–70.

198. Knoppers ("An Achaemenid Imperial Authorization?" 133–34) argues that Nehemiah instituted these laws and edicts without reference to external Persian authorities. Since Nehemiah was *the* Persian authority in Yehud, he could promulgate law under his own initiative. Nehemiah was not acting in his own interests here but in the interests of his Persian masters. For discussion of similar behavior exhibited by Greek tyrants and their

A second way to limit the power of the aristocracy was to create and maintain urban groups.[199] Cities were the source of wealth.[200] The peasants paid their taxes in kind. These perishable goods could not be sent directly from the satrapies in the periphery all the way to Susa. There had to be intermediate levels of exchange and markets whereby these goods could be translated into ingots or coins for transport. Cities provided markets where these exchanges could occur. Only the cities could create this wealth, and the rulers and their agents either established new cities for that purpose or, like Nehemiah, forcibly populated existing ones (Neh 11:1, 2). The bourgeois class thus created was naturally opposed to the landed aristocracy, independent of them, and dependent solely on the imperial governor.

Besides strengthening oppositional strata of society, such as the peasants and the urban class, the ruler also strove to limit the elites' power. A common way was to prevent intermarriages among them. Such a ban has been carried out in other bureaucratic empires with the same objective. Akbar, one of the descendants of Gengis Kahn, established a military occupation in China and forbade intermarriage among the various ethnic groups there.[201] Lucius Aemilius Paulus, a Roman general in 168 B.C.E., divided Macedonia into four separate provinces; he then forbade intermarriage and land-ownership across the boundaries.[202] The deified Augustus established a code of rules for the administration of the Privy Purse, a code maintained for 200 years. This code consisted of over 100 laws that greatly restricted interaction among ethnic groups. The goal was *divide et impera.*[203] Marriages enhanced the power and wealth of patrilineal groups and cemented relations among them. Nehemiah's prohibition of foreign wives (i.e., wives from other provinces of the satrapy) served to prevent these marriages of convenience and to limit the influence and power of these families.

Eisenstadt's model of the political systems of bureaucratic empires provides a useful framework in which to view the political struggle. Like rulers of bureaucratic empires everywhere, the Persian ruler used every means at his disposal to ensure for himself a constant supply of resources, both financial and human. His primary means was to garrison soldiers throughout the cities and

---

comparison with Nehemiah, see Ehrenberg, *From Solon to Socrates,* 56–76; M. Smith, *Palestinian Parties,* 126–47; and Yamauchi, "Two Reformers Compared."

199. Eisenstadt, *The Political Systems of Empires,* 136–37.

200. Herrenschmidt, "L'empire perse achéménide"; de Ste. Croix, *Class Struggle,* 14–15.

201. Duverger, "Le concept d'empire."

202. Livy (45.29); Shallit, "The End of the Hasmonean Dynasty," 41.

203. Lewis, *Life in Egypt under Roman Rule,* 32–33. The code of regulations of the Privy Purse is BGU 1210 at the Berlin Egyptian Museum. Cf. Bagnall and Frier, *The Demography of Roman Egypt,* 28–29.

countryside of his empire. He also restricted the power and influence of the aristocracy and other elites by arrogating to himself their traditional roles and powers. Finally, he strengthened social strata such as the peasantry and the bourgeois, who were traditionally in opposition to local elites. As elsewhere, the aristocracy and priesthood did not submit passively to encroachments upon their traditional powers by the imperial ruler. They strove to oppose and prevent foreign control, and fought for independence and autonomy.

Ezra's Mission

According to the Book of Ezra, in his 7th year, King Artaxerxes sent Ezra to Jerusalem with the following command:[204]

> And you, Ezra, according to the god-given wisdom you possess, appoint magistrates and judges who would judge all the people who are in Beyond the River—all who know the law (דתא) of your god and [all] who do not know, to inform them. All who would not execute the law (דתא) of your god and the law (דתא) of the king zealously, let a judicial verdict (דינה) be executed on him: either for death, or flogging, confiscation of property, or imprisonment. (Ezra 7:25, 26)

Most scholars interpret Artaxerxes' command as an order to Ezra to make the Mosaic Law code legally binding on Jews.[205] They differ on whether it obligated only Jews in Yehud or if it included all the Jews in the entire satrapy of Beyond the River.[206] Ska argues, however, that the law of God could not refer to the Mosaic law code that we have. Nowhere in the Pentateuch is imprisonment mentioned as a sanction for infractions; and stoning, which is often mentioned, is not cited here. There can be no equivalence between "the law of God" and Jewish law, if Ezra 7 differs on such an important point as sanctions. Nor is it likely that the Pentateuch served as an imperially authorized Jewish law. It is in Hebrew, not Aramaic; it contains narrative; and it

204. I assume Artaxerxes II. The following is taken from my article "You Shall Appoint Judges." I discuss the date of Ezra briefly below (p. 223).

205. E.g., Frei, "Persian Imperial Authorization." Frei states (p. 6) that "Ezra was ordered, among other things, to introduce a religiously based law book." He cites as evidence Ezra 7:25–26.

206. Blenkinsopp, *Ezra–Nehemiah*, 152–57; idem, "Was the Pentateuch the Constitution of the Jewish Ethnos?"; Williamson, *Ezra, Nehemiah*, 103–5; Janzen ("The 'Mission' of Ezra") thinks it possible that Ezra was sent to enforce Jewish law on all the Jews in the satrapy but that it is unlikely. Grabbe (*Ezra–Nehemiah*, 153) suggests that the Achaemenids imposed it only on the province of Yehud. According to Grabbe, "it would not be surprising if local Jewish law was allowed to be enforced on the people of the Persian province Yehud."

describes the land of Israel as reaching from the Wadi of Egypt to the Euphrates River! Not very likely under the Persians.[207]

According to the plain meaning of Artaxerxes' letter, Ezra was to appoint judges and magistrates. This was his only assignment.[208] These judges were to judge every people of the entire satrapy of Beyond the River (כל עמה די בעבר נהרה). They would adjudicate the cases of Jew and non-Jew alike ("those who know the law and those who do not"). There would be no provision for separate judges for the separate ethnic groups. The same men would judge each person in the satrapy. As discussed above (pp. 90–92), contemporary documents from Egypt reveal that under the Persians the different ethnic groups appeared before the same judges. These Iranians were either royal (Judges of the King, *TAD* B.5.1:3) or provincial appointees (Judges of the Province, *TAD* A.5.2:4, 7). There were no Egyptian judges for the Egyptians or Jewish judges for the Jews.

In addition to the Iranian judges, data from Egypt reveal that two other sets of officials were involved in the judicial system: *goškiaʾ*, from the Old Persian **gaušaka*, known as the 'king's ears', and the 'police' *typatyaʾ*, from the Old Persian **tipati-* (*TAD* A.4.5:9, 10). The use of Persian loanwords in Egyptian texts implies a completely Persian judicial system in the Egyptian satrapy, with judges, police, and intelligence officers all Iranian. The same would have been true throughout the empire, including the satrapy of Beyond the River and the province of Yehud. A completely Persian judicial system would have been installed, with Iranian judges and magistrates. Governors would have appointed the provincial officials; and the king, or his agent, would have appointed those at the satrapal level—the royal judges. Ezra was that imperial agent; this was his task: to appoint the royal judges for the satrapy Ebar Nahara.[209]

What law did these Persian judges enforce? The phrase "the law (דתא) of your god and the law (דתא) of the king" in Artaxerxes' Letter (Ezra 7:26) parallels the phrase in the Demotic Chronicle #225: "the law (*hp*) of Pharaoh and of the temple."[210] According to this papyrus, Darius collected and

207. Ska, "Persian Imperial Authorization," 167.

208. Steiner, "The *MBQR* at Qumran."

209. We know that the king did not appoint the royal officers himself but, rather, his agents did. After the conquest of Babylon, and after Cyrus's triumphal entrance into the city, the Nabonidus Chronicle continues (III 20; Grayson, "Chronicle 7: The Nabonidus Chronicle," *Assyrian and Babylonian Chronicles*, 110):

> ^{m}*Gubaru* ^{lú}*pāḫatašú* ^{lú}*pāḫ(at)ūti*^{meš} *ina Bābili*^{ki} *ipteqid.*
> Gubaru, his governor, appointed the officials in Babylon.

I suggest that Ezra held this role in Ebar Nahara, not just in Judah, as is stated in v. 25.

210. See the section above on "The Impact of Darius," chap. 3, pp. 75ff.

codified the customs and traditions (*hpw*) that operated in Egypt prior to the Persian conquest.[211]

What was Darius's purpose in codifying Egyptian custom and tradition?

The Role of Law Codes

Darius collected and wrote down the norms (*hpw*) of Egypt that had been practiced prior to the invasion of Cambyses. Perhaps he or his successors did the same in Yehud. As noted above (pp. 51–54, 75), Egypt had no tradition of written law codes, but in the countries of the Fertile Crescent, law collections were common.[212] They proclaimed the rulers' concern "to make justice prevail in the land, to abolish the wicked and the evil, to prevent the strong from oppressing the weak."[213] Darius's collection of the *hpw* of the Egyptians (and perhaps the תורות of the Jews) ought to be placed in the same context as Mesopotamian law collections. Laws were collected for scientific and antiquarian purposes. They were also collected and published as abstract instances of justice to reassure the populace that the new king was concerned to install right order in the land.[214]

Like his Mesopotamian predecessors, Darius portrayed his concern for justice in his inscriptions. The Persian word *dāta* is similar in meaning to Akkadian *kīnātu* and to Egyptian *hp*. Specifically, it refers to order; *dāta* requires that everything be in its rightful place, that everything be as it is intended to be. In a study of the known instances of the term, P. Briant concludes that *dāta* "designates that which has been fixed, that which corresponds to order. . . . The words *dāta, arta* (justice and truth), and *drauga* (its antonym, the lie) refer to a dynastic and religious ethic rather than to a legal reality. Justice is first and foremost fidelity to the rule of Ahura Mazda and to

211. Knoppers ("An Achaemenid Imperial Authorization of Torah in Yehud?" 125–29) points out that the Chronicler, in describing Jehoshaphat's legal reforms, also distinguishes between a legal matter of YHWH and a legal matter of the king (2 Chr 19:8). Knoppers demonstrates that the Chronicler had two separate legal systems in mind, since difficulties in matters of YHWH were brought to Amariah, the chief priest, while difficulties in matters of the king were brought to Zebadiah, the commander of the house of Judah (2 Chr 19:11). Assuming this reflected Persian-period practice, cultic matters would have been brought to the high priest; all other matters were termed 'royal matters' דבר המלך and would have been brought to royal judges and then to the king's local representative, the Persian governor. Knoppers also points out that the Chronicler (1 Chr 26:29–32) assumes that David appointed the same judges to oversee both types of issues, matters of God and matters of the king. I assume that David plays the role of the Persian governor.

212. See the section on law codes in chap. 2 above (pp. 33–35).

213. Code of Hammurabi, quoted from M. Roth, *Law Collections from Mesopotamia*, 13–22, 77.

214. See also Redford, "The So-Called 'Codification' of Egyptian Law under Darius I."

the power of the king."[215] Lecoq finds a "transparent secularization" in the term *dāta*.[216] That is, the law of the king and the law of Ahura Mazda have merged; the will of the king is the will of the god.[217] This is visible in Darius's Behistun inscription:

> Thus says Darius the King: These are the countries which came unto me; by the favor of Ahura Mazda they were my subjects; they bore tribute to me; *what was said unto them by me either by night or by day, that was done.*
>
> Thus says Darius the King: Within these countries, the man who was excellent, him I rewarded well; he who was evil, him I punished well; by the favor of Ahura Mazda these countries showed respect toward my law (*dāta*); *as was said to them by me, thus was it done.* (DB I 17–24)[218]

In Inscription E from Susa:

> Thus says Darius the King: Much which was ill-done, that I made good. Provinces were in commotion; one man was smiting the other. The following I brought about by the favor of Ahura Mazda, that the one does not smite the other at all, each one is in his place. *My law (dāta)—of that they feel fear*, so that the stronger does not smite nor destroy the weak. (DSe 30–41)[219]

In Inscription A from Naqš-i-Rustam, Darius's tomb:

> A great god is Ahura Mazda, who created this earth, who created yonder sky, who created man, who created happiness for man, who made Darius king, one king of many, one lord of many.
>
> I am Darius the Great King, King of Kings, King of countries containing all kinds of men, King in this great earth far and wide, son of Hystaspes, an Achaemenian, a Persian, son of a Persian, an Aryan, having Aryan lineage.
>
> Thus says Darius the King: By the favor of Ahura Mazda these are the countries which I seized outside of Persia; I ruled over them; they bore tribute to me; *what was said to them by me, that they did; my law (dāta)—that held them firm* [then follows a list of countries seized]. (DNa 1–30)[220]

The word of the king—or his delegates—constituted the law of the king. It also constituted the law of the god Ahura Mazda. By his favor to Darius, Ahura Mazda granted the king obedience from the subject peoples. Darius asserts that, by making him king, Ahura Mazda made Darius's word the law of the god among them. This is evident also in the inscriptions of the later kings. Inscription H of Xerxes from Persepolis reads in part:

215. Briant, "Social and Legal Institutions in Achaemenid Iran," 523.

216. That is, "läicisation transparaît," Lecoq, *Les inscriptions de la Perse achéménide*, 167.

217. This is also the finding of Rendtorff, "Esra und das 'Gesetz,'" in a study of the term's biblical occurrences.

218. Kent, *Old Persian*, 119.

219. Ibid., 142.

220. Ibid., 138.

> And among these countries (where I was king) there was (a place) where previously false gods were worshipped. Afterwards, by the favor of Ahura Mazda, I destroyed that sanctuary of the demons, and I made proclamation, "The demons shall not be worshipped!" Where previously the demons were worshipped, there I worshipped Ahura Mazda and Arta reverently.[221]
>
> And there was other (business) that had been done ill; that I made good. That which I did, all I did by the favor of Ahura Mazda. Ahura Mazda bore me aid, until I completed the work.
>
> You who (will be) hereafter, if you will think, "Happy may I be when living, and when dead may I be blessed," have respect for that law (*dāta*) which Ahura Mazda has established; worship Ahura Mazda and Arta reverently. The man who has *respect for that law (dāta) which Ahura Mazda has established,* and worships Ahura Mazda and Arta reverently, he both becomes happy while living, and becomes blessed when dead. (XPh 35–56)[222]

According to this inscription, Ahura Mazda has established law, *dāta.* This *dāta* was *prima facie* the word of the king. It was also order, equity, fairness, and justice. Artaxerxes' Letter demanded that judges judge according to the *dāta* of the king—that is, the word of the king and his surrogates. In addition to this positive law, judges were commanded to base their decisions on "the *dāta* of your (Ezra's) god."[223] This does not imply that the Persian judges were now suddenly to base their decisions on a local law code. That notion was foreign to judicial concepts in the ancient Near East.[224] Rather, "the law of the god" is in fact natural law—the divinely protected but socially derived concepts of fairness and justice (*dāta, arta, hp, kīnātu*). To appoint judges who judge according to this law is to appoint them to judge according to the immutable and impersonal order of the cosmos. It is to judge according to "truth, justice, order, correct procedures, loyalty, fidelity, correctness, etc."

The Persians may have authorized the Jews to collect and transcribe the customs and traditions of Yehud, as they did in Egypt. However, it was not intended that this collection be binding on the decisions of the Iranian judges that Ezra appointed. They were no more binding on them than was Hammurabi's Code on the judges of Babylon or the laws of the Demotic

221. Kuhrt and Sherwin-White, "Xerxes' Destructions of Babylonian Temples," state that "H. Sancisi-Weerdenburg (*Yaunā en Persai*) has presented strong arguments that this inscription is not historical."

222. Kent, *Old Persian,* 151–52.

223. To Artaxerxes, Ezra's god was 'the God of Heaven' אלה שמייא (Ezra 7:12, 21, 23) and likely a local manifestation of Ahura Mazda. See Bolin, "The Temple of יהו at Elephantine." Rendtorff ("Esra und das 'Gesetz' ") suggests the law of the king was the law of the god (and vice versa), no matter who the god or king was.

224. See the sections on law codes above in chaps. 2 and 3, my "You Shall Appoint Judges," and the references cited there.

Chronicle on the Iranian judges in Egypt.[225] As was true everywhere, the judges that Ezra appointed would have judged according to their own socially constructed notions of fairness and justice.

This was Ezra's mission: Ezra, the Persian official, was to appoint royal judges for the satrapy Beyond the River and for each of its provinces. (This command, as stated in Ezra 7:25, 26, suggests an interesting facet of Persian administration. It was not the satraps or the governors who appointed the royal judges in their jurisdiction but a separate official. These Persian judges—appointed independently of the satrap and governors—could then serve as additional "eyes and ears" of the king.)[226] Ezra had no other administrative authority. He was not governor.[227] The judges he appointed were not bound to obey him. Their obligation was to the governor, the satrap, and the king.

Mosaic Laws in Yehud

If law codes were not intended to influence the decisions of judges, how and why were such Mosaic laws as the Sabbath enforced? If the judges were Persian, as they were in Egypt, how would they even know about the Sabbatical laws? How could Persian judges enforce these laws if they judged according to Persian social norms?

The phrase "the law of the king" in Artaxerxes' Letter refers to the edicts of the Great King, but it also refers to delegated power. The law of the king includes the edicts of satraps, provincial governors, and mayors. These local rulers were the source of positive law in their districts; their commands were the "law of the king." If the governors were Jewish, as they seem to have been in Yehud, they could impose Jewish customs upon the people in their province. In Judah, in 445, the Persian provincial governor was the Jew Nehemiah. Nehemiah promulgated Sabbath laws without appeal to a law book, law code, or law collection (Neh 13:15–22). He simply commanded. His authority stemmed not from a law code but from his status as governor. This is evident from the following passage:

225. Pace Berquist, *Judaism in Persia's Shadow,* 55. Berquist offers no evidence for his statement that laws once codified took on imperial force and helped to standardize administration.

226. That judges would be chosen directly by the king (or his agent) rather than by the satrap is reminiscent of Xenophon's remark on the installation of local garrison commanders. These were to be chosen directly by the king as well, not by the satrap. The garrison commanders were appointed directly by the king (or his agent) so that they would serve as "eyes and ears" of the king within the satrapy. It appears that the same function is attested here for the royal judges.

227. Pace Berquist, *Judaism in Persia's Shadow,* 55.

> In those days I saw in Judah people pressing wine on the Sabbath, bringing heaps [of grain] and loading [them] on donkeys (and even wine, grapes, figs, and every kind of burden) and bringing [them] to Jerusalem on the Sabbath. I warned [them] against selling food then.
>
> Even the Tyrians who settled there[228] were bringing fish and every type of merchandise and were selling them on the Sabbath to the Jews in[229] Jerusalem.
>
> I prosecuted (ואריבה) the nobles of Judah, and I said to them, "What is this evil thing you are doing to desecrate the Sabbath? Is this not what your fathers did so that our God brought upon us all this evil and upon this city? And you add wrath upon Israel by profaning the Sabbath?
>
> And it was just as the shadows fell on the gates of Jerusalem before the Sabbath that *I commanded* the doors be closed. *I commanded* they should not be opened until after the Sabbath. *I set some of my men to guard the gates* and not to let anyone bring burdens into the city on the Sabbath. (Neh 13:15–19)

Nehemiah established the Sabbatical law and enforced it by means of the men under his command, soldiers from the garrison. Nehemiah was the source of positive law in his district; as he commanded, so it was done. His commands may have coincided with a Mosaic law code, but the law code was not the source of his authority. As elsewhere throughout the Achaemenid Empire, Nehemiah's authority stemmed from his status as governor and from the soldiers under his command.

Nehemiah also promulgated an edict against intermarriage (Neh 13:23–25):

> And in those days, I saw Jews who married Ashdodite, Ammonite, and Moabite women. Half their children spoke Ashdodite. None of them knew how to speak Judean, but only the language of the various peoples.
>
> I entered into a dispute (אריב) with them, cursed them, beat some of them, pulled out the hair of their beards (ואמרתם), and I made them swear by God [saying], "You shall not give your daughters to their sons nor take their daughters for your sons or for yourselves."[230]

The root ריב used here can denote physical fighting, for example, in Exod 21:18,

228. The Hebrew has בה 'in it', referring to either Judah or Jerusalem.

229. Deleting the *waw.*

230. P. R. Davies ("Minimalists and Maximalists," 72) describes the society reflected in the books of Ezra and Nehemiah as "xenophobic." This passage depicts the society as not being xenophobic enough for Nehemiah's taste. The large amount of intermarriage against which both Nehemiah and Ezra fulminate argues against a xenophobic society. It also argues against the notion of a "culture of resistance" suggested by Smith-Christopher in "The Politics of Ezra"; and against "the attempt [by the גולה community] at inward consolidation of a threatened minority" (idem, "The Mixed Marriage Crisis in Ezra 9–10").

וכי־יריבן אנשים והכה־איש את־רעהו באבן או באגרף ולא ימות ונפל למשכב:

when men struggle (יריבן) and one strikes the other with a stone or fist. . . .

It can also refer to a legal dispute: Isa 3:13: נצב לריב יהוה ועמד לדין עמים 'YHWH stands forth to argue (לריב) his case; he stands to judge peoples'. As in Isaiah, the situation described in Nehemiah refers to a judicial preceding, not a physical struggle. The term might reasonably be translated 'prosecute'.

According to Heltzer:

> In general, we know that in the whole Eastern Mediterranean in ancient time, cutting or plucking of the hair and beard by force was considered to be an act of disgrace and humiliation of free persons and that, to the contrary, special styles of beards and hair coiffures were esteemed as a sign of honor. Taking this into account, it is difficult to imagine that the aristocrats of Judah stood in line, and the governor Nehemiah in person was beating them and plucking their beards.[231]

Rather than an impetuous act, plucking hair from the head and beard was an official punishment in the Achaemenid Empire. According to a cuneiform text from the Murašû archive (CBS 5213), two men agreed by contract to do groundbreaking on the land of Rimūṭ-Maš. The text then states:

> If they have not completed the groundbreaking by the first day of the fifth month, they shall be beaten one hundred times with a *niṭpu*, their beards and hair (of the head) shall be plucked out, and Rībat, son of Bēl-Irība, servant of Rimūṭ-Ninurta, shall keep them in the workhouse.[232]

The text is dated to the fifth year of Darius II, 420 B.C.E. Here we see the punishments of flogging and imprisonment, as well as that of plucking the head and beard.

Nehemiah similarly accused (לריב) some men of marrying foreign women, judged them guilty, and ordered their punishment—all according to Persian law.[233] The men submitted because they had no choice (one possible sanction for disobedience was death). Nehemiah, as Persian governor, had the right and ability to create law, its interpretation, and to execute sanctions for its disobedience.[234] The prohibition against intermarriage may have been

231. Heltzer, "The Flogging and Plucking of Beards." I thank P. Briant for calling this article to my attention.

232. Ibid., 306.

233. Pace Blenkinsopp (*Ezra–Nehmiah*, 364), who considers the incident an example of Nehemiah's "impulsive and even intemperate nature"; and also Williamson (*Ezra, Nehemiah*, 398), who states: "Nehemiah's violent outburst may have been a spontaneous reaction to his discovery; . . . the fact that he beat but 'some of the men' is not suggestive of any kind of judicial procedure."

234. In this sense, here is the "imperial authorization" of which P. Frei speaks. I argue however that Nehemiah, as governor, was its source in Yehud.

part of Mosaic law, and the Persians may have been involved in codifying it. However, no law code could have given Nehemiah the right to prohibit intermarriage. His right lay in his office of governor.

If Ezra 7:25–26 was part of a genuine commission from the Persian king Artaxerxes to a person named Ezra, and I believe it was, then Ezra's assignment in 398 was to appoint judges and magistrates.[235] Like the ones in Egypt, they would have been Iranian and would have judged first according to the *dāta* of the king and his representatives (the satrap or governor) and second according to the *dāta* of the god. The former term refers to positive law, created by edict. The latter term refers to "natural" law. Judges would not have judged according to a law code; the law collections were not *codes* in the modern sense. Rather, they would have made their decisions according to their socially constructed concepts of right, fairness, and justice. These would necessarily be Persian concepts—not Jewish! In 445, however, the governor of Yehud was Nehemiah, the Jew, and he outlawed business on the Sabbath and intermarriage. His authority stemmed not from a law collection but from his office as governor. These edicts could not be undone. The judges that Ezra later appointed were bound by Nehemiah's edicts.

Artaxerxes' Letter puts the behavior of the local leadership (ראשי האבות זקנים) and the local assembly (קהל) in perspective. The sanctions listed in the edict (i.e., the ability to confiscate land and property, to threaten with death, flogging, and imprisonment) were not given to a קהל or to the local leadership. Artaxerxes assigned these powers to Persian officials—to the royal judges and magistrates that Ezra appointed. He did not authorize local leaders or local assemblies to formulate law or to enforce it. As was true throughout the Persian Empire, local leaders and assemblies met only to hear the law imposed upon them by satrap or governor.[236] Persian judges and officials executed that law. There was no self-rule in Judah, as there was none in any province in the empire.

The שרים who informed Ezra of the marriage of Jews to the peoples of the lands (Ezra 9:1); who had the power to order the destruction of property (10:7, 8); and who had the power to impose sanctions for failure to divorce (10:14, 16) would not have been local leaders or local "heads of fathers' houses." Those with power in the Persian Empire were royally appointed satraps, governors, and the Persian judges and magistrates who obeyed them.

235. The date of Ezra's arrival is discussed briefly below (p. 223).

236. Several scholars (e.g., Blenkinsopp, *Ezra–Nehemiah*, n. 7, pp. 174ff.; Williamson, *Ezra, Nehemiah*, n. 8, pp. 127, 280) place Nehemiah 8 (reading the law) between Ezra 8 (Ezra arrives in Judah) and 9 (the people learn they haven't been following the law). Scholars make this change because they realize that the law against intermarriage was not formulated by the people in a popular assembly but was part of an edict officially imposed upon them.

In the case of early-4th-century Yehud, these judges and magistrates were appointed by Ezra, the royal agent.

The Authenticity of Artaxerxes' Letter to Ezra

These conclusions necessarily rest on the historicity of two verses (Ezra 7:25–26) in the so-called Artaxerxes Rescript. Scholars have generally concluded that the Rescript (Ezra 7:11–26) is an authentic letter from the Persian king that had been updated in the Hellenistic period.[237] Porten has shown that the number of contemporary Achaemenid forms and the large number of Persian words in it indicate a genuine document.[238] Grabbe argues that it includes a mixture of early and late morphemes (כון and הום instead of כם and הם; די and דנה instead of זי and זנה/א) and suggests that it may be a genuine document that was updated and perhaps even added to in the Hellenistic period.[239] Muraoka and Porten agree that, although the final *nun* is preferred in the Egyptian papyri for feminine object suffixes, plural morphemes occur with both final *nun* and final *mem* for both masculine and feminine object suffixes.[240] Most of the examples of masculine final *nun* are from the Hermopolis Papyri, which are late 6th or early 5th century, and Muraoka and Porten interpret them as precursors of the corresponding forms that appear in later Aramaic dialects. There is, moreover, the phrase פרסכן ('your salary'—but addressed to a single man!) in a letter dated to the second quarter of the 5th century, and להן ('to them') and ביניהן ('between them') referring to men in letters from the Jewish garrison at Elephantine. These all appear without the *waw.* Regarding a final *m* or *n,* no consistency can be expected.

As for plene or defective spelling, Muraoka and Porten note plene spelling of the morpheme הום in the letter from the Jewish garrison to Judah (לנפשהום, זניהום, עליהום; all in *TAD* A.4.7 and 8). The only morphemes that are not attested in the Egyptian papyri until the 3rd century are הון and כון.

Janzen objects primarily to the use of די throughout the letter rather than זי.[241] However, Aramaic witnesses a gradual sound change during the

237. E.g., Blenkinsopp, "Was the Pentateuch the Civic and Religious Constitution?"; Steiner, "The *MBQR* at Qumran." Janzen argues that the letter is a forgery, since if it were authentic, it would have been initiated by Ezra, and a quotation of the original request would have appeared in the letter. This is not necessary; the response of Bagavahya and Delaiah to the community at Yeb (*TAD* A.4.9) does not quote from the original request. Schwiderski (*Handbuch,* 362–64) argues that the greeting formula in Ezra 7:11, 12 is ל rather than על or אל. The former is characteristic of the Hellenistic period, not the Achaemenid.

238. Porten, "The Documents in the Book of Ezra," 186.

239. Grabbe, "The Law of Moses in the Ezra Tradition," 93.

240. Muraoka and Porten, *A Grammar of Egyptian Aramaic,* 53–54.

241. Janzen, "The 'Mission' of Ezra and the Persian-Period Temple Community."

Achaemenid period from ז to ד, and both זי and די can appear in the same letter (e.g., *TAD* A.2.3).[242] Moreover, as Muraoka and Porten point out:

> Most instructive is . . . *TAD* B 3.4, which has זין ודבב [legal] 'suit or process' (line 17) [yet] דין ודבב [in lines 12, 13, and 14]. The spelling here with ז is best interpreted as a hypercorrection: Haggai [the scribe], on the alert for the common misspelling by ד for the correct ז, here inadvertently writes Zayin instead of the correct Dalet. This would indicate that, by 437 BCE when the document was drawn up, the sound in question was considered better represented by ד than by ז.[243]

With these orthographic caveats in mind, we examine the letter. The decree states in part (Ezra 7:25, 26):

> And you, Ezra, according to the god-given wisdom you possess,[244] appoint magistrates and judges who would judge all the people who are in Beyond the River—all who know the law of your god and [all] who do not know, to inform them. All who would not execute the law of your god and the law of the king zealously, let a judicial verdict be executed on him: either for death, or flogging,[245] confiscation of property, or imprisonment.

None of the contested plural forms occurs in this passage; thus, there seems no reason not to view these verses as an authentic command to Ezra. He was to appoint judges and magistrates; this was his mission.[246]

Working backward, we read v. 24, which provides a clue to the date of the letter and of Ezra's tenure in Yehud:

> Let it be known to you, לכם [i.e., to all you royal treasurers in Beyond the River], that [regarding] all the priests, all the Levites, the singers, the gatekeepers, the temple servants (נתיניא), or cult servants (פלחי בית אלהא) of the house of this god, neither tribute, poll tax, nor land tax shall you be authorized to impose upon them (עליהם).[247]

This passage employs genuine Achaemenid suffix forms throughout and so can also be assumed to stem from an original letter. The list of temple officials may have been added by a Jewish redactor as a gloss on the generic פלחי בית

242. Folmer, *The Aramaic Language in the Achaemenid Period*, 49–63; and Muraoka and Porten, *A Grammar of Egyptian Aramaic*, 2–6.

243. Ibid., 3.

244. Literally: "the wisdom of your god which is in your hand." This translation is suggested by the NRSV.

245. The term *šršw* is Persian and denotes "beating, flogging, caning, or other types of corporeal punishment" (Rundgren, "Zur Bedeutung von *ŠRŠW*").

246. After all, *someone* appointed the judges; Steiner, "The *MBQR* at Qumran."

247. For discussion of these taxes, see Ephʿal, "Syria–Palestine under Achaemenid Rule," 158–59; Schaper, "The Jerusalem Temple," 535–36, and above, pp. 87–88 nn. 186–87.

אלהא ('temple cult servants'). As shown above, exemption of temple officials from taxation and tribute was not unusual in the Persian Empire; it may have been given to the priests of YHWH as a quid pro quo for Ezra's services to the king. The exemptions to the priests of Apollo, the Temple of Neith, and the priests of Marduk in Babylon are other examples. There is no mention here of priestly exemption from corvée labor, but it invariably accompanied exemption from taxes and tribute. If the letter implied priestly exemption from corvée labor, and if it is historical, then Ezra would necessarily have come to Beyond the River after Nehemiah—in the 7th year of Artaxerxes II (398). Nehemiah had imposed corvée labor upon the priests (Neh 3:1), something he could not have done had Ezra given them an exemption earlier.

Working backward, we read v. 23 of the rescript of Artaxerxes:

> All that the God of Heaven commands, let it be done diligently for the house of the God of Heaven lest there be wrath (קצף)upon the kingdom of the king and upon his sons. (Ezra 7:23)

The word for 'diligent' is the Persian *adarazda*, which implies a Persian author for this verse. It means 'religiously eager, devoted' and is most-often restricted to references to Ahura Mazda. It has the connotation of continuing the faith (e.g., Yasna 31.1).[248] This verse most likely was included in Artaxerxes' original letter; the wording is consistent with Persian thought. Zoroaster did not envision Ahura Mazda to be all powerful. Rather, the god received his power from the devotion and sacrifices of his followers. A Zoroastrian daily prayer can be rendered: "Arise for me, Lord! By your most holy spirit, O Mazda, take to yourself might through devotion, swiftness through good gift-offerings, potent force through truth, protection through good purpose."[249] Mankind's devotions and offerings help Ahura Mazda defeat evil.

Janzen suggests, however, that the reference to קצף in the passage appears "odd," since the word never appears in any extrabiblical Aramaic text.[250] However, *kšap* is Persian from Sanskrit *ksap* 'night', and the concept of a hostile "wrath" (Aēšma), the generic night demon, is central to Zoroastrian thought (Y. 29:2; 30:6; 48:12).[251] The Zoroastrian Artaxerxes could certainly have seen the Temple to the God of Heaven in Jerusalem as a Temple to Ahura Mazda.

Working backward again, we come to vv. 21–22 of the rescript:

> And from me (I, Artaxerxes the king) is issued an order to all the treasurers of Beyond the River that (די) whatever Ezra, the priest, scribe of the law of

248. G. Windfuhr, personal communication, April 2000.

249. Boyce, *Zoroastrianism*, 74.

250. Janzen, "The 'Mission' of Ezra." It does appear in the Akkadian of the Armana Letters and is judged Old Canaanite by Hoftijzer and Jongeling, ad loc.

251. Boyce, *A History of Zoroastrianism*, 1.87.

> the God of Heaven, shall ask of you (ישאלנכון), shall be done eagerly up to one hundred talents of silver, one hundred cors of wheat, one hundred baths of wine, one hundred baths of oil, and salt without being counted. (Ezra 7:21–22)

The presence of this late form spelled plene, **ישאלנכון**, suggests at least that this verse was touched up by a copyist. Janzen asserts, however, that the particle **די** 'that', which introduces the command of Artaxerxes, is nowhere used to introduce speech in any of the extrabiblical Persian-period official correspondence. He concludes that this passage and therefore the entire letter is not authentic. Yet we see the same construction in *TAD* A.6.13:4, 5:

> **כעת ארשם כן אמר אנתם הנדרז עבדו לחתובסתי פקיד ורוהי זי עד מנדת בגיא זי ורוהי אספרן והדאבגו יהנפק**

> Now Arsham says thus: You all, issue instruction to Ḥatubasti, official of Varuvahya, *that* he release the rent of the domains of Varuvahya in full and the accrued increment.

This construction is identical to the construction in our verse.[252] It is rare in Biblical Hebrew but does occur in Persian-period texts (e.g., Esth 3:4; Job 36:24; 37:20; 1 Chr 21:18, contrast 2 Sam 24:18). It also occurs in Persian inscriptions. The Persian word *tya* 'that' introduces direct and indirect quotation (DB 1.32, 52; DNa 38f.; DNb 8, 10, 19).[253]

This passage is directed to the relevant powers, the satrapal treasurers. The amount of silver (100 talents) has seemed impossibly high, and some argue that the rescript is therefore not historical.[254] However, Diodorus Siculus states (16.40.2) that "Artaxerxes III, readily acceding to the request (of Thebes), made a gift to (Thebes) of 300 talents of silver." The amount of 100 talents may not be extraordinary, considering the great wealth of the kings of Persia. It has been assumed that the 100 cors of wheat were for the temple's cereal offerings; the 100 baths of wine for its drink offerings; the oil and salt to accompany the temple offerings and the oil for the temple lamp.[255] These amounts would have supplied the temple for about two years.

There is no mention in vv. 21–22 that these items were for the temple, however. They are separate from the silver and gold offered to the temple by the king and his counselors and separate from what is offered to Ezra in Babylon (7:15, 16). Those funds were freewill offerings. They were not to come from the provincial treasuries of the satrapy Beyond the River. Verses

252. I thank B. Porten for pointing this out to me.

253. Kent, *Old Persian*, 93, 187.

254. It has been suggested that 100 talents would weigh more than 3 tons! Blenkinsopp, *Ezra–Nehemiah*, 151; Grabbe, *Ezra–Nehemiah*, 138–41; Williamson suggests an error in transmission (*Ezra, Nehemiah*, 103).

255. Williamson, ibid., 103.

21 and 22, however, are orders to the treasurers of the various provinces in the satrapy. They represent less than one-third of the annual tribute to the king from the satrapy Ebir Nahara (Hdt. 3.91). These items were to be diverted from the king's revenues to pay the judges and other officials of the satrapy Beyond the River whom Ezra appointed. They are exactly the kinds of items that are listed as payments to officials in the Persepolis Tablets.[256] Texts from the time of Ezra reveal that officials were most often paid in wheat and wine but were beginning to be paid in silver as well. While not numerous, references to the payment of oil as part of the monthly rations to officials are not unknown.[257] The Persepolis Fortification Tablets do not mention salt. Perhaps it was distributed as rations but not counted.

It is interesting to note that the treasurers had wheat, wine, and oil at their disposal, as well as silver. Taxes paid in kind were evidently stored for use to pay satrapal officials and not sent on to Susa. This provides an explanation of the ubiquitous stamped jar handles found in Persian-period strata. These handles are stamped with the seal of the governor, with the name of the province, or both, and were most likely used to store these taxes.[258] Silver was usually melted down into ingots and sent on to the Great King.[259] Although coins were available, silver was still weighed out, as it was at Elephantine.

256. Idem, "The Governors of Judah under the Persians," 80. Cf. Cameron, *Persepolis Treasury Tablets*; Hallock, *Persepolis Fortification Tablets*; idem, "The Evidence of the Persepolis Tablets."

257. Hallock, *Persepolis Fortification Tablets*, PF 795, p. 234. Most commentators render the word for 'oil' in the Artaxerxes rescript *mešaḥ* 'anointing oil', giving it cultic connotations. This is not necessary. In Aramaic, it is simply the normal word for 'oil', 'fat', 'goose fat', 'resin', 'pine wood'—any cooking oil or perfumed oil (Jastrow, *Dictionary of the Targumim*, def. III, 851; Hoftijzer and Jongeling, *Dictionary of Northwest Semitic Inscriptions*, 699; *TAD* A.4.7:20). Payment of grain, drink, and oil was also used in Judah. These three items served as rations to the Sidonians and Tyrians for bringing cedar from Lebanon to build the House of YHWH (Ezra 3:7). Here the word for 'oil' is the more usual *šemen*. That an oil for bathing or perfume is meant and not oil for cooking or cultic purposes can be inferred from the LXX's χαρρα = χρῖμα, i.e., 'cream'. This is the meaning of the Aramaic *mešaḥ*.

258. Carter, *The Emergence of Yehud*, esp. pp. 259–68; Christophe, *The Yehud Stamped Jar Handle Corpus*; Stern, *Material Culture*, 196–214. Christophe suggests that the concentration of the finds of the *Yehud* stamped jars in Jerusalem and Ramat Raḥel, rather than scattered over the entire province, implies that the jars were used for trade rather than taxation (pp. 181ff.). Along with Carter (pp. 282–83), my intuitions are the opposite. The large number of inscribed jar handles found at Ramat Raḥel suggests that this town served as a major collection site and holding area in Judah. From here, rations could have been paid out to Persian officials and their employees. The soldiers at Elephantine also received monthly allotments in silver and grain from the royal storehouse (*TAD* B.2–4).

259. Schaper, "The Jerusalem Temple"; Slotsky, *The Bourse of Babylon*.

Working backward, we come to vv. 15–20:

> [You shall] bring silver and gold that the king and his advisors voluntarily offer to the god of Israel who dwells in Jerusalem and any silver and gold that is found in the whole province of Babylon with the contributions of the people and the priests [which] they contribute to the house of their (הם) god that is in Jerusalem. Therefore you shall buy in full with this silver bulls, rams, lambs, their (הון) grain offerings, their (הון) libations, and offer them on the altar of the house of your (כם) god which is in Jerusalem. And whatever is good to you and to your brothers to do with the rest of the silver and gold you may do; according to the wish of your (כם) god you may do. And the vessels that are given to you for the service of the house of your god deliver to the god of Jerusalem. And the rest of the needs of the house of your god that befall you to give, you may give from the house of the treasury of the king. (Ezra 7:15–20)

These verses contain a mixture of early and late constructions; they likely do not stem from the original letter. The Achaemenid rulers did not use *Israel* as the name of the province. Yet, if Ezra's mission from the Persian king to Yehud is at all historical, Artaxerxes would certainly have sent gifts along with him for the temple in Jerusalem.[260]

Working back still further, we come to v. 14:

> Be it resolved that [an order] has been sent from the king and his seven advisors [to you] to supervise over (לבקרא על) [the establishment of a judiciary system] in Yehud and Jerusalem according to the law of your god, which is under your authority.[261] (Ezra 7:14)

Steiner brings to bear several parallels from Aramaic documents at Qumran to conclude that לבקרא על does not mean 'to make an investigation at' or 'to conduct an investigation over' but 'to supervise', 'oversee'.[262] He finds parallels in the Greek term ἐπισκοπέω, which means 'to inspect, examine' but also to 'exercise the office of ἐπίσκοπος'. This office can be a 'supervisor, inspector' but also one sent by Athens to subject states. It has the latter meaning in mid–late-5th-century Athens. In the Athenian decrees, the term is often used to refer to people coming from Athens to establish democratic and judicial arrangements in newly subjected states. The most famous example occurs in Aristophanes, *Birds*, produced in 414 B.C.E., in which the inspector is sent to set up a legal system in Cloudcuckootown. Steiner suggests that לבקרא is to 'exercise the office of מבקר' and that this was the temporary task of setting up a Persian judicial system in Persian subject states. According to Steiner, "a

260. The literature on the Achaemenids' gifts to subordinates is vast. See Briant, *HEP*, chap. 8.

261. The emendation is based on Steiner, "The *MBQR* at Qumran."

262. Ibid.

close reading of the text shows that [Ezra's] authority was limited to setting up a judicial system."[263] This is the view suggested here.

Finally we come to vv. 12 and 13:

> Artaxerxes King of Kings to Ezra (לעזרא) the priest, scribe of the law of the God of heaven: גמיר! And now, from me it is ordered that all who would volunteer from my kingdom from among his people Israel and his priests and Levites to go to Jerusalem with him, let him go. (Ezra 7:12–13)

These verses betray the work of later writers. The use of the preposition ל rather than על or even אל reflects Hellenistic usage.[264] The term "Israel," while typical of Jewish writers from Babylon (e.g., Deutero-Isaiah), seems unlikely to have been used by Persian rulers, who referred to the province as *yhd* or *yhwd.*

It appears then that only vv. 21–26 are from the original letter. If so, vv. 25 and 26 define Ezra's mission. His task was to appoint judges and to supervise a Persian judicial system in Beyond the River.

Yoḥanan the Priest

A single extant silver coin may help to elucidate temple-palace relations in Judea during the Persian period.[265] The reverse bears a legend in Paleo-Hebrew: on left, upward, יוחנן; on right, downward, הכוהן: 'Yoḥanan the priest'. This is the only extant Persian-period Judean coin that bears the title הכוהן. Based on a study of similar Cilician and Samarian coins from datable coin hoards, I was able to conclude that the coin had been minted between 378 and 368.[266] This means that a Yoḥanan was high priest sometime between those dates; a high priest named Yoḥanan is well attested in the biblical texts, the Elephantine Papyri, and Josephus's *Antiquities of the Jews.*

According to Neh 12:22, the priests of the Persian Empire, down to "Darius the Persian," were Eliašib, Yoiada (Yehoiada), Yoḥanan, and Yaddua. Most scholars assume this Darius to be Darius II (423–405) and not Darius III (335–331), the last Persian king.[267] Eliašib was high priest when Nehemiah arrived in Jerusalem in 445 (Neh 3:1). Nehemiah left Jerusalem to go to the king in 432 (Neh 13:6, 7) and returned perhaps after three years (the probable

263. Ibid., 629.

264. Folmer, *The Aramaic Language,* 628; Schwiderski, *Handbuch,* 362. Tellingly, Muraoka and Porten do not discuss the use of *l-* in the address formula, since it never appears in their Egyptian texts.

265. The coin has been published by Barag, "A Silver Coin of Yoḥanan the High Priest"; idem, "A Silver Coin of Yoḥanan and the High Priest"; idem, "Some Notes on a Silver Coin of Joḥanan the High Priest."

266. See my "Silver Coin of Yoḥanan Hakkôhēn."

267. E.g., Barag, "A Silver Coin of Yoḥanan and the High Priest," 11.

stay abroad of Arsames, the Persian satrap). He describes the state of affairs he found at his return (Neh 13:28), "And one of the sons of Yehoiada, son of Eliašib the high priest, married [the daughter of] Sanballat, the Horonite, and I removed him from me." The usual translation of this verse is "One of the sons of Yehoiada, son of the high priest Eliašib. . . ."[268] It is equally possible to read, "One of the sons of Yehoiada, the high priest, son of Eliašib."[269] According to the latter interpretation, Yehoiada was high priest some time after 432, when Nehemiah returned from Babylon. Eliašib may have already been elderly in 445 when Nehemiah arrived; we hear no more of him. Yehoiada may have been high priest from the time of Nehemiah's arrival until Yoḥanan, his son, succeeded him. When would that have been?

A high priest named Yoḥanan is known from an archive found on the Nile Island of Elephantine. As stated above (chap. 3, pp. 99ff.), a letter (*TAD* A.4.7) was sent in 407 from the Jewish garrison there "to our lord Bagavahya, governor of Judah (פחת יהוד)." This letter states that the garrison had sent a letter three years before to Bagavahya but also to Yehoḥanan the high priest (כהנא רבא) and his colleagues, the priests (lines 17–18). Thus, a Yehoḥanan was high priest in Jerusalem in 410, probably the beginning of his term. According to the biblical text, he was the son of Yehoiada, who would have been high priest sometime between 445 and 410. The Jewish garrison at Elephantine must have thought that Yoḥanan had some secular authority, because they appealed to him for help against the Persian officials in Egypt. The answer came only after three years—not from Yoḥanan, but from Bagavahya and Delaiah, Sanballat's son, governors of Judah and Samaria respectively. Yoḥanan's failure to respond may indicate that the high priest had no secular authority to intervene. Or, it may reflect a power struggle between Yoḥanan and Bagavahya early in both their careers. Such a power struggle is suggested by Josephus (*Ant.* 11.297):

> On the death of the high priest Eliasib, his son Jōdas (Ἰώδας/Yehoiada) succeeded him in the high priesthood. And, when he also died, Jōannēs (Ἰωάννης/Yoḥanan), who was his son, assumed this office; it was through him that Bagōsēs, the general of the other Artaxerxes (Βαγώσης ὁ στρατηγός τοῦ ἄλλου Ἀρταξέρξου) defiled the sanctuary and imposed tribute on the Jews, so that before offering the daily sacrifices they had to pay from the public treasury fifty drachmae for every lamb.
>
> The reason for this was the following happening. Jōannēs had a brother named Jēsūs (Yehošuaʿ), and Bagōsēs, whose friend he was, promised to obtain the high priesthood for him. With this assurance, therefore, Jēsūs quar-

268. So the NRSV.

269. This is recognized by many commentaries, e.g., Blenkinsopp, *Ezra–Nehemiah,* ad loc.; Williamson, *Ezra, Nehemiah,* ad loc.

> reled with Jōannēs in the temple, and provoked his brother so far that in his anger he killed him. . . .
>
> Now when Bagōsēs, the general of Artaxerxes, learned that Jōannēs, the high priest of the Jews, had murdered his own brother Jēsūs in the temple, he at once set upon the Jews. . . . Bagōsēs made the Jews suffer seven years for the death of Jēsūs.[270]

If Bagōsēs is Bagavahya, and if Yoḥanan's brother Jesus was the one who married the daughter of Sanballat (Neh 13:28), then Bagavahya, by supporting Sanballat's son-in-law for high priest, indicates that he was cozy with the Sanballat family and was attempting to exclude Yoḥanan from the sources of power. This coziness is further suggested by his collaborating with Delaiah, Sanballat's son (and Jesus' brother-in-law?), on the response to the Jewish community at Elephantine. Bagavahya may have thrown his lot in with the other governors of Beyond the River. If so, then Yoḥanan had sided with the Persians. It may be surmised then that this Yoḥanan, the high priest and the (grand)son of Eliašib, was the very same Yehoḥanan in whose apartment Ezra spent that tearful night (Ezra 10:6).

Scholars question whether the Jōannēs and Bagōsēs in Josephus refer to the Yoḥanan and Bagavahya of the Elephantine Papyri.[271] Williamson suggests that they are not the same, even if the same names lie behind both renditions. He argues that Josephus had a reliable source for the incident but misinterpreted it.[272] The phrase "the other Artaxerxes" refers literally to Artaxerxes II (405–358), but according to Williamson, Josephus may not have known there were several Artaxerxes and conflated them.[273] Moreover, Josephus's Bagōsēs cannot be the Bagavahya of the papyri because the Bagavahya in the papyri is called פחה 'governor', whereas Josephus calls Bagōsēs a military officer, στρατηγός. Williamson argues that another Bagoses, a Persian general of Artaxerxes III, a vicious eunuch (Diodorus 17.3), better fits Josephus's source. Following Cross, he argues for supplementing the biblical high priest list with another Yoḥanan-Yaddua pair who would have been high priests during the time of Artaxerxes III (358–338).[274]

It is likely, however, that Bagavahya was both governor of Yehud and military στρατηγός. In fact, it was common, if not obligatory, for governors

270. This is the translation by R. Marcus, in the Loeb Classical Library.

271. For a discussion of the issues, see Grabbe, "Who Was the Bagoses of Josephus?"

272. Williamson, "The Historical Value of Josephus' *Jewish Antiquities* XI"; idem, "The Governors of Judah under the Persians."

273. There were actually four Artaxerxes. The Persian king Arses (335–333) took the throne name Artaxerxes IV.

274. Cross, "Aspects of Samaritan and Jewish History"; idem, "Papyri and Their Historical Implications"; idem, "A Reconstruction of the Judaean Restoration." This is also argued by Schaper, *Priester und Levitin*, 158. But see VanderKam, "Jewish High Priests."

and satraps to go to battle and to lead a contingent of troops at the king's command. The Achaemenid Empire was in a constant state of war or preparation for war. The Great King had to be ready to deploy huge armies anywhere in its realm—at little cost. There were conquests and rebellions, satrapal revolts, dynastic struggles, and attacks from Grecian cities. The satrap's major responsibility was to maintain an organized battalion that could respond immediately to the command of the king.[275] The governor Bagavahya would have had to lead a contingent in his satrap's army.

The coin minted with the name Yoḥanan indicates that a Yoḥanan was high priest sometime between 378–368. If so, he was likely the same Yoḥanan who was high priest in 410 and in 398, the probable date of Ezra's arrival. There is no reason to doubt a period of 40 years in office for a high priest. Nor is there reason to add other high priests named Yoḥanan to the biblical high priest list. This Yoḥanan would have been the one who killed his brother Yešuaʿ in the temple. In 410, when Yoḥanan was high priest, the Persian governor of Yehud was Bagavahya (i.e., Bagohi or Bagōsēs), known from the Elephantine Papyri. This Bagavahya would have been the Bagōsēs who placed the surtax on the temple priesthood in response to the murder. Josephus reports that the surtax was lifted 7 years later. If it was lifted at the time of Ezra's arrival, which seems likely in view of the instructions in the Letter, then the murder took place in 405, at the time of Cyrus the Younger's revolt. If Bagavahya was away from Yehud leading a contingent in the battle against Cyrus, then it would have been an opportune moment for Yoḥanan to kill his brother.

According to Josephus, Yoḥanan murdered his brother because Bagavahya had promised to give Yešuaʿ the priesthood. The power of the governor to appoint the high priest in Judah is consistent with what has been noted in other satrapies of the Persian Empire. However else we are to understand it, the murder indicates a power struggle between Yoḥanan and the governor. It is curious that Yoḥanan was not executed for the act. He must have had the support of some highly placed Persians—quite likely the king himself. The coins with the legend *Yoḥanan ha-Kohen* may indicate Persian support for Yoḥanan's priesthood over that of the governor Bagavahya, rather than any attempt to usurp power.

If Yoḥanan was high priest from 410 (as indicated in the papyri) to 370 (as suggested from the coin), then it is entirely likely that his son Yaddua followed as high priest from 370 to 333, the time of the Macedonian conquest. It would have been this Yaddua who welcomed Alexander to Jerusalem (*Ant.* 11.326). The list of priests in Neh 12:22 is complete up to Darius the Persian, that is, Darius III, and was written by an editor during the Hellenistic period.

275. Briant, "Guerre, tribut et forces."

If Yoḥanan obtained any secular control, it did not outlast himself. He may have seized power while Bagavahya was away fighting the war against Cyrus the Younger, and demonstrated it by murdering his brother, Bagavahya's favorite. Perhaps he achieved favor with the Persians thereby and was able to mint some coins with his name on them. If he had any secular authority, it was short-lived and illusory. The coins of Yeḥizqiyah הפחה, which closely follow those of Yoḥanan, indicate that Yeḥizqiyah became governor after Bagavahya and held the post under Mazday, the satrap, until the advent of Alexander the Great. Secular control quickly reverted into the hands of Persia.[276]

Alexander

In the spring of 336, a vanguard of 10,000 Macedonians, accompanied by a fleet, crossed the Hellespont. By fall, Philip had been assassinated, and Alexander, at age 20, was declared king of Macedon (Diodorus 16.94–17.2).[277] After avenging his father's death and securing control of Greece, Alexander gathered his army to the Hellespont and crossed with it from Europe into Asia (Diodorus 17.17). Alexander's passage through the Greek cities of Asia Minor was swift and sure. Land owned by the Great King became Alexander's. Tribute due Darius became subject to Alexander's satraps and governors. By the end of that year, Alexander controlled Ephesus, Magnesia, the Tralles, Miletus, and Caria. Persian losses were immense. Its top generals were gone, either grievously wounded, killed in battle, had committed suicide, or had fled. The bulk of the Persian army retreated southward. By September 333, Alexander had captured Cilicia, defeating the combined forces of Cilicia and Beyond the River, led by Mazday, its satrap. Mazday retreated to Issus in northern Syria. There he was joined by the Egyptian army led by Sabakes, the satrap of Egypt, and the royal army led by Darius himself (accompanied by his court). By November of 333, Alexander had defeated these combined Persian armies and had captured the royal mother and wives. Darius fled, retreating southward down the Euphrates with Mazday and the remnants of the Persian army with him. Besides the many killed and captured

276. Spaer ("Jaddua the High Priest?") suggests that a coin with the proto-Aramaic inscription YDWʿ was minted by a Judean high priest in the first half of the 4th century, a priest whose name had dropped out of the list of priests due to haplography. Meshorer has since concluded that these Yadduaʿ coins are Samarian. Meshorer states (personal communication): "Except for the coin published by Spaer and myself, there [are three others]. All come from Samaria. . . . Not only the provenience, but the 'fabric' is decisive. (I wish it were Jerusalem but it is definitely not)."

277. This section is based on Briant, *HEP*, chap. 18; Hammond, *A History of Greece*; and Diodorus Siculus 17.

at Issus, the Persian army lost its Greek mercenaries, who fled back to the motherland.

The way down the Phoenician coast was now open to Alexander. The remnants of the armies of Egypt, Cilicia, and Ebar Nahara had retreated down the Euphrates with Darius. The coastal cities of Lebanon had no choice but to open their gates to him, except for the island city of Tyre, which he besieged. The news of the victory at Issus and the surrender of other Phoenician ports caused the Persian fleet to break up rapidly. Persian squadrons from Rhodes, Lycia, Cilicia, Cyprus, and Phoenicia now joined Alexander, and for the first time, he controlled the sea. With these ships, he blockaded Tyre. After seven months, Alexander landed on the island and took the city (July 332). There was widespread massacre; all not slain were sold into slavery. From Tyre, Alexander marched south, received the formal submission of the inland peoples of Palestine, and laid siege to Gaza, which held out for two months. Again, when the siege was broken, the men were killed, the women and children sold into slavery. A week after the surrender of Gaza, Alexander had reached Pelusium, at the border of the Delta. The Egyptians surrendered without a battle. By November of 332, Alexander was "Pharaoh," and "Son of Re." The western satrapies of the Persian Empire had fallen, and with them Persian control of Judah.

Yaddua, the High Priest of the Jews

According to Josephus (*Ant.* 11.7.2):

> When Joannes departed this life he was succeeded in the high priesthood by his son Jaddus.

This Yaddua, the son of Yoḥanan, would have been high priest from approximately 370 to 333, so that he must have been elderly during the reign of Darius III, the last king of the Persians. According to Josephus, Alexander recognized Yaddua as head of Yehud (*Ant.* 11.317ff.):

> Alexander, coming to Syria, took Damascus, became master of Sidon, and besieged Tyre; from there he dispatched a letter to the high priest of the Jews, requesting him to send him assistance and supply his army with provisions and give him the gifts which they had formerly sent as tribute to Darius, thus choosing the friendship of the Macedonians, for, he said, they would not regret this course.

Alexander's mode of conquest of both Asia Minor and Palestine was to concentrate on the coastal cities. Nevertheless, the inland cities also succumbed. It is highly likely that the approach recorded here for Jerusalem was the same one that was conducted against other inland cities. He would have sent them a message offering peace if they came over to him; otherwise siege and massacre. This was also the tactic of Cyrus the Great in his conquest of the cities of Asia Minor.

How likely is it that he would have sent his embassy to the high priest? In fact, there was no one else. The satrap, Mazday, had fled with Darius down the Euphrates. In that army there were contingents led by the governors of the provinces of Ebar Nahara. The Persian soldiers garrisoned in Jerusalem were either fighting with their governor or, like other soldiers garrisoned throughout the empire, had fled. Yaddua alone was left.

Conclusion

Data from Persian period Yehud yield two primary results: First, the model of Achaemenid rule derived from the western satrapies of Babylonia, Egypt, and Asia Minor applies equally well to Judah. Second, the model of Achaemenid rule proposed by Eisenstadt is a better descriptor of Persian Yehud than the model of self-governance or its variant, the model of imperial authorization of local norms. These models of self-governance are not consistent with the data. A Persian-appointed governor ruled Yehud from its inception at the time of Cyrus until its fall to Alexander in 333. A garrison with imperial troops and an imperial garrison commander was in charge of Jerusalem. As elsewhere in the Empire, Persian governors sought to control the local high priest. As elsewhere, priests were a source of corvée labor until a special decree released them.

Persian-period Judah was not self-governing: There were no assemblies, no Jewish lay bodies to advise the governor, no sanhedrins. There was no vehicle for local control. Neither was Judah a theocracy. Local officials, whether priest or lay, held little real power. The Jewish community in Yehud certainly constructed its identity and its unity around the temple, as they did in Elephantine; the high priest was their spokesman. Nevertheless, power remained in the hands of Persia. The prayer attributed to Ezra aptly describes life in the provinces of the Persian Empire (Neh 9:36–37):

> Behold we, this day, are slaves. The land that you gave to our fathers, to eat its fruit and its goodness, behold, we are slaves on it. Its plentiful yield belongs to the kings that you have set over us, because of our sins. On our backs they rule, and over our beasts, according to their will; and we are in great distress.

Appendix

Kings of Ancient Mesopotamia [1]

THE NEO-BABYLONIAN DYNASTY

1. Nabopolassar	625–605
2. Nebuchadnezzar II	604–562
3. Evil-Merodach	561–560
4. Neriglissar	559–556
5. Labaši-Marduk	556 (3 months)
6. Nabonidus	555–539

THE ACHAEMENID RULERS

1. Cyrus II	559–530
2. Cambyses II	529–522
3. Bardija	522 (6 mos.)
4. Nebuchadnezzar III	522 (2 mos.)
5. Nebuchadnezzar IV	521 (3 mos.)
6. Darius I	522–486
7. Xerxes I	486–465
8. Artaxerxes I	465–424
9. Darius II	424–405
10. Artaxerxes II	405–359
11. Artaxerxes III	358–338
12. Artaxerxes IV	338–336
13. Darius III	336–331
Alexander III	330–323

1. After Oppenheim, *Ancient Mesopotamia*, 340.

Egyptian Pharaohs [2]

DYNASTY 26

1. Necho II	610–595
2. Psammetichus II	595–589
3. Apries (Hofra)	589–570
4. Amasis	570–526
5. Psammetichus III	526–525

DYNASTY 27

1. Cambyses II	525–522
2. Darius I	522–486
3. Xerxes I	486–465
4. Artaxerxes I	465–424
5. Darius II	424–405
6. Artaxerxes II	405–359

DYNASTY 28

1. Amyrtaeus	404–399

DYNASTY 29

1. Nepherites I	399–393
2. Psammuthis	393
3. Achoris	393–380
4. Nepherites II	380

DYNASTY 30

1. Nectanebo I	380–362
2. Tachos	362–360
3. Nectanebo II	360–343

DYNASTY 31 – SECOND PERSIAN PERIOD

1. Artaxerxes III	343–338
2. Artaxerxes IV	338–336
3. Darius III	336–332
4. Khababash	333 (last known indigenous Egyptian ruler)

THE MACEDONIAN DYNASTY

Alexander III	332–323

2. After Grimal, *Ancient Egypt*, 394–95.

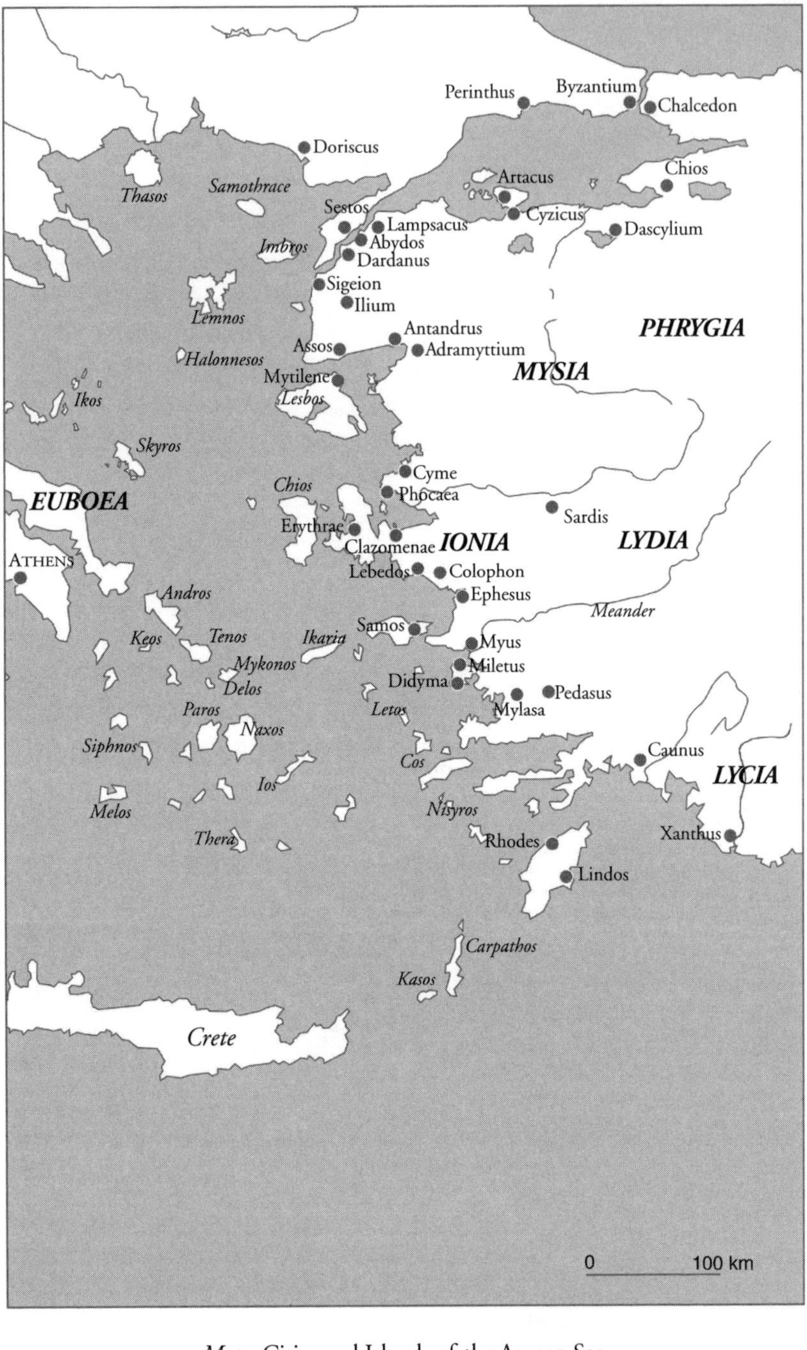

Map. Cities and Islands of the Aegean Sea.

Bibliography

Ackroyd, P. R. "Archaeology, Politics and Religion: The Persian Period." *The Iliff Review* 39 (1982) 5–24.

______. *Exile and Restoration: A Study of Hebrew Thought of the Sixth Century B.C.* OTL. Philadelphia: Westminster, 1968.

______. "The Temple Vessels: A Continuity Theme." Pp. 45–60 in idem, *Studies in the Religious Tradition of the Old Testament.* London: SCM, 1987.

Ager, S. L. *Interstate Arbitrations in the Greek World, 337–90 B.C.* Berkeley: University of California Press, 1996.

Albertz, R. *From the Exile to the Maccabees.* Vol. 2 of *A History of Israelite Religion in the Old Testament Period.* OTL. Louisville: Westminster John Knox, 1994.

Albrektson, B. *History and the Gods: An Essay on the Idea of Historical Events as Divine Manifestations in the Ancient Near East and in Israel.* Lund: C.W.K. Gleerup, 1967.

Allam, S. "Réflexions sur le 'code legal' d'Hermopolis dans l'Égypte ancienne." *CdE* 61 (1986) 50–75.

______. "Richter." Pp. 245–47 in vol. 5 of *Lexikon der Aegyptologie.* Wiesbaden: Harrassowitz, 1972.

Alt, A. "Die Rolle Samarias bei der Entstehung des Judentums." Pp. 316–37 in vol. 2 of *Kleine Schriften zur Geschichte des Volkes Israel.* Edited by A. Alt. Munich: Beck, 1953.

Arnold, D. *Temples of the Last Pharaohs.* Oxford: Oxford University Press, 1999.

Aufrère, S., J.-C. Golvin, and J.-C. Goyon. *L'Égypte restituée: Sites et temples de haute Égypte.* Paris: Editions France, 1991.

Austin, M. "Greek Tyrants and the Persians, 546–479 B.C." *Classical Quarterly* 40 (1990) 289–306.

Avigad, N. *Bullae and Seals from a Post-exilic Judean Archive.* Qedem 4. Jerusalem: Israel Exploration Society, 1976.

Bagnall, R., and B. Frier. *The Demography of Roman Egypt.* Cambridge: Cambridge University Press, 1994.

Balcer, J. "Fifth Century B.C. Ionia: A Frontier Redefined." *REA* 87 (1985) 31–42.

_______. *Herodotus and Bisitun: Problems in Ancient Persian Historiography.* Historia 49. Stuttgart: Steiner, 1987

_______. *Sparda by the Bitter Sea: Imperial Interaction in Western Anatolia.* Chico, Calif.: Scholars Press, 1984.

Barag, D. "A Silver Coin of Yoḥanan and the High Priest." *Qadmoniot* 17 (1984) 55–58. [Hebrew]

________."A Silver Coin of Yoḥanan the High Priest and the Coinage of Judea in the Fourth Century B.C." *INJ* 9 (1986–87) 4–21, pl. 1.

________. "Some Notes on a Silver Coin of Joḥanan the High Priest." *BA* 48 (1985) 166–68.

Barstad, H. "History and the Hebrew Bible." Pp. 37–64 in *Can a "History of Israel" Be Written?* Edited by L. L. Grabbe. JSOTSup 245. Sheffield: Sheffield Academic Press, 1997.

________. *The Myth of the Empty Land.* Oslo: Scandinavian University Press, 1996.

Bean, G. E. "Notes and Inscriptions from Caunus." *JHS* 73–74 (1953–54) 10–35, 85–110.

Beaulieu, P.-A. "An Episode in the Fall of Babylon to the Persians." *JNES* 52 (1993) 241–61.

________. *The Reign of Nabonidus, King of Babylon (556–539 B.C.).* YNER 10. New Haven: Yale University Press, 1989.

Beckerath, J. von. *Handbuch der ägyptischen Königsnamen.* Münchner Ägyptologische Studien 20. Munich: Deutscher Kunstverlag, 1984.

Bedford, P. R. *Temple Restoration in Early Achaemenid Judah.* Leiden: Brill, 2001.

Berger, P.-R. "Der Kyros-Zylinder mit dem Zusatzfragment BIN II Nr. 32 und die akkadischen Personennamen im Danielbuch." *ZA* 64 (1975) 192–234.

________. "Zu den Namen *ššbṣr* und *šnʾṣr.*" *ZAW* 83 (1971) 98–100.

Berquist, J. L. *Judaism in Persia's Shadow: A Social and Historical Approach.* Minneapolis: Fortress, 1995.

Black, J. A. "The New Year Ceremonies in Ancient Babylon: 'Taking Bel by the Hand' and a Cultic Picnic." *Religion* 11 (1981) 39–59.

Blackman, A. M. "Priest, Priesthood (Egyptian)." Pp. 117–44 in *Gods, Priests and Men: Studies in the Religion of Pharaonic Egypt by Aylward M. Blackman.* Edited by A. B. Lloyd. New York: Kegan Paul, 1998.

Blenkinsopp, J. "Did the Second Jerusalemite Temple Possess Land?" *Transeuphratène* 21 (2001) 61–68.

________. *Ezra–Nehemiah: A Commentary.* OTL. Philadelphia: Westminster, 1988.

________. "Was the Pentateuch the Civic and Religious Constitution of the Jewish Ethnos in the Persian Period?" Pp. 41–62 in *Persia and Torah: The Theory of Imperial Authorization of the Pentateuch.* Edited by J. W. Watts. SBL Symposium Series 17. Atlanta: Society of Biblical Literature, 2001.

Bloom, J. A. *Ancient Near Eastern Temple Assemblies.* Ph.D. dissertation, Annenberg Research Institute, 1992.

Boccaccini, G. *Roots of Rabbinic Judaism: An Intellectual History, from Ezekiel to Daniel.* Grand Rapids: Eerdmans, 2002.

Bodi, D. *Jérusalem à l'époque perse.* Paris: Geuthner, 2002.

Boehmer, R. M. "Uruk-Warka." P. 294 in vol. 5 of *OEANE.*

Boffo, L. "La lettera di Dario I a Gadata: I privilegi del tempio di Apollo a Magnesia sul Meandro." *BIDR* 20 (1978) 267–303.

Bolin, T. "The Temple of יהו at Elephantine and Persian Religious Policy." Pp. 127–42 in *The Triumph of Elohim: From Yahwisms to Judaisms.* Edited by D. Edelman. Grand Rapids: Eerdmans, 1995.

Bongenaar, A. C. V. M. *Interdependency of Institutions and Private Entrepreneurs.* MOS 2. PIHANS 87. Leiden: Nederlands Historisch-Archaeologisch Instituut te Istanbul, 2000.

____. *The Neo-Babylonian Ebabbar Temple at Sippar: Its Administration and Its Prosopography.* PIHANS 80. Leiden: Nederlands Historisch-Archaeologisch Instituut te Istanbul, 1997.

Bongrani Fanfoni, L., and F. Israel. "Documenti achemenidi nel deserto orientale egiziano (Gebel Abu Queh—Wadi Hammamat)." *Transeuphratène* 8 (1994) 75–93.

Bontty, M. M. *Conflict Management in Ancient Egypt: Law as a Social Phenomenon*, Ph.D. dissertation, University of California at Los Angeles, 1997.

Borchhardt, J. "Eine Doppelaxtstele aus Limyra: Zur Herrschaft der Karer in Lykien." Pp. 183–91 in *Studien zur Religion und Kulture Kleinasiens: Festschrift für Friedrich Karl Dörner zum 65. Geburtstag am 28 Februar 1976*. Edited by S. Sahin, E. Schwertheim, and J. Wagner. Leiden: Brill, 1978.

Bottéro, J. "The 'Code' of Ḫammurabi." Pp. 156–98 in *Mesopotamia: Writing, Reasoning, and the Gods*. Edited by J. Bottéro. Chicago: University of Chicago Press, 1992.

Boyce, M. *The Early Period*. Vol. 1 of *History of Zoroastrianism*. Leiden: Brill, 1996.

_____. *Under the Achaemenians*. Vol. 2 of *History of Zoroastrianism*. Leiden: Brill, 1982.

_____. *Zoroastrianism: Its Antiquity and Constant Vigour*. New York: Mazda and Bibliotheca Persica, 1992.

Brandenstein, W., and M. Mayrhofer. *Handbuch des Altpersischen*. Wiesbaden: Harrassowitz, 1964.

Breasted, J. H. (trans.). *Ancient Records of Egypt*. 5 vols. Urbana: University of Illinois Press, 2001.

Bresciani, E. "Cambyse, Darius I et le droit des temples égyptiens." *Méditerranées* 6/7 (1996) 103–14.

_____. "The Persian Occupation of Egypt." Pp. 503–28 in vol. 2 of *CHI*.

Briant, P. "Cités et satrapes dans l'empire achéménide: Xanthos et Pixôdaros." *CRAIBL* (1998) 305–47.

_____. "Contrainte militaire, dépendance rurale et exploitation des territoires en Asie achéménide." *Index* 8 (1978–79) 48–98.

_____. "Une curieuse affaire à Elephantine en 410 av. n.e.: Widranga, le sanctuaire de Khnum et le temple de Yahweh." *Méditerranées* 6/7 (1996) 115–35.

_____. *From Cyrus to Alexander: A History of the Persian Empire*. Translated by P. Daniels. Winona Lake, Ind.: Eisenbrauns, 2002.

_____. "Droaphernès et la statue de Sardes." Pp. 205–26 in *Studies in Persian History: Essays in Memory of David M. Lewis*. Edited by M. Brosius and A. Kuhrt. Vol. 11 of *Achaemenid History*. Leiden: Nederlands Instituut voor het Nabije Oosten, 1998.

_____. "Ethno-classe dominante et populations soumise dans l'empire achéménide: Le cas d'Egypt." Pp. 137–74 in *Method and Theory*. Edited by A. Kuhrt and H. Sancisi-Weerdenburg. Vol. 3 of *Achaemenid History*. Leiden: Nederlands Instituut voor het Nabije Oosten, 1988.

_____. "Guerre, tribut et forces productives dans l'empire achéménide." *DHA* 12 (1986) 33–48.

_____. "Histoire et archéologie d'un texte: La *Lettre de Darius à Gadatas* entre Perses, Grecs et Romains." In press in *Licia e Lidia prima dell'ellenizzazione*. Edited by M. Salvini and R. Gusmani. Rome: ISMEO, forthcoming.

_____. *Histoire de l'Empire perse: De Cyrus à Alexandre*. Paris: Fayard, 1996.

_____. "Pouvoir central et polycentrisme culturel dans l'empire achéménide." Pp. 1–31 in *Sources, Structures and Synthesis*. Edited by H. Sancisi-Weerdenburg. Vol. 1 of *Achaemenid History*. Leiden: Nederlands Instituut voor het Nabije Oosten, 1987.

_____. "Social and Legal Institutions in Achaemenid Iran." Pp. 517–28 in vol. 1 of *CANE*. Edited by J. Sasson. New York: Scribner's, 1995.

Briant, P., and C. Herrenschmidt. *Le Tribut dans l'empire perse: Actes de la table ronde de Paris, 12–13 Décembre 1986.* Trav. Inst. d'Etudes Iraniennes de l'Université de la Sorbonne Nouvelle 13. Paris: 1989.

Brugsch, H. "Ein Dekret Ptolemaios' des Sohnes Lagi, des Satrapen." *ZÄS* 9 (1871) 1–13.

Burchardt, M. "Datierte Denkmäler der Berliner Sammlung aus der Achämenidenzeit. Eine Weihinschrift an Darius I." *ZAS* 49 (1911) 69–80; pls. 8–10.

Burkard, G. "Literarische Tradition und historische Realität." *ZAS* 121 (1994) 93–106; 122 (1995) 31–7.

Burkert, W. *Greek Religion.* Cambridge: Harvard University Press, 1985.

Cameron, G. *Persepolis Treasury Tablets.* Chicago: University of Chicago Press, 1948.

_____. "Cyrus the 'Father,' and Babylonia." *Acta Iranica* 1 (1974) 45–48.

Capart, J. "Les Fouilles d'El Kab." *CdE* 23 (1937) 133–46.

Cardascia, G. *Les archives des Murašû.* Paris: Imprimerie Nationale, 1951.

_____. "Armée et fiscalité dans la Babylonie achéménide." Actes du colloque national: Paris, 14–16 octobre 1976. *Armées et fiscalités dans le monde antique* 25 (1977) 1–11.

_____. "Le fief dans la Babylonie achéménide." *Recueils de la société Jean-Bodin, I²: Les liens de vassalités et les immunités* 1 (1958) 55–88.

_____. "Ḫaṭru." Pp. 150–51 in vol. 4 of *RLA.*

Carter, C. E. *The Emergence of Yehud in the Persian Period: A Social and Demographic Study.* JSOTSup 294. Sheffield: Sheffield Academic Press, 1999.

Cauville, S. *Edfou.* Cairo: Publications de l'Institut Français d'Archéologie Orientale du Caire, 1984.

Cavigneaux, I. "Die Statthalter von Suḫu und Mari im 8. Jh. v. Chr." *BaMi* 21 Tab. 35–38 (1914) 321–456.

Cenival, F., de. *Les associations religieuses en Égypte d'aprés les documents démotiques.* Cairo: Publications de l'Institut Français d'Archéologie Orientale du Caire, 1973.

Chaumont, M.-L. "Un nouveau gouverneur de Sardes à l'époque achéménide d'aprés une inscription récemment découverte." *Syria* 67 (1990) 579–608.

Chauveau, M. "La chronologie de la correspondance dite 'de Phérendatès.'" *RdE* 50 (1999) 269–71.

Christophe, J. *The Yehud Stamped Jar Handle Corpus: Implications for the History of Post-Exilic Palestine.* Ph.D. dissertation, Duke University, 1993.

Clarke, S. "El-Kab and Its Temples." *JEA* 8 (1922) 16–40.

Clay, A. T. "Gobryas, Governor of Babylonia." *JAOS* 41 (1921) 466–67.

Cocquerillat, D. *Palmeraies et Cultures de l'Eanna d'Uruk (559–520).* Berlin: Mann, 1968.

Cogan, M. *Imperialism and Religion: Assyria, Judah and Israel in the Eighth and Seventh Centuries B.C.* Missoula, Mont.: Scholars Press, 1974.

Cogan, M., and H. Tadmor. *II Kings.* AB 11. New York: Doubleday, 1988.

Cousin, G. "Correction à l'article initulé 'Lettre de Darius à Gadatas.'" *Bulletin de Correspondence Hellenique* 14 (1890) 646–48.

Cousin, G., and G. Deschamps. "Lettre de Darius, fils d'Hystaspes." *Bulletin de Correspondence Hellenique* 12/13 (1889) 529–42.

Cowan, C. C. "The ʿAraq el-Emir and the Tobiads." *BA* 20 (1957) 63–76.

Cross, F. M. "Aspects of Samaritan and Jewish History in Late Persian and Hellenistic Times." *HTR* 59 (1966) 201–11.

_____. *Canaanite Myth and Hebrew Epic: Essays in the History of the Religion of Israel.* Cambridge: Harvard University Press, 1973.

_____. "The Papyri and Their Historical Implications." Pp. 17–29 in *Discoveries in the Wâdī ed-Dâliyeh.* Edited by P. W. Lapp and N. L. Lapp. AASOR 41. Cambridge, Mass.: American Schools of Oriental Research, 1974.
_____. "A Reconstruction of the Judaean Restoration." *JBL* 94 (1975) 4–18.
_____. "A Report on the Samaria Papyri." Pp. 17–26 in *Congress Volume: Jerusalem, 1986.* Edited by J. A. Emerton. VTSup 40. Leiden: Brill, 1988.
Crowfoot, J. W., K. M. Kenyon, and E. L. Sukenik. *Samaria–Sebaste—Reports of the Work of the Joint Expedition in 1931–1933 and of the British Expedition in 1935, No. 1: The Buildings at Samaria.* London: Palestine Exploration Fund, 1942.
Cruz-Uribe, E. "The Hibis Temple Project." *JARCE* 23 (1986) 157–66.
_____. "The Invasion of Egypt by Cambyses." *Transeuphratène* 25 (2003) 9–60.
Dalley, S. "Anointing in Ancient Mesopotamia." Pp. 19–25 in *Oil of Gladness: Anointing in the Christian Tradition.* Edited by M. Dudley and G. Rowell. London: SPCK, 1993.
Dandamayev, M. "Achaemenid Babylonia." Pp. 296–311 in *Ancient Mesopotamia: A Collection of Studies by Soviet Scholars.* Edited by I. M. Diakonoff. Moscow: "Nauka," 1969.
_____. "Achaemenid Imperial Policies and Provincial Governments." *Iranica Antiqua* 34 (1999) 269–82.
_____. "Achaemenid Mesopotamia: Traditions and Innovations." Pp. 229–34 in *Continuity and Change.* Edited by H. Sancisi-Weerdenburg et al. Vol. 8 of *Achaemenid History.* Leiden: Nederlands Instituut voor het Nabije Oosten, 1994.
_____. "Babylonian Popular Assemblies in the First Millennium B.C." *The Canadian Society for Mesopotamian Studies Bulletin* 30 (1995) 23–29.
_____. *Iranians in Achaemenid Babylonia.* Columbia Lectures in Iranian Studies 6. Costa Mesa, Calif: Mazda and Bibliotheca Persica, 1992.
_____. "The Neo-Babylonian Elders." Pp. 38–41 in *Societies and Languages of the Ancient Near East: FS I. M. Diakonoff.* Edited by M. Dandamaev. Warminister: Aris & Phillips, 1982.
_____. "The Neo-Babylonian *Zazakku.*" *AoF* 21 (1994) 34–40.
_____. *A Political History of the Achaemenid Empire.* Leiden: Brill, 1989.
_____. "Royal *Paradeisoi* in Babylonia." Pp. 113–7 in *Orientalia J Duchesne-Guillemin Emerito Oblata.* Hommages et Opera Minora 9. Leiden: Brill, 1984.
_____. *Slavery in Babylonia, 626–331.* Dekalb, Ill.: Northern Illinois University Press, 1984.
_____. "Social Stratification in Babylonia (7th–4th centuries B.C.)." Pp. 433–44 in *Wirtschaft und Gesellschaft im alten Vorderasien.* Edited by J. Harmatta and G. Komoróczy. Budapest: Kiadó, 1976.
_____. "State and Temple in Babylonia in the First Millennium B.C." Pp. 589–96 in vol. 2 of *State and Temple Economy in the Ancient Near East.* Edited by E. Lipiński. Leuven: Departement Oriëntalistiek, 1979.
_____. "Der Tempelzehnte in Babylonien während des 6–4 Jh. v.u Z." Pp. 82–90 in *Beiträge zur Alten Geschichte und deren Nachleben: Festschr. F. Altheim.* Edited by R. Stiehl and H. E. Stier. Berlin: de Gruyter, 1969.
Dandamayev, M., and V. Lukonin. *The Culture and Social Institutions of Ancient Iran.* Cambridge: Cambridge University Press, 1989.

David, E. "The Oligarchic Revolution at Rhodes, 391–89 B.C." *Classical Philology* 79 (1984) 271–84.

Davies, N. de Garis. *The Temple of Hibis in El Khargeh Oasis.* New York: Metropolitan Museum of Art, 1953.

Davies, P. R. "Minimalists and Maximalists." *BAR* 26 (2000) 24–27, 72–73.

Debord, P. *L'Asie Mineure au IVe Siècle (412–323 a.C.): Pouvoirs et jeux politiques.* Bordeaux: Ausonius, 1999.

Depuydt, L. "Evidence for Accession Dating under the Achaemenids." *JAOS* 115 (1995) 193–204.

_____. "Murder in Memphis: The Story of Cambyses' Mortal Wounding of the Apis Bull (ca. 523 B.C.E.)." *JNES* 54 (1995) 119–26.

_____. "Regnal Years and Civil Calendar in Achaemenid Egypt." *JEA* 81 (1995) 151–73.

Derchain, P. *El Kab.* Vol. 1. Brussels: Fondation égyptologique Reine Elisabeth, 1971.

Deutsch, R. "Six Unrecorded 'Yehud' Silver Coins." *INJ* 11 (1990–91) 4–6.

Devauchelle, D. "Le sentiment anti-perse chez les anciens Égyptiens." *Transeuphratène* 9 (1995) 67–80.

Driel, G. van. "The Edict of Belshazzar: An Alternative Interpretation." *Jaarbericht van Het Voorazieatisch-Eqyptisch Genootschap "Ex Orient Lux"* 30 (1987–88) 61–64.

Dumbrell, W. "The Tell El-Maskhuta Bowls and the 'Kingdom' of Qedar in the Persian Period." *BASOR* 203 (1971) 33–44.

Dupont-Sommer, A. "L'énigme du dieu Satrape et le dieu Mithra." *CRAIBL* (1976) 648–60.

_____. "La stèle trilingue du Letoon: L'inscription araméenne." Pp. 129–78 in vol. 6 of *Fouilles de Xanthos: La stèle trilingue du Létôon.* Edited by H. Metzger. Paris: Klincksieck, 1979.

Duverger, M. "Le concept d'empire." Pp. 5–23 in *Le concept d'empire.* Edited by M. Duverger. Paris: Universitaires de France, 1980.

Ebeling, E. "Beamter." Pp. 441–67 in vol. 1 of *RLA* .

Ehrenberg, V. *From Solon to Socrates: Greek History and Civilization during the Sixth and Fifth Centuries B.C.* London: Methuen, 1973.

Eisenstadt, S. N. *The Political Systems of Empires.* New York: Free Press of Glencoe, 1963.

Ellis, R. S. *Foundation Deposits in Ancient Mesopotamia.* New Haven: Yale University Press, 1968.

Engelmann, H., and R. Merkelbach. *Die Inschriften von Erythrai und Klazomenai.* Vol 1. Bonn: Rudolf Habelt, 1972.

Ephʿal, I. "On Warfare and Military Control in the Ancient Near Eastern Empires: A Research Outline." Pp. 76–106 in *History, Historiography, and Interpretation.* Edited by H. Tadmor and M. Weinfeld. Jerusalem: Magnes, 1984.

_____. "Syria–Palestine under Achaemenid Rule." Pp. 139–64 in vol. 4 of *CHI.*

Fensham, F. C. *The Books of Ezra and Nehemiah.* NICOT. Grand Rapids: Eerdmans, 1982.

Fishbane, M. *Biblical Interpretation in Ancient Israel.* Oxford: Clarendon, 1985.

Fleming, D. "The Biblical Tradition of Anointing Priests." *JBL* 117 (1998) 401–14.

Folmer, M. L. *The Aramaic Language in the Achaemenid Period.* Orientalia Lovaniensia Analecta 68. Leuven: Peeters, 1995.

Foster, B. "Akkadians." Pp. 49–54 in vol. 1 of *OEANE.*

Frame, G. *Babylonia 689–627 B.C.: A Political History.* Istanbul: Nederlands Historisch-Archaeologisch Instituut te Istanbul, 1992.

_____. "Nabonidus, Nabû-Šarra-Uṣur, and the Eanna Temple." *ZA* 81 (1991) 31–86.

_____. "Some Neo-Babylonian and Persian Documents Involving Boats." *OrAnt* 25 (1986) 29–50.

Frankfort, H. *Ancient Egyptian Religion: An Interpretation.* New York: Harper & Row, 1948.

_____. *Kingship and the Gods: A Study of Ancient Near Eastern Religion as the Integration of Society and Nature.* Chicago: University of Chicago Press, 1948; rev. ed., 1978.

Frei, P. "Persian Imperial Authorization: A Summary." Pp. 5–40 in *Persia and Torah: The Theory of Imperial Authorization of the Pentateuch.* Edited by J. W. Watts. SBL Symposium Series 17. Atlanta: Society of Biblical Literature, 2001.

_____. "Die persische Reichsautorisation: Ein Überblick." *ZABR* 1 (1995) 1–35.

_____. "Zentralgewalt und Lokalautonomie im achämendischen Kleinasien." *Transeuphratène* 3 (1990) 157–71.

_____. "Zentralgewalt und Lokalautonomie im Achämenidenreich." Pp. 8–131 in *Reichsidee und Reichsorganisation im Perserreich.* Edited by P. Frei and K. Koch. OBO 55. Fribourg: Universitätsverlag, 1984; 2nd ed., 1996.

Frei P. and K. Koch (eds.). *Reichsidee und Reichsorganisation im Perserreich.* OBO 55. Fribourg: Universitätsverlag, 1984; 2nd ed., 1996.

Fried, L. S. "The *ʿAm Hāʾāreṣ* in Ezra 4:4 and Persian Imperial Administration." In *Judah and Judaeans in the Achaemenid Period.* Edited by O. Lipschits and M. Oeming. Winona Lake, Ind.: Eisenbrauns, forthcoming.

_____. "Cyrus the Messiah? The Historical Background of Isaiah 45:1." *HTR* 95 (2002) 373–93.

_____. "A Governor of Byblos from Sippar." *NABU* 36 (2003).

_____. "The High Places (Bāmôt) and the Reforms of Hezekiah and Josiah: An Archaeological Investigation." *JAOS* 122 (2002) 437–65.

_____. "The Land Lay Desolate: Conquest and Restoration in the Ancient Near East." Pp. 21–54 in *Judah and the Judeans in the Neo-Babylonian Period.* Edited by O. Lipschits and J. Blenkinsopp. Winona Lake, Ind.: Eisenbrauns, 2003.

_____. "The Political Struggle of Fifth-Century Judah." *Transeuphratène* 24 (2002) 61–73.

_____. "A Silver Coin of Yoḥanan Hakkôhēn." *Transeuphratène* 25 (2003) 47–67, pls. 2–5.

_____. "You Shall Appoint Judges: Ezra's Mission and the Rescript of Artaxerxes." Pp. 63–89 in *Persia and Torah: The Theory of Imperial Authorization of the Pentateuch.* Edited by J. W. Watts. SBL Symposium Series. Atlanta: Society of Biblical Literature, 2001.

Gardiner, A. *Egypt of the Pharaohs.* New York: Oxford University Press, 1961.

Garland, R. *Introducing New Gods: The Politics of Athenian Religion.* London: Duckworth, 1992.

Gauthier, H., and H. Sottas. *Un décret trilingue en l'honneur de Ptolémée IV.* Cairo: Impr. de l'Institut français d'archéologie orientale, 1925.

George, A. R. *House Most High: The Temples of Ancient Mesopotamia.* Mesopotamian Civilizations 5. Winona Lake, Ind.: Eisenbrauns, 1993.

Gera, D. "On the Credibility of the History of the Tobiads (Josephus, *Antiquities* 12, 156–222, 228–236)." Pp. 21–38 in *Greece and Rome in Eretz Israel.* Edited by A. Kasher, U. Rappaport, and G. Fuks. Jerusalem: Yad Izhak Ben-Zvi, 1990.

Gesenius, W. *Gesenius' Hebrew Grammar.* 2nd ed. Edited by E. Kautzsch. Translated by A. E. Cowley. Oxford: Clarendon, 1910.

Giovinazzo, G. "The Tithe *ešrû* in Neo-Babylonian and Achaemenid Period." Pp. 95–105 in *Le tribut dans l'Empire perse.* Edited by P. Briant and C. Herrenschmidt. Paris: Peeters, 1989.

Goldstein, J. A. *I Maccabees.* AB 41. New York: Doubleday, 1976.

Grabbe, L. L. "The Authenticity of the Persian 'Documents' in Ezra." Paper read at the Aramaic Section of the Society of Biblical Literature Annual Meeting, San Fransisco, November 1992.

_____. " 'The Exile' under the Theodolite: Historiography as Triangulation." Pp. 80–100 in *Leading Captivity Captive.* Edited by L. L. Grabbe. JSOTSup 278. Sheffield: Sheffield Academic Press, 1998.

_____. *Ezra–Nehemiah.* Old Testament Readings. New York: Routledge, 1998.

_____. "The Law of Moses in the Ezra Tradition: More Virtual than Real?" Pp. 91–113 in *Persia and Torah: The Theory of Imperial Authorization of the Pentateuch.* Edited by J. W. Watts. SBL Symposium Series 17. Atlanta: Society of Biblical Literature, 2001.

_____. "Who Was the Bagoses of Josephus (*Ant.* 11.7.1, §§297–301)?" *Transeuphratène* 5 (1992) 49–55.

Grayson, A. K. *Assyrian and Babylonian Chronicles.* Locust Valley, N.Y.: Augustin, 1975. Repr., Winona Lake, Ind.: Eisenbrauns, 2000.

Greengus, S. "Legal and Social Institutions of Ancient Mesopotamia." Pp. 469–84 in vol. 1 of *CANE.* Edited by J. Sasson. New York: Scribner's, 1995.

_____. "Some Issues Relating to the Comparability of Laws and the Coherence of the Legal Tradition." Pp. 77–87 in *Theory and Method in Biblical and Cuneiform Law: Revision, Interpolation and Development.* Edited by B. M. Levinson. Sheffield: Sheffield Academic Press, 1994.

Grelot, P. *Documents Araméens d'Egypt.* Paris: Cerf, 1972.

Griffith, F. L. " 'Papyri from El Hibeh,' and 'The Petition of Peteesi.' " Pp. 37–112 in *Catalogue of the Demotic Papyri, III.* John Rylands Library 9. Manchester: University Press / London: Quaritch, 1909.

Grimal, N. *A History of Ancient Egypt.* Translated by I. Shaw. Oxford: Blackwell, 1992.

Gschnitzer, F. "Eine persische Kultstiftung in Sardeis und die 'Sippengötter' Vorderasiens." Pp. 45–54 in *Im Bannkreis des Alten Orients* (FS K. Obenhuber). Edited by W. Meid und H. Trenkwalder. Innsbruck: Institut für Sprachwissenschaft der Universität Innsbruck, 1986.

Habicht, C. "Falsche Urkunden zur Geschichte Athens im Zeitalter der Perserkriege." *Hermes* 89 (1961) 1–35.

Hallock, R. T. "The Evidence of the Persepolis Tablets." Pp. 588–609 in *The Median and Achaemenian Periods.* Vol. 2 of *CHI.*

_____. *Persepolis Fortification Tablets.* Chicago: University of Chicago Press, 1969.

Halpern, B. *The Constitution of the Monarchy in Israel.* Atlanta: Scholars Press, 1981.

_____. *David's Secret Demons: Messiah, Murderer, Traitor, King.* Grand Rapids: Eerdmans, 2001.

_____. "A Historiographic Commentary on Ezra 1–6: Achronological Narrative and Dual Chronology in Israelite Historiography." Pp. 81–142 in *The Hebrew Bible and Its Interpreters.* Edited by W. H. Propp, B. Halpern, and D. N. Freedman. Biblical and Judaic Studies 1. Winona Lake, Ind.: Eisenbrauns, 1990.

_____. "The Ritual Background of Zechariah's Temple Song." *CBQ* 40 (1978) 167–89.

Hammond, N. G. L. *A History of Greece to 322 B.C.* New York: Oxford University Press, 1986.

Hansen, O. "The Purported Letter of Darius to Gadates." *Rheinisches Museum für Philologie* 129 (1986) 95–96.

Hanson, P. D. *Dawn of Apocalyptic.* Philadelphia: Fortress, 1975.

Harmatta, J. "Modéles littéraires de l'édit babylonien de Cyrus." *Acta Iranica* 1 (1974) 29–44.

Harris, R. "On the Process of Secularization under Hammurapi." *JCS* 15 (1961) 117–20.

Harrison, C. M. *Coins of the Persian Satraps.* Ph.D. dissertation, University of Pennsylvania, 1982.

Heltzer, M. "The Flogging and Plucking of Beards in the Achaemenid Empire and the Chronology of Nehemiah." *AMI* 28 (1995–96) 305–7.

_____. "Some Questions about Royal Property in the Vth Satrapy and Profits of the Royal Treasury." *Transeuphratène* 19 (2000) 127–29.

Hensley, C. L. V. *The Official Persian Documents in the Book of Ezra.* Ph.D. dissertation, University of Liverpool, 1977.

Hermann, P. "Mystenvereine in Sardeis." *Chiron* 26 (1996) 315–41.

Herrenschmidt, C. "L'empire perse achéménide." Pp. 69–102 in *Le concept d'empire.* Edited by M. Duverger. Paris: Presses Universitaires de France, 1980.

Hinz, W. "Darius und der Suezkanal." *AMI* 8 (1975) 115–21.

Hölbl, G. *A History of the Ptolemaic Empire.* London: Routledge, 2001.

Hoftijzer, J., and K. Jongeling. *Dictionary of the North-West Semitic Inscriptions.* Handbuch der Orientalistik 1/21. Leiden: Brill, 1995.

Hoglund, K. G. *Achaemenid Imperial Administration in Syria–Palestine and the Missions of Ezra and Nehemiah.* SBL Dissertation Series 125. Atlanta: Scholars Press, 1992.

Holloway, S. W. *The Case for Assyrian Religious Influence in Israel and Judah: Inference and Evidence.* Vol. 2. Ph.D. dissertation, University of Chicago, 1992.

Hornblower, S. *Mausolus.* Oxford: Clarendon, 1982.

Hout, M. van den. "Studies in Early Greek Letter-Writing." *Mnem.* 2 (1949) 19–41, 138–53.

Hüttenbach, F. Lochner von. "Brief des Königs Darius an den Satrapen Gadatas (Toleranzedikt fremde Götter betreffend)." Pp. 91–98 in *Handbuch des Altpersischen.* Edited by W. Brandenstein and M. Mayrhofer. Wiesbaden: Harrassowitz, 1964.

Hughes, G. "The So-Called Pherendates Correspondence." Pp. 75–86 in *Grammatica Demotica: FS E. Lüddeckens.* Edited by H.-J. Thissen und K.-T. Zauzich. Würzburg: Zauzich, 1984.

Hughes, G., and R. Jasnow. *Oriental Institute Hawara Papyri.* OIP 113. Chicago: Oriental Institute, 1997.

Hurowitz, V. (A.) *I Have Built You an Exalted House: Temple Building in the Bible in Light of Mesopotamian and Northwest Semitic Writings.* JSOTSup 115. Sheffield: Sheffield Academic Press, 1992.

_____. "The Priestly Account of Building the Tabernacle." *JAOS* 105 (1985) 21–30.

_____. "Temporary Temples." Pp. 37–50 in *Kinattūtu šā Dārâti: Raphael Kutscher Memorial Volume.* Edited by A. F. Rainey. Tel Aviv: Institute of Archaeology, 1993.
Jacobsen, T. "Review of *Lamentation over the Destruction of Ur* by S. N. Kramer." *American Journal of Semitic Languages and Literature* 58 (1940) 219–24.
Jameson, M. H. "A Decree of Themistocles from Troizen." *Hesperia* 29 (1960) 198–223.
Janssen, J. J. "The Role of the Temple in the Egyptian Economy during the New Kingdom." Pp. 505–15 in vol. 2 of *State and Temple Economy in the Ancient Near East.* Edited by E. Lipiński. Louvain: Departement Oriëntalistiek, 1979.
Janzen, D. "The 'Mission' of Ezra and the Persian-Period Temple Community." *JBL* 119 (2000) 619–43.
Japhet, S. "Sheshbazzar and Zerubbabel against the Background of the Historical and Religious Tendencies of Ezra–Nehemiah." *ZAW* 94 (1982) 66–98.
Jastrow, M. ספר מלים: *A Dictionary of the Targumim, Talmud Babli, Yerushalmi and Midrashic Literature.* New York: Judaica, 1989.
Joannès, F. "À propos du *zazakku* à l'époque neo-babylonienne." *NABU* 103 (1994).
_____. "Pouvoirs locaux et organizations du territoire en Babylonie achéménide." *Transeuphratène* 3 (1990) 173–89.
_____. "Relations entre intérêts privés et biens des sanctuaires à l'époque néo-babylonienne." Pp. 25–41 in *Interdependency of Institutions and Private Entrepreneurs.* Proceedings of the Second MOS Symposium. Edited by A. C. V. M. Bongenaar. Leiden: Nederlands Historisch-Archaeologisch Instituut te Istanbul, 2000.
_____. *Textes économiques de la Babylonie récente (Étude des textes de TBER—Cahier Nr 6).* Paris: Editions Recherche sur les civilisations, 1982.
Johnson, J. "The Demotic Chronicle as an Historical Source." *Enchoria* 4 (1974) 1–17.
_____. "Is the Demotic Chronicle an Anti-Greek Tract?" Pp. 107–24 in *Grammata demotica: Festschrift für Erich Lüddeckens zum 15. Juni 1983.* Edited by H.-J. Thissen and K.-T. Zauzich. Würzburg: Zauzich, 1984.
_____. "The Persians and the Continuity of Egyptian Culture." Pp. 149–59 in *Continuity and Change.* Edited by H. Sancisi-Weerdenburg et al. Vol. 8 of *Achaemenid History.* Leiden: Nederlands Institute voor het Nabije Oosten, 1994.
Johnstone, S. *Disputes and Democracy: The Consequences of Litigation in Ancient Athens.* Austin: University of Texas Press, 1999.
Jones, A. H. M. *The Greek City: From Alexander to Justinian.* Oxford: Clarendon, 1940.
Jursa, M. *Das Archiv des Bēl-rēmanni.* Vitgaven van het Nederlands Historisch-Archaeologisch Instituut te Istanbul 86. Leiden: Nederlands Historisch-Archaeologisch Instituut te Istanbul, 1999.
_____. "Bogenland schon under Nebukadnezar II." *NABU* 124 (1998).
_____. *Der Tempelzehnt in Babylonien vom siebenten bis zum dritten Jahrhundert v. Chr.* Münster: Ugarit-Verlag, 1998.
Kaiser, W., et al. "Zur Frage persischer Zerstörungen in Elephantine." *MDAIK* 53 (1997) 178–82.
Kamal, A. *Stèles ptolémaïques et romaines.* Cairo: Imprimérie de l'Institut français d'archéologie orientale, 1904–5.
Kapelrud, A. "Temple Building, a Task for Gods and Kings." *Orientalia* 32 (1963) 56–62.
Kaufmann, Y. *From the Babylonian Captivity to the End of Prophecy.* Vol. 4 in *History of the Religion of Israel.* New York: Ktav, 1977.

Keen, A. *Dynastic Lycia: A Political History of the Lycians and Their Relations with Foreign Powers, C. 545–362.* Leiden: Brill, 1998.

Kees, H. *Probleme der Aegyptologie: Das Priestertum im ägyptischen Staat vom neuen Reich bis zur Spätzeit.* Leiden: Brill, 1953.

Kent, R. G. *Old Persian: Grammar, Texts, Lexicon.* AOS 33. New Haven: American Oriental Society, 1953.

Kenyon, K. *Royal Cities of the Old Testament.* London: Barrie & Jenkins, 1971.

Kern, O. *Inscriptiones Graecae.* Bonn: A. Marcus et E. Weber, 1913.

Kervran, M., et al. "Une statue de Darius découverte à Suse." *Journal Asiatique* 260 (1972) 235–66.

Kessler, K. *Uruk: Urkunden aus Privathäusern. Die Wohnhäuser westlich des Eanna-Tempelbereichs. Teil I. Die archive der Söhne des Bēl-ušallim, des Nabû-ušallim, und des Bēl-supê-muḫur.* AUWE 8. Mainz am Rhein: Zabern, 1991.

Kienitz, F. *Die politische Geschichte des Aegyptens vom 7. bis zum 4 Jhdt. v. d. Zeitwende.* Berlin: Akademie-Verlag, 1953.

Kitchen, K. *The Third Intermediate Period in Egypt (1100–650).* Warminster: Aris & Phillips, 1973.

Knoppers, G. N. "An Achaemenid Imperial Authorization of Torah in Yehud?" Pp. 115–34 in *Persia and Torah: The Theory of Imperial Authorization of the Pentateuch.* Edited by J. W. Watts. SBL Symposium Series 17. Atlanta: Society of Biblical Literature, 2001.

Kümmel, H. M. *Familie, Beruf und Amt im spätbabylonischen Uruk: prosopogrische Untersuchungen zu Berufsgruppen des 6. Yahrhunderts v. Chr. in Uruk.* Berlin: Abhandlungen der Deutschen Orient-Gesellschaft 20. Berlin: Mann, 1979.

Kuhrt, A. *The Ancient Near East c. 3000–330* BC. Vol. 2. New York: Routledge, 1995.

_____. "Nabonidus and the Babylonian Priesthood." Pp. 119–55 in *Pagan Priests: Religion and Power in the Ancient World.* Edited by M. Beard and J. North. London: Duckworth, 1990.

Kuhrt, A., and H. Sancisi-Weerdenburg (eds.). *Method and Theory.* Proceedings of the London 1985 Achaemenid History Workshop. Vol. 3 of *Achaemenid History.* Leiden: Nederlands Institute voor het Nabije Oosten, 1988.

Kuhrt, A., and S. Sherwin-White. "Xerxes' Destruction of Babylonian Temples." Pp. 69–78 in *The Greek Sources.* Edited by H. Sancisi-Weerdenburg and A. Kuhrt. Vol. 2 of *Achaemenid History.* Leiden: Nederlands Institute voor het Nabije Oosten, 1987.

Kutsch, E. "Salbung as Rechtsakt." *ZAW*Sup 87 (1963) 1–72.

Kutsko, J. F. *Between Heaven and Earth: Divine Presence and Absence in the Book of Ezekiel.* Biblical and Judaic Studies 7. Winona Lake, Ind.: Eisenbrauns, 2000.

Laato, A. *The Servant of YHWH and Cyrus: A Reinterpretation of the Exilic Messianic Programme in Isaiah 40–55.* Coniectanea Biblica Old Testament Series 35. Stockholm: Almqvist & Wiksell, 1992.

Lacey, W. K. *The Family in Classical Greece.* Ithaca: Cornell University Press, 1968.

Landsberger, B. "Die babylonischen Termini für Gesetz und Recht." Pp. 219–34 in *Symbolae ad Iura Orientis Antiqui.* Edited by T. Folkers et al. Leiden: Brill, 1939.

_____. *Brief des Bischofs von Esagila an König Asarhaddan.* Mededeelingen der Koninklijke Nederlandsche Akademie van Wetenschappen n.s. 28/6. Amsterdam: Noord-Hollandsche, 1965.

Lapp, N. L. (ed.). *The Excavations at Araq el-Emir.* Vol. 1. AASOR 47. Cambridge, Mass.: American Schools of Oriental Research, 1983.

Lapp, P. W. "ʿIraq el-Emir." Pp. 527–31 in vol 2 of *Encyclopedia of Archaeological Excavations in the Holy Land.* Edited by M. Avi-Yonah. Englewood Cliffs, N.J.: Prentice-Hall, 1976.

Lapp, P. W., and N. L. Lapp (eds.). *Discoveries in the Wadi ed-Daliyeh.* AASOR 41. Cambridge, Mass.: American Schools of Oriental Research, 1974.

Laroche, E. "L'inscription lycienne." Pp. 49–127 in vol. 6 of *Fouilles de Xanthos: La stèle trilingue du Létôon.* Edited by H. Metzger. Paris: Klincksieck, 1979.

Lecoq, P. *Les inscriptions de la Perse achéménide: Traduit du vieux perse, de l'élamite, du babylonien et de l'araméen, présenté et annoté.* Paris: Gallimard, 1997.

Lemaire, A. "Un nouveau roi arabe de Qedar." *RB* 81 (1974) 63–72.

_____. "Populations et territoires de la Palestine à l'époque perse." *Transeuphratène* 3 (1990) 31–74.

_____. "The Xanthos Trilingual Revisited." Pp. 423–32 in *Solving Riddles and Untying Knots: Biblical, Epigraphic, and Semitic Studies in Honor of Jonas C. Greenfield.* Edited by Z. Zevit, S. Gitin, and M. Sokoloff. Winona Lake, Ind.: Eisenbrauns, 1995.

_____. "Zorobabel et la Judée à la lumière de l'épigraphie (fin du VIe s. av. J.C.)." *RB* 103 (1996) 48–57.

Lemaire, A., and H. Lozachmeur. "*Bîrāh/Bîrtāʾ* en araméen." *Syria* 64 (1987) 262–66.

_____. "La *bîrtāʾ* en Méditerranée orientale." *Semitica* 43–44 (1995) 75–78.

_____. "Remarques sur le plurilinguisme en Asie Mineure à l'époque perse." Pp. 91–123 *Mosaïque de langues—mosaïque culturelle: Le bilinguisme dans le proche-orient ancien.* Antiquités Sémitques 1. Edited by F. Briquel-Chatonnet. Paris: Librairie d'Amérique et d'Orient, 1996.

Lewis, N. *Life in Egypt under Roman Rule.* Oxford: Clarendon, 1983.

Lichtheim, M. "Statue Inscription of Udjahorrensne." Pp. 36–41 in *The Late Period.* Edited by M. Lichtheim. Vol. 3 of *Ancient Egyptian Literature.* Berkeley: University of California Press, 1980.

_____. "The Victory Stela of King Piye." Pp. 66–84 in *The Late Period.* Edited by M. Lichtheim. Vol. 3 of *Ancient Egyptian Literature.* Berkeley: University of California Press, 1980.

Lindenberger, J. "Razing of Temple and Petition for Aid." Pp. 63–68 in idem, *Ancient Aramaic and Hebrew Letters.* Writings from the Ancient World 4. Atlanta: Scholars Press, 1994.

_____. "What Ever Happened to Vidranga?: A Jewish Liturgy of Cursing from Elephantine." Pp. 134–57 in *Studies in Language and Literature in Honour of Paul-Eugène Dion.* Vol. 3 of *The World of the Aramaeans.* JSOTSup 326. Edited by P. M. M. Daviau, J. W. Wevers, and M. Weigl. Sheffield: Sheffield Academic Press, 2001.

Lipiński, E. "Shadday, Shadrapha et le dieu Satrape." *Zeitschrift für Althebraistik* 8 (1995) 247–74.

Lipiński, E. (ed.). *State and Temple Economy in the Ancient Near East.* 2 vols. Louvain: Departement Oriëntalistiek, 1979.

Lipschits, O., and J. Blenkinsopp (eds.). *Judah and the Judeans in the Neo-Babylonian Period.* Winona Lake, Ind.: Eisenbrauns, 2003.

Lloyd, A. B. "Cambyses in Late Tradition." Pp. 195–204 in *The Unbroken Reed: Studies in the Culture and Heritage of Ancient Egypt.* Edited by C. Eyre, A. Leahy, and L. Montague-Leahy. London: Egypt Exploration Society, 1994.

_____. "Herodotus on Cambyses: Some Thoughts on Recent Work." Pp. 55–66 in *Method and Theory.* Edited by A. Kuhrt and H. Sancisi-Weerdenburg. Vol. 3 of *Achaemenid History.* Leiden: Nederlands Institute voor het Nabije Oosten, 1988.

_____. *Herodotus, Book II: A Commentary.* Leiden: Brill, 1975.

_____. "The Inscription of Udjaḥorresnet: A Collaborator's Testament." *JEA* 68 (1982) 166–80.

_____. "The Late Period (664–332 BC)." Pp. 369–94 in *The Oxford History of Ancient Egypt.* Edited by I. Shaw. Oxford: Oxford University Press, 2000.

_____. "Nationalist Propaganda in Ptolemaic Egypt." *Historia* 31 (1982) 33–55.

Lorton, D. "Legal and Social Institutions of Pharaonic Egypt." Pp. 345–62 in vol. 1 of *CANE.* Edited by J. Sasson. New York: Scribner's, 1995.

_____. "The Supposed Expedition of Ptolemy II to Persia." *JEA* 57 (1971) 160–64.

_____. "The Treatment of Criminals in Ancient Egypt through the New Kingdom." *JESHO* 22 (1977) 2–64.

Lozachmeur, H. "Un nouveau graffito araméen provenant de Saqqâra." *Semitica* 48 (1998) 147–49.

Lundquist, J. M. *Studies on the Temple in the Ancient Near East.* Ph.D. dissertation, University of Michigan, 1983.

MacGinnis, J. D. A. "A Further Note on the *Zazakku.*" *NABU* 29 (1996).

_____. *Letter Orders from Sippar and the Administration of the Ebabbara in the Late Babylonian Period.* Poznan, Poland: Bonami, 1995.

_____. "Qīpu's Receive." *NABU* 93 (1993).

_____. "The Royal Establishment at Sippar in the 6th Century B.C. " *ZA* 84 (1994) 198–219.

_____. "A Royal Share in the Meals of Šamaš." *NABU* 90 (1994).

Machinist, P. "The First Coins of Judah and Samaria: Numismatics and History in the Achaemenid and Early Hellenistic Periods." Pp. 365–79 in *Continuity and Change.* Edited by H. Sancisi-Weerdenburg, A. Kuhrt, and M. C. Root. Vol. 8 of *Achaemenid History.* Leiden: Nederlands Institute voor het Nabije Oosten, 1994.

Machinist, P., and H. Tadmor. "Heavenly Wisdom." Pp. 146–51 in *The Tablet and the Scroll: Near Eastern Studies in Honor of William W. Hallo.* Edited by M. E. Cohen, D. C. Snell, and D. B. Weisberg. Bethesda, Md.: CDL, 1993.

Mariette, A. *The Monuments of Upper Egypt.* Alexandria: Amourès, 1877.

Martin, C. "The Demotic Texts." Pp. 277–385 in *The Elephantine Papyri in English: Three Millennia of Cross-Cultural Continuity and Change.* Edited by B. Porten. New York: Brill, 1996.

Maystre, C. *Les grands prêtres de Ptah de Memphis.* OBO 113. Fribourg: Universitätsverlag / Göttingen: Vandenhoeck & Ruprecht, 1992.

Mazar, B. "The Tobiads." *IEJ* 7 (1957) 137–45, 229–38.

McEvenue, S. "The Political Structure in Judah from Cyrus to Nehemiah." *CBQ* 43 (1981) 353–64.

Meeks, D. "Les donations aux temples dans l'Égypte du Ier millénaire avant J.-C." Pp. 605–87 in vol. 2 of *State and Temple Economy in the Ancient Near East.* Edited by E. Lipiński. Louvain: Departement Oriëntalistiek, 1979.

Meiggs, R., and Lewis, D. *A Selection of Greek Historical Inscriptions to the End of the Fifth Century* BC. Oxford: Clarendon, 1969.
Meissner, B. *Babylonien und Assyrien.* Heidelberg: Carl Winter, 1925.
Menu, B. "Les juges égyptiens sous les dernières dynasties indigènes." Pp. 233–46 in vol. 2 of *Récherches sur l'histoire juridique, économique et sociale de l'ancienne Égypt.* Edited by B. Menu. Cairo: Institut Français d'Archéologie Orientale, 1998.
Meshorer, Y. *Persian Period through Hasmonaeans.* Vol. 1 of *Ancient Jewish Coinage.* New York: Amphora, 1982.
Meshorer, Y., and S. Qedar. *The Coinage of Samaria in the Fourth Century* BCE. Jerusalem: Numismatic Fine Arts. 1991.
Metzger, H. *L'Acropole lycienne.* Vol. 2 of *Fouilles de Xanthos.* Paris: Klincksieck, 1963.
_____. "L'inscription grèque." Pp. 31–48 in *La stèle trilingue du Létôon.* Vol. 6 of *Fouilles de Xanthos.* Edited by H. Metzger. Paris: Klincksieck, 1979.
_____. "Le sanctuaire de Leto." Pp. 9–28 in *La stèle trilingue du Létôon.* Vol. 6 of *Fouilles de Xanthos.* Edited by H. Metzger. Paris: Klincksieck 1979.
Metzger, H. (ed.). *La stèle trilingue du Létôon.* Vol. 6 of *Fouilles de Xanthos.* Paris: Klincksieck, 1979.
Meyer, E. *Die Entstehung des Judentums.* Hildesheim: Olms, 1965. [Reprinted from the 1896 impression]
Meyers, C. L., and E. M. Meyers. *Haggai, Zechariah 1–8.* AB 25B. Garden City, N.Y.: Doubleday, 1987.
Meyers, E. M. "The Shelomith Seal and the Judean Restoration: Some Additional Considerations." *ErIsr* 18 (Avigad volume; 1985) 33–38.
Mieroop, M. van de. *The Ancient Mesopotamian City.* New York: Oxford University Press, 1997.
_____. "The Government of an Ancient Mesopotamian City: What We Know and Why We Know So Little." Pp. 139–61 in *Priests and Officials in the Ancient Near East.* Edited by K. Watanabe. Heidelberg: Carl Winter, 1999.
Mildenberg, L. "Notes on the Coin Issues of Mazday." *INJ* 11 (1990–91) 9–23.
_____. "Yehud: A Preliminary Study of the Provincial Coinage of Judaea." Pp. 183–96 and pls. 21–22 in *Greek Numismatics and Archaeology: Essays in Honor of Margaret Thompson.* Edited by O. Mørkholm and N. M. Waggoner. Wettern, Belgium: NR, 1979.
Motyer, J. A. *The Prophecy of Isaiah.* Leicester: Inter-Varsity, 1993.
Moursi, M. *Die Hohenpriester des Sonnengottes von der Frühzeit Aegyptens bis zum Ende des Neuen Reiches.* Münchner Aegyptologische Studien 26. Munich: Deutscher Kunstverlag, 1972.
Mowinckel, S. *He That Cometh.* Oxford: Blackwell, 1956.
_____. *The Psalms in Israel's Worship.* Oxford: Blackwell, 1962.
Muffs, Y. *Studies in the Aramaic Legal Papyri from Elephantine.* Leiden: Brill, 1969.
Muraoka, T., and B. Porten. *A Grammar of Egyptian Aramaic.* New York: Brill, 1998.
Murnane, W. *Texts from the Amarna Period in Egypt.* Atlanta: Scholars Press, 1995.
_____. *The Penguin Guide to Ancient Egypt.* 9th ed. New York: Penguin, 1996.
Myers, J. M. *Ezra–Nehemiah.* AB 14. New York: Doubleday, 1965.
Myśliwiec, K. *The Twilight of Ancient Egypt: First Millennium* B.C.E. Ithaca: Cornell University Press, 2000.

Naville, E. *Mound of the Jew and the City of Onias.* London: Egypt Exploration Society, 1890.

_____. "La stele de Pithom." *ZAS* 40 (1902) 66–75, pls. 3–5.

_____. *The Store-City of Pithom and the Route of the Exodus.* London: Trubner, 1885.

Nims, C. "The Term *hp*, 'Law,' 'Right,' in Demotic." *JNES* 7 (1948) 243–60.

Noth, M. *The History of Israel.* New York: Harper, 1960.

Nurmela, R. *The Levites: Their Emergence as a Second-Class Priesthood.* University of South Florida Studies in the History of Judaism 119. Atlanta: Scholars Press, 1998.

O'Connor, D. "New Kingdom and Third Intermediate Period, 1552–664 BC." Pp. 183–278 in *Ancient Egypt: A Social History.* Edited by B. Trigger et al. New York: Cambridge University Press, 1983.

Olmstead, A. T. "Tattenai, Governor of 'Across the River.'" *JNES* 3 (1944) 46.

Oppenheim, A. L. *Ancient Mesopotamia: Portrait of a Dead Civilization.* Chicago: University of Chicago Press, 1977.

_____. "The Babylonian Evidence of Achaemenid Rule in Mesopotamia." Pp. 540–41 in vol. 2 of *CHI.*

_____. "A Fiscal Practice of the Ancient Near East." *JNES* 6 (1947) 116–20.

Parke, H. W. "The Massacre of the Branchidae." *JHS* 105 (1985) 59–68.

Perrot, J., et al. "La porte de Darius à Suse." *Cahiers de la délégation archéologique française en Iran* 4 (1974) 43–56.

Pestman, P. W. "L'origine et l'extension d'un manuel de droit égyptien." *JESHO* 26 (1982) 14–21.

_____. *Les papyrus démotiques de Tsenhor (P. Tsenhor): Les archives privées d'une femme égyptienne du temps de Darius 1er.* Leuven: Peeters, 1994.

Petersen, D. L. *Haggai and Zechariah 1–8: A Commentary.* OTL. Philadelphia: Westminster, 1984.

_____. "Zerubbabel and Jerusalem Temple Reconstruction." *CBQ* 36 (1974) 366–72.

Petit, T. "L'évolution sémantique des termes hébreux et araméens *pḥh* et *sgn* et accadiens *pāḫatu* et *šaknu.*" *JBL* 107 (1988) 53–67.

_____. *Satrapes et satrapies dans l'empire achemenide de Cyrus le Grand a Xerxes Ier.* Paris: Les Belles Lettres, 1990.

Petropoulou, K. "The *Eparche* Documents and the Early Oracle at Oropus." *GRBS* 22 (1981) 39–63.

Piccirilli, L. *Gli arbitrati interstatali greci.* Vol. 1. Pisa: Marlin, 1973.

Pilgrim, C. von. "Der Tempel des Jahwe." *MDAIK* 55 (1999) 142–45.

Pinches, T. "Two Late Tablets of Historical Interest." *PSBA* 38 (1916) 27–34.

Porciani, L. *La forma proemiale: Storiografia e pubblico nel mondo antico.* Pub. della Classe di Lettere e filosofia 18. Pisa: Scuola Normale Superiore di Pisa, 1997.

Porten, B. "The Address Formulae in Aramaic Letters: A New Collation of Cowley 17." *RB* 90 (1983) 396–415.

_____. *Archives from Elephantine: The Life of an Ancient Jewish Military Colony.* Berkeley: University of California Press, 1968.

_____. "The Documents in the Book of Ezra and the Mission of Ezra." *Shnaton* 3 (1978–79) 174–96. [Hebrew]

_____. "Elephantine Papyri." Pp. 445–55 in vol. 2 of *ABD.*

_____. *The Elephantine Papyri in English: Three Millennia of Cross-Cultural Continuity and Change.* New York: Brill, 1996.

Porten, B., and A. Yardeni. *Letters; Contracts; Literature, Accounts, Lists; and Ostraca.* Vols. 1–4 of *Textbook of Aramaic Documents from Ancient Egypt.* Jerusalem: Hebrew University, 1986–99.

Posener, G. *La première domination perse en Égypte.* Cairo: Institut français d'archéologie orientale, 1936.

Postgate, J. N. *Early Mesopotamia: Society and Economy at the Dawn of History.* London: Routledge, 1992.

_____. *Taxation and Conscription in the Assyrian Empire.* Rome: Pontifical Biblical Institute, 1974.

Quaegebeur, J. "*Phritob* comme titre d'un haut fonctionnaire ptolémaïque." *Ancient Society* 20 (1989) 159–68.

Rabinowitz, I. "Aramaic Inscriptions of the Fifth Century B.C.E. from a North-Arab Shrine in Egypt." *JNES* 15 (1956) 1–9.

Redford, D. *The Akhenaten Temple Project.* Warminster: Aris & Philips, 1976.

_____. "Pathros." P. 178 in vol. 5 of *ABD.*

_____. *Pharaonic King-Lists, Annals and Day-Books: A Contribution to the Study of the Egyptian Sense of History.* SSEA 4. Mississauga, Ont.: Benben, 1986.

_____. "The So-Called 'Codification' of Egyptian Law under Darius I." Pp. 135–59 in *Persia and Torah: The Theory of Imperial Authorization of the Pentateuch.* Edited by J. W. Watts. SBL Symposium Series 17. Atlanta: Society of Biblical Literature, 2001.

Rendtorff, R. "Esra und das 'Gesetz.'" *ZAW* 96 (1984) 165–84.

Rigsby, K. J. *Asylia: Territorial Inviolability in the Hellenistic World.* Berkeley: University of California Press, 1996.

Roaf, M. *Cultural Atlas of Mesopotamia and the Ancient Near East.* Oxfordshire: Andromeda Oxford, 1996.

Robert, L. *Documents de l'Asie Mineure.* BEFAR 239. Paris: Boccard, 1987.

_____. "Une nouvelle inscription grèque de Sardes: Réglement de l'autorité relatif à un culte de Zeus." *CRAIBL* (1975) 306–30.

Roebuck, D. *Ancient Greek Arbitration.* Oxford: Holo, 2001.

Roeder, G. *Die ägyptische Götterwelt.* Zurich: Artemis, 1959.

Rooke, D. W. *Zadok's Heirs: The Role and Development of the High Priesthood in Ancient Israel.* Oxford: Oxford University Press, 2000.

Root, M. C. *The King and Kingship in Achaemenid Art: Essays on the Creation of an Iconography of Empire.* Acta Iranica 19; 3rd series 9. Leiden: Brill, 1979.

Rose, W. H. *Zemah and Zerubbabel: Messianic Expectations in the Early Postexilic Period.* JSOTSup 304. Sheffield: Sheffield Academic Press, 2000.

Roth, A. M. "The Organization and Functioning of the Royal Mortuary Cults of the Old Kingdom in Egypt." Pp. 133–40 in *The Organization of Power: Aspects of Bureaucracy in the Ancient Near East.* Edited by M. Gibson and R. D. Biggs. Chicago: Oriental Institute of the University of Chicago, 1987.

Roth, M. T. *Law Collections from Mesopotamia and Asia Minor.* 2nd ed. SBL Writings from the Ancient World Series 6. Atlanta: Scholars Press, 1997.

Rougemont, G. *Lois sacrées et réglements religieux.* Vol. 1 of *Corpus des inscriptions de Delphes.* Paris: Boccard, 1977.

Rundgren, F. "Zur Bedeutung von *ŠRŠW*: Ezra vii 26." *VT* 7 (1957) 400–404.

Ruzicka, S. *Politics of a Persian Dynasty: The Hecatomnids in the Fourth Century B.C.* Norman, Okla.: University of Oklahoma Press, 1992.

Sack, R. H. *Cuneiform Documents from the Chaldean and Persian Periods.* London: Associated University Presses, 1994.
Saggs, H. W. F. "Two Administrative Officials at Erech in the 6th Century B.C." *Sumer* 15 (1959) 29–38.
_____. "Assyrian Warfare in the Sargonic Period." *Iraq* 25 (1963) 145–54.
Sahin, M. C. "Two New Inscriptions from Lagina (Koranza)." *Anadolu/Anatolia* 17 (1973) 187–95.
Sahin, S. "Ein attisches Dekret für Erythrai." *Turk Tarih Belleten* 40 (1976) 569–71.
Salonen, E. *Über den Zehnten im alten Mesopotamien: Ein Beitrag zur Beschichte der Besteuerung.* Studia Orientalia 43. Helsinki: Societas Orientalis Fennica, 1972.
Sancisi-Weerdenburg, H. (ed.). *Sources, Structures and Synthesis.* Vol. 1 of *Achaemenid History.* Leiden: Nederlands Institute voor het Nabije Oosten, 1987.
_____. *Yaunā en Persai: Grieken en Perzen in een ander perspectief.* Groningen: Dijkstra Niemeyer, 1980.
Sancisi-Weerdenburg, H., and A. Kuhrt (eds.). *Asia Minor and Egypt: Old Cultures in a New Empire.* Vol. 6 of *Achaemenid History.* Leiden: Nederlands Institute voor het Nabije Oosten, 1991.
_____. *The Greek Sources.* Vol. 2 of *Achaemenid History.* Leiden: Nederlands Institute voor het Nabije Oosten, 1987.
Sancisi-Weerdenburg, H., A. Kuhrt, and M. Cool Root (eds.). *Continuity and Change.* Vol. 8 of *Achaemenid History.* Leiden: Nederlands Institute voor het Nabije Oosten, 1994.
Sanders, E. P. *Judaism: Practice and Belief, 63 BCE–66 CE.* Philadelphia: Trinity, 1992.
San Nicolò, M. *Beiträge zu einer Prosopographie neubabylonischer Beamten der Zivil- und Tempelverwaltung.* SBAW 2. Munich: Bayerische Akademie der Wissenschaften, 1941.
_____. "Zur Verproviantierung des kgl. Hoflagers in Abanu durch den Eanna-Tempel in Uruk." *ArOr* 17 (1949) 323–30.
Sarna, N. "Psalm 89: A Study in Inner Biblical Exegesis." Pp. 29–46 in *Biblical and Other Studies.* Edited by A. Altmann. Cambridge: Harvard University Press, 1963.
Sauneron, S. *Les prêtres de l'ancienne Égypte.* Paris: Seuil, 1957.
Sauneron, S., and H. Stierlin. *Edfou et Philae: Derniers temples d'Égypte.* Paris: Chêne, 1975.
Schaper, J. "The Jerusalem Temple as an Instrument of the Achaemenid Fiscal Administration." *PEQ* 45 (1995) 528–39.
_____. *Priester und Leviten im achämenidischen Juda.* FAT 31. Tübingen: Mohr Siebeck, 2000.
Schaudig, H. *Die Inschriften Nabonids von Babylon und Kyros' des Grossen samt den in ihrem Umfeld entstandenen Tendenzschriften: Textausgabe und Grammatik.* AOAT 256. Münster: Ugarit-Verlag, 2001.
Schiel, V. "Le Gobryas de la Cyropédie et les textes cunéiformes." *RA* 11 (1914) 165–74.
Schmitt, R. "Bemerkungen zu dem sog. Gadatas-Brief." *ZPE* 112 (1996) 95–101.
Schniedewind, W. *Society and the Promise to David.* Oxford: Oxford University Press, 1999.
Schwiderski, D. *Handbuch des nordwestsemitischen Briefformulars: Ein Beitrag zur Echtheitsfrage der aramäischen Briefe des Esrabuches.* BZAW 295. Berlin: de Gruyter, 2000.

Seidl, E. *Aegyptische Rechtsgeschichte der Saiten- und Perserzeit.* Glückstadt: Augustin, 1968.

Sekunda, N. "Achaemenid Colonization in Lydia." *REA* 87 (1985) 7–30.

Sethe, K. *Hieroglyphische Urkunden der griesche-römischen Zeit.* Vol. 2. Leipzig: Heinrichs, 1904.

Shafer, B. E. "Temples, Priests, and Rituals: An Overview." Pp. 1–30 in *Temples of Ancient Egypt.* Edited by B. E. Shafer. Ithaca: Cornell University Press, 1997.

Shallit, A. "The End of the Hasmonian Dynasty and the Rise of Herod." Pp. 44–70 in vol. 7 of *World History of the Jewish People.* Edited by M. Avi-Yonah. New Brunswick, N.J.: Rutgers University Press, 1975.

Shaw, I. *The Oxford History of Ancient Egypt.* Oxford: Oxford University Press, 2000.

Shupak, N. "A New Source for the Study of the Judiciary and Law of Ancient Egypt: 'The Tale of the Eloquent Peasant.'" *JNES* 51 (1992) 1–18.

Ska, J. L. "'Persian Imperial Authorization': Some Question Marks." Pp. 161–82 in *Persia and Torah: The Theory of Imperial Authorization of the Pentateuch.* Edited by J. W. Watts. SBL Symposium Series 17. Atlanta: Society of Biblical Literature, 2001.

Slotsky, A. L. *The Bourse of Babylon: Market Quotations in the Astronomical Diaries of Babylonia.* Bethesda, Md.: CDL, 1997.

Smith, M. "II Isaiah and the Persians." *JAOS* 83 (1963) 415–21.

_____. *Palestinian Parties and Politics That Shaped the Old Testament.* New York: Columbia University Press, 1971.

Smith, S. *Babylonian and Historical Texts Relating to the Capture and Downfall of Babylon.* London: Methuen, 1924.

Smith-Christopher, D. "The Mixed Marriage Crisis in Ezra 9–10 and Nehemiah 13: A Study of the Sociology of the Post-exilic Judaean Community." Pp. 243–65 in *Temple and Community in the Persian Period.* Edited by T. C. Eskenazi and K. H. Richards. Vol. 2 of *Second Temple Studies.* Sheffield: Sheffield Academic Press, 1994.

_____. "The Politics of Ezra: Sociological Indicators of Postexilic Judaean Society." Pp. 73–97 in *Persian Period.* Edited by P. Davies. Vol. 1 of *Second Temple Studies.* Sheffield: Sheffield Academic Press, 1991.

Spaer, A. "Jaddua the High Priest?" *INJ* 7 (1986) 1–3.

Spalinger, A. "The Concept of the Monarchy during the Saite Epoch: An Essay in Synthesis." *Orientalia* 47 (1978) 12–37.

Spiegelberg, W. *Demotische Inschriften und Papyri.* Vol. 3 of *Die demotischen Denkmäler.* Leipzig: Drugulin, 1932.

_____. "Drei demotische Schreiben aus der Korrespondenz des Pherendates des Satrapen Darius' I., mit den Chnum-Priestern von Elephantine." *SPAW* (1928) 604–22.

_____. *Die sogenannte demotische Chronik des Pap. 215 der Bibliothéque Nationale de Paris.* Leipzig: Hinrichs, 1914.

Ste. Croix, G. E. M. de. *The Class Struggle in the Ancient Greek World: From the Archaic Age to the Arab Conquests.* Ithaca: Cornell University Press, 1981.

Steiner, R. C. "The *MBQR* at Qumran, the *Episkopos* in the Athenian Empire, and the Meaning of *LBQR'* in Ezra 7:14: On the Relation of Ezra's Mission to the Persian Legal Project." *JBL* 120 (2001) 623–46.

Stern, E. *The Assyrian, Babylonian, and Persian Periods (732–332 B.C.E.).* Vol. 2 of *Archaeology of the Land of the Bible.* ABRL. New York: Doubleday, 2001.

_____. "The Archeology of Persian Palestine." Pp. 88–114 in vol. 1 of *The Cambridge History of Judaism.* Edited by W. D. Davies and L. Finkelstein. Cambridge: Cambridge University Press, 1984.

_____. "Between Persia and Greece: Trade, Administration and Warfare in the Persian and Hellenistic Periods (539–63 BCE)." Pp. 432–45 in *The Archaeology of Society in the Holy Land.* Edited by T. Levy. Leicester: Leicester University Press, 1995.

_____. *Material Culture of the Land of the Bible in the Persian Period, 538–332.* Warminster: Aris & Philips, 1982.

_____. "Seal-Impressions in the Achaemenid Style in the Province of Judah." *BASOR* 202 (1971) 6–16.

Stern, M. *Greek and Latin Authors on Jews and Judaism.* Jerusalem: Magnes, 1976–84.

Stolper, M. *Entrepreneurs and Empire: The Murašû Archive, the Murašû Firm and Persian Rule in Babylonia.* Leiden: Nederlands Historisch-Archaeologisch Instituut te Istanbul, 1985.

_____. "The Governor of Babylon and Across-the-River in 486 B.C." *JNES* 48 (1989) 283–305.

_____. "The Neo-Babylonian Text from the Persepolis Fortification." *JNES* 43 (1984) 299–310.

Tadmor, H. "Temple Cities and Royal Cities in Babylon and Assyria." *Milhemet kodesh u-ma'tirologiyah be-toledot Yisra'el.* Jerusalem: Ha-ḥevrah ha-historit ha-Yisra'elit, 1967. [Hebrew]

_____. "Was the Biblical *Sārîs* a Eunuch?" Pp. 317–26 in *Solving Riddles and Untying Knots: Biblical, Epigraphic, and Semitic Studies in Honor of Jonas C. Greenfield.* Edited by Z. Zevit, S. Gitin, and M. Sokoloff. Winona Lake, Ind.: Eisenbrauns, 1995.

Tappy, R. "Samaria." Pp. 463–67 in vol. 4 of *OEANE.*

Taylor, J. "The Third Intermediate Period, 1069–664 BC." Pp. 330–68 in *Oxford History of Ancient Egypt.* Edited by I. Shaw. Oxford: Oxford University Press, 2000.

Tcherikover, V. "Palestine under the Ptolemies: A Contribution to the Study of the Zenon Papyri." *Mizraim* 4–5 (1937) 1–90.

Tcherikover, V., and A. Fuks. *Corpus Papyrorum Judaicarum.* Cambridge: Harvard University Press, 1957.

Teixidor, J. "The Aramaic Text in the Trilingual Stele from Xanthos." *JNES* 37 (1978) 181–85.

Théodorides, A. "La 'Coutume' et la 'Loi' dans l'Égypte Pharaonique." *Recueils de la Societé Jean Bodin* (1990) 39–47.

Thiers, C. "Civils et militaires dans les temples: Occupation illicite et expulsion." *BIFAO* 95 (1995) 493–516.

Thompson, S. "The Anointing of Officials in Ancient Egypt." *JNES* 53 (1994) 15–25.

Thureau-Dangin, F. *Rituels accadiens.* Paris. Leroux, 1921.

Tod, M. N. *A Selection of Greek Historical Inscriptions: From the Sixth Century B.C. to the Death of Alexander the Great in 323 B.C.* Vols. 1–2. Oxford: Clarendon, 1948.

Torrey, C. C. *Ezra Studies.* Reprinted. New York: Ktav, 1970.

Traunecker, C. "Un document nouveau sur Darius Ier à Karnak." Pp. 209–13 in *Cahiers de Karnak Vol. VI (1973–1977).* Paris: Éditions Recherche sur les civilisations, 1981.

Tuplin, C. "The Administration of the Achaemenid Empire." Pp. 109–66 in *Coinage and Administration in the Athenian and Persian Empires.* Edited by I. Carradice. British

Archaeological Reports International Series 343. Oxford: British Archaeological Reports, 1987.

_____. "Darius' Suez Canal and Persian Imperialism." Pp. 237–83 in *Asia Minor and Egypt: Old Cultures in a New Empire.* Edited by H. Sancisi-Weerdenburg and A. Kuhrt. Vol. 6 of *Achaemenid History.* Leiden: Nederlands Institute voor het Nabije Oosten, 1991.

_____. "Persian Garrisons in Xenophon and Other Sources." Pp. 67–70 in *Method and Theory.* Edited by A. Kurht and H. Sancisi-Weerdenburg. Vol. 3 of *Achaemenid History.* Leiden: Nederlands Instituut voor het Nabije Oosten, 1988.

_____. "Xenophon and the Garrisons of the Persian Empire." *AMI* 20 (1987) 167–245.

Ungnad, A. "Keilinschriftliche Beiträge zum Buch Esra und Ester." *ZAW* 58 (1940–41) 240–44.

Valbelle, D. "L'Égypte pharaonique." Pp. 11–177 in *L'état et les institutions en Égypte des premiers pharaons aux empéreurs romains.* Edited by G. Husson and D. Valbelle. Paris: Armand Colin, 1992.

Vanderhooft, D. S. *The Neo-Babylonian Empire and Babylon in the Latter Prophets.* HSM 59. Atlanta: Scholars Press, 1999.

VanderKam, J. C. "Jewish High Priests of the Persian Period: Is the List Complete?" Pp. 67–91 in *Priesthood and Cult in Ancient Israel.* Edited by G. A. Anderson and S. M. Olyan. Sheffield: Sheffield Academic Press, 1991.

Vaux, R. de. "Le roi d'Israël, Vassal de Yahvé." Pp. 152–80 in *The Bible and the Ancient Near East.* Edited by R. de Vaux. Garden City, N.Y.: Doubleday, 1971.

Verbrugghe, G. P., and J. M. Wickersham. *Berossos and Manetho: Native Traditions in Ancient Mesopotamia and Egypt.* Ann Arbor: University of Michigan Press, 1996.

Viganò, L. "Rituals at Ebla II, ì-giš sag: A Purification Ritual or Anointing of the Head?" *JNES* 59 (2000) 13–22.

Vittmann, G. "Der demotische Papyrus Rylands 9, Teil 1 und 2." *Ägypten und Altes Testament* 38 (1998).

_____. "Eine mißlungene Dokumentenfalschung: Die 'Stelen' des Peteese I (P. Ryl. 9, XXI–XXIII)." *EVO* 17 (1994).

Voigtlander, E. N. von. *The Bisitun Inscription of Darius the Great: Babylonian Version.* Corpus Inscriptionum Iranicarum. London: Lund Humphries, 1978.

_____. *A Survey of Neo-Babylonian History.* Ph.D. dissertation. University of Michigan, 1963.

Walker, C. B. F. "A Recently Identified Fragment of the Cyrus Cylinder." *Iran* 10 (1972) 158–59.

Waltke, B. K., and M. O'Connor. *An Introduction to Biblical Hebrew Syntax.* Winona Lake, Ind.: Eisenbrauns, 1990.

Waterman, L. "The Camouflaged Purge of Three Messianic Conspirators." *JNES* 13 (1934) 73–78.

Watts, J. W. (ed.). *Persia and Torah: The Theory of Imperial Authorization of the Pentateuch.* SBL Symposium Series 17. Atlanta: Society of Biblical Literature, 2001.

Weinberg, J. P. "Zentral- und Partikulargewalt im achämenidischen Reich." *Klio* 59 (1977) 25–43. = "Central and Local Administration in the Achaemenid Empire." Pp. 105–26 in *The Citizen-Temple Community.* Edited by J. P. Weinberg. Translated by D. L. Smith-Christopher. JSOTSup 151. Sheffield: Sheffield Academic Press, 1992.

Weinfeld, M. "Cult Centralization in Israel in the Light of a Neo-Babylonian Analogy." *JNES* 23 (1964) 202–12.

Weisberg, D. "Polytheism and Politics: Some Comments on Nabonidus' Foreign Policy." Pp. 547–56 in *Crossing Boundaries and Linking Horizons: Studies in Honor of Michael C. Astour on His 80th Birthday.* Edited by G. D. Young, M. W. Chavalas, and R. E. Averbeck. Bethesda, Md.: CDL, 1997.

Weiskopf, M. *The So-Called "Great Satraps' Revolt," 366–360 B.C.: Concerning Local Instability in the Achaemenid Far West.* Historia 63. Stuttgart: Franz Steiner, 1989.

Wellhausen, J. *Prolegomena to the History of Ancient Israel.* New York: Meridian, 1957.

Westbrook, R. "Biblical and Cuneiform Law Codes." *RB* 92 (1985) 247–64.

_____. "What Is the Covenant Code?" Pp. 15–26 in *Theory and Method in Biblical and Cuneiform Law: Revision, Interpolation, and Development.* Edited by B. M. Levinson. JSOTSup 181. Sheffield: Sheffield Academic Press, 1994.

Whitehead, J. D. *Early Aramaic Epistolography: The Arsames Correspondence.* Ph.D. dissertation, University of Chicago, 1974.

Widengren, G. "The Persian Period." Pp. 489–538 in *Israelite and Judean History.* Edited by J. Hayes and J. Maxwell Miller. Philadelphia: Westminster, 1977.

Wiesehöfer, J. "Zur Frage der Echtheit des Darios-Briefes an Gadatas." *RhM* 130 (1987) 396–98.

_____. "*PRTRK, RB ḤYLʾ, SGN* und *MRʾ:* Zur Verwaltung südägyptens in achaïmenidischer Zeit." Pp. 305–9 in *Asia Minor and Egypt: Old Cultures in a New Empire.* Edited by H. Sancisi-Weerdenburg and A. Kuhrt. Vol. 6 of *Achaemenid History.* Leiden: Nederlands Institute voor het Nabije Oosten, 1991.

Williamson, H. G. M. *The Book Called Isaiah: Deutero-Isaiah's Role in Composition and Redaction.* Oxford: Oxford University Press, 1994.

_____. "The Composition of Ezra I–VI." *JTS* n.s. 34 (1983) 1–30.

_____. *Ezra, Nehemiah.* WBC. Waco, Tex.: Word, 1985.

_____. "The Governors of Judah under the Persians." *Tyndale Bulletin* 39 (1988) 59–82.

_____. "The Historical Value of Josephus' *Jewish Antiquities* XI." 297–301." *JTS* 28 (1977) 49–66.

Winlock, H. E., et al. *The Temple of Hibis in el-Khargeh Oasis.* New York: Metropolitan Museum of Art, 1953.

Winnicki, J. K. "Carrying Off and Bringing Home the Statues of the Gods: On an Aspect of the Religious Policy of the Ptolemies towards the Egyptians." *The Journal of Juristic Papyrology* 24 (1994) 149–90.

Wuttmann, M., et al. "ʿAyn Manāwīr (oasis de Kharga): Deuxième rapport préliminaire." *BIFAO* 98 (1998) 367–462.

_____. "Prémier rapport préliminaire des travaux sur le site de ʿAyn Manāwīr (oasis de Kharga)." *BIFAO* 96 (1996) 385–451.

Wuttmann, M., T. Gonon, and C. Thiers. "The Qanats of ʿAyn-Manâwîr (Kharga Oasis, Egypt)." *JASR* 1 (2000) (*www.achemenet.com*).

Yamauchi, E. M. "Two Reformers Compared: Solon of Athens and Nehemiah of Jerusalem." Pp. 269–92 in *The Bible World: Essays in Honor of Cyrus H. Gordon.* Edited by G. Rendsburg et al. New York: Ktav and The Institute of Hebrew Culture and Education of New York University, 1980.

Yardeni, A. "Maritime Trade and Royal Accountancy in an Erased Customs Account from 475 B.C.E. on the Aḥiqar Scroll from Elephantine." *BASOR* 293 (1994) 67–78.

Yoffee, N. "Orienting Collapse." Pp. 1–19 in *The Collapse of Ancient States and Civilizations.* Edited by N. Yoffee and G. L. Cowgill. Tuscon: Univeristy of Arizona Press, 1988.

Younger, K. L. *Ancient Conquest Accounts: A Study in Ancient Near Eastern and Biblical History Writing.* JSOTSup 98. Sheffield: Sheffield Academic Press, 1990.

Yoyotte, M. J. "Les inscriptions hiéroglyphiques Darius et l'Égypte." *Journal Asiatique* 260 (1972) 253–65.

_____. "Le nom égyptien du 'ministre de l'économie'—de Saïs à Méroé." *CRAIBL* (1989) 73–90.

Zadok, R. *The Jews of Babylonia during the Chaldean and Achaemenian Periods according to the Babylonian Sources.* Haifa: University of Haifa Press, 1979.

Zauzich, K.-T. *Ägyptische Handschriften.* Teil 2. Verzeichnis der orientalischen Handschriften in Deutschland 19. Wiesbaden: Franz Steiner, 1971.

_____. "Die demotische Papyri von der Insel Elephantine." Pp. 421–35 in *Egypt of the Hellenistic World: Proceedings of the International Colloquium, Leuven: 24–26 May 1982.* Edited by E. van 't Dack, P. Van Dessel, and W. van Gucht. Studia Hellenistica 27. Louvain: Studia Hellenistica, 1983.

_____. *Papyri von der Insel Elephantine.* Vols. 1 and 3 of *Demotische Papyri aus den Staatlichen Museen zu Berlin.* Berlin: Akademie-Verlag, 1978–93.

_____. "Weitere Fragmente eines juristischen Handbuches in demotischer Schrift." *EVO* 17 (1994) 327–32.

Zawadzki, S. "Cyrus-Cambyses Coregency." *RA* 90 (1996) 171–83.

Zgusta, L. "Iranian Names in Lydian Inscriptions." *Charisteria Orientalia* (Prague, 1957) 397–400.

Zimmerli, W. *Ezekiel 1.* Hermenia. Philadelphia: Fortress, 1979.

Indexes

Index of Authors

Ackroyd, P. R. 167–168, 198, 203–204
Ager, S. L. 127
Albertz, R. 190–191, 200
Albrektson, B. 159
Allam, S. 52–53
Alt, A. 184, 187
Arnold, D. 77
Aufrère, S. 77
Austin, M. 122
Avigad, N. 164, 183–184, 186, 188

Bagnall, R. 211
Balcer, J. 73, 124
Barag, D. 186–187, 227
Barstad, H. 158, 177
Bean, G. E. 147
Beaulieu, P.-A. 15, 22–23, 25–28, 36, 42
Beckerath, J. von 63
Bedford, P. R. 159, 163–164, 170, 174, 182–183
Berger, P.-R. 20–21, 184
Berquist, J. L. 217
Black, J. A. 30
Blackman, A. M. 50, 56, 58–59
Blenkinsopp, J. 52, 118, 147, 164, 166–167, 170, 183, 189, 191, 195, 207, 212, 219–221, 224, 228
Bloom, J. A. 32
Boccaccini, G. 207
Bodi, D. 194
Boehmer, R. M. 28
Boffo, L. 108, 113
Bolin, T. 164, 216
Bongenaar, A. C. V. M. 8, 13, 17–18, 41–42, 44–45
Bongrani Fanfoni, L. 87, 111
Bontty, M. M. 75
Borchhardt, J. 146, 151
Bottéro, J. 34
Boyce, M. 133, 223
Brandenstein, W. 108
Breasted, J. H. 55
Bresciani, E. 73, 75–76
Briant, P. 31, 66, 82, 102–103, 105, 108–114, 116–119, 121–122, 124, 130, 134, 137–138, 140–142, 146, 151–152, 189, 196, 214–215, 219, 226, 230–231
Brugsch, H. 71
Burchardt, M. 67
Burkard, G. 69–70
Burkert, W. 134

Cameron, G. 28, 225
Capart, J. 77
Cardascia, G. 43, 208
Carter, C. E. 164, 184, 187, 198, 225
Cauville, S. 78
Cenival, F. de 57–58
Chaumont, M.-L. 136
Chauveau, M. 81–82, 84
Christophe, J. 184, 225
Clarke, S. 77
Clay, A. T. 44
Cocquerillat, D. 36–38, 209
Cogan, M. 26, 72, 159, 167

Index of Scripture

New Testament